Building a Sustainable Political Economy: SPERI Research & Policy

Series Editor
Colin Hay, SPERI, University of Sheffield, Sheffield, UK

The Sheffield Political Economy Research Institute (SPERI) is an innovation in higher education research and outreach. It brings together leading international researchers in the social sciences, policy makers, journalists and opinion formers to reassess and develop proposals in response to the political and economic issues posed by the current combination of financial crisis, shifting economic power and environmental threat. Building a Sustainable Political Economy: SPERI Research & Policy will serve as a key outlet for SPERI's published work. Each title will summarise and disseminate to an academic and postgraduate student audience, as well as directly to policy-makers and journalists, key policy-oriented research findings designed to further the development of a more sustainable future for the national, regional and world economy following the global financial crisis. It takes a holistic and interdisciplinary view of political economy in which the local, national, regional and global interact at all times and in complex ways. The SPERI research agenda, and hence the focus of the series, seeks to explore the core economic and political questions that require us to develop a new sustainable model of political economy at all times and in complex ways.

speri.

More information about this series at
http://www.palgrave.com/gp/series/14879

Adam Barber

UK Banks and the Lessons of the Great Financial Crisis

palgrave
macmillan

Adam Barber
Department of Economics
Policy and International Business
Manchester Metropolitan University
Manchester, UK

Building a Sustainable Political Economy: SPERI Research & Policy
ISBN 978-3-030-70253-3 ISBN 978-3-030-70254-0 (eBook)
https://doi.org/10.1007/978-3-030-70254-0

This Palgrave Macmillan imprint is published by the registered company Springer Nature Switzerland AG
The registered company address is: Gewerbestrasse 11, 6330 Cham, Switzerland

For Jade Josephine Wei Ming

Acknowledgements

My interest in the Great Financial Crisis and bank reform first began in the summer of 2008 when as an undergraduate student at the University of Hull, I returned home for the summer holidays to find that my Dad had lost his job as a direct result of the crisis. It baffled me that a mechanic working in Barnsley, South Yorkshire could somehow be caught up in the catastrophic events that were unfolding in the City and on Wall Street. We would later find out that the company that my Dad had worked for had been bought by a subsidiary owned by RBS that, faced with mounting losses and in an attempt to raise capital, had liquidated its assets—including the garage where my Dad had worked since he was sixteen. Thankfully, by the time that I returned to my studies in the autumn Dad had secured a new job—others would not be so lucky! Yet the events of that summer would stick with me and sparked a certain curiosity that persists today. Many of the questions that I found myself asking that summer would later underpin the rational for this book: why had the crisis been allowed to happen, why had no one seen it coming; why had the banks' reckless and often criminally negligent behaviour gone largely unpunished; and what lessons if any had the banks learned—were all issues that I found myself grappling with over the coming months and years. This curiosity would lead me to go onto read for a Master's degree in International Political Economy, also at the University of Hull, with Simon Lee and Richard Woodward feeding my natural inquisitiveness and encouraging me to towards Ph.D. study.

In September 2013, I joined the Sheffield Political Economy Institute (SPERI) at the University of Sheffield and began working on my Ph.D. thesis that, unbeknownst to me at the time, would inform and later transform into the manuscript before you today. At SPERI, I found a natural home that provided me with the intellectual stimulus, encouragement and general good company needed to pursue my research. I am grateful to all my friends and former colleagues at Sheffield. I am particularly indebted to Andrew Baker, Dan Bailey, Craig Berry, Colin Hay, Tom Hunt, Tony Payne, Scott Lavery and the late Mick Moran who encouraged me to convert my various thoughts and musings on the Great Financial Crisis and bank learning into book form. I owe Andrew Hindmoor a special debt of gratitude for his unwavering support, patience and helpful comments on earlier drafts, and his constructive advice on how to improve them.

Though this book was conceived at the University of Sheffield, it has been written, in the main, at Manchester Metropolitan University (MMU) where in February 2018 I would join the Future Economies research centre. At MMU, I would find myself working with new colleagues and some familiar faces. In particular, I am grateful to Rory Shand and Kathryn Simpson who provided invaluable advice and support in getting this book to publication. I am also grateful to Donna Lee who has given me the intellectual freedom and space to pursue this project. My time at MMU would see me reunite with some of my former colleagues from Sheffield including Dan Bailey, David Beel, Sean MacDaniel and Craig Berry who I am equally indebted to. Craig has been a constant source of encouragement and has challenged me to develop me understanding of the political economy. I feel truly lucky to know Craig both as colleague and as a friend.

I also want to thank Tim Jackson and Sophia Kuehnlenz whose shared interest in banking and the financial crisis has led to many a lively conversation as we have put the banks, the British economy and world to rights.

I am grateful to Nick Barclay and Rebecca Roberts at Palgrave Macmillan for their interest in this project. I am particularly indebted Balaji Varadharaju at Springer Nature whose patience, understanding and general encouragement have helped see the book through to publication.

Finally, I owe a great debt of gratitude to all my family and friends for their constant love and unwavering support. I am particularly grateful to Emma, Dawn, Ben, Lucas, Megan, Steve, Bev and Holly. A special thanks to Riki. Finally, Mum and Dad who taught me the importance of education and hard work and spent hours reading with me as a child. Thank you.

To Jade, thank you for always being there for me, for your patience and understanding, to pick me up when I am down and to share the good times and bad. You are my rock and the love of my life.

Praise for *UK Banks and the Lessons of the Great Financial Crisis*

'Barber's book offers a hugely important contribution to the field of political economy – and social science more generally. The novel "learning" framework Barber applies to UK banks in the wake of the 2008 crisis is both sensible and innovative, and enables a fresh set of insights about the diverse – and diversifying – characteristics of the UK banking sector. I have learned a lot from Barber's research, and the book deserves to be widely read.'

—Craig Berry, *Future Economies Research Centre, Manchester Metropolitan University, UK*

'Adam Barber observes that regulators, bankers and politicians have all promised to learn lessons from the 2008 financial crisis. This book asks whether, more than a decade on, they have done so. The answer he provides is nuanced and convincing and moves us beyond the binary alternatives of arguing that everything has changed or that nothing has changed.'

—Andrew Hindmoor, *Deputy Vice President, Education, University of Sheffield, UK*

'Britain's "Big Four" banks – RBS, Lloyds, Barclays and HSBC – were at the centre of the maelstrom of 2008. In this book, Adam Barber expertly charts how the crisis impacted differentially on the business models and internal governance structures of these major banking institutions. Extensive empirical work and a robust theoretical framework combine to illuminate important continuities and changes within these systemically important financial institutions. This book will be of great utility to anyone interested in banking, finance, institutionalism, British political economy as well as the wider legacy of the 2008 crash.'

—Scott Lavery, *Lecturer in the Department of Politics and International Relations, University of Sheffield, UK*

Contents

Abbreviations

ABCP	Asset-Backed Commercial Paper
ABS	Asset Backed Securities
AGM	Annual General Meeting
AML	Anti-Money Laundering
BIS	Bank for International Settlements
BoE	Bank of England
CAPM	Capital Asset Pricing Model
CDO	Collateralise Debt Obligation
CDS	Credit Default Swaps
CEO	Chief Executive Officer
CFTC	Commodity Futures Trading Commission
CMBS	Commercial Mortgage Backed Securities
CRO	Chief Risk Officer
DoJ	Department of Justice
FCA	Financial Conduct Authority
FINMA	Financial Market Supervisory Authority
Forex	Foreign Exchange
FPC	Financial Policy Committee
FSA	Financial Services Authority
GCE	Group Chief Executive
HBOS	Halifax Bank of Scotland
IMF	International Monetary Fund
Libor	London Interbank Offered Rate
MTM	Mark-to-Market
OBSV	Off-Balance Sheet vehicles
PCBS	Parliamentary Commission on Banking Standards

PPI	Payment Protection Insurance
PRA	Prudential Regulation Authority
RBS	Royal Bank of Scotland
REPOs	Repurchase Agreements
RMBS	Residential Mortgage Backed Securities
ROE	Return on Equity
RWA	Risk Weighted Assets
SFO	Serious Fraud Office
SIV	Structured Investment Vehicles
SMEs	Small and Medium-sized Enterprises
SPV	Special Purpose Vehicles
VAR	Value At Risk

CHAPTER 1

Introduction

The devastating events that beset financial markets in the summer of 2007 led to a huge contraction in global economic output and left the financial and banking systems in the core economies of the UK, United States and Europe on the brink of destruction. Mervyn King, former governor of the Bank of England, has pointed out that while financial markets have been plagued by crises and crashes with an almost 'depressing regularity' throughout history, the events of 2007 and 2008 were unprecedented in size and scale, leaving almost no domestic economy unaffected (King, 2009: 1). The ensuing fallout from 'arguably the greatest crisis in the history of financial capitalism' (Turner, 2009: 5) has led to a protracted global economic and political crisis with austerity (Clark, 2016); the European Sovereign Debt Crisis (Tooze, 2018); Brexit (Darling, 2017) and global Trumpism (Blyth & Matthijs, 2017) all being concomitant with the Great Financial Crisis (GFC henceforth).

In the decade that has followed the GFC there has been an attempt by policy-makers and regulators across the globe to strengthen the balance sheets of the world's largest banks. The introduction of more stringent capital and liquidity requirements for institutions deemed as being globally systemically important has meant that banks are now better capitalised than in 2008 with more diversified and 'deeper' sources of funding (Geithner, 2017). Such reforms promised to strengthen the balance sheets of the world's largest banks that would be better placed to withstand

A. Barber, *UK Banks and the Lessons of the Great Financial Crisis*, Building a Sustainable Political Economy: SPERI Research & Policy, https://doi.org/10.1007/978-3-030-70254-0_1

large-scale economic crises (ibid.). However, this somewhat shallow institutional focus by policy-makers and regulators has meant that many of the wider systemic factors that contributed to, and compounded the effects of, the GFC have gone largely unchecked. Though the balance sheets of the world's largest institutions have shrunk dramatically following the GFC, with many banks reducing their global footprint and trimming back non-core businesses, banks and banking markets are now more concentrated (World Bank, 2017) and 'collectively less safe' than in 2008 (Bell & Hindmoor, 2018: 2). As such, and despite regulatory reforms, banks continue to be systemically important and lie at the very heart of the global economy with the Bank of England concluding that banks remain 'prime movers' within financial markets (Bank of England, 2014: 1).

Consequently, the structural and regulatory context within which banks operate post-2008 may not be sufficient to insulate the real economy from shocks originated in the banking sector. For example, Sam Woods of the Bank of England has noted that in order to be effective, regulation must also be met with a 'healthy dose of judgement' on the part of institutions, adding that regulators 'will not spot everything' (Woods, 2017: 20–22). Woods also argues that the 'role of the supervisor is to observe' whereas the role of the 'firm - and the individuals running it – is to meet the intention of regulation' (ibid.). Moreover, institutional reforms have neglected wider post-crisis structural shifts in banking markets that have led to greater regulatory arbitrage as banks look to shift their actives in such a way as to reduce the impact of regulation and effectively 'game' the system (Bell & Hindmoor, 2018). Indeed, Baily et al. (2015) have concluded that constant innovation in banking markets has forced regulators into a never-ending game of catch-up as they seek to mitigate against the potential harmful impact of innovative financial instruments. Meanwhile, Thomas Rixen (2013) has argued that post-crisis attempts at regulatory reform are weak and ineffective. Moreover, despite regulatory efforts, banks in the UK are still too-big-to-fail and retain the ability to trigger and amplify stresses within the economy (Carney, 2016, 2017a, 2017b). Accordingly, the corporate culture, business models and behaviour of banks and bankers are of consequence for the everyday lives of individuals that rely upon the sound functioning of markets (Driga & Dura, 2014).

The Empirical Puzzle

In the wake of the GFC bankers, politicians and regulators have all spoken candidly about the need for lesson learning. In 2009, RBS 'accepted' and 'apologise[d]' for its role in the crisis insisting that it had 'learned lessons' and mended its ways (RBS, 2009). Former Barclays Chairman Marcus Agius likewise noted that Barclays had 'reviewed the lessons learnt from the financial crisis' and had subsequently made 'a number of changes' (Agius, 2010: 151). Stephen Green, former HSBC Chairman, similarly observed that the GFC had highlighted 'important lessons to learn' and the 'need for urgent change' (Green, 2010: 8). More recently, Mark Carney has stressed the importance of banks not losing sight of the lessons of the GFC (Carney, 2017c). Meanwhile, former Prime Minister Gordon Brown believes that banks have failed to learn many of the lessons of the crisis (Brown, 2017).

While leading policy-makers, bankers and politicians have all discussed at length the need and willingness of banks to learn, a key question post-crisis is whether banks have truly undergone a fundamental change. Insights drawn from the organisational studies literature suggests that institutions that fail to act in their own 'enlightened self-interest' (Macartney & Calcagno, 2019: 633) and implement reform in the light of lessons learned will suffer from suboptimal financial performance (Frogman, 1997; Resnick et al., 2006; Ross et al., 1996). Likewise, reputational damage, while not easily quantifiable, has a real bearing upon the commercial and financial viability of a firm (Frogman, 1997; Karpoff, 2012). As such, it stands to reason that following the GFC we may have expected banks to have learned lessons and reform accordingly given the huge financial and reputational losses sustained.

However, at the heart of this 'problem-centred' approach to the research (Shapiro, 2004) lies an assumption that banks want to learn and are capable of learning as rational processors of information. One line of reasoning would suggest that banks took huge risks in the decade before the GFC and have paid few penalties for their actions, because they have been bailed out with few catches. From a macro-vantage point therefore, we may expect that there are few incentives for large banks to learn because there remains a too-big-to-fail issue writ large with state finances as the backstop. This problem has never been fully addressed, and we need to allow for the possibility that some banks have become rent seeking and extracting behemoths (Baker, 2015; Shaxson, 2018), with this so ingrained in their micro-cultures that they cannot learn and cannot change.

Research Questions

The interrogation of this incentive and motivation problem lies at the heart of this research. Over a decade on from the GFC, this book asks: Have banks in the UK learned lessons from the 2008 Great Financial Crisis? Bank learning in the UK after the crisis is something we need to know more about. Whether banks are now safer and more likely to aid rather than disrupt the economy are important questions of social relevance. The book uses original empirical research to reveal the learning experience of UK banks and veracity of these approaches. The book directly addresses and answers a number of important questions:

- Have banks learned lessons from the 2008 Great Financial Crisis?
- What lessons have been learned?
- How have lessons been drawn?
- What has impeded lesson learning?

While extensive reform following the crisis has meant that the regulatory context within which banks operate has changed significantly since 2008 (Baker, 2013; Bell & Hindmoor, 2014; Tucker et al., 2013), supervisory interventions alone may not be sufficient to ensure the safety and stability of banks. Historically low interest rates (IMF, 2017), diminished share price valuations (Bell & Hindmoor, 2018), regulatory arbitrage (Brazier, 2017) and innovative financial products (Erturk, 2017) have meant that banks have both the commercial incentive and means to effectively sidestep regulation (Bell & Hindmoor, 2015a, 2015b; Brazier, 2017; Johal et al., 2014). Thus, it is the banks and not the supervisor that are the regulatory agenda setters (Baily et al., 2015; Brazier, 2017; Woods, 2017). Hence, reform of the financial system may require institutions to recognise the lessons of the past and change accordingly. As such, the question of whether banks in the UK have learned lessons from the GFC is an important one.

By applying a range of learning literatures drawn from the social sciences to the public pronouncements and activities of the UK's largest banks, the book establishes a clear account of what has happened inside these systemically important institutions. The analysis reveals significant insights into the stability of banks post-crisis, the motivation behind any behavioural changes—and the veracity of these approaches—and the implication of change, or lack thereof, for the future of banking and financial markets.

Methods and Theory of Work

This research involves a series of empirical studies and surveys the UK's four largest banks—RBS, Lloyds, Barclays and HSBC—over a ten-year period (2008–2018) following the GFC. These banks dominate the UK banking sector—which is the largest banking market in Europe and fourth largest in the world (UK Finance, 2018)—with 77 per cent of current accounts and 85 per cent of business accounts being held at one of these institutions (CMA, 2016). The banks are also internationally important having been recognised by the Financial Stability Board as 'global systemically important institutions' (FSB, 2016, 2017). Moreover, RBS, Lloyds, Barclays and HSBC are all ranked within the top 25 largest global banks and top 10 largest European banks (S&P Global, 2018).

Due to the sample size, the research does not present a traditional case study analysis from which general musings and broad assumptions about the systemic nature of the UK banking sector can be drawn or applied. However, a survey of the banks presented in the book will make an important contribution to current debates on financial stability, growth and the structural importance of financial services to the UK economy. As such, the question of whether RBS, Lloyds, Barclays and HSBC have learned lessons from the GFC is an important one, not least because of the potential risk that, *prima facie*, these banks still pose to the real economy given their size and role in both domestic and international markets.

The value of the research offered in this book lies in presenting an empirically rich original contribution to the literature that penetrates the business models, corporate culture and behaviour of the UK's four biggest banks in the decade since the GFC. In detailing the inner workings of RBS, Lloyds, Barclays and HSBC—exposing the nature of power located within individual institutions, the dynamics of structural constraints, the logic of authority and control and the interplay between values, success and failures—in the post-crisis decade, we are able to gain valuable insight into the nature of bank learning, the structural and instrumental power of banks in the UK and how the role and influence of banks post-crisis has been challenged by regulatory reforms. Though the research analyses the dynamic qualities of each bank on an individual basis, proportionate relationships between observable factors will be explored and elucidated to the reader where appropriate. I do not believe the small sample size to be a significant factor in the overall logic of the research's major objectives.

Given a post-crisis surge in interest in the banks—the way they operate, how they are regulated and their role within globalised financial markets—by academics, practitioners, the press and public alike, there is now a rich source of information available in the public domain. However, this information remains fragmented with academics and practitioners working within their own narrow disciplinary and policy silos. I overcome these shortcomings by synthesising data from various sources to present a unique study that cuts across disciplinary and policy divides. The four empirical chapters of the book are drawn from a documentary analysis of over 400 strategy documents produced by the four banks; financial market infrastructure providers; government bodies; regulatory authorities; lobbying groups; trade associations; and the media. In addition, the book uses data collated and published by Bankscope to conduct a comparative balance sheet analysis.[1] Collectively, this information will be used to explain and disseminate key changes in the organisational logic and behaviour of banks post-crisis and their capacity for learning. In this respect, the book offers the reader an empirically rich understanding of the intricacies that have pervaded the banking world post-2008 that is missing form current contributions.

To make the collection, analysis and presentation of the empirical material more manageable, the book introduces the evidence for each bank on a case-by-case basis. Each of the empirical chapters, and the material contained there within, is further divided into three broad categories namely, *matters of governance and regulation*, *remuneration and bonuses*, and *the balance sheet*. Due to the complex nature of banking, discussions of post-crisis governance and regulation, remuneration and bonuses, and

[1] Bankscope is published by Bureau van Dijk. All the data cited here was last accessed in December 2016. In January 2017, Bureau van Dijk withdrew Bankscope replacing it with a new service: Orbis Bank Focus. Unfortunately, this new service only reports on bank data since 2011. See: http://www.bvdinfo.com/en-gb/our-products/company-information/international-products/bankscope.

balance sheets cannot be neatly compartmentalised into just a single category with many issues overlapping due to the unique and multifaceted structure of the banks' businesses models. By dividing the analysis in this way, I am able to present the empirical material in an ordered and consistent fashion.

Limitations of the Research

The book also has limitations: I do not study all UK banks or major banks located in Europe and the United States, the latter of which is home to the world's premier global financial centre—New York (Z/Yen & CDI, 2018). The findings presented here are also provisional because, even today, many of the structural and institutional dynamics of the GFC are still being played out. Likewise, while I recognise that banks are capable of learning and change, institutions can also revert to previous behaviours or create entirely new patterns of reasoning not yet witnessed, and as such, the banks may yet change again in the future.

Though the book focuses principally upon banks—specifically UK banks—I do not suppose that banks were the only actors that caused the GFC. Indeed, an array of economic and political considerations, that likewise contributed to, and compounded the effects of, the GFC also need to be accounted for. Similarly, I recognise that the presence of learning at UK banks, or not as the case may be, will not necessarily insulate the global economy from future distress. History has taught us that financial and economic crises can originate from a plethora of sources, many of which lie outside the control of banks and banking markets (Anderson, 2013; Kindleberger & Aliber, 2011). In particular, post-crisis regulatory arrangements; tax reforms in the United States; increased global business leverage and invest debt; sustained global imbalances; debt fuelled growth; expanding Chinese credit markets; Brexit trade negotiations; the environmental crisis; and the ensuing health and economic crisis related to the COVID-19 global pandemic, all similarly warrant further investigation.

The varieties of capitalism literature (Hall & Soskice, 2001) form an important part of contemporary discussions within political economy upon the nature of capitalism and whether a reimaging of capitalism has—or indeed should have—taken place following the crisis. However, I do not directly address current debates on the state of capitalism and the implications of the GFC for the present neoliberal capitalist order.

Despite these limitations, a focus on post-GFC bank learning will make an important and original contribution to the field of political economy. The book offers an empirically rich picture of how interactions between agents (bankers), institutions (banks) and structures (financial markets) have operated in such a way as to elicit certain behavioural responses, biases and beliefs and how these have been translated into real-world outcomes. Likewise, the analysis of bank learning, and the implication of change, presented here will speak to broader themes concerning financial stability, growth and the sound functioning of markets, due to the huge role that these systemically important institutions continue to play in the global economy. In this respect, the themes explored in the book also address the financialisation and varieties of capitalism literatures.

Contribution to the Literature

This research offers a number of distinct contributions to the existing literature. First, the book situates self-directed bank learning within wider post-crash structural debates surrounding growth, the sound functioning of markets and regulatory reform. Building on an expanded historical institutionalist theoretical framework, the book problematises current regulatory and macroprudential responses to the crisis. For example, the role of the banks in the GFC has been well documented (see, e.g., Bernanke, 2009; 2012; Cohan, 2009, 2011; Lewis, 2011; Sorkin, 2009) and we know that banks were one of the key actors in the crisis. Yet, an element missing from the literature is the question of self-directed bank reform. Current contributions have instead focused upon unravelling the many causes of the crisis (see, e.g., Blinder, 2014; Davies, 2010; Stiglitz, 2010; Wolf, 2015), the issue of regulation (see, e.g., Geithner, 2017; Helleiner, 2014; Rixen 2013) and macroprudential reform (see, e.g., Baker, 2015; Eatwell, 2009; Mugge, 2011). However, these contributions are also problematic as they fail to account for the agency of the banks and bankers in shaping their proximate environment (Bell & Hindmoor, 2015a). This book seeks to rebalance the debate by moving beyond questions of regulation and macroprudential policy. Instead, the book adopts a bank-centric comparative analysis of the UK's four largest banks (RBS, Lloyds, Barclays and HSBC) that recognises the vital role played by these systemically important institutions in driving the reform process post-crisis.

Second, the book also contributes to a wider critical political economy literature concerning the financialisation of markets (van der Zwan, 2014) and the structural importance of financial services to the UK's economy (Krippner, 2011). A reluctance on the part of political leaders and policy-makers in the UK to introduce more sweeping structural reforms in the wake of the crisis reveals important insights about the UK's finance-led growth model. The prevailing financialisation of the UK's economy from the 1980s onwards has had the effect of both strengthening banks while at the same time constraining policy-makers (Bell & Hindmoor, 2015a, 2018). By placing banks at the centre of the UK's 'finance-led regime of accumulation' (Macartney & Calcagno, 2019: 631), financialisation has reinforced the power of the banks to resist more radical reform due to their privileged position at the heart of a finance-led growth model (Krippner, 2011). At the same time, the agency of political leaders and policy-makers has been inhibited by the capital-intensive nature of a highly financialised economic structure that state managers both helped create but are also increasingly beholden to (Bell &d Hindmoor, 2015a, 2018). My research outlines the ways in which behavioural forms and patterns of learning by the banks may undermine the UK's finance-led growth model and precarious economic recovery.

Third, the book advances the first comprehensive treatment of Britain's 'big four' banks in the post-crisis decade (2008–2018). Through documentary analysis and a detailed examination of the behaviour and performance of banks, the book establishes a clear account of what has happened inside these institutions. By examining the business models, culture and decision-making processes of the banks, the book reveals important insights about the motivation behind any behavioural changes post-crisis. As such, a systemic coverage of learning by major UK banks will make an original and important contribution to the current literature and ongoing debates surrounding the regulation and the sound functioning of financial markets, the social utility of an oversized financial sector and financial stability.

Selection and Justification of Theoretical Framework

In this section of the chapter, I introduce the theoretical framework against which the book's key themes and research questions will be explored. I build upon an expanded version of historical institutionalism first developed by Bell (2011), Bell and Feng (2014) and Bell and Hindmoor (2015a), that seeks to use the methods of political science to study the behaviour of agents within an institutional and structural context. Drawing upon institutional theory, and in particular the expanded version of historical institutionalism explored by Bell (2011), Bell and Feng (2014) and Bell and Hindmoor (2015a), I am able to make distinctions between structures (financial markets), institutions (banks) and agents (bankers) in order to study how these 'mutually-shaping interactions' are played out through time (Bell & Hindmoor, 2015a: 21–22). The theoretical framework explored and developed in this section of the book will provide my research with a rich theoretical underpinning against which the behaviour of banks and bankers, along with their capacity for learning will be examined. Though my research is firmly situated within the institutionalist school, the application of historical institutionalism towards the study of post-crisis banking, institutional learning and the politics of reform is novel. To date, no academic books have been published that focus directly on post-crisis bank learning. Indeed, there appear to be very few, if any, texts that consider a bank-centric approach to growth, the sound functioning of markets and regulatory reform more generally. As such, the expanded version of historical institutionalism utilised here will make a major contribution to a very large field that will benefit from the book's unique theoretical perspective.

The meaning applied to institutions and structures within the social sciences literature has often been blurred, with these key terms having frequently being used interchangeably and thereby leading to a great deal of ambiguity and confusion (see Cortell & Peterson, 1999). Given the emphasis that historical institutionalism places upon agents, institutions and structures, it is pertinent to the ensuing discussion that we first, albeit briefly, examine how the institutionalist school distinguishes between agents, institutions and structures. According to Hodgson (2006: 18) institutions are 'systems of established and embedded social rules that structure social interactions'. These rules form the basis of recognised norms, ideational biases, values and underlying philosophies that are simultaneously adopted, reproduced and reshaped by members belonging to a particular group (Fleetwood, 2008: 15). Within the context of this research, it is the banks that embody these ideational preferences, beliefs and underlying values. In this respect, RBS, Lloyds, Barclays and HSBC signify the institutional dynamics that will be examined.

Structures on the other hand are understood to be the broader situational environment within which institutions operate (Bell & Hindmoor,

2015a). Structures are often used to explain how constituent parts of a whole relate to one another (Elder-Vass, 2006: 10) and may include power relations, material incentives and sanctions or 'other rationalities or pressures' that may shape the preference choice of agents (Bell & Hindmoor, 2015a: 23). Put simply, structures are the 'templates for action' that inform the human condition and decision-making process by endowing agents with information relating to consequences of a particular action (Lopez & Scott, 2000: 30). In terms of this research, structures are understood as being the wider context within which post-crisis discussions of bank learning, along with the broader themes of this book, will take place. For example, financial markets, regulatory constraints, competition between banks, political considerations and the rewards and disincentives associated with specified behaviours are all representative of the structural setting within which bank learning and this research is positioned.

The significance of defining and separating institutions and structures is twofold. First, such a distinction gives the research a robust theoretical grounding upon which the subsequent investigations, arguments and conclusions of the book can be built and tested. Second, by delineating institutions and structures, the research will be well positioned to identify changes that have occurred at the banks independently of structural constraints—and which subsequently may be indicative of learning—from those that have been mandated by the wider operating environment, such as changes in regulatory requirements. By detaching institutions from structures, we will similarly gain insight into those conditions that affect learning, but remain outside of the immediate environment and control of agents.

Situating Historical Institutionalism

Before I move on to discuss the practical application of expanded historical institutionalism to my own research, it is important we first situate historical institutionalism within the broader literature and specifically the institutionalist school to which it owes its intellectual roots. Historical institutionalism, along with rational choice theory and sociological institutionalism, belongs to the 'new institutionalist' approach of studying the social sciences (Meyer & Rowan, 1977; DiMaggio & Powell, 1983; North, 1990). While all three fields of thought are concerned with the study of institutional 'rules', 'norms' and 'common understandings' (Cairney, 2012: 70), what separates these contending theories is the extent to which they ascribe meaning to the ability of agents to shape and be shaped by contextual factors. For example, rational choice theorists suggest that agents are essentially self-seeking individuals that when faced with a particular decision or situation will always look to maximise returns while minimising the associated costs (Steinmo, 2012: 126). Rational choice theory views institutions as a framing mechanism that shapes an agent's decision-making process by presenting individuals with both the costs and benefits—embedded within institutional norms and rules—of their behavioural decisions (Hindmoor, 2006). As such, rational choice theory suggests that an individual's actions can be accurately predicted based upon the 'expected utility' of a specific path and agents' propensity towards maximising returns (Green & Shapiro, 1994: 17–30).

Conversely, sociological institutionalists view agents as being fundamentally social beings that behave in routine ways that are neither totally rational nor deliberately self-serving (King, 2004). In this respect, institutions are framed as being the 'social norms that govern everyday life and social interaction' (Steinmo, 2012: 126). According to this view, institutions act as a 'key reference point' for agents whom it is assumed will both 'obey' and be 'guardians' of the predominant rules and norms (March & Olsen, 2006: 7). Sociological institutionalists suggest that when confronted by rules and principles, agents will not look to maximise their own self-interest but will behave in a manner that is most appropriate or socially acceptable with individuals being free to interpret the 'meaning of their institutional commitments' (Peters, 2005: 26).

Historical institutionalists situate themselves somewhere in the middle of these two contending schools, believing agents to be simultaneously 'norm abiding rule followers and self-interested rational actors' (Steinmo, 2012: 126). Historical institutionalism distinguishes itself from other new institutionalist theories, which Pierson (2000: 93) suggests overemphasise the paralysis of institutions over agents by limiting an individual's 'room to manoeuvre', by developing a theoretical framework that allows the study of the delicate interplay between agents and the 'formal rules, compliance procedures and standard operating procedures' that govern institutions (Hall cited in Thelen & Steinmo, 2008: 188). Essentially, historical institutionalism puts agents back into institutional analysis and allows us to study how interactions between agents and the institutions that they inhabit are manifest in real-world situations.

Expanded Historical Institutionalism and the Importance of Agency

Scholars such as Blyth (1997), Hay (2006) and Schmidt (2008) have all raised concerns over the application of historical institutionalism to the study of the social sciences with Hay (2006: 590) suggesting that historical institutionalism tends towards the 'lock-in' effects associated with institutional path dependency. Likewise, Blyth (1997: 230) contends that institutions 'constrain rather than enable political action'. Meanwhile Schmidt (2008: 313) purports that institutionalism holds an 'overly sticky' conception of institutions. Similarly, North (1990) has argued that institutions, while conceived by humans, can act as a powerful constraining force that ultimately shapes and determines the trajectory of an agent's behaviour.

The work of Bell (2011), Bell and Feng (2014) and Bell and Hindmoor (2015a), looks to overcome these shortcomings which Bell (2011) argues places too much emphasis upon the '*institutional*' of historical institutionalism. By moving beyond traditional applications of historical institutionalism and firmly situating their theoretical framework within the structure and agency approach of studying the social sciences, Bell and Hindmoor (2015a) situate institutions, such as banks, as an arbitrator of the interactions between agents and structures. Importantly however, the scholars stress that agents are not simply banal actors but instead possess their own unique ideas and perceptions about the world and which determines how agents behave when confronted by structures (ibid.: 24). Likewise, Streeck (2009), due to the rapidly changing trajectory of capitalism over the past three decades, has similarly called for the Academy to move beyond purely institutionalist approaches to studying political science, arguing for the need to contemplate both structural and institutional considerations.

My own research utilises an historical institutionalist theoretical framework but, following in the tradition of Streeck (2009) and Bell and Hindmoor (2015a), moves beyond the constraints of an overly institutionalist approach. One of the strengths of institutionalism is the recognition of agents as being responsible for the creation of institutions. However, institutionalist accounts of structure and agency are also problematic, as they tend to overplay the stifling effect of institutions (Bell & Hindmoor, 2015a). Likewise, an exaggerated intuitionalist approach to the study of political science fails to recognise the authoritative and independent nature of 'interpretive agents' and their ability to overcome institutional barriers (Bell, 2011). Indeed, Weyland (2008: 281) contends that institutionalist analyses tend to be overly 'static' and 'linear' making it difficult to explain political change. Likewise, Schmidt (2008: 314) similarly argues that institutionalist approaches have been guilty of 'subordinating' human agency to structures resulting in 'unthinking' actors.

In order to overcome the shortcomings associated with a purely institutionalist approach to the research, my own work will not limit or overlook the role of agency in the analytical process. I move beyond traditional applications of institutional theory that can limit the scope of agency and is better suited to the study of static institutions that are epitomised by continuity and predictability (Bell & Hindmoor, 2015a), as opposed to the shifts and shocks we associate with banks and financial markets. Instead, I undertake a careful and detailed examination of both agents and institutions in the post-crisis decade. In particular, I focus upon how key 'interpretive agents' (Bell, 2011) within the banks are shaped by, and are able to shape, the institutions within which they operate and thereby steering the structures that they helped to create.

Structures, Institutions and Agents

The theoretical framework that I advance here does not reject or abandon institutionalism, instead I look to cast a new light on how we view and conceptualise institutions and their role in the study of the social sciences. Such an approach will equip my research with the freedom to move beyond the constraints of institutionally based conceptions of learning. In doing so, I will be free to draw-out and make key analytical divisions between structures, institutions and agents. The importance of these distinctions is emphasised by Bell (2011) who concludes that institutions are best viewed as taking on a mediating role between agents and structures, a division that is often conflated and lost within purely institutionalist approaches. Such an approach will provide my research with a rich theoretical underpinning against which post-crisis banking, institutional learning and the politics of reform will be explored.

Though I recognise the importance of structures in the analytical process, I likewise avoid the trappings of overly structuralist approach that tends to exaggerate the deterministic or constraining forces of structures (Hindmoor & McGeechan, 2013). Instead, I argue that structures endow agents with both restraints and freedoms. Here I turn to the work of Bell and Hindmoor (2015a) to whom my own theoretical approach owes its intellectual roots. For example, in their account of the GFC, Bell and Hindmoor (2015a) demonstrate how the financialisation of global markets from the 1980s onwards was, on the one hand, representative of the growing structural significance of international finance. On the other hand, the authors argue that a shift in the growing magnitude of global finance did not occur independently but was instead arbitrated by key agents (ibid.: 26–27). Indeed, it appears that a series of financial innovations conceived of by agents, and supported by governments keen to harness the perceived benefits of greater economic liberalisation, shifted the structural power of global capitalism towards agents and institutions—bankers and banks—in the years preceding the GFC.

Scholars such as Barnett and Duvall (2005) also suggest that structures have the power to distribute and align the costs or benefits of a specific path or action. The authors argue that as a result, agents may be less willing to challenge structurally imposed power relations and will be more inclined to accept certain structural dynamics (ibid.). However, my analysis joins that of Bell and Hindmoor (2015a: 28) in arguing that while resignation may be one resulting factor of the inherent power of mediating structures, power can also be returned to individuals through the cognition of agents to 'create an ideational or discursive order' that aligns the self-interests of multiple agents. By interpreting, manipulating and influencing structural power dynamics in this way, agents are able to skew the benefits of structures to their own advantage (ibid.). In this instance, the unique structural power relations between agents, institutions and structures are not manifest through sanctions or a certain kind of coercive power but through agents' own willingness to accept and support structural relations due to the perceived material payoff that such an alignment would bring. Such a conception of the role of structures and agents will allow my own work to move beyond a purely structuralist approach to the research.

Likewise, though my work is situated within the tradition of institutionalism, I look to broaden my approach beyond either the new institutionalist or structuralist school by again incorporating the theoretical framework first established by Bell and Hindmoor (2015a). Utilising the work of Margaret Archer (1995, 2000, 2003), the authors are able to make four important analytical distinctions between agents, institutions and structures that will aid my analysis of post-crisis bank learning in the UK. *First*, the authors argue that agents, institutions and structures each possess unique properties that are analytically and methodologically different and as such, one cannot be reduced to the other; *second*, the institutional and structural settings within which agents act are 'pre-given at any point in time'; *third*, agents, institutions and structures are constantly engaged in a 'dialectically' mutually shaping relationship; *fourth*, institutional and structural effects are played out and arbitrated through agents (Bell & Hindmoor, 2015a: 24).

The practical application of Bell and Hindmoor's (2015a) expanded historical institutionalism and the distinction between agents, institutions and structures made by the authors, will be of central importance to my own analysis. I argue that in the post-crisis decade bankers have been key agents of reform with the ability steer institutions and markets. Importantly however, institutional and structural factors have not merely been supplanted by the agency of individuals. Indeed, I demonstrate that the authority of agents is also dependent upon institutions and structures, which empower agents. As we shall see in the coming chapters, powerful agents within the banks have the ability to steer organisations but are also beholden to powerful institutional and structural dynamics that in some instances have dictated the pace and extent of reform. For example, in response to institutional and structural incentives and pressures, bankers have looked to re-engineer their balance sheets in the decade that has followed the crisis. An increasing reliance upon short-term wholesale funding, a growth in trading liabilities along with an expansion of off-balance sheet trading activity has exposed the banks and bankers to new as well as old forms of systemic risk. In this respect, though agents have the ability to shape institutional and structural dynamics, there is also present a delicate interplay between agents, institutions and structures that has dictated the learning trajectory of banks in the post-crisis decade.

These theoretical delineations demonstrate how institutions can empower and 'liberate' agents that, in turn, can lead to structural change. Moreover, the theoretical framework unpacked above is indicative of the importance of studying agents, institutions and structures—which act as a mediating force of prevailing ideas and material interest—within political science. The expanded version of historical institutionalism first pioneered by Bell (2011), Bell and Feng (2014) and Bell and Hindmoor (2015a), and built upon here, will equip my own analysis with the theoretical tools needed to analyse and understand the structural and institutional context within which autonomous agents learn. Such distinctions are important as they will provide my research with the intellectual apparatus needed to explain inter-bank variations in learning and the degree to which agents have been able to steer some institutions clear of the most harmful effects of the GFC and resist structural pressures. It is against this backdrop that this book, the research questions and general theorising will be situated.

The Chapters

In Chapter 2, I look at the idea of learning. Using literature gathered from across the social sciences, the chapter 'unpacks' the concept of learning and sets out a clear definition of what learning entails—the mechanisms by which agents and institutions learn and how we account for structural considerations in the learning process. In particular, the account of learning presented in Chapter 2 will be used to identify the key characteristics of learning while also familiarising the reader with those conditions most conducive towards learning. Specifically, the chapter will stress the importance of double-loop learning which dictates a positive behavioural change in an organisation's values, philosophies and procedures. The chapter will also stress the importance of both 'learning space'—the dedication of time and resources to the learning process—and 'dissatisfaction' as being key detriments in the learning trajectory of institutions.

Chapter 3 provides the reader with a detailed account of the central causes of the GFC. It will consider how a series of socio-economic and socio-political synergies, coupled with a system predicated upon risk, combined to create the 'perfect storm'. In particular, it will be argued that competition, along with a plethora of mutually shaping non-exclusive causes, was a key factor in the financial meltdown of 2007/2008 and remains today one of the greatest obstacles to learning. As well as situating the structural background against which post-crisis bank learning will take pace, the purpose of Chapter 3 is to create and detail a series of benchmarks against which the progress of banks can be assessed. Those factors that gave rise to and magnified the crisis will be the key measures against which the ensuing empirical evidence will be tested.

Chapter 4 will present the first of the empirical studies and will discuss the extent to which learning has taken place at RBS. The evidence presented in this chapter will suggest that despite making some positive changes including reducing the group's bonus pool by 72 per cent, retrenching the business on UK domestic markets and exiting or reducing exposures within a number of non-core businesses, RBS has on the whole failed to learn lessons from the crisis. The evidence presented in this chapter will suggest that RBS' lack of learning can be attributed to the group failing to orient the necessary learning space towards the reflexive process inherent in learning. Instead, it will be argued that the group has been consumed with the trivial detail of specific failures that have diverted time and resources away from an overall strategic review of the business. As such, RBS' underlying philosophies, objectives and standard operating procedures have undergone little reform following the GFC.

Chapter 5 will present the empirical evidence in relation to Lloyds Banking Group. In this chapter, I argue that despite a catastrophic merger with Halifax Bank of Scotland, which resulted in a state-sponsored bailout worth more than £20 billion, Lloyds do appear to have learned lessons from the GFC. It will be demonstrated that post-2008 Lloyds has increased customer deposits and reduced short-term funding, reduced its leverage ratio, increased regulatory capital and exited multiple foreign markets. While Lloyds, like all the banks in this study, has not been without its problems, especially in relation to internal governance, the evidence shows that when confronted with failures, or moments of dissatisfaction, Lloyds has been quick to deal with matters, and has applied institutional resources—learning space—towards the reflexive process associated with learning. Moreover, it will be demonstrated that by acting quickly and decisively the group has been free to concentrate on drawing lessons from the GFC, which has resulted in a positive learning experience for the bank.

In Chapter 6, I examine Barclays that presents a rather interesting case with the evidence suggesting that the group may have undergone a double U-turn post-2008. For example, in the years that immediately followed the GFC, Barclays demonstrated little evidence of learning or change. However, after a series of governance failures, the most notable of which was the group's implication in the rigging of Libor, Barclays commissioned an independent evaluation of the business in the form of the Salz Review. As a result, the group launched a series of initiatives aimed at restoring trust in the Barclays brand—putting 'values' back into the business and de-risking the balance sheet. A significant part of this new regime would involve the scaling back of the investment bank, which was identified as the driving force behind much of the nefarious culture that had infected the entire group. Consequently, it appeared that Barclays were beginning to show signs of learning and change. However, its investors became uneasy with the new business model and soon began to grow impatient. Following a boardroom coup in July 2015, Anthony Jenkins, the group chief executive that had been responsible for much of Barclays' turnaround, was terminated. Jes Staley, a career investment banker, was sought as his replacement who quickly began to rebuild the investment bank and roll-back many of the initiatives that had been implemented under the tenure of his predecessor. The picture unfolded in Chapter 6 is of particular interest as it stresses the role of competitive structural pressures, the interpretation of these structures by agents, and the impact of these structural and institutional dynamics upon the learning trajectory of banks.

Chapter 7 presents the final empirical study of the book and details for the reader the evidence relating to HSBC. It will be shown that following the crisis HSBC has learned different lessons in relation to different areas of the business with this learning taking place at dissimilar speeds. Archer's (2003, 2012) thesis on the meta-reflexives will be used to explain how, in relation to the balance sheet, there appears to be evidence of learning despite the absence of notable change. It will be demonstrated that HSBC has learned lessons but in this instance, substantive change is neither required nor productive. Conversely, evidence presented in relation to remuneration will suggest a rather conflated story of learning and change. This may be attributed to structural competitive pressure and HSBC's perceived diminished ability to attract and retain the brightest banking talent. Evidence will be discussed which suggests that while all the banks in this study are subject to structural competitive pressures, these have been felt more acutely at HSBC and Barclays. This can be attributed to the banks' continued exposure to non-EU markets that have subsequently brought the banks into direct competition with institutions not held to the same domestic and European regulatory standards. The contribution of the evidence presented in this chapter will be important to the research as it leads us to two very important conclusions surrounding learning. First, in accordance with Archer's (2003, 2012) work on the meta-reflexives learning may be possible despite tangible change. Second, structures, interpreted through institutions by key agents, clearly matter in the learning trajectory of the banks.

The concluding chapter will draw together the evidence presented in the empirical sections of the book and will determine that RBS and Barclays have largely failed to learn lessons from the GFC. Conversely, the chapter will find that Lloyds and HSBC have generally demonstrated evidence of learning and change. However, it will be stressed that we must approach such conclusions with caution and avoid making generalisations as it will be shown that there is no single or uniform answer to the questions posed by this research. Instead, it will be noted that each bank should be considered on its own merit with the complexity of institutions meaning that different banks have learned different lessons in relation to contending areas of both their own business and the banking sector in general.

Notwithstanding these institutional variations, the book will conclude that there are identifiable amongst the banks a number of recurring themes or ideas that appear to have been significant in the learning trajectory of institutions. It will be shown that dissatisfaction—defined as when institutional aspirations outstrip outcomes—plays an important role in learning with a degree of dissatisfaction needed to propel banks from a static state towards the progress of learning. However, it will be demonstrated that too much dissatisfaction can be crippling and retard the learning process with the level of dissatisfaction being particular to each individual bank.

Likewise, the analysis will find that the application of 'learning space'—institutional resources—both human and fiscal capital—to the reflexive process inherent in learning, has been a mitigating factor of post-crisis bank learning. For example, banks such as Lloyds and HSBC have been successful learners because they have oriented sufficient learning space towards the undertaking of a fundamental re-evaluation of their underlying principles, philosophies and key strategical practices in the light of the causes of the crisis. Importantly however, it will be observed that the degree of learning space enjoyed by an organisation has largely been determined by institutional interpretations and responses to organisational failures and the GFC more generally.

This leads us to a further conclusion of the research, namely, that both structure and agency matter in the learning process. Yet, while the extent to which structural determinants influence learning at the banks appears to be subject to the interpretations of situational agents, some structural pressures seem to be too great to overcome even when change is recognised as being desirable by these key agents. Subsequently, the book utilises the work of Margaret Archer to conclude that in some cases learning can occur despite the presence of substantive change particularly when the associated cost of change is deemed to be too high. In this instance, the analysis finds that institutions can learn but the lesson learned is about the cost of reform to the perceived competitive position of the bank.

Due to the small sample size, as discussed above, we should avoid applying these conclusions to UK banks and banking markets in general, with the chosen institutions being representative as opposed to systemic. Nonetheless, conclusions drawn from this research remain important due to the systemically important nature of the banks surveyed—as demonstrated through both their domestic dominance and international holdings—with institutions still considered too-big-to-fail (Kay, 2016). Moreover, the bank-centric approach adopted by this research and subsequent conclusions will inform current debates on financial stability and growth, addressing a key gap in the literature. The book also stresses that it is important that we keep in mind that not only can banks change but that they can also revert back to previous behaviours and change again in the future. That is to say, we should not assume that institutions such as RBS and Barclays that have generally failed to learn lessons would not learn and change in the future. Indeed, as we shall see within the empirical chapters, RBS and Barclays do present some limited evidence or 'pockets' of learning in certain areas of the business. Conversely, Lloyds and HSBC while generally displaying positive signs of learning may also change in the future to the detriment of financial stability. Essentially, the analysis presented here is provisional because while cultures at the banks may be set this does not mean that they are permanent.

References

Agius, M. (2010) Barclays corporate governance report: Group chairman's introduction. In *Barclays [Barclays banking group PLC] Annual report and accounts 2009*. Available at: https://home.barclays/content/dam/home-barclays/documents/investor-relations/annualreports/ar2009/barclays-plc-annual-report-2009.pdf, pp. 151–152.

Anderson, S. (2013). A history of the past 40 years in financial crises. In International financing review, 2000 issue 40 years in review. Thomas Reuters (pp. 48–52). Available at: http://edition.pagesuite-professional.co.uk/Launch.aspx?EID=b2eb69c3-7774-4d35-a0ff-c70b03f7288f.

Archer, M. (1995). *Realist social theory: The morphogenetic approach*. Cambridge: Cambridge University Press.

Archer, M. (2000). *Being human: The problem of agency*. Cambridge: Cambridge University Press.

Archer, M. (2003). *Structure, agency and the internal conversation*. Cambridge: Cambridge University Press.
Archer, M. (2012). *The reflexive imperative in late modernity*. Cambridge: Cambridge University Press.
Baily, M., Holmes, S., & Bekker, W. (2015, May 26). *The big four banks: The evolution of the financial sector, part I*. Brooking Institute. Available at: https://www.brookings.edu/wp-content/uploads/2016/06/big_four_banks_evolution_financial_sector_pt1_final.pdf.
Baker, A. (2013). The new political economy of the macroprudential ideational shift. *New Political Economy, 18*(1), 112–139.
Baker, A. (2015). *The bankers paradox: The political economy of macroprudential regulation* (SRC Discussion Paper No. 37). The London School of Economics and Political Science.
Bank of England. (2014). *The financial policy committee's powers to supplement capital requirements: a policy statement by the financial policy committee*. London: Bank of England. Available at: http://www.bankofengland.co.uk/financialstability/Documents/fpc/policystatement140113.pdf.
Barnett, M., & Duvall, R. (2005). Power in international politics. *International Organization, 59*(1), 39–75.
Bell. S. (2011). Do we really need a new 'constructivist institutionalism' to explain institutional change? *British Journal of Political Science, 41*(4), 883–906.
Bell, S., & Feng, H. (2014). How proximate and 'meta-institutional' contexts shape institutional change: Explaining the rise of the people's bank of China. *Political Studies, 62*(1), 197–215.
Bell, S., & Hindmoor, A. (2014). The ideational shaping of state power and capacity: Winning battles but losing the war over bank reform in the us and uk. *Government and Opposition, 49*(3), 342–368.
Bell, S., & Hindmoor, A. (2015a). *Masters of the universe, slaves of the market*. Cambridge MA: Harvard University Press.
Bell, S., & Hindmoor, A. (2015b). Masters of the universe but slaves of the market: Bankers and the great financial meltdown. *British Journal of Politics and International Relations, 17*(1), 1–22.
Bell, S., & Hindmoor, A. (2018). Are the major global banks now safer? Structural continuities and change in banking and finance since the 2008 crisis. *Review of International Political Economy, 25*(1), 1–27.
Bernanke, B. (2009, November 17). *Testimony before the national commission on the causes of the financial and economic crisis in the United States*. Available at: http://som.yale.edu/sites/default/files/files/Bernanke_Ben_Financial_Crisis_Inquiry_Commission_11-17-09.pdf.

Bernanke, B. (2012, April 13). *Some reflections on the crisis and the policy response*. Speech at the Russell Sage Foundation and the Century Foundation Conference on Rethinking Finance, New York. Available at http://www.federalreserve.gov/newsevents/speech/bernanke20120413a.htm.

Blinder, A. (2014). *After the music stopped: The financial crisis, the response, and the work ahead*. New York: Penguin Books.

Blyth, M. (1997). Any more bright ideas? The ideational turn of comparative political economy. *Comparative Politics, 29*(2), 229–250.

Blyth, M., & Matthijs, M. (2017). Black swans, lame ducks, and the mystery of IPE's missing macroeconomy. *Review of International Political Economy, 24*(2), 203–223.

Brazier, A. (2017, Monday 24 July). *'Debt strikes back' or 'the return of the regulator'?*. Alex Brazier executive director, financial director for financial stability strategy and risk member of the financial policy committee bank of England University of Liverpool, Institute for Risk and Uncertainty. Available at: http://www.bankofengland.co.uk/publications/Documents/speeches/2017/speech992.pdf.

Brown, G. (2017). *Gordon Brown my life, our times*. London: Bodley Head.

Cairney, P. (2012). *Understanding public policy: Theories and issues*. Basingstoke: Palgrave.

Carney, M. (2016, February). *Bank of England inflation report press conference* [online]. Available at: http://www.bankofengland.co.uk/publications/Pages/webcasts/latest.aspx.

Carney, M. (2017a, September 28). *Opening remarks to the bank of England 'independence—20 years on'*. Conference Remarks given by Mark Carney, Governor of the Bank of England. Available at: https://www.bankofengland.co.uk/-/media/boe/files/speech/2017/opening-remarks-at-the-boe-independence-20-years-on-conference.pdf?la=en&hash=4D7358410C6E5852A401EC6EF0DEEE7A00D4F0F9.

Carney, M. (2017b, Tuesday). *Financial stability report press conference* [online]. Available at: https://www.bankofengland.co.uk/-/media/boe/files/financial-stability-report/2017/transcript-june-2017.pdf?la=en&hash=AF4E73FFEE23818E5CC4B3D8B479968E2AF9ADFD.

Carney, M. (2017c, April 20). *What a difference a decade makes*. Remarks at the institute of International Finance's Washington Policy Summit, the Reagan Centre, Washington DC [online]. Available at: https://www.bankofengland.co.uk/-/media/boe/files/speech/2017/what-a-difference-a-decade-makes.

Clark, D. (2016). *The global financial crisis and austerity: A basic introduction*. Bristol: Polity Press.

CMA [Competition & Markets Authority]. (2016). *Retail banking Market investigation: Final report august 2016*. Available at: https://assets.publis

hing.service.gov.uk/media/57ac9667e5274a0f6c00007a/retail-banking-market-investigation-full-final-report.pdf.

Cohan, W. (2009). *House of cards: A tale of hubris and wretched excess on wall street*. New York: Doubleday.

Cohan, W. (2011). *Money and power: How goldman sachs came to rule the world*. New York: Doubleday.

Cortell, A., & Peterson, S. (1999). Altered states: Explaining domestic institutional change. *British Journal of Political Science, 29*(1) (January), 177–203.

Darling, A. (2017, September 13). Between a rock and a hard place: 10 years on from Northern rock. *Resolution Foundation* [online]. Available at: https://www.youtube.com/watch?v=hBTI4GQT_OI&feature=youtu.be.

Davies, H. (2010). *The financial crisis: Who is to blame?*. Cambridge: Polity Press.

DiMaggio, P., & Powell, W. (1983). The iron cage revisited: Institutional isomorphism and collective rationality in organizational fields. *American Sociological Review, 48*(2), 147–160.

Driga, I., & Dura, C. (2014). *The financial sector and the role of banks in economic development*. Annals of the University of Petrosani, pp. 598–603. Available at: http://www.upet.ro/simpro/2014/proceedings/09%20-%20ECONOMICS%20AND%20PUBLIC%20ADMINISTRATION/9.2.pdf.

Eatwell, J. (2009). Practical proposals for regulatory reform. In P. Subacchi & A. Monsarrat (Eds.), *New ideas for the London summit: Recommendations to the G20 leaders* (pp. 11–15). London: Royal Institute for International Affairs Chatham, The Atlantic Council.

Elder-Vass. D. (2006). Re-examining Bhaskar's three ontological domains: the lessons from emergence. In C. Lawson, J. Latsis, & N. Martins (Eds.), *Contributions to social ontology*. London: Routledge.

Erturk, I. (2017). Shadow banking: A story of the doppelganger (the Double) in science of finance. *Journal of Cultural Economy* (16 November 2016), 1–16.

Fleetwood, S. (2008). Institutions and social structures. *Journal for the Theory of Social Behaviour, 38*(3).

Frogman, J. (1997). Socially irresponsible and illegal behavior and shareholder wealth: A metaanalysis of event studies. *Sage, 36*(3), 221–249.

FSB [Financial Stability Board]. (2016, November 21). *2016 List of Global Systemically Important Banks (G-SIBs)* [online]. Available at: https://www.fsb.org/wp-content/uploads/2016-list-of-global-systemically-important-banks-G-SIBs.pdf.

FSB [Financial Stability Board]. (2017, November 21). *2017 List of Global Systemically Important Banks (G-SIBs)* [online]. Available at: https://www.fsb.org/wp-content/uploads/P211117-1.pdf.

Geithner, T. (2017). Are we safe yet: How to manage financial crises? *Foreign Affairs, 96*(1), 54–72.

Green, S. (2010). *Group chairman's statement: 2009: A year of transition*. In HSBC [HSBC Holdings PLC] Annual report and accounts 2009: Strong, steadfast, sustainable. Available at: www.hsbc.com/-/media/hsbc-com/.../financialresults/2009/hsbc2009ara0.pdf, pp. 8–11.

Green, D. P., & Shapiro, I. (1994). *Pathologies of rational choice theory: A critique of applications in political science*. New Haven: Yale University Press.

Hall, P., & Soskice, D. (2001). *Varieties of capitalism: The institutional foundations of comparative advantage*. Oxford: Oxford University Press.

Hay. C. (2006). Globalization in public policy in rein. In M. Moran, & R. Goodin (Eds), *Oxford handbook of public policy*. Oxford: Oxford University Press.

Helleiner, E. (2014). *The status Quo crisis: Global financial governance after the 2008 meltdown*. Oxford: Oxford University Press.

Hindmoor, A. (2006). *Rational choice*. London: Palgrave Macmillan.

Hindmoor, A., & McGeechan, J. (2013). Luck, systematic luck and business power: Lucky all the way down or trying hard to get what it wants without trying? *Political Studies, 61*(4), 834–849.

Hodgson, G. (2006). What are institutions. *Journal of Economic, 40*(1), 1–25.

International Monetary Fund [IMF]. (2017, April). *Global financial stability report: Getting the policy mix right*. Available at: https://www.imf.org/en/Publications/GFSR/Issues/2017/03/30/global-financial-stability-report-april-2017.

Johal, S., Moran, M., & Williams, K. (2014). Power, politics and the city of London after the great financial crisis. *Government and Opposition, 49*(3), 400–425.

Karpoff, J. M. (2012). Does reputation work to discipline corporate misconduct? In T. Pollock & M. Barnett (Eds.), *The Oxford handbook of corporate reputation*. Oxford: Oxford University Press.

Kay, J. (2016). *Other people's money*. London: Profile Books.

Kindleberger, C. P., & Aliber, R. Z. (2011). *Manias, panics, and crashes, a history of financial crises*. Basingstoke: Palgrave Macmillan.

King, A. (2004). *The structure of social theory*. London: Routledge.

King, M. (2009, March 17). *Finance—A return from risk*. Speech to the Worshipful Company of International Bankers. London. Available at http://www.bis.org/review/r090319a.pdf.

Krippner, G. (2011). *Capitalizing on crisis: The political origins of the rise of finance*. Cambridge, MA: Harvard University Press.

Lewis, M. (2011). *The big short*. London: Penguin.

Lopez, J., & Scott, J. (2000). *Social structure*. Buckingham: Open University Press.

Macartney, H., & Calcagno, P. (2019). All bark and no bite: The political economy of bank fines in Anglo-America. *Review of International Political Economy, 26*(4), 630–665.

March, J. G., & Olsen, J. P. (2006). The logic of appropriateness. In M. Moran, M. Rein, & R. E. Goodin (Eds.), *The Oxford handbook of public policy*. Oxford: Oxford University Press.

Meyer, J., & Rowan, B. (1977). Institutionalized organizations: Formal structure as myth and ceremony. *American Journal of Sociology, 83*(2), 340–363.

Mugge, D. (2011). From pragmatism to dogmatism: European union governance, policy paradigms and financial meltdown. *New Political Economy, 16*(2), 185–206.

North, D. (1990). *Institutions, institutional change and economic performance*. New York: Cambridge University Press.

Peters, G. B. (2005). *Institutional theory in political science* (2nd ed.). Bloomsbury Academic: Bloomsbury.

Pierson, P. (2000). Not just what, but when: Timing and sequence in political processes. *Studies in American Political Development, 14*(1), 72–92.

RBS [Royal Bank of Scotland]. (2009). *Annual report and accounts 2009*. Available at: http://investors.rbs.com/~/media/Files/R/RBS-IR/annual-reports/rbs-group-accounts-2009.pdf.

Resnick, P., Zeckhauser, R., Swanson, J., & Lockwood, K. (2006). The value of reputation on eBay: A controlled experiment. *Experimental Economics, 9*(2), 79–101. https://doi.org/10.1007/s10683-006-4309-2.

Rixen, T. (2013). Why reregulation after the crisis is feeble: Shadow baking, offshore financial centres, and jurisdictional competition. *Regulation and Governance, 7*(4), 435–459.

Ross, S., Westerfield, R., & Jaffe, J. (1996). *Corporate finance*. Boston: Irwin.

S&P Global. (2018, April 6). *S&P Global market intelligence: Data dispatch: The world's 100 largest banks. [online]*. Available at: https://platform.mi.spglobal.com/web/client?auth=inherit#news/article?id=44027195&cdid=A-44027195-11060.

Schmidt, V. (2008). Discursive institutionalism: The explanatory power of ideas and discourse. *Annual Review of Political Science, 11*(1), 303–326.

Shapiro, I. (2004). Problems, methods, and theories in the study of politics, or: What's wrong with political science and what to do about it. In I. Shapiro, R. Smith, & T. Masoud (Eds.), *Problems and methods in the study of politics* (pp. 19–41). Cambridge: Cambridge University Press.

Shaxon, N. (2018). *The finance curse: How global finance is making us all poorer*. London: Bodley Head.

Sorkin, A. (2009). *Too big to fail: Inside the battle to save wall street*. London: Allen Lane.

Steinmo. S. (2012). Historical institutionalism. In D. Della Porta & M. Keating (Eds.), *Approaches and methodologies in the social sciences*. Cambridge: Cambridge University Press.

Stiglitz, j. (2010). *Freefall: America, free markets and the sinking of the world economy*. New York: W.W. Norton.

Streeck, W. (2009). *Re-forming capitalism: Institutional change in the German political economy*. Oxford: Oxford University Press.

Thelen. K., & Steinmo. S. (2008). Historical institutionalism in comparative politics. In S. Steinmo, K. Thelen, & F. Longstreth (Eds.), *Structuring politics: Historical institutionalism in comparative analysis (Cambridge studies in comparative politics)*. Cambridge: Cambridge University Press.

Tooze, A. (2018). *Crashed: How a decade of financial crises changed the world*. London: Allen Lane.

Tucker, P., Hall, S., & Pattani, A. (2013). Macroprudential policy at the Bank of England. *Bank of England Quarterly Bulletin, Bank of England, 53*(3), 192–200.

Turner, A. [Turner Review]. (2009). *The turner review: A regulatory response to the global banking crisis*. London: FSA. Available at http://www.fsa.gov.uk/pubs/other/turner_review.pdf.

UK Finance. (2018, September). *United Kingdom's banking sector: Facts & figures* [online]. Available at: https://www.ebf.eu/united-kingdom/.

van der Zwan, N. (2014). Making sense of financialisation. *Socio-Economic Review, 12*, 99–129.

Weyland, K. (2008). Toward a new theory of institutional change. *World Politics, 60*(2), 281–314.

Wolf, M. (2015). *The shifts and the shocks*. London: Penguin.

Woods, S. (2017, May). *Looking both ways*. Speech given by Sam Woods Sam Woods, Deputy Governor, Prudential Regulation and Chief Executive Officer, Prudential Regulation. Available at: http://www.bankofengland.co.uk/publications/Documents/speeches/2017/speech988.pdf.

World Bank. (2017). *Global financial development database*. Washington, DC: The World Bank Group. Retrieved from http://data.worldbank.org/data-catalog/global-financial-development.

Z/Yen and CDI. (2018). *The global financial centres index 23*. Z/Yen Group/China Development Institute: London/Shenzhen.

CHAPTER 2

How Do Banks Learn?

Introduction

This chapter offers a highly original account of learning and details the mechanisms and processes by which banks learn and change. The chapter will 'unpack' the concept of learning and will set out a clear definition of what learning entails and how we should account for structural considerations in the learning process. Drawing upon debates within the social sciences, the chapter will account for and situate the process of learning. The concept of learning is crucial to the research presented in this book because, in order to determine if and how banks have learned following the GFC, we must first understand what learning is—the processes, mechanism and typologies of learning. To this extent, the account of learning presented in this chapter will be used to identify the key characteristics of learning while also familiarising the reader with those conditions most conducive towards learning. This information will be important as it will allow us to identify examples of learning within the coming empirical chapters and subsequently answer the guiding research question.

Given the importance of post-GFC bank learning to financial stability, the sound functioning of markets and the UK's finance led-growth model, it is not enough to simply observe that change has occurred at the banks in question. Instead, I will look to isolate change that has happened as a result of the process of learning, from responses to exogenous structural factors—the changing nature of financial markets, investor appetite

A. Barber, *UK Banks and the Lessons of the Great Financial Crisis*, Building a Sustainable Political Economy: SPERI Research & Policy, https://doi.org/10.1007/978-3-030-70254-0_2

and regulatory requirements. To this end, the importance of the texts and scholarship on learning accounted for in this chapter of the book lies in identifying the key processes of learning against which causal inferences will be made to the extent that I might isolate positive examples of learning and change. In this respect, the chapter will extricate the central debates and key theories of learning located within the field of political science, organisational studies, economics, psychology, educational studies, sociology and anthropology. These typologies of learning will be used to not only answer the overarching research question, but will also help us to understand the differences and similarities in the learning trajectories of institutions.

The literature accounted for in this section of the book has been selected following a thorough library-based examination of a range of works, including books, book chapters and journal articles. As such, the preparation of this review has considered a wide collection of texts. Yet, the literature presented in this chapter is not an all-encompassing or exhaustive list. Instead, the review focuses upon a number of classic works that have been selected due to their standing as key texts, serving as the foundation for individual disciplines. Nevertheless, as the reader will observe where appropriate I also present and discuss more recent studies that have built upon these seminal texts. The purpose of this chapter is to determine a definition of learning that will also help us to understand the various conditions, markers and processes of learning. Furthermore, the account of learning presented here will give the research a rigorous academic underpinning against which my own thoughts, ideas and lines of inquiry can be built upon, tested and contextualised as I develop my own dialogue with the literature and its theoretical foundations.

A Definition of Learning

In this chapter of the book, I demonstrate that 'change' is central to learning and often the end result of the learning process. Indeed, a common theme that runs throughout the literature accounted for in this chapter is the idea that learning entails a series of cognitive responses, by agents and institutions, to new information that results in a shift in the frames, preferences and meanings applied by actors to their situational environment (see, e.g., Cyert and March, 1963; Cangelosi and Dill, 1965; Argyris and Schon, 1978; Duncan and Weiss, 1979; Fiol and Lyles 1985; Levitt and March, 1988; Huber, 1991; Sabatier, 1988;

Weick and Roberts, 1993). These ideational changes subsequently give rise to an expanded range of potential behaviours from which actors draw upon (Huber, 1991; May, 1992), resulting in improved policy actions, behavioural patterns and normative preferences (Easterby-Smith and Araujo, 1999; Sabatier, 1993).

Consequently, the literature on learning recognises that learning is inextricably linked to a self-reflexive process (Smith, 2011, 2013) that results in a series of positive changes in the behavioural outcomes of actors that stress an effective response to new information. For example, we shall see that Bracken et al. (2005) build upon the classic work of Tversky and Kahneman (1974) and suggest that past losses and a fear of future catastrophe will evoke within actors a strong behavioural response that seeks to mitigate future damage (Bracken et al., 2005). In this instance, previous losses or 'deep regret anchors' cause the learning subject, in our case banks and key agents within institutions, to effectively step back and appraise all relevant information with such considerations being centred upon the fear of imminent catastrophe and 'history repeating itself' (ibid, pp. 23–24). In response to the processing of this information, actors will develop powerful new schemas, and subsequently behavioural norms and patterns, that will look to prevent such events from happening again (Bracken et al., 2005: 25).

Similarly, the chapter will detail the work of Argyris and Schon (1978, 1996) who also emphasise the importance of change in the learning process. The authors propose that the starting point for all institutional learning is dissatisfaction. Dissatisfaction occurs when previously established routines fail to produce predictable or desirable outcomes (ibid). The ensuing void between that which is desirable and that which is achievable then becomes the stimulus for learning as policy-makers look to close this gap (May, 1992). As such, institutions must overcome this problem by orienting and applying its resources—time and human and fiscal capital—to the search for alternatives that will allow it to create new patterns of reasoning and move beyond previously established underlying theories-in-use—these being an organisation's guiding principles, philosophies and standard operating procedures (Argyris et al., 1985; Argyris and Schon 1996; Edmondson, 1996; Edmondson and Monigeon, 1999). Put simply, in order to learn, new information must be sought, evaluated and then applied.

The Framing of Learning in this Chapter

Before we move on to look at learning in more detail, it is important that we first frame the analysis that is to follow. In order to do this I turn briefly to consider the work of Herbert A Simon (1957, 1958, 1983) on bounded rationality. Classic economic theory suggests that actors are rational beings with access to perfect information that informs their decision-making process (Simon, 1959: 254). Armed with this perfect information and a rational mind, mainstream economics suggest that it is possible to predict the behaviour of actors who will always look to maximise outcomes (ibid). However, Simon (1959: 256) rejects this notion arguing that due to the complexity and shifting nature of the economic environment that frames the 'choices that economic man faces', perfect information is rarely available. Consequently, Simon (1957, 1958, 1959, 1983) argues that though humans are rational thinkers, this rationality is bound by certain and sure limitations (Simon, 1983: 22). Subsequently, human behaviour, including learning, is premised upon the notion that while agents possess the ability to formulate responses to problems and are capable of multifaceted thoughts, these actions are framed by a lack of access to complete information and as such, agents are 'boundedly rational' in their decision-making processes (Simon, 1957, 1958, 1983).

Simon's work on bounded rationality (1957: 270) suggests that human choice to follow the 'optimal path' is hampered by individuals' lack of 'wits' and the 'senses' needed to determine and uncover such a path—assuming that an optimal route exists. Instead, the author argues that an agent's decision-making process involves a series of 'rational adjustments' leading humans to follow a 'satisficing path' that delivers acceptable rather than optimal results (ibid. p. 271). In this context, the choice to pursue rational outcomes—and thereby achieve optimal results—is framed by a lack of complete information that leads agents to make a series of trade-offs and re-adjustments. Consequently, though agents are free to choose the optimal path, the choices faced by individuals are inherently bounded in their rationality (Simon, 1957, 1958, 1983). Put simply, bank learning in the post-crisis decade may not produce 'optimal results' but should lead to improved policy actions based upon all relevant information.

Single- and Double-Loop Learning

Single- and double-loop learning theory is drawn from the literature on organisational studies and is most closely associated with the work of Argyris and Schon (1978, 1996). The relevance of organisational studies in application to my own work lies in the multi-disciplinary approach that the field has adopted over time including, but not restricted to, management, economics, business, history and psychology (Dodgson, 1993). Organisational studies offers us a robust and well-rounded theory in explaining not only how institutions learn but also how various mechanisms applied at the organisational level may improve or inhibit the learning trajectory of institutions.

Single- and double-loop learning theory suggests that the starting point for institutional learning is dissatisfaction, with undesirable outcomes causing the necessary stimulation to seek alternatives to established routines, behaviours and standard operating procedures (Argyris and Schon, 1978). According to the theory, when dissatisfaction arises an organisation will attempt to reconcile this discontent in one of two ways. *First*, if the error identified can be corrected in such a way that it allows institutions to carry on working undisrupted and in pursuit of the same core policy intentions and outcomes, then the error detection/correction process is described as 'single-loop learning' (ibid. p. 2). *Second*, if the appropriate correctional response to the error demands that the organisation significantly alter or modify its core objectives, strategies and institutional norms then this gives rise to a secondary response known as 'double-loop learning' (Argyris and Schon, 1978: 2).

Single-loop Learning

Single-loop learning is concerned with making modest and incremental change in the light of new information that amends the strategies of institutions in such a way as to preserve established underlying ideas and 'theories of action' (Argyris and Schon, 1996: 20). Single-loop learning takes place when an institution identifies an error within either a single or multiple facets of its standard operating procedures (ibid. p. 21). These routines are subsequently modified and adapted in such a way as to maintain the direction and performance of the institution that is in keeping with current organisational directives (Argyris and Schon, 1996: 21). In this respect, single-loop learning does not evoke radical reform of an institution's values and norms. Instead, alterations to an organisation's operating procedures will be done in such a way as to preserve the *status quo* (Argyris and Schon, 1978, 1996).

Thus, an institution that has learned to the extent that single-loop learning may be identified can be said to have learned, but only to the point that it has learned new strategies or procedures that allow it to continue to act without serious revision to 'particular goals or values' (Usher and Bryant, 1989: 87). As such, single-loop learning can be identified when 'goals, values and strategies' remain unquestioned in the light of new information, with an institution instead focusing upon making pre-existing procedures more effective (ibid. p. 88). Consequently, single-loop theory suggests that learning does not necessitate an extensive search for information. Instead, learning is reducible to an exercise in the ability of an institution to adapt and fit already established programmes to new circumstances and environments (Dodgson, 1993). Simply put, single-loop learning describes change at the margins of an organisation that, while important, does not result in the substantial reform of an institution's underlying core concepts and philosophies and resultantly may leave room for potential errors to be repeated.

In terms of a practical application to post-crisis bank learning in the UK, single-loop learning is desirable but only to the extent that it is a precursor to more substantive double-loop learning—explored below. Given the magnitude of the GFC and the role of the banks in the crisis, a fundamental reappraisal of the way in which banks operate—their business models, corporate culture and decision-making processes—may be necessary to avert future catastrophe and mitigate the risk posed to financial markets by these systemically important institutions. To this end, the empirical chapters that follow will look to identify policies implemented by the banks that overhaul an institution's underlying theories and governing values.

Double-loop Learning

In contrast, double-loop learning may be said to be present at an institution when the extent of the learning process effects a definitive change in an organisation's 'values of theory-in-use' (Argyris and Schon, 1996: 21). An institution's theories-in-use are described by Argyris et al. (1985: 82) as being an organisation's underlying governing values and philosophies that can be 'inferred from action'. These fundamental 'conceptions and philosophies' are subsequently manifest through an institution's practical and strategical policies and standard operating procedures (Kerr, 2010: 3). Double-loop learning within an institutional setting can be observed when an organisation first recognises discrepancies between the group's theories-in-use and desirable outcomes (Argyris and Schon, 1996). Again, like many of the theories examined in this chapter, it is dissatisfaction—the gap between aspiration and results—that is the driving force behind learning. According to double-loop theory, following the identification and detection of a failure, the learning subject will reassess and then alter its fundamental conceptions and philosophies in the light of new information in such a way as to avoid further losses and deliver desirable outcomes (ibid).

As both single- and double-loop learning share many of the same properties, it is important that we are able to distinguish between the more cosmetic variation of learning, single-loop, and the more applied version, double-loop, in order to determine the extent to which banks have learned from the GFC. To this end Smith (2011, 2013) suggests that while both processes represent a degree of learning, single-loop theory professes adherence to a familiar routine and present norms with only minimal revisions. In contrast, double-loop learning requires innovation and analytical inquiry into the organisation's values and norms. Here it is possible to draw parallels with Hall's (1993: 279) third-order change that similarly stresses a 'paradigm shift' in the underlying principles that guide policy objectives. For Hall (ibid), third-order change is a 'disjunctive process' which results not only in 'discontinuities in policy' but an overhaul in the thinking of how policies are made, perceived and evaluated. In the context of post-crisis bank learning explored throughout my work, double-loop learning, unlike the single-loop theory, necessitates a clear and observable positive change in a bank's underlying theories-in-use—these being the core conceptions, philosophies and values that govern an institution. To this end, the empirical analysis that follows will look to identify examples of where an institution has implemented policies and procedures that are emblematic of a change in the bank's governing values and which aligns strategic operations to newly conceived underlying core conceptions and philosophies (Argyris and Schon, 1996).

The Learning Space Theory

The work of Edmondson and Monigeon (1999: 160) argues that institutional learning is extremely difficult and almost 'impossible' in highly pressurised situations. This is because, according to the authors, when faced with an environment where the stakes are high and a great deal rests upon making the correct decision key agents—that embody institutions (Sabatier, 1988)—are more likely to strictly adhere to institutional policies and organisational 'theories-in-use' for fear of sanction (Edmondson and Monigeon, 1999). The consequence of such behaviour is that agents and institutions are inhibited from learning when learning is most sorely needed, with the process of individual reasoning leading to a lack of information exchange (ibid).

This suggests that the complex nature of an institution may inhibit its capability to learn under times of increased pressure. Indeed, only when an institution is able to move beyond the restrictions imposed by its own 'theories-in-use' will it have the freedom and innovation to learn and remedy problems. Edmondson and Monigeon (1999) argue that in order to overcome these institutional biases and norms, the learning subject—in our case banks—must dedicate sufficient 'space' to the learning process. In this context, 'learning space' is understood as being the application of both time and resources—human and fiscal capital—towards the reflexive process inherent in learning (ibid). Consequently, learning space theory dictates that in order to learn, an institution must undergo an evaluative process aimed at deconstructing a particular problem and finding suitable solutions. In this respect, the work of Edmondson and Monigeon (1999) stresses that learning is predicated upon the need for institutions to seek, evaluate and apply new information.

The practical application of the learning space theory to an analysis of post-GFC bank learning in the UK means that I will look to identify the extent to which banks have applied institutional resources—learning space—to the evaluative process integral to learning. This may include the use of independent reviews and audits as well as engaging in dialogue with institutional investors such as shareholders. In this respect, I would expect to see those institutions with a greater propensity towards learning not only utilising reviews, but also designing and applying institutional systems aimed at changing and instilling a new set of governing values. Put simply, the empirical chapters of this book will look for evidence of the banks seeking, evaluating and applying new information resulting in substantive change.

Policy Learning

As we can see, learning is premised upon a number of factors that affects how, when and under what circumstances agents, and the institutions that they embody, learn. How quickly institutions learn, the lessons drawn from specific situations and how likely an organisation is to retain those lessons is equally dependent upon numerous determinants. It is here that we turn to the literature on policy learning drawn from the discipline of political science and most closely associated with the work of Richard Rose (1991, 1993, 2005). Policy learning has been selected for my own research as it can help us to better understand how institutional ideas, policies and norms, framed within a specific political epoch and sphere, can aid learning through the formulation of alternative organisational rules and practices. Moreover, Day and Klein (1989: 350) argue that the central importance of Rose's (1991, 1993, 2005) work lies in its ability to endow the researcher with a framework robust enough to tackle institutional learning within a 'truly unpredictable' structural setting. Policy learning is centred upon the notion that lessons can be drawn by examining previously established programmes already in existence elsewhere and that through a careful and detailed assessment of these programmes it is possible to determine expected gains (Rose, 1991, 1993, 2005).

For Rose (1993) policy-makers will always favour inaction over action, the status quo over radical new ideas and a stationary state over the uncertainty of progress. This is because, according to the functionalist scholar Karl Deutsch (1963), whose work had great influence on Rose, to follow the previously established path is efficient, if not always effective. As such, to 'stick to what is known' can be desirable as such a path leads to predictable and expected outcomes with 'routine' allowing policy-makers the freedom to invest their time in matters which they believe to carry a higher value (ibid. p. 111). Consequently, procedure ordains policy-makers with the 'ability to afford not to learn' (Deutsch, 1963: 112).

Like the literature on single- and double-loop learning, policy learning similarly suggests that what transforms policy-makers from a perpetual state of stasis into an effective and active learner is dissatisfaction (Rose,

1991, 1993, 2005). Indeed, Rose (1993: 57) argues that dissatisfaction is a 'necessary condition of lesson-drawing'. Within the policy learning framework, dissatisfaction is described as arising when established routines become fractured and no longer produce predictable or desirable outcomes (Rose, 1991, 1993, 2005; May, 1992). The gap between objectives and outcomes subsequently forces policy-makers to seek new forms of knowledge. The result of this search for new information subsequently gives rise new policies, programmes and ideas as policy-makers look to close the gap between aspirations and achievement (May1992). Sabatier (1988) also stresses the motivating force of dissatisfaction, arguing that undesirable outcomes resulting from specific policy initiatives will propel agents to seek alternatives and instigate new policy paradigms. Moreover, the degree of dissatisfaction determines the intensity of the search for alternatives, or in other words, the greater the dissatisfaction the greater the search for alternatives (Rose, 1993).

Similarly, the literature on punctuated equilibrium, associated with the work of Jones and Baumgartner (1993, 2005, 2009), also stresses the importance of dissatisfaction, with a 'crisis or trigger event' that undermines institutional routines being central to learning (Jones and Baumgartner, 1993: 10). The authors build upon the work of Herbert A. Simon and suggest that boundedly rational actors do not respond to signals proportionately due to the 'great number of real tangible problems… which can only be attended to one at a time' (ibid. p. 10). Due to the limited capacity of agents to process vast amounts of information, signals relating to policy failures can become lost with key indicators going unrecognised. This in turn leads to a build-up of unanswered questions concerning the effectiveness of policies until a point of punctuation or 'burst'. At this point, policy-makers will become critically aware of signals and new information—previously unnoticed—that highlights the gap between outcomes and current institutional procedures (Jones and Baumgartner, 1993). This burst subsequently gives rise to dissatisfaction which in turn entreaties policy-makers to focus more intently upon the cause of dissatisfaction and to move from general musings to the specific (ibid, 2005). True et al. (2007) similarly argue that policy change within institutions is typically a slow-moving and cumbersome task that, following a prolonged period of stasis, is prone to rapid and dramatic 'bursts' and shifts in policy orientation and structure. This account of learning, in application to the analysis of bank learning, would suggest that institutions that have recognised the causes of the GFC, and interpreted these signal effectively—implementing specific policies aimed at addressing these key triggers—would have a greater propensity for learning.

Accordingly, the policy learning framework drawn, in the main, from political science, may explain why some banks demonstrate a greater propensity for learning than others. In particular, we may hypothesise that those banks that have undergone the greatest dissatisfaction—having experienced significant upheavals—in the post-crisis decade, may also be the greatest learners, with the rate of dissatisfaction determining the search for new information. However, this hypothesis stands in contrast to the learning space theory, discussed in the above section, which suggests that learning in highly pressurised situations—such as following a catastrophe or moments of crisis—is extremely difficult. While not impossible to overcome, institutions must apply learning space in order to move beyond, and resist the pull to fall back upon, previously established routines. The empirical analysis that follows will test these contending frameworks—the learning space and dissatisfaction theories—in order to determine the accuracy and validity of the hypotheses extended.

To aid us in the identification of learning, Rose (1991, 2005) outlines five key factors or processes of learning. The first of these is *photocopying*. Photocopying occurs when an institution copies a policy or programme already in existence elsewhere with very few, if any, changes made between the original and the new policy (Rose, 2005). However, Rose (ibid. p. 82) warns that photocopying may not always prove successful because, just as 'institutions… are not the same', policies cannot be identical. Therefore, Rose (1991, 2005) stresses the importance of his second proposal of *copying*. Copying takes place when an institution adopts a certain policy from an adjacent organisation and uses this as a 'blueprint' for new institutional policies (Rose, 2005: 82). Copying will typically allow for small variations between the policy being copied and the formulation of a new policy. Importantly, however, copying requires a detailed exploration of the seminal ideas and philosophies that underpin the policy in question (Rose, 1991, 2005). Accordingly, when copying a policy from either an adjacent institution or from an historical in-house initiative, institutions will disseminate very specific details surrounding the implementation of the policy in question including administrative processes, standard operating procedures and key performance indicators that are used to evaluate the success of the chosen programme (ibid).

Third, Rose (1991, 2005) discusses the prospect of *hybrid learning*. Hybrid learning takes place when several harmonious factors, extricated from two or more individual policies, are combined to create a new policy (Rose, 2005). However, the author goes on to stress that hybrid learning is distinct and separate from his fourth proposal of *synthesis learning*, insomuch as it combines similar factors from different policies which share the same objectives (ibid. p. 81). Synthesis learning on the other hand may be present when factors drawn from differing policies, which do not necessarily share the same underlying utility, are combined to create an alternative policy (Rose, 1991). However, Rose (ibid) warns that synthesis learning ultimately results in an artificial policy with no proven track record and as such, the expected return or efficiency of the policy will be impossible to predict.

Finally, *selective imitation* may be said to be present when an institution selects a policy or policies from a rival organisation with underlying norms and values that are 'congenial' to its own (Rose, 2005: 84). However, measuring selective imitation is not without its problems. This is because, according to Rose (ibid) in recognising the success of a rival institution, the learning subject, in our case banks, will be forced to confront its own weaknesses and failures and as such, selective imitation is laden with political costs (Rose, 1991, 2005).

As such, we can see that the policy learning framework and the typologies of learning espoused by Rose (1991, 2005) are intimately bound to an evaluative process whereby learning is predicated upon making a judgement about a specific policy or programme in place within a given time or space. Similarly, May's (1992: 335–336) thesis on instrumental policy learning also stresses a 'new understanding about the viability of policy interventions' along with an 'increased understanding of policy instruments [and] implementation' as being central to learning. However, lesson learning is not simply about blindly borrowing or condemning policies with a proven track record of either success or failure. Instead, learning entails a reflexive critical process that must account for the institutional as well as structural setting where new information concerning policy formation has been sought, and will be applied (May, 1992). Hence, lesson learning within the context of the policy learning framework emphasises the importance of an increased understanding of the application of newly acquired information and is subsequently applied and used to inform and improve outcomes (May, 1992).

A practical application of the policy learning framework to my research means that we may expect to see those banks that have undertaken a fundamental reappraisal of their institutional policies and procedures, for example through the use of internal and external reviews, to have a greater propensity towards learning. The importance of formal reviews as a means of measuring and testing learning within my work is stressed by Rose (1991: 19–20) who asserts that in order for an institution to enter into the evaluative process associated with learning, it must first gather a raft of new knowledge concerning its policy options. Likewise, Baumgartner and Jones (2009) also note that the 'burst' of a punctuated point in time often leads to the legitimisation of actors that are typically held outside of problem solving circles. In this instance, the drive for change and search for effective policy responses means that agents traditionally excluded from an institution's central policy-making unit are now seen not only as a valuable source of information but are actively encouraged to feed into the solution of problems (ibid).

Moreover, in light of the policy learning framework, I will not only be looking at the behaviour of banks—which is important in the learning process—but importantly, I will examine the underlying processes behind any changes and how information gathered has been used. Indeed, Etheredge (1981: 77) has argued that learning can only be said to have taken place if the subject demonstrates sufficient knowledge and an 'increased intelligence and sophistication of thought' when applying new forms of information to the framing or solving of problems. As such, I will look to identify how information has been applied to such an extent that we can recognise a re-alignment of group philosophies. Put simply, the policy learning framework when applied to the question of post-GFC bank learning dictates that institutions seek, evaluate and apply new information in a way that results in a series of improved policy actions aimed at shifting or re-aligning an institution's underlying values.

Cognition and Schema

This section of the chapter draws on the literature on learning taken from the discipline of psychology and in particular social psychology. The field of psychology is of importance to my research, and the broader subject of learning, because it recognises that learning is not only an individual but also an institutional process that similarly accounts for structures. Psychologists working within the field of education and learning have sought to identify and explain how different institutional and structural variants may alter and affect how agents learn and how the broader structural environment may shape the methods and techniques pertinent to learning. Like the performance-based insights drawn from the literature on policy learning, the discipline of psychology similarly proposes that the history of past events can greatly influence human behaviour and learning (Minsky 1975; Bandura, 1977; Fiske and Taylor, 1991; Jitendra et al., 2007; Pendry, 2008).

Bandura (1977) suggests that all agents possess an intrinsic cognitive process that helps humans recognise certain key situational indicators and which determine what behaviour is preferable or appropriate at a specific event or point in time. This cognitive process enables agents to judge the likely outcome of responses and the consequences of specified behaviours (ibid). These cognitive processes are formed upon and underpinned by a series of schemas, which are responsible for storing knowledge and forming relationship paths between a certain stimulus and those previously held ideas and information (Fiske and Taylor, 1991). The schema can be simply defined as a piece of information, concerning expectancies based on history about people, objects or situations, that has previously been established and is held in the memory (Pendry, 2008). As such, individuals are endowed with an understanding of how they must behave or respond within certain institutional and structural contexts in order to achieve desirable outcomes and avert unsatisfactory results (Bandura, 1977). Jitendra et al (2007) argue that schema-based learning takes place when an individual or institution first identifies a problem and then undergoes a search for new information or ideas that will correct the issue. According to Minsky's (1975) *frame theory*, altering and adding information to the already established schema is possible when a series of cognitive processes are utilised to inform pre-existing knowledge slots during the search for corrective information (also see: Mayer, 1999; Desoete et al., 2003).

However, while learning is to some extent seen as an individual process, the literature on cognition and schema also recognises the potency of structures. For example, cognition-based learning is premised upon the assumption that all humans are social beings. In order to assimilate into their respective groups, individuals must acquire and adopt the cultural rules or norms that govern that society and which are transmitted via structures (Elkjaer, 1999). The success of an individual becoming a fully functioning member of a particular group or society is rested upon their ability to interpret and understand social knowledge and to absorb the cultural history of a given group (ibid). This internalisation is aided by the schema which equips agents with a prior framework to which new, or similar, experiences and information can be grafted (Fiske and Taylor, 1991). Once a schema has been established, it will affect how quickly information is absorbed and assimilated into memory. How agents distinguish situational characteristics, how new ideas are interpreted and what conclusions can be drawn about the similarities and differences in new experiences are all likewise governed by the schema and how effectively new ideas can be grafted to old memories (Fiske and Taylor, 1991).

This account of learning therefore stresses the role of structures in the learning process and which equip agents, and the institutions that they embody, with the cultural rules and norms to succeed. As such, we should not discount the role of structures in determining the learning trajectory of banks. For example, actors may be wary of breaking social conventions—built in to structures—due to the assuredness that rules and norms give agents by dictating what is expected of them in a given situation (Fiske and Taylor, 1991). In application to my analysis of bank learning in the post-crisis decade, financial markets bring both certainty to banks—determining what is expected of them—but also, due to their highly competitive nature, have the ability to punish institutions that stray from the established path. In this respect, financial markets and highly mobile capital—upon which bank rely—may incentivise or penalise a certain behavioural decision, which in turn may encourage or retard the learning process.

Given the fact that schemas are deeply embedded within an individual's cognitive reasoning, shaping an agent's understanding and experience of the numerous social worlds we inhabit and information encountered, it may therefore be judged that the schema would inhibit rather than enable learning. For example, when an actor encounters new knowledge, the social schema may quickly assimilate or 'rationalise' that information to fit an already established schema (Elkjaer, 1999: 82). In this case, an individual's cognitive reasoning can potentially close off agents from new and viable sources of knowledge as the schema falsely interprets or rejects new information (Elkjaer, 1999).

Likewise, when agents encounter information that is at odds with the pre-existing schema or information slot, then a cognitive bias may cause an individual to disregard new information. For example, in their investigation into the Columbia space shuttle disaster Boin and Fishbacher-Smith (2011) found that NASA did not wilfully ignore or disregard safety concerns from engineers that the shuttle's thermal protection system had been damaged and would fail upon re-entering the Earth's atmosphere. Instead, the authors conclude that NASA 'did not know' how to assimilate the information being relayed to them (ibid. p. 84). Indeed, NASA's past safety record was exemplary without the loss of a single astronaut (CAIB, 2003). Moreover, similar technical issues that had affected previous space flights had resulted in the most negligible results (ibid). As such, Boin and Fishbacher-Smith (2011: 84) note that it was not 'the loss of a safety culture' but, a 'disciplined adherence to proven safety systems' at NASA that led to the catastrophe.

One potential way of overcoming these barriers to learning presented by cognition and the schema can be found in the psychology sub-discipline of heuristics and signalling which looks at how information or signals are interpreted by individuals. The work on heuristics by Tversky and Kahneman (1974: 1124) asserts that when faced with uncertain events, individuals will turn to a number of heuristics or signals that 'reduce the complex task of assessing probabilities and predicting values'. As such, Tversky and Kahneman (1974) argue that heuristics may be a useful tool in the processing of complex information, leading to desirable outcomes. Indeed, building upon the work of Tversky and Kahneman (1974), Bracken et al. (2005), writing from within the discipline of strategic management, suggest a number of practical ways that will aid in the interpretation of signals and hence learning.

First, the authors propose that no one individual should be responsible for interpreting and disseminating information (Bracken et al., 2005). Instead, it is argued that in order to minimise the chances of information being misinterpreted or disregarded, multiple actors should be tasked with the interpretation of signals (ibid). Likewise, no single decision maker should have absolutely autonomy over an institution, instead power and authority over the strategic orientation of an organisation should be shared by multiple actors (Bracken et al., 2005). In application to my own work, this would suggest that it is necessary to examine how key decision makers are held to account. In particular, I will look at how corporate governance is structured within the banks and any changes that may or may not have been made to these structures post-2008. Moreover, the account of learning proposed by Bracken et al. (2005) suggests that those banks that have multiple layers to their strategic decision-making processes, and which hold material decision makers to account, would have a greater propensity towards correctly interpreting information—that may otherwise be disregarded by pre-set cognitive biases—and hence learning.

Secondly, the authors propose that within an institution, separate teams or divisions should be responsible for holding one-another to account (Bracken et al., 2005). It is argued that such measures foster an environment of competition between divisions. The result of which is that individuals and teams will focus more intently upon the situational environment for key signals and dedicate themselves fully to the interpretation of this information for fear of 'letting the side down' or being labelled as the 'weak link' (Bracken et al., 2005: 22). As such, my research will look to identify examples of banks that have implemented and actively encouraged mechanisms such as cross-divisional appraisals, which the literatures suggests should lead to learning.

A *third* factor that Bracken et al.(2005: 22) propose may better inform agents' and institutions' understanding and interpretation of new information or signals is what the authors call 'deep regret anchors' (Bracken et al., 2005: 22). The central premise of this idea is that individuals will look to minimise losses even at the expense of losing gains with past losses and a fear of future catastrophe, built into a previously established schema, being the central force behind institutional learning (Bracken et al., 2005). In this instance, past losses or 'deep regret anchors' cause the learning agent or organisation to effectively step back and appraise all relevant information before making a decision with such considerations being centred upon the fear of imminent catastrophic losses and 'history repeating itself' (ibid. p. 23). This may lead us to conclude that banks that have critically appraised and reflected upon the causes of the GFC, within both their own institutions and the wider banking industry, may demonstrate a greater aptitude for learning. This is because, according to the deep regret anchors theory, institutions that are able to reflect upon all relevant information, identifying the source of losses and how to avoid future catastrophe, will be more efficient processors of information and subsequently, better placed to make informed decisions.

Like the single- and double-loop, learning space and policy learning theories, the work on cognition and schema similarly suggests that learning takes place through a process of error detection and error correction. The result of which is an observable changes to an institution's underlying theories, values and philosophies. Nonetheless, we should keep in mind that learning is always punctuated by a certain kind of rationality. As a result, the learning experience of the UK's largest banks in the post-crisis decade may not necessarily produce optimal outcomes. Indeed, we should remind ourselves here of Simon's (1957: 259) thesis which suggests that agents become 'satisfied' with a particularly clumsy kind of rationality which is premised upon using rough approximations to compensate for key information gaps. According to the author, this kind of rationality typically involves refining and limiting the 'planning horizon' by making assumptions concerning the optimal outcome of a specific path (ibid). Agents and institutions will take stock of early returns before making incremental revisions until an outcome which is both acceptable and obtainable is reached (Simon, 1957). This kind of rational adjustment leads to what humans find to be 'good enough' as opposed to opportunity maximising (ibid. p. 260). However, a failure to produce maximum returns should not be considered as a failure to learn lessons, particularly when there is clearly evidence of a revision to an institution's underlying theories-in-use and preferred policy actions.

Structure and Agency

So far, this chapter has looked at how different scholars from across the social sciences define learning, how and why learning happens and the different kinds of learning delineated within various disciplines. However, any attempt to understand learning and how different typologies of learning can be used to evaluate the post-crisis experience of UK banks would be incomplete without contextualising this learning within both an individual and structural setting. Indeed, the account of learning detailed thus far could be accused of overstating agency in the learning process and underplaying the role of structures in determining the learning trajectory of institutions. To this end, the following section of the chapter will look to rebalance the debate. *First*, it will be suggested that all learning, be it at an agential or institutional level, takes place within structural settings that have the potential to inhibit the ability to learn. *Second*, I argue that agents are indeed capable of overcoming structural forces in order to learn and change. *Third*, it shall be demonstrated that the learning process cannot simply be reduced to either a structural or an agential-based exercise but is instead akin to a constant state of interaction between both structures and agents. *Finally*, drawing on the work of Margaret Archer (2003, 2007, 2012), I posit that, contrary to the account of learning presented so far, learning may not necessitate an overall behavioural change.

The literature on structure and agency is drawn from the discipline of sociology. The contribution of theories of learning rooted in the structure and agency debate to my work are particularly important as they recognise the delicate interplay between both sociocultural and individual considerations in the learning process. Indeed, theories of learning associated with the discipline of psychology tend to overplay learning as being a purely individual experience (see Marton, 1975; Marton and Saljo, 1976; Watkins, 1983). Conversely, the social constructivist tradition emphasises social structures as being the key conduit in the learning experience (see Vygotsky, 1962, 1978). However, the structure and agency literature recognises both structure and agency as being equally important in the learning trajectory of institutions. The importance of considering both structure and agency in the research process is highlighted by Ashwin (2008: 151–152) who suggests that a rejection of the structure and agency thesis would severely limit the 'explanatory power' of institutional and agency based research. The author goes on to note that a focus by researchers upon both structures and agents greatly improves the 'quality of explanations' in detailed empirical research (ibid. p. 153).

The roots of the structure and agency thesis can be traced back to critical realism and the work of Roy Bhaskar (1979, 1993). Bhaskar (1993) suggests that agency follows structure but stresses that agency is not 'locked in' or predetermined by structures which are a necessary precondition of agency. Indeed, the author argues that 'society is both the ever present condition (material cause) and the continually reproduced outcome of human agency' (Bhaskar, 1979: 44). As such, critical realism suggests that social structures are constantly adopted by agents who then reproduce and reinforce these structures through social rules, norms, cultures and traditions which are the product and exercise of human agency (Bhaskar, 1979: 44–45). Essentially, critical realism suggests that the propagation of structures is reliant upon the actions of autonomous agents and that these very actions are in of themselves only made possible by structures (Baert, 1998).

Similarly, Hartwig (2007) also suggests that we must not fall foul to reducing human interaction to a single operating sphere. Instead, the author stresses that society is founded upon and constrained by a 'stratified nature of reality' with multiple and simultaneous interactions and facets of knowledge shaping the relationship between the 'knower and [what is] known' (ibid. p. 240). As such, critical realism recognises that human agency, social interactions and how actors interpret the world is not wholly independent of the 'objects, processes, and events' which construct reality (ibid). Indeed, Bhaskar (1979: 45) recognises that countless 'structural conditions' underpin all human action and stresses that 'society does not exist independently of human activity... but it is not the product of it' either.

King (2000, 2004, 2005) build upon the work of Bhaskar (1979, 1993) and critical realism by suggesting that while on the surface, human action may appear to be hedged in or underpinned by structural forces, agents retain a sure degree of autonomy and are free to exercise certain behaviours in any way they see fit (King, 2005). King (2000) rejects Giddens's (1988, 1995) structuration theory which suggests that agents, consciously aware of their own social systems, adopt a series of routine actions which reinforce pre-existing social structures. Instead, King (2005: 216) argues that even the most basic examination of one's own everyday experience will highlight the numerous interactions between structures and our own sense of agency. While the author suggests that 'family, class, income bracket, culture, religious background' are all structural factors which may constrain the way in which agents behave, the extent to which individuals conform to and adopt these behavioural norms is ultimately determined by autonomous thinkers (ibid, 2004: 16). Moreover, the author goes on to suggest that

> Life is not the struggle of the individual against structure, nor the reproduction of the structure by the agent, but an eternal round of interactions through which social relations between humans are made, transformed and destroyed. (King, 2004: 17)

Though King (2000, 2004, 2005) recognises the importance of structures and agency in human interaction, the author's work tends to overstate the ability of agents to overcome structures, which while not impossible, can prove extremely difficult to break free of (Bell and Hindmoor, 2015). Similarly, the work of Bhaskar (1979, 1993) also recognises the significance of both structure and agency, but tends towards a greater emphasis of the constraining nature of structures. In this respect, the author tends to relegate human agency to a reproductive role with individuals exercising their agency but only to the extent to replicate or modify the structures by which they are framed.

The wok of Margaret Archer (1995, 2000, 2003, 2007, 2012) possesses a much greater balance between structures and agents than that of King (2000, 2004, 2005) or Bhaskar (1979, 1993). Archer's work is important to my research and the conceptualisation of learning as it develops a model that explains the way in which agents are able to exercise their autonomy while at the same time recognising the potential constraining power of structures. Indeed, Kahn et al. (2012: 860) have suggested that Archer's work on structure and agency 'offers a promising basis to help explain [the] interplay between personal and socio-cultural factors within... learning'.

Archer's (1988) early work emphasises the importance of considering both structure and agency in social life. The author successfully separates agency, culture and structures by arguing that these critical domains are 'substantially' different and 'autonomous' from one another (Archer, 1988: 9). According to Archer (ibid), to ignore these differences and simply reduce society to one or another of these factors would be to reduce the complexity of social life into a 'simple' amalgamation that would undermine attempts to understand the human condition.

Similarly, in her later work Archer (2003: 130) suggests that all human behaviour is determined by an 'internal conversation' in which agents reflexively consider their position in relation to external social conditions, such as structures. According to the internal conversation thesis, all agents are free thinkers with a distinct personality unique to them and as such are able to determine their thoughts, which are guided or underpinned by personal morals, values and goals (Archer, 2003). When confronted with structures, agents, due to their unique set of personal characteristics and the freedom of thought, will exercise the power of reasoning, in accordance with a personal position, to make a judgement (ibid). Agents will then formulate a strategic response centred upon what they deem to be the most pleasing and of the greatest importance (Archer, 2003).

Though an initial reading of Archer (1988) may appear to overstate agency, the author's work on the internal conversation stresses the importance of not discounting structural forces, which can be particularly salient in shaping human life (ibid.: 2003). For example, in everyday life agents will first gather information about their unique social context from structures before devising a unique response (Archer, 2003). Specifically, an agent's response to structures will be centred upon both personal objectives and, more importantly, the possibilities and limitations which those structures hold (ibid. p. 133). Subsequently, an agent's morals, values and goals will be revised and reinterpreted in the light of structural constraints and opportunities, as actors create appropriate responses according to what will equip them with the greatest opportunity to achieve their ambitions (Archer, 2003: 133). This would suggest that agents can be reflexive to the extent that they first consider their position in relation to structures, and then exercise their autonomy in order to realise their goals but with structural constraints an ever present consideration.

The importance of reflexivity in the learning process is similarly highlighted by the educational studies literature. In their work, Booth and Anderberg (2005) demonstrate a positive correlation between critical reflection and enhanced learning capabilities. The authors found that participants who were able to reflect critically upon their position and role within the wider system (structures) were more likely to consider a broad range of strategic factors when learning. This expanded awareness of the wider situational context subsequently resulted in more effective and efficient, and ultimately, successful learners (ibid. p. 381). Building upon this work, Kahn et al. (2012) also found a positive correlation between a greater consciousness of an agent's immediate operating environment and learning. Intrinsically, the authors concluded that the capabilities of agents could be attributed to the extent to which individuals exercised their 'personal powers' of reflection (Kahn et al., 2012: 865).

While Archer's (2003) internal conversation model introduces the importance of individual reflexivity, the author further elaborates upon this key issue by highlighting four distinct forms or types of reflexive consideration: *communicative reflexives; autonomous reflexives; fractured reflexives;* and *meta-reflexives.* While communicative, autonomous and fractured reflexives are all important factors in the internal conversation, I will focus my attention upon meta-reflexives. The meta-reflexives thesis will help us to address a major underlying question within my research, and which stands in contrast to much of the literature already examined, namely, *is learning possible despite the absence of behavioural change?*

The meta-reflexives describe agents who are able to consider their own reflexive position in the decision-making process. For example, an individual's internal conversational is typified by a series of mental exchanges, namely, actors will ask themselves a question internally and then seek out an internal answer (Archer, 2003). However, meta-reflexivity occurs when agents question the answer that they have provided themselves with and which subsequently gives rise to an internal deliberative process. However, with the meta-reflexivity consideration, the internal conversation is no longer concerned with establishing a correct answer, but is instead focused upon discovering and challenging the process used to establish the particular answer reached (ibid). Importantly, Archer (2012: 206) states that in considering our own reflexive process, the meta-reflexive instinct leads agents to become acutely aware of the 'situational logic of opportunity'. In this instance, structures, rather than being blindly internalised and reproduced, are instead problematised with actors demonstrating a greater understanding of both the possibilities and limitations of their own agency and structural forces (ibid. p. 207).

In application to my research, this suggests that reflexive agents may, in reaction to the GFC, first establish that learning is necessary, but following the internal deliberative process, which considers the 'situational logic of opportunity', calculate that the structural environment, in our case financial markets, would punish them if they change dramatically. As such, through the exercise of their own agency, banks may choose not to alter their behaviour radically. Indeed, Caetano (2014: 6) argues that meta-reflexive agents develop a 'critical vision' that informs the understanding and development of behaviours that are deemed to be most appropriate and beneficial to the learning subject's position. When applied to post-crisis bank learning, it may be that the banks have indeed learned lessons following the GFC, but that the lessons learned are about the costs and dangers of reform. In this respect, we may hypothesise that one of the outcomes of the crisis is that banks may have learned that in this instance radical change is neither desirable nor of benefit. In essence, Archer's (2003, 2012) thesis on the meta-reflexives indicates that an increased awareness of the situational logic of opportunity presented by the structural environment may have limited the capacity of the banks for reform. While this may not necessarily be the most desirable outcome, it still represents a greater sophistication of thought, and hence learning, and can explain why some banks have learned despite the absence of substantive change.

When applying the structure and agency thesis, and in particular Archer's (2003, 2012) work, to bank learning, I will carry forward two important factors that will be employed in the analytical process to follow. The *first* is the notion that banks and bankers are not separated or detached from the structures within which they operate, namely financial markets, yet, at the same time retain a great deal of autonomy. It is against this backdrop of individual and sociocultural factors that learning takes place, with agents and structures being neither 'co-extensive nor co-variant' (Archer, 1995: 66). The *second* is the idea that the reflective capabilities of agents in the learning process do not necessitate a dramatic or observable behavioural change and that meta-reflexives about the learning process itself are important.

Conclusion

In this chapter, I have set out an account of learning drawing from the literature located within the social sciences. The material outlines a description of learning, those conditions most conducive to learning and how a practical application of these ideas may be translated into a critical analysis of post-crisis bank learning. While there are a number of contending typologies of the concept of learning, single- and double-loop learning will be crucial in answering the question posed in this research as it equips us with the theoretical tools with which to distinguish between more superficial (single-loop) and deeper (double-loop) conceptions of learning.

The literature on single- and double-loop learning stresses that single-loop learning, while perhaps an important precursor to more substantive double-loop learning, is a more ostensible kind of learning which fails to tackle the root cause of problems. Instead, single-loop learning entails making slight and incremental changes to the fringes of current practices and norms. Conversely, double-loop learning stresses the presence of a thorough reflexive and evaluative process, which results in positive tangible changes to the underlying governing philosophies and rationale. The importance of single- and double-loop learning lies in the ability that it endows my research with to identify and isolate examples of leaning which have resulted in a change of an institution's policy objectives with those which have produced a reorientation of strategic goals, values and underlying group principles.

The account of learning presented in this chapter also stresses that both agential and institutional variations of learning are predicated upon and framed by bounded rationality. Because agents rarely have access to perfect information, they are prone to making clumsy approximations to compensate for key gaps in information. Moreover, the ability of the learning subject—in our case banks and bankers—to process information is further hampered their limited computational abilities. As such, while following the optimal path is desirable, it is not always possible because actors are prone to settle for what is 'good enough' and as a result are 'boundedly rational' learners. Consequently, the literature on bounded rationality tells us that while learning may be desirable amongst the banks and bankers, it may not always be achievable because agents and the institutions that they embody have a propensity to settle and become 'satisficers' as opposed to pursuing optimal outcomes.

The path towards maximising outcomes may be further complicated when we account for the fact that structures are also a mitigating factor in the learning process. For example, learning is set within broader structural constraints, which while not impossible to overcome, exert a great deal of influence over the learning process. Indeed, it is important that we keep in mind the temporal and shifting nature of both structures and agents. For example, structures are constantly moving and evolving. A case in point here would be the structural regulatory environment that banks are situated in. Since the GFC, the regulatory landscape has shifted significantly and as such, banks have been forced to adapt their behavioural patterns accordingly. Likewise, agent-based learning at banks in the post-crisis decade is similarly time-based. Indeed, as we shall see in the coming empirical chapters of the book, it is possible that key 'interpretive agents' (Bell, 2011) may have learned lessons, subsequently implementing change accordingly, only to be replaced by another set of individuals that may not have learned lessons or learned different lessons. Such instances will be distinguished within the empirical chapters accordingly.

The work of Archer (2003, 2012) on meta-reflexives shows us that while the desire to change may be one outcome of the learning process, this desire may not necessarily translate into proportionate actions if the associated cost of change is perceived as being too high. In this instance the internal conversation, while recognising that learning is needed, identifies that change—or to deviate too far from the established path—would place the learning agent at a disadvantage and thus prove costly. In this respect, learning may be present despite the absence of tangible change, with the lesson learned by agents and institutions being about their own capacity for change. In relation to the analysis of post-GFC bank learning, the meta-reflexives suggests the need to account for how agents and institutions perceive the wider structural environment.

While establishing a number of benchmarks or measures of learning against which the coming empirical evidence on each bank will be tested, this chapter of the book and the account of learning presented therein, also endows us with a theoretical grounding that can explain inter-bank variations in lesson learning. *First*, the literature stresses that dissatisfaction—this being when aspiration outstrips outcomes, and a desire to rectify unfavourable results will prompt learning resulting in a positive behavioural change. Therefore, we may hypothesise that those banks that have undergone the greatest dissatisfaction and experienced the largest losses may also be the greatest learners as the level of dissatisfaction at these institutions will be will higher. *Second*, learning requires space—being the dedication of both time and resources to the learning process. Subsequently, those banks that have applied the greatest institutional resources—learning space—to the self-reflexive process inherent in learning may have a greater propensity towards learning. These two important facets will be tested throughout the empirical chapters.

References

Archer, M. (1988). *Culture and agency: The place of culture in social theory*. Cambridge: Cambridge University Press.

Archer, M. (1995). *Realist social theory: The morphogenetic approach*. Cambridge: Cambridge University Press.

Archer, M. (2000). *Being human: The problem of agency*. Cambridge: Cambridge University Press.

Archer, M. (2003). *Structure, agency and the internal conversation*. Cambridge: Cambridge University Press.

Archer, M. (2007). *Making our way through the world*. Cambridge: Cambridge University Press.

Archer, M. (2012). *The reflexive imperative in late modernity*. Cambridge: Cambridge University Press.

Argyris, C., & Schon, D. A. (1978). *Organizational learning: A theory of action perspective*. Reading, MA: Addison-Wesley Publishing.

Arygris, C., & Schon, D. A. (1996). *Organizational learning II: Theory, method, and practice*. Reading, MA: Addison-Wesley Publishing.

Argyris, C., Putnam, R., & Smith, D. (1985). *Action science*. San Francisco: Jossey-Bass.

Ashwin, P. (2008). Accounting for structure and agency in 'close-up' research on teaching, learning and assessment in higher education. *International Journal of Educational Research, 47*, 151–158.

Baert, P. (1998). *Social theory in the twentieth century*. Cambridge: Polity Press.
Bandura, A. (1977). Self-efficacy: Towards a unifying theory of behavioural change. *Psychological Review, 84*(2), 191–215.
Bell, S. (2011). Do we really need a new 'constructivist institutionalism' to explain institutional change? *British Journal of Political Science, 41*, 883–906.
Bell, S., & Hindmoor, A. (2015). *Masters of the universe, slaves of the market*. Cambridge, MA: Harvard University Press.
Bhaskar, R. (1979). *The possibility of naturalism*. Harvester: Brighton.
Bhaskar, R. (1993). *Dialectic: The pulse of freedom*. London: Verso.
Boin, A., & Fishbacher-Smith, D. (2011). The importance of failure theories in assessing crisis management: The *Columbia* space shuttle disaster revisited. *Policy and Society, 30*(2011), 77–87.
Booth, S., & Anderberg, E. (2005). Academic development for knowledge capabilities: Learning, reflecting and developing. *Higher Education Research & Development, 24*(4), 373–386.
Bracken, P., Bremmer, I., & Gordon, D. (2005). *Managing strategic surprise: Lessons from risk management and risk assessment*. Cambridge: Cambridge University Press.
Caetano, A. (2014, September 10). Defining personal reflexivity: A critical reading of archer's approach. *European Journal of Social Theory, 15*(1), 93–115.
Cangelosi, V., & Dill, W.R. (1965). Organizational learning. Observations toward a theory. *Administrative Science Quarterly, 10*(2), 175–203.
Columbia Accident Investigation Board [CAIB]. (2003). *Columbia accident investigation report*. Available at: http://www.nasa.gov/columbia/home/CAIB_Vol1.html.
Cyert, R.M., & March, G. (1963). *A behavioral theory of the firm*. Englewood Cliffs, N.J: Prentice-Hall.
Day, P., & Klein, R. (1989). Interpreting the unexpected: The case of AIDS policy making in Britain. *Journal of Public Policy, 9*(3), 337–353.
Desoete, A., Roeyers, H., & De Clercq, A. (2003). Can offline metacognition enhance mathematical problem solving? *Journal of Educational Psychology, 95*, 188–200.
Deutsch, K. W. (1963). *The nerves of government*. New York: Free Press.
Dodgson, M. (1993, May). Organizational learning: A review of some literatures. *Organization Studies, 14*, 375–394.
Duncan, R., & Weiss, A. (1979). Organisational learning: Implications for organisational design. In B. M. Staw & L. L. Cummings (Eds.), *Research in organisational behaviour* (pp. 75–123). Greenwish, CT: JAI Press.
Easterby-Smith, M., & Araujo, L. (1999). Organizational learning: Current debates and opportunities. In M. Easterby-Smith, B. Burgoyne & L. Araujo

(Eds.), *Organizational learning and the learning organization* (pp. 1–21). London: Sage.

Edmondson, A. (1996). Learning from mistakes is easier said than done: Group and organizational influences on the detection and correction of human error. *The Journal of Applied Behavioural Science, 32*(1): 5–28.

Edmondson, A., & Moingeon, B. (1999). Learning, trust and organizational change. In M. Easterby-Smith, J. Burgoyne & L. Araujo (Eds.), *Organizational learning and the learning organization: Developments in theory and practice* (Chapter 9, pp. 157–176). London: Sage Publications.

Elkjaer, B. (1999). In search of a social learning theory. In M. Easterby-Smith, B. Burgoyne & L. Araujo (Eds.), Organizational learning and the learning organization: Developments in theory and practice (Chapter 5, pp. 75–91). London: Sage Publications.

Etheredge, L. S. (1981). Government learning: An overview. In S. Long (Ed.), *The hand-book of political behaviour* (Vol. 2, pp. 73–161). New York: Plenum Press.

Fiol, C. M., & Lyles, M. A. (1985). Organizational learning. *Academy of Management Review, 10*(2), 803–813.

Fiske, S. T., & Taylor, S. E. (1991). *Social cognition.* New York: McGraw-Hill.

Giddens, A. (1988). *Central problems in social theory.* London: Macmillan.

Giddens, A. (1995). *The constitution of society.* Cambridge, UK: Polity.

Hall, P. (1993). Policy paradigms, social learning, and the state: The case of economic policymaking in Britain. *Comparative Politics, 25*(3) (April), 275–296.

Hartwig, M. (2007). *Dictionary of critical realism.* London: Routledge (online)

Huber, G. P. (1991). Organisational learning: The contributing process and the literature. *Organization Science, 2*(2), 88–115.

Jitendra, A. K., Griffin, C. C., Haria, P., Leh, J., Adams, A., & Kaduvettoor, A. (2007). A comparison of single and multiple strategy instruction on third-grade students' mathematical problem solving. *Journal of Educational Psychology, 99*(1), 115–127.

Jones, B. D., & Baumgartner, F. R. (1993). *Agendas and instability in American politics.* Chicago: University of Chicago Press.

Jones, B. D., & Baumgartner, F. R. (2005). *The Politics of attention: How government prioritizes problems.* Chicago: University of Chicago Press.

Jones, B. D., & Baumgartner, F. R. (2009). *Agendas and instability in American politics* (2nd ed.). Chicago: Chicago University Press.

Kahn, P., Qualter, A., & Young, R. (2012). Structure and agency in learning: A critical realist theory of the development of capacity to reflect on academic practice. *Higher Education Research & Development, 31*(6) (December), 859–871.

Kerr, P. (2010). Espoused theories and theories-in-use of information literacy: A model for reflection and evaluation. *Proceedings of the American Society for Information Science and Technology, 46*(1), 1–7.
King, A. (2000). The accidental derogation of the lay actor a critique of giddens's concept of structure. *Philosophy of the Social Sciences, 30*(3), 362–383.
King, A. (2004). *The structure of social theory*. London: Routledge.
King, A. (2005). Structure and agency. In A. Harrington (Ed.), *Modern social theory* (pp. 215–232). Oxford. Oxford University Press.
Levitt, B., & March, J. G. (1988). Organisational learning. *Annual Review of Sociology, 14*, 319–340.
Marton, F. (1975). On non-verbatim learning. I. Level of processing and level of outcome. *Scandinavian Journal of Psychology, 16*(1) (September), 273–279.
Marton, F., & Saljo, R. (1976). On qualitative differences in learning. I. outcome and process. *British Journal of Educational Psychology, 46*, 4–11.
May, P. J. (1992). Policy learning and failure. *Journal of Public Policy, 12*(4), 331–354.
Mayer, R. E. (1999). *The promise of educational psychology: Vol. 1. learning in the content areas*. Upper Saddle River, NJ: Merrill Prentice Hall.
Minsky, M. (1975). A framework for representing knowledge. In P. Winston (Ed.), *The psychology of computer vision*. New York: McGraw-Hill.
Pendry, L. (2008). Social cognition. In M. Hewstone, W. Stroebe & K. Jonas (Eds.), *Introduction to social psychology: A European perspective*. Fourth Edition. Oxford: Blackwell.
Rose, R. (1991). What is lesson-drawing? *Journal of Public Policy, 11*(1), 3–30.
Rose, R. (1993). *Lesson-drawing in public policy: A guide to learning across time and space*. Chatham, New Jersey: Chatham House Publishers.
Rose, R. (2005). *Learning from comparative public policy: A practical guide*. London: Routledge.
Sabatier, P. A. (1988). An advocacy coalition framework of policy change and the role of policy-orientated learning therein. *Policy Sciences, 21*, 129–168.
Sabatier, P.A. (1993). Policy change over a decade or more. In P.A. Sabatier & H.C. Jenkins- Smith (Eds.), Policy change and learning, an advocacy coalition approach, pp. 13–39. Boulder: Westview Press.
Simon, H. A. (1957). *Models of man*. New York: John Wiley and Sons.
Simon, H. A. (1958). *Administrative behaviour* (2nd ed.). New York: Macmillan.
Simon, H. A. (1959). Theories of decision-making in economics and behavioural science. *The American Economic Review, XLIX*(3), 253–283.
Simon, H. A. (1983). *Reason in human affairs*. California: Stanford University Press.

Smith, M. K. (2011, 2013). Chris argyris: Theories of action, double-loop learning and organizational learning. *The encyclopaedia of informal education*. Available at: http://infed.org/mobi/chris-argyris-theories-of-action-double-loop-learning-and-organizational-learning/. Accessed 11 April 2014.

True, J. L., Jones, B. D., & Baumgartner, F. R. (2007). Punctuated equilibrium theory. In P. Sabatier (Ed.), *Theories of the policy process*. Cambridge, MA: Westview Press.

Tversky, A., & Kahneman, D. (1974, September 27). Judgement under uncertainty: Heuristics and biases. *Science, 185*(4157), 1124–1131.

Usher, R., & Bryant, I. (1989). *Adult education as theory, practice and research: The captive triangle*. London: Routledge.

Vygotsky, L. S. (1962). *Thought and language*. Cambridge, MA: MIT Press.

Vygotsky, L. S. (1978). *Mind and society: The development of higher mental processes*. Cambridge, MA: Harvard University Press.

Watkins, D. (1983). Depth of processing and the quality of learning outcomes. *Instructional Science, 12*, 49–58.

Weick, K. E., & Roberts, K. H. (1993). Collective mind in organizations: Heedful interrelating on flight decks. *Administrative Science Quarterly, 38*(3), 357–381.

CHAPTER 3

The Great Financial Crisis

Overview

Though banking crashes and financial crises have plagued markets throughout history, the extent to which the Great Financial Crisis of 2008 devastated the global economy was unprecedented. The fallout from the GFC was virtually instantaneous and led to a crippling depression of economic activity that affected almost every corner of the globe (King, 2009). Unlike previous crises, the GFC was not the result of a downturn in economic activity in the real economy. Instead, the roots of the crisis can be traced to bank losses triggered by the US subprime mortgage crisis, which subsequently spread to the real economy (Bell & Hindmoor, 2015). Following the GFC, Andrew Haldane of the Bank of England concluded that financial markets had greatly increased the privatisation of return while amplifying and the 'socialisation of risk' (Haldane, 2011: 2).

This section of the book offers an account of the origins of the GFC. The chapter considers the role that the banks played in the crisis and how institutions were able to exploit socio-economic and political frailties in order to create and 'game' a system predicated upon risk. The chapter argues that competition, along with a plethora of other mutually shaping non-exclusive causes, was a key factor in the GFC and remains today one the greatest obstacles to learning. As well as situating the structural background against which learning takes place, the chapter will also establish

A. Barber, *UK Banks and the Lessons of the Great Financial Crisis*, Building a Sustainable Political Economy: SPERI Research & Policy, https://doi.org/10.1007/978-3-030-70254-0_3

the key lessons that can be taken from the crisis. The purpose of this exercise is twofold. *First*, in order to judge if the banks have learned lessons from the crisis we must first understand the causes of the GFC. To this end, the chapter will consider and explore those factors considered within the literature as being the key triggers of the crisis. *Second*, the causes of the GFC accounted for here will then be carried forward into the empirical chapters that follow and used as a series of benchmarks or yardsticks against which learning can be tested. While this chapter offers the reader an exploration of those conditions that gave rise to the crisis, it is worth noting that the analysis put forward in this section is not intended to be a comprehensive analysis of every contributing factor to the GFC, indeed, there is a multitude of other triggers that presupposed the crisis. Instead, the analysis examines the problems which, in the light of the objective of the book, can be isolated and individually managed by the banks and against which learning will subsequently be tested.

The importance of the account of the GFC presented here lies not simply in highlighting the triggers of the crisis but how the banks' business models—their corporate culture, remunerative practices and balance sheets—worked in such ways as to compound and magnify the effects of the GFC. It will be demonstrated how failures within one particular facet of the banking industry were able to spread to and pervade the entire system because of the unique way in which banks, and the markets in which they operated, were structured. As such, the chapter will focus on the key vulnerabilities that built up over time, highlighting how structural flaws within the banks, along with the regulatory environment, worked in such a way as to give rise to the causal mechanisms that triggered the crisis, and greatly amplified the associated costs.

I do not assume that a correcting of the failures associated with the GFC, detailed in this chapter, by the banks will prevent future financial crises. Indeed, as discussed in the Introduction, we know that historically crises have emerged from a number of different facets within the global economy. The current health and economic crisis stemming from the COVID-19 global pandemic is just one example of an emerging crisis that remains separate from bank learning and the GFC. As such, I recognise that future crises may not necessarily be tied directly to the banks. Likewise, we know that while banks can indeed learn and change, they can also revert to previous behaviours or create entirely new patterns of reasoning not yet witnessed. Therefore, even though the banks surveyed in this study may present evidence of learning in relation to those factors outlined in this chapter, this is not to say that future crises will not happen. Yet, the account of the GFC presented here, along with the question of post-crisis bank learning, remains important due to the extent to which the banks, and those practices detailed below, played in precipitating arguably the greatest economic and financial crisis in recent history, the effects of which are still being felt today (King, 2016).

Causes of the Great Financial Crisis

The causes of the GFC are deep and varied with many of these factors sharing countless of the same properties and being closely related. For example, the role of leverage and wholesale funding in the crisis are interrelated and can be contrasted with the short-termism of the bonus culture that pervaded institutions in the years preceding the GFC. As such, this chapter should not be read as a mono-causal exposition of the crisis, with many of the causes of the crisis augmenting and compounding one another. Indeed, attributing the crisis to an isolated or singular event or trigger would only serve to mislead the reader. Instead, the aim of the chapter is to unfold an accurate and detailed analysis of the delicate interplay between several key factors that should not be considered in isolation.

Excessive Competition

One of the underlying features of the GFC, and from which many of the other triggers of the crisis would flow, is the extent to which banks, over the course of the two decades before the crisis, became exposed to ever-increasing structural competitive pressures. In response to these growing pressures, banks reengineered their balance sheets in order to protect their share price and return on equity (ROE), held by many financial analysists as the two fundamentals of a bank's worth and which subsequently became key determinants of employee remuneration.

Banks had always played a key role in the economy, acting as a go-between for customers in the transfer of payments, providing a secure home for savings, and funding future investments through loans (Bell & Hindmoor, 2015). These activities provided institutions with a steady yet modest profit stream that was further enhanced by favourable levels of equity capital and substantial cash reserves. As such, the business models once employed by banks proved for a banking system that was highly liquidised with low rates of leverage (Haldane, 2011). However, deregulation under the neoliberal agenda—pursued on both sides of the Atlantic from the 1980s onwards—exposed banks to fresh levels of competition which had not been witnessed before. New rules meant that national, regional and international institutions were now all thrown into the same arena to vie for capital, which had simultaneously become ever more liquid due to the erosion of capital controls (Gamble, 2014).

Following the deregulation of the City, the dominance of Britain's 'Big Four' banks', while still accounting for an overwhelming majority of the market share, was directly challenged by large international players, keen to establish and expand their UK presence (Bell & Hindmoor, 2015). Technological innovation also equipped smaller challenger banks and building societies with the tools needed to launch an assault on their larger counterparts' market share thus, further ramping up competition levels. This was then compounded by a belief amongst senior bankers that the only way to protect their business and maintain ROEs and share price valuations, as well as potential takeovers from rival institutions, was to grow their balance sheets exponentially (Perman, 2013).

These factors worked in such a way as to increase competition between the banks that was then realised on three mutually non-exclusive fronts. *First*, growth options became limited resulting in banks having to rely on their assets in place to generate profits (Bustamante & Donangelo, 2014). This method of profit generation had always been an integral part of banking, however what changed following the deregulation of the City was the extent to which activity of this kind, along with a shift towards financial trading, came to dominate and displace more traditional banking models, becoming the default source of profit (Gowan, 2009). As a result, banks became proficient in creating and benefitting from the volatility of asset prices, buying up assets and creating speculative bubbles, making a profit before exiting the market and bursting the bubble and thus, contributing towards a financial system which was increasingly predicated upon risk (ibid.).

Second, increased competition within markets and between the banks resulted in reduced profit margins. In response, banks increased their leverage ratios as a means of protecting their margins (Bustamante & Donangelo, 2014). However, in doing so institutions significantly diminished their ability to absorb losses and service debts by eroding the reserves which lower rates of leverage—higher capital holdings—had afforded them (ibid.). For example, banks would use their short-term capital to 'gear-up' their balance sheets and exploit asset bubbles in order to meet expected ROE targets (Haldane, 2011: 12). When this proved successful, more short-term capital flooded into the system creating yet more incentive to increase leverage further (ibid.). When the crisis hit, banks found that their loss absorbing capacity had been almost wiped out due to the now huge leverage ratios they were operating with. This subsequently led to paralysis in the markets as banks were unable to service their debts due to diminished liquidity (Hale & Santos, 2013).

Third, highly mobile capital, facilitated by the liberalisation movement, meant that in the years preceding the crisis shareholder value became highly skewed towards short-termism with average holdings in the UK and United States falling from approximately 3 years to 3 months in the decade before the GFC (Haldane, 2011: 12). This was then compounded by the rise of so-called quarterly capitalism whereby analysis by private investors, financial institutions and the media placed intense scrutiny on the banks' ability to create shareholder value (Haldane, 2011; Bell & Hindmoor, 2015). One of the results of this unrelenting analysis was that banks became swept up in so-called herding behaviour with institutions seeking to emulate successful rivals (Greenspan, 2013). Competitive emulation and herding behaviour was particularly harmful as on seeing the apparent success of their competitors, banks became evermore willing to ignore their own intuitive warning signs for fear of losing ground and thereby exacerbating market deficiencies (ibid.).

While structural competitive pressures remain, to some extent, outside the control of institutions, and cannot necessarily be managed and isolated by the banks, there are certain measures that the banks can take to mitigate these factors and which may be indicative of learning. For example, banks that have rebalanced their remuneration away from structures that are heavily skewed towards increasing share price values and ROE, which have in the past compounded structural pressures, may demonstrate a greater propensity towards learning. Likewise, an increased loss absorbing capacity and reduced leverage ratios may also be indicative of the presence of learning.

True Belief in the Efficiency of Markets

Another fundamental cause of the crisis can be found in the belief, and misplaced confidence, that in the years preceding the GFC, the growing complexity of institutions and financial markets had been matched by sophisticated mathematical algorithms that had effectively allayed risk

(Turner, 2009). In particular, it was believed that the Capital Asset Pricing Model (CAPM) and the Value At Risk (VAR) methodologies had meant that financial markets and institutions were both efficient and accurate in determining prices (Davies, 2010). These models were particularly salient in the crisis because they endowed senior bankers with a belief that markets were effective and that mark-to-market (MTM) pricing, whereby assets are endlessly re-evaluated against the market, rather than book, were an accurate reflection of the true value of an asset (Bootle, 2011).

However, the risk models used by many of the banks were seriously flawed with capital markets extremely under-priced, risk premiums being exceptionally low and a false assumption that risk had been effectively dispersed when in fact it had become more concentrated (Gowan, 2009). Resultantly, information within the financial system came to be largely distorted by such models with financial actors basing their decisions on incomplete or inaccurate information (Blinder, 2014). This reliance upon mathematical models was not, contrary to the common depiction, solely motivated by greed or a 'don't care attitude' but was instead the product of 'true believers' who thought that complex models had all-but removed risk from the system (Bell & Hindmoor, 2015: 15). Indeed, Friedman (2009) argues that bankers overwhelmingly favoured lower yielding, safer AAA securities over more hazardous, higher return AA rated securities, thus demonstrating both imprudence and a belief in the accuracy of the market to correctly price risk.

In the sphere of economics, it is well documented that the efficiency of financial markets is largely dependent upon the dissemination of information (Fama, 1970; Lucas, 1980; Forstater, 2007). Information is important to the sound functioning of markets as it allows investors to make decisions based upon the correct pricing of assets, identifying losses within the system and discerning both individual and market liabilities (Acharya et al., 2009). However, risk models such as CAPM and VAR removed much of the need for individual investors to exercise their own discretion by promising a method that accurately priced assets (Davies, 2010).

This reliance upon what we now know to be flawed mathematical models was then further compounded by the fact that many senior bankers had backgrounds in economics (Davies, 2010). For example, rational expectations—a branch of microeconomics—suggests that market processes and the institutions which embody these methods are much more accurate in judging and pricing risk than centrally imposed regulators (Engelen et al., 2011). The rational expectations theory had been a mainstay of the business schools and universities from which the top banks drew their graduates. As such, banks lacked both the technical and theoretical expertise to thoroughly test and question underlying assumptions (Davies, 2010). Furthermore, academia and market practice became increasingly intertwined in the years before the crisis as leading academics came to hold senior consultancy positions within both private and public institutions (Engelen et al., 2011). This 'corporatization' of the economics profession gave credence to the business strategies employed by the banks with the risk models used by institutions going unquestioned due to the academic authority enjoyed by senior economists (ibid.).

These factors combined to create a system centred upon asymmetric information, resulting in the mispricing of risk and a rational reliance upon the market to make what we now know to be incorrect calculations. Consequently, armed with inaccurate information agents and institutions wrongly allocated resources thereby creating significant skews and instability that, when the crisis hit, determined both the scale and speed with which the downturn happened.

Leverage

There is little doubt that over the course of the last century banks have dramatically grown their balance sheets often, as discussed above, in response to increasing competition from rival institutions. Haldane et al. (2010: 84) suggest that in the decade before the crisis, the balance sheets of the world's 1,000 largest banks grew by approximately 150 per cent. However, this rapid expansion was not accompanied by a growth of equity bases, resulting in large disparities in the capital ratios of many institutions (ibid.). Intense competition coupled with greater free movement of capital following the 'big bang' of the City of London, meant that in the years preceding the crisis, banks saw their share price and ROE being increasingly eroded (Clark, 2016). In this pressure cooker environment institutions sought to grow their balance sheets, as a means of reversing their fortunes, by significantly increasing their leverage. The banks were aided in their endeavours by regulatory stipulations, or a lack thereof, such as the Basel II capital standards framework which Adair Turner (2016: 30) argues allowed banks to maximise 'scarce' capital in an effort to extend more credit into the real economy. As a result, banks became highly skilled in working within regulatory requirements to ramp up leverage ratios through the use of innovative financial products (Erturk, 2017).

Banks would utilise off-balance sheet vehicles, for example, which were frequently secured against long-term debts held in structured investment vehicles (SIVs) (Acharya & Schnabl, 2009). One of the associated benefits of these financial instruments, which was accompanied by an expansion into the so-called shadow banking sector, was that banks were able to move assets off their balance sheets and as such were no-longer required to hold capital against them (Erturk, 2017). However, in order to make these conduits attractive to buyers, banks would extend liquidity and credit guarantees to counterparties (Acharya & Richardson, 2009). Effectively, institutions would insure the underlying credit by absorbing any potential risk and in effect bring the items back on to the balance sheet but, importantly, without the necessary capital requirements (ibid.). As these instruments carried little need for capital, banks were able to ramp up leverage ratios to levels five times higher than what would ordinarily be allowed on a balance sheet (Acharya & Schnabl, 2009). For example, before the crisis hit RBS had a leverage ratio of 31:1; Lloyds 29:1; Barclays 33:1 and HSBC 24:1.

These innovative products would ultimately prove costly for the banks as the creation and retention of risk remained with the issuing bank. For instance, because many of the products carried with them implicit liquid and credit guarantees they were subject to the highest possible approval from the relevant credit rating agencies, typically having been rated AAA (Acharya & Richardson, 2009). And because these instruments had the highest possible rating they were open to investment from lucrative money markets funds which gave banks access to readily available capital and thus, enabled them to fund the conduits with unusually low interest rates (Acharya & Richardson, 2009; Engelen et al., 2011). Consequently, liquid and credit guarantees gave investors a degree of recourse against the banks, meaning that investors could simply return the assets if or when losses began to occur. In the third quarter of 2007, this is exactly what happened. A downturn in the market led many investors to return the assets to the banks that were now faced with the reality of moving these largely diminished products back onto their balance sheets which lacked the necessary capital to cover the ensuing losses (Acharya & Schnabl, 2009; Acharya & Richardson, 2009: 201).

Greenspan (2013) argues that when dealing with assets, banks have a natural propensity to avoid pooling products into a particular facet of highly leveraged portfolios and will instead look to diversify risk through a number of alternate mechanisms. However, in the decade preceding the GFC banks became exposed to highly leveraged products. Greenspan (2013) speculates that the cause of this excessive risk-taking can be directly linked to the 'true believers' hypothesis, discussed above, and a notion amongst the banks trading in these assets that their products were structured in such a way, and carried enough security, that gearing up leverage ratios was safe.

However, at a time when greater liquidity risks had permeated the banking system, banks were gambling on their own liquidity by selling and borrowing against assets, which in the event of a crisis or reversal of market trends could prove difficult to move (Davies, 2010). As a result, banks and bankers had unwittingly exposed themselves to potential liquidity shocks. As Friedman (2009: 146) has pointed out, 'with leverage comes not only the promise of larger gains, but the risk of greater losses'. Thus, excessive leverage is something that we should not consider in isolation. Instead, massively geared up leverage ratios at many of the banks was emblematic of the wider structural and agent-led landscape at the time of the crisis. Moreover, excessive competition and a true belief in the efficiency of markets acted to reinforce such harmful practices.

Consequently, the build-up of excessive leverage within the financial system, like many of the factors discussed in this chapter, demonstrates that banks and bankers were not the only actors in the GFC. Indeed, regulators—whose job it was to monitor institutions, shareholders—who flooded the system with more and more capital—and a number of other actors and financial market infrastructure providers all played an important part. However, given the huge role banks and bankers had in the crisis and their continued contribution to financial stability, not only as key financial intermediaries but also as systemically important institutions, the question of whether banks have learned lessons from the crisis remains crucial to current debates on financial stability, growth and reform.

Moreover, excessive leverage and the manner in which banks used innovative financial products to circumvent regulatory stipulations in the years which proceeded the crisis further demonstrates the need to move beyond questions of regulation and stresses the necessity for assuming a bank-centric approach to reform. For instance, we know from the above discussion that banks, while perhaps not in compliance with the 'spirit' of regulation, were (generally) operating within the letter of the law. While post-crisis regulatory reform now requires institutions to hold greater levels of capital and has introduced more stringent controls on leverage ratios, competition within markets and between banks still persists (IMF, 2017; Bell & Hindmoor, 2018). As such, banks have both the incentives and means to sidestep regulation, which may lead to future regulatory arbitrage[1] (Brazier, 2017; Erturk, 2017).

Shadow Banking

The overambitious and undercapitalised business strategies associated with ever-increasing leverage ratios and competition-based financial innovations were greatly aided by the growth in the shadow banking sector. The trade in and origination of shadow banking instruments facilitated much of the banks' inorganic growth strategies and which further exacerbated the crisis by exposing banks to new levels of risk which were almost impossible to calculate (Gowan, 2009). For example, what distinguishes the shadow banking sector from more traditional banking markets is the extent of regulations concerning capital and deposit guarantees. A proliferation in the use of shadow banking instruments, such as Asset Backed Commercial Paper (ABCP) and Repurchase Agreements (REPOs), proved so harmful because these innovative products did not carry the same implicit minimal capital standards and requirement to increase equity in-line with assets as instruments and institutions governed by traditional bank markets (Bernanke, 2012). This was further augmented by the fact that much of the shadow banking industry was located and routed through tax havens which are themselves shrouded in secrecy and opacity with little regulatory oversight (Hampton & Christensen 2002; Woodward, 2006; Palan et al., 2009; Urry, 2014).

Because products within the shadow banking sector could be set up with minimal capital they appeared to be a very efficient, and hence a lucrative investment, with traders quickly buying up these instruments (Bernanke, 2012). This in turn both drove up demand but also flooded banks with even more cheap credit. Banks responded to this demand, aided by access to ever readily available funding, by originating even more products and thus fuelling the cycle further (ibid.). However, the unique

[1] A factor which may explain the growth in off-balance sheet items and the shadow banking sector discussed in the coming empirical chapters.

way in which the shadow banking sector was, and still is, structured meant that while there was an implied division between shadow and non-shadow banks, in practice more traditional 'on-shore' markets quickly became intertwined with the murky 'off-shore' world (Chrisensen et al., 2016). For example, shadow banking instruments held by the banks were rarely kept 'on balance sheet' and were typically held in off-balance-sheet Special Purpose Vehicles (SPV) (Urry, 2014). As a result, these off-balance-sheet items did not share the luxury of robust regulatory scrutiny and state-sponsored security nets (Ramskogler, 2015). Instead, shadow banks employed devices such as placing restrictions upon portfolios and relying on the prudence of rating agencies (Bernanke, 2012). This belief in the prudence of the ratings agencies to correctly price instruments and portfolios turned out to be disaster when competition between agencies led to products being priced according to the needs of the banks rather than at fair value (Lewis, 2011). When markets began to falter in 2007 and MTM pricing undermined confidence in the shadow banking sector, the market experienced widespread flight as investors scrambled to offload their position (Bernanke et al., 2019). Once-AAA-rated securities were downgraded as 'toxic' and became worthless leaving banks with little option but to bring them back on to their balance sheets which were by then significantly undercapitalised (Acharya et al., 2009).

Turner (2012: 16–17) identifies four key ways in which shadow banking instruments contributed to and exacerbated instability within financial markets. *First*, because shadow banking relied on MTM pricing as opposed to more traditional secured lending practices, this led to asymmetries of procyclical credit creation. *Second*, shadow banking instruments intensified the problem of complex intermediation chains which are inherently prone to funding runs and maturity mismatches. *Third*, due to the absence of explicit capital guarantees the risk between funding liquidity and market liquidity was heightened leading to greater chances of contagion across markets. *Finally*, because shadow banking relied heavily upon 'self-referential' pricing models, fair value assessments became skewed and blinkered thus further increasing procyclical instability.

Resultantly, we can see how shadow banking and the trade in off-balance-sheet products, which encapsulated these markets, played a central role in the GFC. Moreover, a series of mutually reinforcing factors, such as a failure to correctly regulate and price risk and an increased willingness on the part of the banks to operate with enhanced leverage ratios, likewise worked in such a way as to magnify and compound the effects of the crisis.

Wholesale Funding

The expansion of the shadow banking sector along with investment banking and the growing magnitude of more traditional banking activities in the global economy in the years leading up to the crisis was fuelled by a reliance upon short-term, often overnight, wholesale funding which facilitated a banking and financial system with a growing propensity towards risk. Indeed, in the years before the GFC, many of the major global banks increasingly came to rely on alternative forms of funding, as opposed to traditional funding sources such as customer deposits and savings, in order to pursue their expansionary goals (Bernanke, 2010). Much of this funding came by way of the wholesale markets in which banks and other financial institutions would lend and borrow money between one another on a short-term basis (Clark, 2016). However, funding of this kind would prove to be the Achilles' heel for banks when, in late 2007 and early 2008, inter-bank markets froze.

Funding made available through wholesale markets meant that banks were able to develop large maturity mismatches, namely by borrowing short-term in order to hold and fund long-term investments (King, 2016). This was accompanied by a belief that wholesale markets were a relatively safe and secure way of funding long-term assets. However, when markets began to falter, panic and suspicion began to spread throughout wholesale markets as banks and financial institutions, keen to protect themselves from potentially bad debtors, began to withdraw credit (Bell & Hindmoor, 2015). In response, banks began to hoard liquidity by shortening the terms of their inter-bank loans or calling in the debt of the loan in its entirety (Haldane & May, 2011). As more and more institutions began to cut their loans and withdraw credit, others similarly followed suit leading to a 'funding liquidity shock' as overnight credit all but evaporated from the system (ibid.: 353).

This problem was further compounded by the fact that, as discussed above, many of the banks were now operating with significantly ramped up leverage ratios. Banks and bankers had presumed that in the event of a liquidity squeeze, excessive leverage ratios could be, at least partially, offset by the selling assets thereby increasing overall liquidity (Bell & Hindmoor, 2015). However, this turned out to be erroneous leaving the banks with large maturity mismatches and unable to service their debts (ibid.). As Davies (2010) points out, banks that relied upon the selling of assets in order to increase their liquidity pools were extremely vulnerable to MTM pricing which subsequently downgraded the value of assets. As the GFC began to gather pace and spread, confidence evaporated along with liquidity and shortly thereafter readily available capital all but disappeared (King, 2016).

One of the reasons why a withdrawal of liquidity from wholesale markets was so catastrophic was because of the systemic risks associated with inter-bank lending. Wholesale markets greatly amplified highly unstable and opaque linkages between the banks increasing the prospect of potential counter-party risk, with the failure of any one bank having the potential to bring down the entire system (Acharya et al., 2009). When market confidence began to turn in mid-2007 these complex linkages manifested themselves as banks and other financial institutions struggled to fully understand or identify the extent to which losses at other institutions could potentially affect them (Acharya et al., 2009; Bernanke et al., 2019). The result of this was that markets quickly became illiquid as banks were unable to attain short-term funding. With cash reserves depleted and inter-bank markets in paralysis, governments across the globe faced little option but to step in and recapitalise the entire banking system.

Remuneration

One of the principle charges levied against the banks in the aftermath of the GFC is that questionable business strategies concerning shadow banking instruments, capitalisation and leverage ratios, to name but a few, were in part driven by the banks' remuneration structures. Indeed, in the decade preceding the crisis employee compensation was increasingly skewed towards short-term and often high-risk trades, with an explicit focus upon growing ROE and share price valuations (Admati & Hellwig, 2013; Clark, 2016). This result of this was that bankers were incentivised to pursue ambiguous financial activities that would ensure that targets were met and bonuses awarded.

For example, growth in ROE and a bank's share price were a frequent measure of increased equity yields and were used as a standard for determining employee performance and target setting by senior management (Haldane, 2011). In order to meet these targets and achieve the resulting lucrative bonuses, bank employees sought ever riskier, short-term yields on investments (Admati & Hellwig, 2013). When employees met these targets, by delivering favourable returns, investors and the senior management of banks sought to boost their short-term profits further by increasing targets and thereby motivating employees to engage still further in ever riskier behaviour (Haldane, 2011), in what Haldane (2012c: 6) has described as a 'system with in-built incentives for self-harm'.

Similarly, variable remuneration within investment and trading divisions of banks was progressively linked to both the number of trades made by an employee and the net asset value of particular funds under management (Acharya & Richardson, 2009). Put simply, the higher the number of trades or the greater the value of a fund, the greater the bonus. As such, bankers had strong incentives to take on excessive risks, with ramped up leverage ratios linked to Collateralised Debt Obligations (CDOs), Credit Default Swaps (CDS) and other securitisation instruments offering the greatest prospect of higher rewards (Davies, 2010). However, this in turn created a vicious cycle whereby high equity yields and lucrative remuneration packages became mutually reinforcing (Haldane, 2012a).

However, Mervin King (2009), former Governor of the Bank of England, argues that the speculative nature of the banking system, reinforced by skewed remuneration structures, cannot be solely attributed to a minority of greedy bankers. Instead, Lord Kind (2009) suggests that we must also account for the role shareholders and investors that, keen to see favourable returns on their capital, helped to manufacture remuneration structures that placed a premium upon the financial 'ends' but paid little attention as to how result were delivered. Indeed, Haldane (2011: 12) draws attention to the fact that under joint stock banking, whereby shareholders are liable for any incurring debts, ownership and control are 'divorced'. Consequently, Haldane (2011) argues that in order to regain a certain amount of control over the business decisions of senior bankers, shareholders progressively sought to align senior pay and shareholder interests. This is evidenced by the fact that when senior managers and their staff returned huge profits, shareholders responded by increasing their investment in the bank, pumping more and more money into the system in the hope of replicating previous success and thus encouraging bankers to enter into ever larger trades (Haldane, 2012c). While King (2009: 3) concedes that investors did not necessarily grasp the complexity of the trades that were being made on their behalf, it appears that when times were good and record profits were being reported, no-one stopped to ask what the downside risk was and whether such practices were in the long-term interest of the bank. Thus, excessive risk-taking and the reward of questionable business strategies became both the norm and mutually reinforcing (PCBS, 2013: 9).

Corporate Governance and Risk

While excessive competition, rampant leverage ratios and the trade of complex financial instruments, facilitated by the shadow banking sector, all played a huge role in the GFC, it has been hypothesised that the fallout from these factors could have been mitigated had the corporate governance and risk control functions of institutions been more robust (Bell & Hindmoor, 2015, 2018). The lack of an appropriate risk management framework at a number of banks in the years before the crisis meant that many institutions had failed to implement even the most basic of business rules concerning diversification and capitalisation. Consequently, banks were left with portfolios that were highly concentrated, highly leveraged and extremely sensitive to volatility (Sabato, 2009).

This deficiency in business best practice has been linked to the way in which banks' internal governance was structured. In particular, traditional risk management controls, which relied heavily upon the prudence and sound judgement of highly specialised risk analysists and the chief risk officer, had, in the years preceding the crisis, been increasingly subordinated to VAR and CAPM models which, as discussed previously, were laden with risk (Turner, 2009). In their study, Ellul and Yerramilli (2010) surveyed 72 of the largest US banks over a 15-year period (1994–2009). The authors found that the chief risk officer (CRO) at 85 per cent of banks surveyed was not in the top five highest-paid employees (ibid.). Likewise, at 43 per cent of banks, the CRO was not a member of the executive committee and was scarcely seated on the board of directors, with 33 per cent of banks surveyed having no CRO at all (Ellul & Yerramilli, 2010). The growing exclusion of the CRO from the upper-echelons of corporate governance meant that it was very difficult for these key agents' voices to be heard, with broken or fractured lines of communication between the CRO and group chief executive, the board and other senior management (Sabato, 2009).

Moreover, the effectiveness of the CRO was often compromised by group reporting mechanisms that frequently saw risk managers answering to divisional or regional heads as opposed to the group chief executive. As such, the escalation of risk was dependent upon the judgement of senior managers, many of whom did not fully understand the risk posed or were insufficiently incentivised to escalate matters (Sabato 2009; Moore, 2015). Likewise, because the CRO typically sat outside the inner circle of senior executives, they frequently suffered from a lack of access to pertinent data and were instead dependent upon secondary information, the timing and accuracy of which could be open to errors (Moore, 2015). Indeed, Kashyap (2010) demonstrates that banks where the presence of the CRO was less prominent had larger exposures to securities, bigger trading books and a greater proportion of derivatives, all of which had a detrimental effect on the health of the bank when the crisis hit.

The diminishing role of the CRO coupled with a reliance upon VAR models was then further exacerbated by the fact that the rapid expansion of institutions had not been met with a similar sophistication of internal group controls. As a result, many aspects of internal risk management became compartmentalised and 'siloed' with little communication between departments, heads and individual risk officers (Ashby, 2010; Moore, 2015). The result of this was that while individual risk mechanisms may have maintained their effectiveness, the data generated and any possible correlation between a bank's activities and risk failed to be communicated effectively leading to huge asymmetries in information. Consequently, risk management teams found it increasingly difficult to both effectively feedback information and access support needed due to the dislocation between risk managers and overarching group governance structures (Ashby, 2010). Resultantly, CROs were left with a fractured picture of group-wide risk that made it impossible to make accurate judgements and identify emerging threats in a timely manner.

Authoritative CEOs

A closely related factor to the failure of internal group governance, and which further intensified many of the causes outlined in this chapter, is the extent to which chief executive officers (CEOs) and senior executives wielded exceptional power and control over institutions and members of staff (Bank of England, 2015). In its investigation into the GFC, the Parliamentary Commission on Banking Standards (PCBS) noted that major deficiencies in banks' internal governance controls were a direct result of the authoritative and hierarchical nature which characterised many institutions (PCBS, 2013). The report goes on to suggest that while some banks appeared to display effective internal oversight, this was in fact a facade as non-executive directors lacked both the 'capacity and incentives' to question the decisions of senior managers and executives (ibid.: 10). Indeed, in many cases it appears that those individuals who were specifically tasked with holding senior managers to account consistently failed to do so and instead conducted themselves in such a way as to give further credence and confirmation to the business strategies being pursued (Davies, 2010; Fraser, 2014; Moore, 2015).

One of the reasons why such circumstances were allowed to persist can be attributed to the fact that those members of staff whose job it was to question and interrogate the strategies of senior management were often excluded from such conversations due to a lack of status stemming from an absence of technical expertise. For example, many non-executive board members were from a non-finance background (PCBS, 2013) and as such, often lacked the relevant skills and understanding of financial markets, which by the mid-2000s had become a minefield of technical information, exotic financial products and contracts, to adequately judge or challenge senior management (Davies, 2010). Moreover, non-executive directors who were charged with overseeing the overall direction of banks have been accused of not dedicating enough time to their duties and operating with a very 'hands-off' or light-touch approach to internal governance (Davies, 2010; Bell & Hindmoor, 2015). The unique way in which non-executive directors and senior managers interacted meant that high-ranking individuals were free to impart their own views upon the entire bank and lead the company in the direction they thought most appropriate with little or no opposition (Bell & Hindmoor, 2015).

The authority enjoyed by CEOs and senior managers, who often had the individual power to dismiss employees, further diminished the willingness or ability of both non-executive directors and staff to challenge senior management (Davies, 2010; Fraser, 2014; Moore, 2015; Augar, 2018). The unique linkages which epitomise the world of banking and finance, meant that employees' careers effectively lied in the hands of a small number of powerful agents. For example, members of staff who had been dismissed from a company could quickly find their reputation and career damaged beyond repair with so-called bad eggs being shunned by the banking community thereafter (Bell & Hindmoor, 2015; Moore, 2015). Thus, in the years preceding the crisis, we find that employees within banks were increasingly reluctant to voice any concerns or challenge the business decisions of senior managers for fear of professional reprisals.

This was then further compounded by a distinct lack of whistle-blowing facilities within institutions. Subsequently, employees who were acting in a way that was harmful or contradictory to good governance practices were often left to carry on until a point in time when irreversible damage had been caused (Medland, 2013; PCBS, 2013). Those who did attempt to address their concerns and raise issues were often brushed aside or met with outright hostility (Martin, 2014; Moore, 2015). As a result, while many key individuals within the banks may have been acutely aware of the technical warning signings that preceded the GFC, the voices of these central figures were largely silenced by the domineering position of senior executives and the governance structures that facilitated them, and against which individuals had little recourse.

Excessive Financial Trading

As addressed previously, the decade preceding the GFC witnessed ever-greater innovation by the banks, that came up with a plethora of financial products that allowed them to grow their balance sheets exponentially. This growth was fuelled, primarily, by an expansion of trading operations particularly within the investment banking divisions of institutions, which moved away from traditional activities such as wealth management and mergers (Davies, 2010). By late 2007, the investment banking operations of all major global banks had grown dramatically and was now a key driver of group profit (Bernanke et al., 2019). This propensity towards trading activities meant that banks significantly increased their exposure to 'investment in [and] sponsorship of hedge funds or private equity funds [and] proprietary trading' (Davies, 2010: 80). However, these funds were sought purely for their profitability and while highly lucrative, they exposed banks to new forms of systemic risk.

The expansion into and growth of financial trading was facilitated by technological advances which reduced and all but removed the barriers which were once associated with both the cost and speed at which financial trades could be made (Engelen et al., 2011). Furthermore, technological and financial innovation combined to create a system, which in the decade leading up to the crisis, was characterised by an abundance of highly mobile capital and instantaneous trading and in which new and sophisticated financial products constantly promised the potential of unprecedented yields for investors (King, 2016).

Initially, the move towards high volume financial trading, and the associated growth of investment banking, was heralded as a success. It was thought that trading in financial instruments allowed investors greater freedom to allocate capital towards products that matched their risk appetites, thereby increasing the volume and frequency in which private entrepreneurs would be willing to engage with the market (Davies, 2010). Similarly, it was believed that trading in innovative products had the effect of dispersing risk more broadly thus allowing banks to shed some of the underlying exposure typically associated with the holding or warehousing of products on balance sheets (ibid.). However, the huge volume at which investment banks were trading meant that by 2007, the composition of bank balance sheets had significantly altered the risk profile of institutions (King, 2016). By the summer of 2007, trading activities in the investment banking divisions of institutions had dwarfed more traditional operations and as a result, when the crisis struck banks quickly found that their investment banking divisions had compromised the entire institution (Admati & Hellwig, 2013).

Moreover, the ascendency of investment banking and the associated expansion of financial trading meant that many banks had turned to the unregulated sector, such as the shadow banking industry, to fund their expansionary goals (Archarya et al. 2009). This was amplified by the fact that financial trading and investment banking proved to be highly profitable for both banks and investors, which in turn spurred a greater appetite amongst institutions to increase their trading activities further (King, 2016). However, the sheer scale in which banks were using the unregulated sector to develop and originate financial trades in order to meet the demand of investors meant that the banks would unwittingly make a largely unregulated facet of the financial sector a cornerstone of the global economy (Archarya et al., 2009).

When the crisis broke, the magnitude and pace at which financial products were being traded, along with the opacity of instruments, meant that it was impossible to determine counter-party risk and which resulted in a freezing of credit markets (Archarya et al., 2009). While institutions did not abandon traditional banking models in the run up to the GFC, the move towards greater financial trading and the associated expansion of investment banking did result in a significant re-engineering of balance sheets (Bell & Hindmoor, 2018). This in turn meant that the capital structure of banks became extremely fragile due to the unregulated origin of many of the products being traded and which now accounted for a huge part of the banks' operations (Wolf, 2015). While profits surged, the complexity that beset institutions due to riskier trading activities became the downfall of the banks. When investment banking activities turned sour, contamination quickly spread to other 'safer' areas of retail and commercial banking, creating losses and fear of loss amongst depositors and leaving governments with little option but to nationalise and recapitalise compromised institutions (Haldane, 2012b).

Too-Big-to-Fail

The growth of bank balance sheets, as a response to many of the factors already discussed in this chapter, in the decade that preceded the GFC resulted in a banking system dominated by a handful of institutions. Haldane and Piergiorio (2009) demonstrate that in 2008, 16 per cent of all global banking assets were held by just five banks. Meanwhile in the UK, by 2007 the total assets of the nation's three largest banks equated to approximately 200 per cent of the country's GDP (Haldane, 2011). The dominance of these monolithic institutions was driven, in part, by the liberalisation of markets and the emergence of a number of challenger banks that threatened the market share of established institutions in more traditional and safer areas, namely deposits and mortgage lending (Perman, 2013; Martin, 2014). While the balance sheets of these challenger banks remained relatively modest in comparison with larger banks, they did, nonetheless, make an impact by cutting precisely into the markets that were considered 'safe' for larger banks (Bell & Hindmoor, 2015). The biggest banks responded by growing their balance sheets even further, as we have already seen, through the use of exotic financial instruments including securitisation products (Haldane & Piergiorio, 2009). At the apex of 2007/2008 the balance sheets of a handful of global banks had reached such a magnitude that when the GFC struck, these once modest institutions had been transformed into colossal entities which, given the size of their assets, had ultimately become too-big-to-fail.

The problem of too-big-to-fail occurs when a large institution, such as the major banks in 2008, accumulates assets to the extent that its failure would lead to a systemic catastrophe and destabilise the domestic or global economy (Brindley et al, 2008). Faced with such a disaster, the host government is forced to take action usually in the form of an institutional or system wide bailout (ibid.). As such, the recapitalisation of banks in the aftermath of the GFC was not done out of some kind of kindness or sympathy but, rather, intervening governments recognised that the consequence of letting banks fail would be much more disastrous and costly than putting together a rescue deal (Bernanke, 2010; Bernanke et al., 2019).

The presupposition that a government will rescue an institution deemed too-big-to-fail in the event that investments turn bad has given rise to concerns that such a guarantee has removed hard budget constraints that would otherwise serve as a check on performance and has led to a certain 'moral hazard' (King, 2009). Moral hazard is best described as the engagement in risky, undesirable or immoral behaviour which increases the likelihood of an institution failing (Mishkin, 2004: 33). Moral hazard resulting from an implicit state guarantee, due to an institution becoming too-big-to-fail, can be particularly harmful for both institutions and markets as it creates asymmetries in information and potential risk-taking.

For instance, if creditors believe that troubled institutions will receive state support and will not be allowed to fail, then the funding demands by creditors will be much lower than if an implicit guarantee was not present (Bernanke, 2010). As a result of lower funding costs, banks were able to utilise their capital base to expand their operations, grow their balance sheets and become yet more deeply embedded within the financial system, thus exacerbating the too-big-to-fail problem (Haldane, 2012b). In the decade before the crisis, the balance sheets of some of the world's largest banks had reached critical mass resulting in suspicion by both investors and the banks themselves that in the event of a failure they would receive a state-backed bailout thereby encouraging institutions to take on evermore risk (Brummer, 2015). Indeed, it appears that investors favoured banks, particularly in the United States, considered too-big-to-fail (Kay, 2016). As a result, senior bankers, keen to garner institutional investment, failed to devote both the necessary time and human and fiscal capital towards the correct pricing of risk, resulting in the mispricing of investments and thereby distorting market information (King, 2009).

This had a threefold effect. *First*, debt-holders lacked both the incentive and means to correctly calculate risk price and failed to adjust for the fact that prices had been distorted by inefficient markets (Haldane, 2011). *Second*, while regulators will always try to curtail the extent to which institutions engage in risky behaviour (Bernanke et al., 2019), imperfect market information meant that the authorities likewise had a skewed picture of the risk-taking activities of the banks making it difficult to effectively regulate institutions (Bernanke, 2010). *Third*, the implicit state guarantee endowed shareholders with an assurance that institutions would be bailed-out if things went drastically wrong (Haldane, 2011). Intrinsically, institutional investors became complacent and failed to hold the board to account, leaving senior executives free to engage in riskier behaviour and thus greatly amplifying systemic risk (Gup, 2004).

Silo Effect

The extent to which failures in one part of the global financial system, and individual institutions, quickly infected and spread to the entire global economy highlights how linkages within financial markets and between banks greatly amplified the effects of the GFC (Davies, 2010). In the wake of the crisis, it has been suggested that the degree to which these relationships caused irreparable damage, to both financial markets and institutions, could have been lessened if communication within individual banks had been more effective.

As outlined above, for example, in the years preceding the crisis, institutions became too-big-to-fail, amassing huge balance sheets and expanding their operations across several continents with multiple individual departments and thousands of employees. However, managing institutions of this size undoubtedly caused problems for both internal communication and co-ordination leading to a 'silo-effect' within organisations (Tett, 2015). The silo-effect describes an institution that lacks effective organisational oversight, has an absence of clear articulated goals and little communication between departments and the institution at large (Halversson, 2010). In this instance, different departments within an institution become fractured and 'siloed' from the main body of the organisation and other divisions, leading to different units operating with their own set of rules, standards and underlying theories-in-use (ibid). In the decade before the crisis this is exactly what happened within major global banks. As banks grew their balances sheets and became too-big-to-fail, institutions became ever more complex and compartmentalised, embodied by multiple and separate 'legal entities', and increasingly impossible to manage (Haldane & Vasileius, 2012).

The lack of effective communication within institutions subsequently had a harmful impact upon the ability of senior managers to maintain control over their institutions. Halversson (2010) suggests that siloed institutions are characterised by increased opacity and difficulties associated with access to 'in-house' information. Moreover, these factors are further compounded and magnified when we consider that silos are often formed within silos (Tett, 2015). For instance, once a department grows to the extent that it becomes disjointed from the main body of the organisation, it is often the case that this silo does not remain a complete entity itself and instead becomes broken into several smaller silos (Halversson, 2010). As a result, communication within the silo becomes further fragmented and extremely intricate with multiple managers, teams and staff, whose communications are at best stretched and more often than not totally absent, finding it increasingly difficult to penetrate information held with an alternative 'sub-silo' (Halversson, 2010; Bell & Hindmoor, 2015; Tett, 2015).

As the GFC began to take hold, risk managers and CEOs had to go on prolonged fact-finding missions in order to establish what risks had been taken and what assets were on the balance sheet (*The Economist*, 2009a). Such information should have been readily available and accessible within minutes, however due to the silo effect, gathering information became a vast project stretching to days' worth of research and communication between departments (Tett, 2015). Indeed, Haldane and Vasileius (2012: 17–18) argue that banks grew to such an extent that they became unmanageable due to increased complexities associated with the evolution of 'opaque, intra-financial system chains of exposure' making it impossible to accurately ascertain an institution's exposures. The result of this was that when banks needed to react quickly to the market and know their own position they were inhibited from responding to new threats due to a lack of access to pertinent information (*The Economist*, 2009a).

The silo effect would appear to stress the need for banks post-crisis to enhance their internal communication mechanisms. Indeed, Bell and Hindmoor (2015, 2018) argue that even after the crisis, the size and complexity of institutions means that many institutions have outstripped old forms of internal oversight and central control embodied by the traditional role of CEOs and senior managers. Haldane and Vasileius (2012: 4) believe that the key to avoiding complexity in institutions and overcoming the negative effects of so-called siloing is to 'simplify' and 'streamline' the immediate environment by implementing practical measures such as enhanced communication channels like down-the-line reporting and whistle-blowing facilities.

Regulation

While the focus of this chapter has been primarily upon the banks and how the business models of institutions contributed and led to the GFC, it is equally important that we consider the role that supervisors and regulatory interventions, or lack therefor, played in the events of 2008. Many of the causes outlined so far in this chapter were allowed to reach the magnitude and scale which they did because regulators did not act, or in other words, and to borrow Davies's (2010) analogy, regulators were 'the guard dog that failed to bark'.

Bell and Hindmoor (2015: 222) argue that the unique structural environment in which bankers and bankers operated, fostered by external powers whose responsibility it was to administer proper checks and balances, not only failed to adequately monitor and rein in senior bankers but actually created a 'supportive…environment' which allowed harmful practices to flourish. One of the causal factors that led to such a unique set of circumstances can be attributed to the ascending power of global financial capital. Clark (2016: 45) argues that following market liberalisation in the 1980s, the 'economic weight' and 'political influence' of banks grew exponentially with cities such as London and New York becoming hugely influential and important in both domestic and international markets. This growing magnitude of financial services empowered banks as regulators were reluctant to implement more stringent controls for fear of stifling innovation and disrupting the finance-led growth models that had become central to governments (Crouch, 2011; Hay, 2013).

In the UK, following the 1997 general election which saw the Labour Party victorious, the newly formed Financial Services Authority (FSA) took over responsibility for banking supervision and promised a 'light touch' and 'principles-based' approach to regulation (Martin, 2014). Indeed, it appears that the prevailing thought at the FSA in the decade before the crisis was that MTM pricing and market discipline was the most effective form of regulation and which would allow the City of London to flourish (Bell & Hindmoor, 2015). Likewise, it was believed that banks, with in-depth knowledge and access to market information, coupled with huge risk management teams on which sat the brightest economic minds of the time, would prove to be a more effective regulator than any independent body (Martin, 2014).

Despite the FSA's light touch approach, it still came under political fire as senior politicians, keen to advance the City's competitive advantage sought to roll back the powers of the newly formed regulator. In May 2005, then Prime Minister Tony Blair lambasted 'over-zealous' enforcement and promised to 'reduce regulatory burdens [for] business' (Blair, 2005). This was similarly echoed by Blair's Chancellor of the Exchequer Gordon Brown who, as part of his Better Regulation Plan, promised 'not just a light touch but a limited touch' (Brown, 2005).

However, a 2015 report published by the Bank of England concluded that the FSA's approach to regulation had significantly contributed to the collapse of both the Royal Bank of Scotland (RBS) and Halifax Bank of Scotland (HBOS), by failing to adequately 'supervise…challenge or review' the banks' inner workings (Bank of England, 2015: 32). The report would go on to state that the FSA's role in the application of regulation at a more general level across the entire banking sector, lacked substantive resources, failed to consider the primary areas of risk—particularly asset quality and liquidity—and showed insufficient attention to institutions' risk management structures (ibid.).

A lack of regulatory oversight was further exacerbated by the actions of auditors who were tasked with ensuring that adequate checks and balances were in place at institutions and which served as an important line of defence in safeguarding banks from excessive risk-taking. However, it appears that auditors themselves were lacking both the expertise and will to challenge banks on their spiralling balance sheets and lack of risk aversion. Lord Myners has subsequently noted that many auditors lacked the technical skill to even begin to grasp what was happening within institutions and instead relied upon some kind of character test whereby judgements regarding balance sheets were made based on if a person was 'honest' (Myners 2013 in Bell & Hindmoor, 2015: 224).

Domestic regulation is however situated within a broader international supervisory framework. The Bank for International Settlements' (BIS) Basel Committee on Banking Supervision is the premium global standard setter and acts as an anchor point for domestic and international regulators. At the time of the GFC, the Basel Committee, under the Basel II framework, dictated that banks should hold a minimum of 8 per cent capital against risk-weighted assets (RWA) (BIS, 2006: 1). However, the banks did not favour holding capital and as a result came up with novel ways to circumvent regulatory requirements, for example using securitisation instruments and expanding into the shadow banking sector (Perman, 2013). The result of this was that when the crisis hit many banks were massively undercapitalised and unable to absorb losses

(Brown, 2010). Thus, it is possible to conclude that much like the UK's domestic regulator and the auditors, the BIS failed to adequately understand or investigate the intricacies of banks' business models and appear to have been out-of-step with institutional innovations. Indeed, it seems that in the boom years before the crisis no-one, through a lack of will or technical knowhow, was either willing or able to apply the brakes to the speeding juggernaut that was international finance.

Conclusion

As we can see, the GFC cannot be attributed to a single factor but should instead be considered as a series of interrelated failures that combined to create the 'perfect storm'. Structural, institutional and agency-based innovations in finance facilitated the rapid expansion of bank balance sheets which meant that by the mid-2000s, banks had become the cornerstone of the global economy leading to new forms of systemic risk. This was accompanied by sense of optimism amongst bankers, markets analysts, shareholders, politicians and regulators that risk had been dispersed, that liquidity and credit would remain free-flowing and that market discipline would ensure optimal outcomes. Consequently, when the crisis struck losses sustained by these systemically important institutions were quickly transmitted to the real economy.

The causes of the GFC accounted for in this chapter suggest that at a time when bankers, regulators, politicians and institutional investors should have been focusing intently upon the intricacies of banks' business models, which were now centred upon in-organic growth strategies, they were instead celebrating the triumph of financialisation and revelling in the seeming success of institutions. However, when markets began to falter and stall in late 2007 and early 2008, investors who had been enjoying the supposed triumph of the banks quickly began to withdraw from markets leaving institutions with the reality of diminished assets, a lack of access to credit and spiralling funding costs and with little option but to accept state aid.

The objective of this chapter has been to examine and map the agential, institutional and structural causes of the crisis. In doing so, the chapter uncovers a series of lessons or benchmarks that will be applied to the empirical analysis to follow and which will allow me to draw conclusions concerning the extent to which banks in the UK have learned lessons from the GFC. Though the degree to which the banks surveyed in my research engaged in the practices and contributory factors outlined above varies, it is nonetheless important that we consider these dynamics against the broader empirical evidence. In doing so, the research will draw wider conclusions surrounding post-crisis reform, financial stability and growth.

References

Acharya, V., & Richardson, M. (2009). *Restoring financial stability: How to repair a failed system*. New Jersey: Wiley.

Acharya, V., & Schnabl, P. (2009). How banks played the leverage game. In V. Acharya & M. Richardson (Eds.), *Restoring financial stability: How to repair a failed system* (pp. 83–100). New Jersey: Wiley.

Acharya, V., Philippon, T., Richardson, M., & Roubini, N. (2009). Prologue: A bird's eye view—The financial crisis of 2007-2009. In V. Acharya & M. Richardson (Eds.), *Restoring financial stability: How to repair a failed system* (pp. 1–56). New Jersey: Wiley.

Admati, A., & Hellwig, M. (2013). *The bankers new clothes*. Princeton, NJ: Princeton University Press.

Ashby. S. (2010, January). *The 2007–09 financial crisis: Learning the risk management lessons*. Available at: https://www.nottingham.ac.uk/business/businesscentres/crbfs/documents/researchreports/paper65.pdf.

Augar, P. (2018). *The bank that lived a little: Barclays in the age of the very free market*. London: Allen Lane.

Bank of England. (2015, November). *The failure of HBOS plc (HBOS) a report by the Financial Conduct Authority (FCA) and the Prudential Regulation Authority (PRA)*. Bank of England. Available at: http://www.bankofengland.co.uk/pra/Documents/publications/reports/hbos.pdf.

Bell, S., & Hindmoor, A. (2015). *Masters of the universe, slaves of the market*. Cambridge, MA: Harvard University Press.

Bell, S., & Hindmoor, A. (2018). Are the major global banks now safer? Structural continuities and change in banking and finance since the 2008 crisis. *Review of International Political Economy, 25*(1), 1–27.

Bernanke, B., Geithner, T., & Paulson, H. (2019). *Firefighting: The financial crisis and its lessons*. London: Profile Books.

Bernanke, B. (2010, September 2). *Statement by Ben S. Bernanke before the financial crisis inquiry commission [transcript]*. Available at: http://fcic-static.law.stanford.edu/cdn_media/fcic-testimony/2010-0902-Bernanke.pdf.

Bernanke, B. (2012, April 13). *Some reflections on the crisis and the policy response*. Speech at the Russell Sage Foundation and the Century Foundation Conference on Rethinking Finance, New York. Available at: http://www.federalreserve.gov/newsevents/speech/bernanke20120413a.htm.

BIS [Bank for International Settlements]. (2006). *Part 2: The first pillar—Minimum capital requirements*. Available at: https://www.bis.org/publ/bcbs128b.pdf.

Blair, T. (2005, May 26). Full text: Tony blair's speech on compensation culture. *The Guardian*. Available at: http://www.theguardian.com/politics/2005/may/26/speeches.media.

Blinder, A. (2014). *After the music stopped: The financial crisis, the response, and the work ahead*. New York: Penguin Books.

Bootle, R. (2011). *The trouble with markets*. London: Nicholas Brealey.

Brazier, A. (2017, Monday 24 July). *'Debt strikes back' or 'the return of the regulator'?*. Alex Brazier executive director, financial director for financial stability strategy and risk member of the financial policy committee bank of England University of Liverpool, Institute for Risk and Uncertainty. Available at: http://www.bankofengland.co.uk/publications/Documents/speeches/2017/speech992.pdf.

Brindley, B. Butler, D. Clutterbuck, B. Johnson, B. Lewis, P. Owen, G. Sidwell, G. Walters, R. M., Wood, A., & Wright, M. (2008). *Oxford dictionary of finance and banking*. Oxford: Oxford University Press.

Brown, G. (2005, November 28). Full text: Gordon brown's speech to the CBI. *Financial Times*. Available at: http://www.ft.com/cms/s/2/9073a120-600d-11da-a3a6-0000779e2340.html#axzz3ttxP5SYf.

Brown, G. (2010). *Beyond the crash: Overcoming the first crisis of globalisation*. London: Simon & Schuster.

Brummer, A. (2015). *Bad banks: Greed, incompetence and the next global crisis*. Random House Business: London.

Bustamante, M. C., & Donangelo, A. (2014, February). *'Product market competition and industry returns' financial markets group* (Discussion Paper No. 728). At: http://www.lse.ac.uk/fmg/workingPapers/discussionPapers/fmgdps/DP728-final.pdf.

Christensen, J., Shaxson, N., & Wigan, D. (2016). The finance curse: Britain and the world economy. *The British Journal of Politics and International Relations, 18*(1), 255–269.

Clark, D. (2016). *The global financial crisis and austerity: A basic introduction*. Bristol: Polity Press.

Crouch, C. (2011). *The strange non-death of neoliberalism*. Cambridge: Polity Press.

Davies, H. (2010). *The financial crisis: Who is to blame?*. Cambridge: Polity Press.

Ellul, A., & Yerramilli, V. (2010, January). *Stronger risk controls, lower risk: Evidence from U.S. bank holding companies* (Axa Working Paper Series No. 1 Discussion Paper No. 646). Available at: http://www.lse.ac.uk/fmg/workingPapers/discussionPapers/Stronger%20Risk%20Controls,%20Lower%20Risk%20Evidence%20from%20US%20Bank%20Holding%20Companies.pdf.

Engelen, E., Erturk, I., Froud, J., Johal, S., Leaver, A., Moran, M., et al. (2011). *After the great complacence: Financial crisis and the politics of reform*. Oxford: Oxford University Press.

Erturk, I. (2017). Shadow banking: A story of the doppelganger (the Double) in science of finance. *Journal of Cultural Economy* (16 November 2016), 1–16.

Fama, E. (1970). Efficient capital markets: A review of theory and empirical work. *Journal of Finance, 25*(2), 383–417.

Forstater, M. (2007). *Little book of big ideas economic*. London: A&C Black Publishers.

Fraser, I. (2014). *Shredded: Inside RBS the bank that broke Britain*. Birlin: Edinburgh.

Friedman, J. (2009). A crisis of politics, not economics: Complexity, ignorance and policy failure. *Critical Review, 21*(2–3), 127–83.

Gamble, A. (2014). *Crisis without end? The unravelling of western prosperity*. London: Palgrave Macmillan.

Gowan, P. (2009). Crisis in the heartland. *New Left Review, 55*, 5–30.

Greenspan, A. (2013). *The map and the territory: Risk, human nature, and the future of forecasting*. London: Allen Lane.

Gup, B. (2004). What does too big to fail mean? In B. Gup (Ed.), *Too big to fail: Policies and practices in government bailouts* (pp. 29–49). London: Praeger.

Haldane, A. (2011, October 24). *Control rights (and wrongs)*. Speech to the Wincott Annual Memorial Lecture, Westminster. Available at: http://www.bankofengland.co.uk/publications/Documents/speeches/2011/speech525.pdf.

Haldane, A. (2012a, April 14). *Financial arms races, based on a speech to institute for new economic thinking*, Berlin. Available at: http://www.bankofengland.co.uk/publications/Documents/speeches/2012/speech565.pdf.

Haldane, A. (2012b, October 25). *On being the right size*. The 2012 Beesley Lectures, Institute of Economic Affairs. Available at: http://www.bankofengland.co.uk/publications/Documents/speeches/2012/speech615.pdf.

Haldane, A. (2012c, October 29). *A leaf being turned*. Occupy Economics, Socially Useful Banking, London. Available at http://www.bankofengland.co.uk/publications/Documents/speeches/2012/speech616.pdf.

Haldane, A., & Alessandri, P. (2009, September 25). *Banking on the state*. Paper presented to the Federal Reserve Bank of Chicago Twelfth Annual International Banking Conference on 'The International Financial Crisis: Have the Rules of Finance Changed'. Chicago. Available at: http://www.bis.org/review/r091111e.pdf.

Haldane, A., & Madouros, V. (2012, August 31). *The dog and the frisbee*. Speech to the Federal Reserve Bank of Kansas City's 366th Economic Policy Symposium on 'The Changing Policy Landscape'. Jackson Hole, Wyoming. Available at: http://www.bis.org/review/r120905a.pdf.

Haldane, A., & May, R. (2011). Systemic risk in banking ecosystems. *Nature, 469*(20), 351–355.

Haldane, A., Brennan, S., & Madouros, V. (2010). What is the contribution of the financial sector: Miracle or mirage? In A. Turner et al. (eds.), *The future of finance: The LSE report* (Chapter 2, pp. 64–105). London: The London School of Economics and Political Science.

Hale, G., & Santos, J. (2013). *Do banks propagate debt market shocks?* Federal reserve bank of San Francisco (Working Paper 2010–08). Available at: http://www.frbsf.org/economic-research/files/wp10-08bk.pdf.

Halversson, E. (2010). *The "silo effect"—Symptoms, causes, cure and prevention.* Offshore Investment February 2010 issue 203. Available at: http://www.offshoreinvestment.com/pages/index.asp?title=issue_203#sthash.lGcyRLgo.dpuf.

Hampton, M. P., & Christensen, J. E. (2002). Offshore pariahs? Small island economies, tax havens and the reconfiguration of global finance. *World Development, 30*(9), 1657–1673.

Hay, C. (2013). *The failure of anglo-liberal capitalism.* London: Palgrave Macmillan.

International Monetary Fund [IMF]. (2017, April). *Global financial stability report: Getting the policy mix right*. Available at: https://www.imf.org/en/Publications/GFSR/Issues/2017/03/30/global-financial-stability-report-april-2017.

Kashyap. A. (2010, February 27). *Lessons from the financial crisis for risk management*. Paper Prepared for the Financial Crisis Inquiry Commission. Available at: http://faculty.chicagobooth.edu/anil.kashyap/research/papers/lesson_for_fcic.pdf.

Kay, J. (2016). *Other people's money.* London: Profile Books.

King, M. (2009, March 17). *Finance—A return from risk.* Speech to the Worshipful Company of International Bankers. London. Available at: http://www.bis.org/review/r090319a.pdf.

King, M. (2016). *The end of alchemy: Money banking and the future of the global economy*. London: Little Brown.

Lewis, M. (2011). *The big short*. London: Penguin.

Lucas, R. (1980). Equilibrium in a pure currency economy. *Economic Inquiry, 18*(2), 203–220.

Martin, I. (2014). *Making it happened: Fred Goodwin and the men who blew up the British economy.* London: Simon & Schuster.

Medland, D. (2013,, June 5). Whistleblowing almost killed me. *Financial Times*. Available at: http://www.ft.com/cms/s/0/2dd0f0de-ab70-11e2-8c63-00144feabdc0.html?siteedition=uk#axzz35SZlyUbZ.

Mishkin, F. S. (2004). *The economics of money, banking, and finance* (7th ed.). Pearson: Addison-Wesley.

Moore, P. (2015). *Crash bank wallop: The memoirs of the HBOS whistle-blower*. London: New Wilberforce.

Palan, R., Murphy, R., & Chavagneux, C. (2009). *Tax havens: How globalization really works*. Cornell: Cornell University Press.

Parliamentary Commission on Banking Standards (PCBS). (2013). *Changing banking for good. (HC 175-I, First Report of Session 2013–14)—Volume 1: summary, and conclusions and recommendations*. London: TSO. Available at: http://www.parliament.uk/documents/banking-commission/Banking-final-report-volume-i.pdf.

Perman, R. (2013). *HUBRIS, how HBOS Wrecked the best Bank in Britain*. Birlinn Limited: Edinburgh.

Ramskogler, P. (2015). Tracing the origins of the financial crisis. *OECD Journal: Financial Market Trends, 2014/2*. Available at: http://www.oecd-ilibrary.org/finance-and-investment/tracing-the-origins-of-the-financial-crisis_fmt-2014-5js3dqmsl4br?crawler=true.

Sabato, G. (2009, August). *Financial crisis: Where did risk management fail? article in SSRN electronic journal*. Available at: https://www.researchgate.net/publication/228126967_Financial_Crisis_Where_did_Risk_Management_Fail.

Tett, G. (2015). *The silo effect: The peril of expertise and the promise of breaking down barriers*. New York: Simon & Schuster.

The Economist. (2009a, December 3). *Silo but deadly*. Available at: http://www.economist.com/node/15016132.

Turner, A. [Turner Review]. (2009). *The turner review: A regulatory response to the global banking crisis*. London: FSA. Available at: http://www.fsa.gov.uk/pubs/other/turner_review.pdf.

Turner, A. (2012, March 14). *Shadow banking and financial instability*. CASS Lecture 2012. CASS Business School. Available at: https://corpgov.law.harvard.edu/2012/04/16/shadow-banking-and-financial-instability/.

Turner, A. (2016). *Between debt and the devil, money, credit, and fixing global finance*. Princeton, NJ: Princeton University Press.

Urry, J. (2014). *Offshoring*. London: Polity Press.

Wolf, M. (2015). *The shifts and the shocks*. London: Penguin.

Woodward. R. (2006, December). Offshore strategies in global political economy: Small islands and the case of the EU and OECD harmful tax competition initiatives. *Cambridge Review of International Affairs, 19*(4).

CHAPTER 4

RBS: Learning to Fail and Failing to Learn

Introduction

In 1998, the Royal Bank of Scotland recorded a modest pre-tax profit of £1 billion (Royal Bank of Scotland, 1998). By 2007, the now renamed and rebranded RBS posted an enormous pre-tax profit of £9.9 billion (RBS, 2007). Yet, just one year later, and amidst the turmoil of the GFC, the group would record a £25 billion loss—the largest in UK corporate history—and require a series of state-sponsored bailouts amounting to a staggering £46 billion and that would leave the UK taxpayer as an 84% stakeholder in the bank (Fraser, 2014).

A series of domestic and international takeovers by RBS throughout the late 1990s and 2000s meant that by 2007 RBS had total assets of £1.9 trillion and were the world's fifth largest bank (Rayner, 2009). By market capitalisation, RBS was 'worth more than Coca-Cola and more than Sony and Apple combined' (Fraser, 2014: xiii). When the crisis hit in 2007/2008 RBS' position was fatally compromised by the fact that much of its expansion programme had been completed without the necessary due diligence (Lambert, 2011). A tacit board that failed to hold the group's bombastic CEO—Fred Goodwin—and his executive team to account (Wilson et al., 2011), coupled with a bonus culture that encouraged staff to prioritise 'increasing revenues, profits, assets and leverage' over 'capital, liquidity and assets quality', only compounded RBS' precarious situation (Lambert, 2011).

A. Barber, *UK Banks and the Lessons of the Great Financial Crisis*, Building a Sustainable Political Economy: SPERI Research & Policy, https://doi.org/10.1007/978-3-030-70254-0_4

In their account of the GFC, Bell and Hindmoor (2015) detail the perilous position that RBS' aggressive expansion policy had left the group in, revealing a balance sheet that was highly exposed to trading activities, overleveraged, undercapitalised and lacked a stable funding base. This precarious situation meant that as the crisis began to take hold, RBS quickly found that's its 'growth at all costs' approach had undermined the group's entire operation as the bank began taking huge losses (Fraser, 2014: 28). RBS' position was compromised yet further by the fact that the group had continued to aggressively buy-up securitised assets from distressed institutions even as the crisis was unfolding, this was despite the fact that demand for such products had practically disappeared (Martin, 2014). Just weeks after purchasing these assets, many of the securitised instruments became toxic, leaving RBS with products that were now worth 'fire sale' prices and with no market to sell to (Bell & Hindmoor, 2015). By October 2008, customer deposits were at an all-time low of just 35%, and with the group borrowing £49 billion from wholesale markets on an overnight basis, RBS were 'unable to get to the end of the day' leaving the UK Government little option but to step in (King, 2016: 37).

Chapter Overview

Over a decade on from RBS' unprecedented bailout, there is little doubt that the group has undergone significant change, not least of which can be witnessed in the leadership of the bank with no member of the 2008 group board, including the influential and controversial former GCE Fred Goodwin, being present at the bank today. However, this chapter will suggest that, despite making some incremental changes following its recapitalisation in 2008, RBS has ultimately failed to learn lessons. It will be argued that much of the progress made by the bank post-GFC can be attributed to exogenous structural factors with subsequent change being largely in keeping with the single-loop learning theory.

Post-GFC, RBS has been embroiled in a series of scandals that have exposed deficiencies in the group's internal governance mechanisms: in 2011 NatWest were fined by the Financial Services Authority (FSA) for failing to deal with customer complaints in a satisfactory manner; in 2012 Coutts Bank was penalised for failing to implement appropriate anti-money laundering (AML) controls; in 2014 RBS was criticised over its handling of small businesses owners placed within the group's Global Restructuring Group. The bank has also been implicated and fined for its involvement in the rigging of Libor, Yen Libor and Forex rates; failing to report share dealings; mis-selling PPI and not observing the appropriate industry standards when offering mortgage advice to clients.

RBS has made some headway on remuneration, reducing the overall employee bonus pool by 72% at the group level and 92% in the investment bank (RBS, 2008, 2010, 2015, 2018). However, the evidence examined in this chapter indicates that the greatest changes to the way in which employees are rewarded have come in response to exogenous influences. In particular, the introduction of the European Parliament's CRD IV Article 90(1)(ca) and (d)—which looks to limit the amount of variable remuneration employees can receive—appears to have had the greatest influence on employee pay and may explain reductions in the bonus pool.

Similarly, RBS appear, *prima facie*, to have made some good progress on the structure and composition of the balance sheet—reducing leverage, increasing customer deposits, decreasing wholesale borrowing and exiting 25 of 38 foreign markets while reducing the size of the investment bank by 76% (RBS, 2008, 2015, 2018). Yet, it will be argued that these changes have to a greater extent been motivated by structural dynamics. Specifically, EU rules on state aid that have required RBS to shed approximately £1 trillion of assets from its balance sheet. As such, a shrinking of the business and the related restructuring of the balance sheet must be considered in the light of these structural constraints.

Factors Explaining RBS' Failure to Learn

In this chapter, I argue that RBS' failure to learn can be attributed to successive regulatory and governance failures that have led the bank on a series of 'firefighting' missions. As a result, RBS has failed to dedicate sufficient institutional resources—human and financial capital—towards the search for, and evaluation of, new information. Put simply, RBS has failed to apply its learning space towards the undertaking of a thorough evaluation of the group's underlying theories-in-use in light of the lessons of the GFC.

The work of Edmondson and Monigeon (1999)—detailed in Chapter 2—suggest that double-loop learning—being the undertaking of a deep and thorough reappraisal of an institution's underlying theories-in-use—does not just happen independently of the learning subject but requires the dedication of learning space. Space is understood as being the application of both time and resources to the learning process (ibid.: 162).

Equally, Simon (1983: 19) also contends that learning requires space. The author argues that in order for substantive learning to take place a learning subject must commit to the seeking, evaluation and application of new information as it is presented (ibid.).

Both Edmondson and Monigeon (1999) and Simon (1983) conclude that without the necessary 'learning space' agents and institutions will be unable to accurately judge, evaluate or appraise their current working methods. Under such circumstances, the exchange of information and ideas will ultimately break down, leaving individuals or organisations to revert to already established procedures and policies as the learning subject seeks reassurance in the status quo, thus failing to learn (Edmondson & Monigeon, 1999). This chapter contends that RBS' lack of learning can be attributed to the group failing to orient sufficient institutional time and resources, or learning space, to the learning process. Instead, the group has focused its attention rather narrowly on individual facets of the business and the minutiae of distinct failures. Moreover, such undertakings have yielded little change with pre-existing structures and normative frames in place at the time of the GFC going largely unchanged. RBS' failure to manage these incidents effectively has meant that the bank has allowed its learning space to be diverted away from a self-reflexive examination of the group's underlying theories-in-use in the light of those deficiencies highlighted by the GFC, and which forms a central part of the learning process (Smith, 2011, 2013). As such, RBS may yet prove to be a threat to financial stability and the real economy.

Governance and Regulation

This section of the chapter will suggest that a series of internal governance and regulatory failures has led RBS on multiple of 'firefighting missions', swallowing up huge amounts of time, resources and human capital as the group has struggled to contain a catalogue of governance issues. The mismanagement of these failures by RBS has ultimately eroded the bank's learning space that could otherwise have been applied to learning lessons from the GFC more broadly. For example, rather than treating problems holistically, appraising the group's underlying governing values and theories-in-use in the light of those deficiencies highlighted by the crisis, RBS has instead dealt with failures on a case-by-case basis. The effect of this is that the group has expended vast institutional resources on mitigating the fallout of specific cases with little tangible change. As such, this section will show that RBS has failed to effectively manage and apply its learning space towards the undertaking of a group-wide appraisal of its business model, standard operating procedures and group policies. In this respect, RBS has failed to enter in to the evaluative process associated with learning and explains why the group has failed to learn, with post-GFC change at the bank having been driven by exogenous factors.

Compliant Handling and Money Laundering

In 2011, both the Royal Bank of Scotland and NatWest banks were hit with fines by the FSA for failing to handle customer complaints in a satisfactory manner (Insley, 2011). The regulator fined RBS £2.8 million after it was revealed that a substantial number of customer complaints had been handled incorrectly or were rejected without proper consideration or explanation, with many customers also being denied access to an appeals process (ibid.). Following an investigation, the FSA revealed that of the cases that it had reviewed, 53% demonstrated a failure to handle the complaint adequately, 62% were in breach of FSA requirements on timelines and 31% were deemed to have an unfair customer outcome (FSA, 2011). Moreover, the FSA concluded that staff at both the Royal Bank of Scotland and NatWest banks were not given adequate training in complaint handling, with oversight of such matters being severely deficient (FSA, 2011).

Likewise, in 2012 Coutts Bank, part of RBS' private banking arm, was fined £8.75 million by the FSA after it was found that the bank had serious deficiencies in its anti-money laundering (AML) procedures (Treanor, 2012a). The FSA concluded that as late as 2010 the bank's AML controls had presented 'serious' and 'systemic' failings that had resulted in an exceptionally high probability that Coutts had been handling the proceeds of crime (FSA, 2012). The FSA found that AML breaches at the bank were 'significant' and 'widespread', with Coutts failing to implement sufficient controls when dealing with new or 'politically exposed persons' with a lack of consistency in the level and application of oversight safeguards (Kar-Gupta, 2012). Moreover, the FSA revealed that AML arrangements at Coutts were significantly out of step with best practice legislation and procedures (FSA, 2012). Coutts were keen to stress that there was no evidence which suggested money laundering had taken place but conceded that the systems put in place by the bank to combat such abuses was 'totally inadequate' but that subsequent actions had been taken to rectify the problem (Treanor, 2012a).

However, in February 2017 Coutts' AML controls would once again be called into question over the bank's dealings with the Malaysian sovereign wealth fund,1Malaysia Development Bhd. Following an investigation by the Swiss Financial Market Supervisory Authority (FINMA), it was revealed that between 2009 and 2013 Coutts had engaged in 'numerous high-risk transactions' and was 'in serious breach of its duty to ensure proper business conduct' (FINMA, 2017).[1] The Swiss regulator noted that Coutts had failed to carry out the proper due diligence on a number of large and high-risk transactions and had ignored its own internal warnings from employees who had raised concerns over suspicious transactions (ibid.). Coutts would eventually report such concerns to authorities but this would come over two years after the original transactions had been completed (Ross, 2017). The bank would eventually be forced to disgorge £5.2 million in profits made from the illicit transactions with FINMA also referring the case to the FSA (ibid.).

While these incidents came to light, for the most part, in the immediate aftermath of the GFC, and at a time when it could be argued that RBS was at the very beginning of its learning journey, these events are nonetheless important due to the subsequent knock-on effect on the group's ability to learn. For example, following each of the failures, RBS' response was to carry out a separate and distinct review of the appropriate business area—requiring the dedication of both time and resources. While strategic and policy reviews form an important part of the learning process (Rose, 1991, 1993, 2005), these appraisals would yield little change with pre-existing governance structures and normative frames in place at the time of the crisis going largely unchanged. Moreover, RBS' failure to manage these incidents effectively meant that the group would lack sufficient resources to apply to the undertaking of a large-scale, timely and reflexive evaluation of the group's underlying theories-in-use in the light of the lessons of the GFC. As such, the failure at Coutts, Royal Bank of Scotland and NatWest highlights not only a deficiency in internal governance standards but also the importance of the effective application of institutional resources in the learning process.

[1] We should note that while RBS would eventually sell the international arm of Coutts to Union Bancaire Privée, the incident in question occurred while Coutts was still a part of the RBS group (for further discussion see Arnold, 2015).

Libor, Share Dealing and 'Sanctioned' Transfers

Further evidence of a failure to learn and the subsequent erosion of learning space can be seen in 2013 when RBS' governance framework would once again be called into question over the bank's involvement in the Libor rate-rigging scandal in both the UK and United States. Following an investigation by the FSA and Commodity Futures Trading Commission (CFTC), it was revealed that RBS employees had been complicit in the manipulation of the inter-bank lending rate, along with a host of other UK banks including Lloyds and Barclays, in order to profit a small group of inside traders (McDonald, 2019). Both City and Wall Street regulators would eventually impose fines totalling approximately £390 million. The subsequent publication of transcripts of conversations between traders at RBS and other institutions would reveal that RBS employees had been deliberately influencing Libor for at least 3 years between mid-2007 and late 2010 (*BBC News*, 2013). As result of RBS' involvement in the rate-rigging scandal John Hourican, head of RBS's investment bank, subsequently left the group.[2]

Commenting on the incident RBS stated that since 2011, when events were first brought to its attention, the group had undertaken a number of key actions including: 'strengthening the systems and controls governing submissions of LIBOR and other trading rates'; creating an independent ring-fenced rate setting team; introducing new 'preventative and detective' statistical controls which monitor submissions for irregularities; and establishing a 'rate setting review board' tasked with overseeing the submissions process (RBS Online, 2013).

Similarly in July 2013, RBS was fined £5.62 million by the FCA for failing to accurately file reports relating to share dealings carried out by the group's investment bank (Rankin, 2013). The resulting investigation by the City regulator concluded that RBS had failed to correctly report share transactions between November 2007 and February 2013 (FCA, 2013). Furthermore, the outcome of the investigation revealed that from November 2007 to February 2012 the group failed entirely to report some 804,000 transactions that accounted for approximately

[2] It must be stressed that Mr Hourican was in no way directly implicated in such matters nor is there any evidence that he had any prior knowledge as to what was happening.

37% of RBS' trades of this kind (ibid.).[3] As such, it was determined that RBS had significantly violated regulatory reporting requirements, with the FCA concluding that the event had brought to light clear deficiencies in the group's internal management controls (FCA, 2013). While commentators have agreed that RBS' conduct was neither 'deliberate' nor 'profit making' the incident does highlight the fact that the group failed to adequately manage internal checks and balances, a key cause of the GFC, over a prolonged period (Rankin, 2013). Moreover, it was revealed that in 2010 RBS had been made aware of the problem but failed to tackle the issue, with breaches in reporting controls occurring as late 2013 (ibid.). In response to the fallout, RBS admitted that there had been a failure within its internal reporting structures and that the bank would make 'significant investments' in improving controls to ensure that such matters would not persist (RBS cited in Wilson, 2013).

In December 2013, it was announced that RBS would once again be fined. This time the group would be hit with a £75 million penalty by US regulators for providing transfers with sanctioned countries such Iran, Sudan and Cuba between 2005 and 2009 (Scannell, 2013).[4] Investigations by the US Treasury found that RBS had deliberately 'instructed employees to list the actual name of the Iranian financial institution rather than the Bank Identifier Code in the beneficiary bank field of the payment instructions' so as to conceal the intended country of receipt from authorities (US Department of the Treasury, 2013). This allowed RBS to deal with nations explicitly sanctioned by the United States, with RBS providing

> written instructions containing a step-by-step guide on how to create and route US dollar payment messages involving sanctioned entities through the United States to avoid detection.
>
> (*BBC News Online*, 2013)

[3] The reporting of such transactions is particularly important to the effective functioning of markets because, while there is no evidence that RBS' transgressions led to any nefarious activity, such failures can often facilitate criminal acts such as insider trading and other questionable market-based behaviour (Wilson, 2013).

[4] We should note that Lloyds, Barclays and HSBC have all been found guilty by regulators for similar dealings.

This incident, along with deficiencies relating to Libor and the misreporting of share dealings, suggests that not only has RBS failed to learn lessons in relation to internal governance and regulatory oversight—with some events occurring up to five years after the GFC and the institutional shortcomings that the crisis highlighted—but, that the group's management of these events may have contributed to the bank's lack of learning. For example, while internal reviews are a key element of the process of learning (Rose, 1991, 1993, 2005), the fact remains that RBS has focused its time, resources and capital on very narrow and specific areas of the business as the group has sought to contain individual breaches. As such, RBS has failed to dedicate sufficient institutional resources towards the undertaking of a group-wide critical reflection aimed at re-evaluating the bank's underlying theories-in-use in response to the challenges and institutional failures stressed by the crisis. Thus, these incidents and RBS' failure to apply learning space to the self-reflexive evaluative process essential in learning may account for a lack of substantive change.

Mortgage Advice, PPI, Global Restructuring Group and Forex Rigging

Further evidence of governance failures at RBS were highlighted in August 2014 when the FCA announced that it would be fining the bank £14.5 million for breaching industry best practices when giving mortgage advice (Press Association, 2014). The FCA fine came following a 2012 investigation into the bank's selling of mortgages, which revealed that NatWest customers had received insufficient or substandard advice when applying for a mortgage (FCA, 2014). A subsequent review of sales carried out by the regulator highlighted that approximately 50% of NatWest mortgage customers had been either misinformed or given advice that was unsuitable or entirely wrong (ibid.). It was determined that in many cases staff had failed to adequately assess the financial background of clients before making a mortgage offer, with employees neglecting to carry out 'affordability assessments', 'failing to advise customers who were looking to consolidate debt properly' and not offering customers suitable advice on the term of their mortgage (FCA, 2014). Moreover, like its previous sanction issued by the FCA over the reporting of share dealings, it was revealed that RBS had been warned about the issue previously. In 2011, the FCA had raised concerns that staff were failing to meet approved standards when giving advice and approving mortgages (Pickford, 2014). When the FCA discovered that over a year later no action had been taken by the bank, it undertook further investigations and subsequently fined RBS (ibid.).

Commenting on the issue, group CEO Ross McEwan said that such failings were 'unacceptable and should never have happened', adding that since the incident the bank had 'completely overhauled [its] processes' and that bank staff had undergone 'extensive' training in order to remedy the situation (McEwan cited in *BBC News*, 2014). However, Mr McEwan and RBS have consistently failed to provide specific details concerning the overhaul of group processes and the extent of staff training. As such, it is difficult to accurately judge the degree to which RBS may have changed its internal procedures and employee training in light of such failures.

Similarly, and like many of its contemporaries, RBS has also been implicated in the mis-selling of Payment Protection Insurance (PPI) when, following an FSA investigation, it was brought to light that the bank had mis-sold customers PPI on its loans, mortgages and credit cards (Brinded, 2013). The FSA's inquiry discovered that many customers that had been approved products had often come under great pressure from the bank to take out PPI insurance, and in some cases, the insurance premium was simply added without the express knowledge or permission of the client (Wearden, 2011). Of all the banks caught up in the scandal, RBS had the third-largest exposure, behind Lloyds and Barclays, at £6.2 billion[5] (Dunkley, 2016c; Mcgaw, 2019a). Speaking to Greig Cameron of *The Herald Scotland*, group CEO Ross McEwan commented that

> At the peak of the financial crisis, RBS was the biggest bank in the world…When the crisis broke the bank was involved in a number of different businesses in multiple countries that have subsequently faced heavy scrutiny by customers and regulators...The scale of the bad decisions during that period means that some problems are still just emerging. The good news is we are now a much stronger bank and can manage these costs while still supporting our customers.
>
> (McEwan cited in Cameron, 2014)

Further penalties for the mis-selling of products would be levied against the bank throughout 2017 and 2018 as RBS this time faced sanctions

[5] In this case, exposure to the scandal has been measured in terms of the size of the compensation package that has been set aside.

from US authorities over the bank's issuance, underwriting and selling of toxic mortgage-backed securities in the years preceding the GFC. Following a long-running investigation led by the US Department of Justice (DoJ), RBS was found to have misled customers about the quality of US subprime RMBS being sold by the bank. A report by the DoJ concluded that between 2005 and 2008, RBS had deliberately withheld information from customers regarding the financial position of underwriters issuing the securities in question; had broken rules on how bad loans were categorised; failed to disclose how many bad loans the bank could exempt from securitised bonds; invented fictional third-party sellers to increase commissions; and fabricated the selling price of securities (Arnold, 2017; Megaw, 2018a). In doing so, RBS mislead customers in to buying products that the bank knew were unsuitable and carried much greater risk than had been disclosed. Transcripts of conversations between RBS employees revealed by the DoJ showed how traders had joked about 'destroying' the US housing market in an attempt to 'redistribute wealth to Wall Street' (anonymous cited in Megaw, 2018a).

The scandal would eventually cost RBS more than £10 billion in fines and compensation packages as part of a settlement agreement struck with US authorities (Arnold, 2017; Dunkley, 2017a; Megaw, 2018a; Shubber, 2018). While RBS would agree terms with various US regulators, the bank would stop short of admitting guilt with Ross McEwan commenting that these 'settlement[s] date[d] back to the period between 2005 and 2007' and that there was 'no place for the sort of unacceptable behaviour *alleged* by the DoJ at the bank we are building today' (McEwan, 2018).

Much like the PPI case discussed above, the mis-selling of subprime RMBS relates to the pre-crisis period and consequently does not necessarily represent a failure to learn. However, in a similar vein to the PPI scandal, RBS has had to commit a staggering degree of institutional resources to rectifying legacy issues with the group once again failing to enter into the evaluative process following these incidents. Consequently, it may be argued that the burden of the US subprime scandal, along with that of the PPI saga, and its drain on the bank's resources, has negatively affected the group's learning space by consuming human and financial capital that could otherwise have been dedicated towards learning from the key lessons of the GFC.

In 2014, RBS would once again become embroiled in controversy when it was announced that it would be closing its Global Restructuring

Group (GRG) following a damning report published by former Government advisor Dr Lawrence Tomlinson. In his report, Dr Tomlinson revealed how the bank had profited from small businesses in distress by unnecessarily pushing some companies into default (Brinded, 2014). The report detailed how RBS had forced many of its struggling small- and medium-sized enterprise (SME) customers into the specialist GRG unit in exchange for continued access to credit (Tomlinson, 2013). It is purported that once placed within the GRG, RBS would then essentially assume control of the business and charge extortionate handling and advisement fees which were 'beyond what can be considered reasonable' (Tomlinson, 2013: 2). Unable to pay such exorbitant charges, businesses would fall in to default to the extent that the excessive fees charged by RBS became the 'key contributing factor to the business' financial deterioration' (ibid.). RBS would then use its influence to force the struggling businesses to sell its assets at a hugely discounted price, which the bank would subsequently buy (Tomlinson, 2013: 2–3).

A subsequent review carried out by the FCA found that RBS had taken inappropriate action in 92% of all cases referred to the GRG unit (Dunkley, 2017b). Moreover, a series of leaked internal memos would detail how managers within the unit had devised a 'tip sheet' for staff on how to extricate additional profits from struggling businesses by using high pressure tactics to ramp-up fees (Binham, 2018a). Staff were warned that 'missed opportunities [would] mean missed bonuses' and that 'sometimes you need to let customers hang themselves' (RBS cited in Treasury Select Committee, 2018).

Despite the damning evidence, RBS have failed to demonstrate any substantive indication of learning or change in relation to this incident. For instance, during its investigation of the GRG saga, the FCA reported that RBS had been obstructively 'defensive' and had impeded investigations (Binham, 2018b). Likewise, when asked to appear before a Treasury Select Committee in 2018, that was conducting its own investigation of the GRG, RBS chairman Sir Howard Davies and the GCE Ross McEwan, were accused by Clive Lewis MP of deliberately misleading the committee in an attempt to conceal how widespread abuses had been at the bank (Binham, 2018c).

In November 2016, RBS announced that it would be putting together a voluntary £400 million compensation scheme to recompense victims of the GRG scandal (Treanor, 2016). However, just one year later it would come to light that the bank had excluded almost 70% of the 12,000 victims identified by the FCA from the scheme (Binham & Dunkley, 2017). RBS claimed that around 8,000 SME customers would not be eligible for compensation as the bank had extended alternative forms of credit to the struggling businesses beyond the GRG and as such customers had not been adversely affected by the rouge unit (ibid.).

Likewise, while the GRG was summarily closed, RBS would go on to establish the newly formed RBS Restructuring Unit (RBS, 2019). Thirty of the 32 GRG senior managers would be transferred to the new unit—including the GRG's most senior manager, Laura Barlow who now heads RBS Restructuring—with 136 the GRGs former 182 employees likewise being relocated to the new division (Binham & Dunkley, 2017). As such, there appears to be little evidence to suggest that RBS has applied institutional resources—learning space—to the search for alternatives that has allowed it to move beyond previously established underlying theories-in-use, with a distinct lack of improved policy actions, behavioural patterns and normative preferences.

In a further incident in May 2015, RBS made known that it had reached a settlement with US authorities over its involvement in the rigging of foreign exchange rates (Forex), agreeing to pay fines totalling £535 million (RBS.com, 2015). After an investigation by US regulators, RBS admitted that between 2007 and late 2013 bank employees had colluded with traders at other institutions to manipulate Forex rates and had conspired to conceal the true nature of profits that had been generated as a result (Binham et al., 2015). Commenting on the issue Ross McEwan stated that

> The serious misconduct that lies at the heart of today's announcements has no place in the bank that I am building. Pleading guilty for such wrongdoing is another stark reminder of how badly this bank lost its way and how important it is for us to regain trust…We are determined to learn the lessons from our past mistakes and to hold those responsible fully to account for their actions.
>
> (McEwan, 2015b)

The Forex scandal did result in some improved policy action at the bank, including restricting employee access to chat rooms and internet messaging services, the banning of mobile phones on the trading floor and improving the disclosure of information to clients. While such changes form an important process in RBS' learning journey and may suggest some limited evidence of learning and change, these reforms appear to be an exception and are not necessarily typical of the group's wider post-GFC approach to governance and regulatory oversight. Indeed, though RBS may present some 'pockets' of learning in relation to governance, the group has, on the whole, failed to demonstrate substantive evidence of learning and change with such examples of reform being confined to the fringes of the business as the frames, preferences and meanings applied by the bank to its situational environment remain broadly intact.[6]

These events not only represent a series of firefighting missions that have consumed the group's attention, acting as a barrier to learning by preventing vital information exchange, they also highlight RBS' failure to adequately manage risks through its internal governance structures. RBS have failed to detail how much time has been dedicated towards the resolution of events or the exact financial costs, measured in terms of staff, lost working hours and reputational damage, thus making it difficult to quantify the extent to which time and resources have been spent on these breaches. Nonetheless, the incidents detailed above suggest not only the absence of learning, but also that RBS has failed to apply institutional resources—learning space—to the search for alternatives. As such, the bank has failed to create new patterns of reasoning and normative preferences in the light of the lessons of the GFC with pre-established underlying theories-in-use persisting at the group. In this respect, RBS has failed to seek, evaluate and apply new information—central to the learning process. This may likewise indicate that though dissatisfaction is crucial in the learning process, without the necessary application of learning space, dissatisfaction can impair learning by eroding the learning space.

Remuneration and Bonuses

In this section of the chapter, I argue that despite making some impressive strides in relation to remuneration, with the group bonus pool falling by 72% between 2010 and 2018, and 92% within the investment bank over the same period (RBS, 2008, 2010, 2018), RBS has ultimately failed to learn. Instead, the most significant changes to pay have come

[6] Most notably, RBS has failed to enhance whistle-blowing facilities at the bank which may have, and may yet still, prevent future governance failures.

in response to exogenous structural factors, namely the implementation of CRD IV and external pressures from the UK Government as the majority shareholder. I posit that the governance failures highlighted in the previous section, and which resulted in the erosion of time and resources, has led RBS to fall back upon previously established institutional norms. In particular, a series of institutional path dependencies concerning competition over the recruitment and retention of talent—interpreted by 'situational agents' (Bell, 2011)—has worked in such a way as to distort the lessons of the GFC and subvert change. As a result, RBS has failed to respond effectively to new information concerning the detrimental effect that remuneration structures can have on banks and financial markets—as stressed by the GFC—with a distinct absence of endogenously originated improved policy action. Instead, post-crisis remuneration structures have closely resembled models in place at the time of the GFC.

Simon (1957: 259) has argued that in order to achieve optimal results, a learning subject needs access to 'perfect' information in order to maximise outcomes. However, when the exchange or transmission of information breaks down, as is the case when the learning space is eroded, the learning subject is with left key gaps and as such will rely on making clumsy approximations to compensate (ibid.: 259–260). Resultantly, agents and institutions will fall back upon pre-established norms and patterns of reasoning as associated with so-called satisficing behaviour (Simon, 1995, 1998). In the case of RBS, the bank has reverted to path dependencies forged in the immediate aftermath of the GFC—concerning competition over pay—due to a perceived lack of alternatives. Consequently, the work of Simon (1957, 1995, 1998) also stresses the need for a learning subject to seek out and evaluate new information in order to learn. Yet, as discussed above, RBS has failed to orient sufficient resources to the evaluative process inherent in learning and which may explain why the group has failed to move beyond previously established institutional norms.

A very distinct strand within the literature on institutional path dependency that may also shed light on why RBS has failed to learn is the idea of 'imprinting' (Stinchcombe, 1965). Imprinting suggests that institutions may continue to adhere to specific behaviours in spite of information that suggests that practices are outdated, erroneous or inefficient (ibid.). This is because, according to Marquis and Tilcsik (2013: 3), certain behaviours or organisational norms formed and adopted at a time of heightened 'institutional sensitivity'—being a period of 'transition, upheaval, and instability'—such as in the aftermath of the GFC, tend to give an organisation meaning, direction and a sense of purpose (ibid.: 9). As such, certain practices are ascribed great importance and institutional value to the point that they become ingrained and 'infused' within an institution and persist beyond their natural lifespan (Selznick, 1957: 16–17). Such ideas then become a 'lasting part of the organisation' despite the presence of contending information that may prove such practices flawed or unproductive (Marquis & Tilcsik, 2013: 2). Moreover, once a particular idea or behaviour has been imprinted on an organisation, this will tend to persevere to the extent that the 'influence of early experience resists extinction to a high degree' (Immelmann, 1975: 22).

Consequently, ideas concerning structural competitive pressures in relation to pay, formed at the time of the crisis, may have a greater propensity to resist change due to the institutional value ascribed to these practices despite opposing information. Likewise, *imprinting* may similarly explain why institutional norms have persisted in spite of the fact that RBS has retrenched operations on UK domestic markets which, due to regulatory equivalency standards, we would expect to have become less competitive with the adoption of CRD IV[7] guaranteeing a more level playing field.

Before we move on to examine the empirical evidence in relation to pay at RBS, I will briefly remind the reader of some of the major regulatory changes that have dictated the level of variable pay at institutions post-2008. While brief, this *aide-mémoire* will be of particular importance to the argument set out in this section, along with coming chapters, and against which hypotheses can be tested.

Since the GFC, regulators in the UK and EU have sought to tackle the short-termism that pervaded institutions by introducing a series of

[7] The presence of certain institutional path dependencies at RBS may also explain why perceived structural competitive pressures have been more punctuated at the bank than at rival institutions such as Lloyds that have similarly retrenched operations on domestic markets. For example, regulatory equivalency standards set out by CRD IV have introduced new upper limits on variable remuneration across both EU and UK markets (James & Quaglia, 2020). As such, we may expect those institutions that have retrenched operations on domestic and European markets to be less sensitive to competition than those banks that have maintained or extended their international exposure, such as Barclays and HSBC, and which has subsequently brought them into competition with rival institutions that are not held to the same regulatory standards.

reforms that would mitigate many of the vulnerabilities associated with pre-crisis remuneration structures. In particular, the Prudential Regulation Authority's Remuneration Code (2011), working in parallel with the Financial Conduct Authority's (Revised) Remuneration Code (2011), and the European Parliament's CRD IV Article 90(1) (ca) and (d) have all looked to limit variable pay and curb excessive risk-taking by implementing a number of measures that seek to better align incentive structures. These reforms include the use of such instruments as: retention periods for bonuses; the limiting of variable pay to a fixed ratio of base salary; restrictions on cash awards and greater use of non-cash instruments; and mandatory clawback stipulations (McDonald, 2019; Macartney & Calcagno, 2019; Prudential Regulation Authority, 2017). For example, the PRA and FCA remuneration codes dictate that at least 40% of all variable remuneration paid to strategically important persons or material risk-takers should be subject to a deferment period of at least three years.[8] For senior managers and personnel receiving bonuses in excess of £500,000, 60% of awards should be locked away for up to a three-year deferral period (FCA, 2017; PRA, 2017).

Relatedly, the European Parliament's CRD IV Article 90(1)(ca) and (d)[9] (introduced 1st January 2014) requires all European headquartered banks to cap variable remuneration at 100% of annual pay or 200% of fixed salary with the majority consent of shareholders (bankofengland.co.uk; PwC, 2013). These regulatory changes have subsequently dictated the level of variable pay at institutions post-GFC and are of particular importance to the hypothesis extended in this section.

Annual Incentive

In 2008, variable remuneration at RBS was divided along three distinct lines; short-term annual incentive; long-term incentive plan and options (RBS, 2007: 106–107). Under the short-term annual incentive (AI hereafter) executive directors could typically expect a bonus of up to 200% of base salary, the exception being the GCE and chief executive of

[8] This will be extended to four years under CRD V (introduced December 2019 with an implementation date of December 2020). For further discussion see: Samuels (2019).

[9] We should note that such regulatory requirements were established before the UK's withdrawal from the EU. The UK has now entered into a transition period, due to end on 31 December 2020, during which EU law continues to apply.

Corporate Markets and Retail Markets who would be eligible of a bonus of up to 250% of base salary (ibid.). Immediately following the GFC, RBS announced that from 2009 onwards any award made under the AI would be deferred into RBS shares and would be subject to a three-year holding period and clawback stipulations (RBS, 2008). The group claimed that such an initiative would 'align the reward of participants with the long-term interests of shareholders' (RBS, 2009a: 226). The maximum potential number of shares made under the AI would be 6 million for the GCE and 3.75 million for the group finance director (RBS, 2010).

While such provisions may, upon first reading, be indicative of positive change at the bank, we should note that depending upon the performance of RBS stock, employees could potentially earn a maximum bonus that would be substantially greater than the previous upper limit of 200% or 250% of base salary respectively (RBS, 2007, 2010). Following these modifications, the structure of the AI would remain unchanged until 2014 when RBS would be forced to amend its policies in order to meet the requirements set out by CRD IV. Accordingly, we witness relatively little change in the overall structure and composition of the AI following the GFC with RBS retaining a degree of consistency with pre-crisis norms—as in keeping with the path dependency hypothesis.

Long-Term Incentive

The second element of variable remuneration in place at RBS in 2008 was the long-term incentive plan (RBS, 2007). This was divided between two separate awards, namely the Medium-Term Performance Plan (MPP) and Options. Under the MPP, employees would be eligible for awards payable in the form of shares or share equivalents of up to 100% of base salary, with the GCE earning up to 150% of salary (ibid.). Under the Options element, personnel could receive share options of up to three times base salary with the award also being subject to a three-year performance condition (RBS, 2007).

In 2009, RBS announced that it would be overhauling its long-term variable element of remuneration and that from 2010 onwards both the MPP and Options would be replaced by a single long-term bonus (RBS, 2009a). Under the new Long-Term Incentive Plan (LTIP), all awards would be structured as performance vesting deferred shares with participants having an option to receive either shares or market value share options, with all rewards being subject to clawback stipulations (ibid.). The maximum potential of awards allowed under the newly formed LTIP would remain at 400% of base salary (RBS, 2010).

Accordingly, we can see that between 2008 and 2013—the final year before the introduction of CRD IV—the way in which employees were rewarded at RBS remained broadly in-line with pre-crisis models. While there is some evidence of change, reforms during this period were consigned to the very fringes of pre-existing institutional structures. As such, RBS appear to have adhered to its former underlying theories-in-use. Moreover, remuneration structures in place at the group have allowed RBS to continue to make exorbitant bonus payments to select members of staff that appear to be out-of-step with performance and which may be indicative of a lack of cultural transformation.

In 2009 for instance, just months after the GFC had taken hold and the group reported pre-tax losses of £2.6 billion, RBS clashed with UK Financial Investments (UKFI), the company set up to manage the UK Government's 84% shareholding in the bank, over plans to award employees bonuses totalling £1.5 billion (Inman, 2009). Given the precarious economic situation of both RBS and the British economy as a whole, UKFI[10] warned that the bank's plans to make multi-million pound awards to staff would send the wrong message to the UK taxpayer and that more reserved rewards would be appropriate (Treanor, 2009). RBS responded by stating that any attempt to cap the bonuses of staff would result in *en-masse* resignations, adding

> Depending on UKFI's approach to recommendations made by the board in respect of that bonus pool, this requirement may adversely impact RBS's ability to attract and retain senior managers and other key employees and thereby place RBS at a significant competitive disadvantage against its competitors as well as increasing the risks facing RBS and weakening management's ability to deal with them.
>
> (RBS, 2009b)

Again in 2009, RBS caused outrage when it acquired eleven fixed investment income traders from Bank of America Merrill Lynch at the cost of approximately £5 million by guaranteeing the traders' first-year bonuses

[10] In June 2018, UKFI would be absorbed into UK Government Investments (for further discussion see Jenkins, 2018).

of £500,000 each (Aldrick, 2009). What is more, just months earlier RBS had appointed Antonio Polverino from Merrill Lynch to head up the group's Financial Institutions and Strategic Financing division with the promise of £7 million in guaranteed bonuses for the former bond trader (Fraser, 2014). Stephen Hester, then GCE, told reporters that while such payments were not desirable, they were essential in attracting and retaining talented staff members, adding that to be the best and provide maximum return for its shareholders it was inevitable that RBS would have to pay more than acceptable (Hester cited in *Telegraph*, 2009).

In late 2010, despite the UK taxpayer holding an 84% stake in the bank and RBS reporting a third consecutive year-end pre-tax loss of £1.1 billion, the group awarded more than one hundred of its investment bankers bonuses in excess £1 million, with total bonuses for the group that year totalling almost £1 billion (Treanor, 2010a). Again, Stephen Hester would defend these payments, telling the press that he would like to pay his investment bankers more and that the bonus pool agreed between RBS and UKFI was hindering the group's ability to recruit and retain the best banking talent (Hester cited in Treanor, 2010b). Meanwhile, Mr Hester was awarded a bonus of £2.5 million in cash and shares for his performance in 2010, bringing his total remuneration for the year to £6.8 million despite RBS' mounting losses (Quinn & Wilson, 2011).

In 2012, RBS would again attract criticism over its remuneration policies when the group announced plans to reward employees, chiefly within the investment bank, bonuses totalling £250 million despite the bank's implication in the rigging of Libor[11] (Parker & Jenkins, 2013). Penny Hughes, chair of the group's remuneration committee, once again stressed competitive pressures as being a mitigating factor in the level of remuneration determined by the group. Ms Hughes noted that the remuneration committee had continued to receive 'regular encouragement' to 'improve the delivery of market competitive remuneration', adding that the level of 'restraint' currently shown by RBS in relation to remuneration was reflective of the 'the nature of our ownership' (Hughes in RBS, 2012).

While at times these events appear a little dated, they are nonetheless pertinent to the argument being presented in this section of the chapter. This because, while remuneration at RBS has undoubtedly undergone

[11] Discussed above.

change and reform following the introduction of CRD IV, structural competitive pressures imprinted upon the group have continued to play a major role in shaping both remuneration and RBS' ability to learn and change. Indeed, those path dependencies forged in the years immediately following the GFC have become so ingrained within RBS's culture that such ideas and attitudes have resisted change even in the face of contending information. As such, in the decade since the crisis competition over pay has continued to be a significant factor in RBS' ideational preferences in relation to pay.

The persistence of long-held beliefs and attitudes, concerning competition over pay, beyond their 'natural lifespan' (Selznick, 1957) can be further witnessed in how RBS responded to the introduction of CRD IV. In 2013, RBS announced that from 2014 onwards it would be abandoning the AI and would consolidate all variable pay into a single LTIP payment (RBS, 2013: 77). The LTIP would see the group use its full regulatory allocation of variable pay, that being 100% of fixed salary, and thereby meeting the requirements set out in CRD IV (RBS, 2014a: 77). Although compliant with CRD IV, RBS did not welcome the European regulation stating that the introduction of a 'hard cap' on bonuses was not something that RBS could endorse or approve of but would endeavour to remain amenable with both the 'spirit' and 'letter' of the law (RBS, 2013: 67).

Though the introductionof CRD IV would inevitably result in a reduction of variable remuneration with the bonus pool falling by £203 million at the group level and £166 million in the investment bank between 2013—the final year before the introduction of the CRD IV—and 2014—the first year of the hard cap,[12] the bonus pool could have been higher were it not for the intervention by the UKFI. For example, under CRD IV banks must seek shareholder approval to extend annual bonuses beyond 100% of fixed pay, with the upper limit being 200% of base salary (bankofengland.co.uk). In April 2014, RBS followed the likes of Barclays and HSBC[13] and sought shareholder approval to increase variable pay to the upper limit of 200% of base salary telling shareholders that

[12] We should note that the controversial 'fixed share allowance' (discussed below) does not fall under 'variable remuneration' and as such is excluded from these figures.

[13] Lloyds are the only bank in this study that have not sought shareholder approval to increase fixed pay to the upper limit of 200% of base salary.

> The Board believes the best commercial solution for RBS is to have the flexibility on variable to fixed pay ratios that is now emerging as the sector norm. This would also allow RBS to maintain the maximum amount of compensation that could be subject to performance conditions including claw back for conduct issues that may emerge in future.
>
> (RBS, 2014b)

The UKFI would ultimately rejected the board's recommendations, meaning that variable remuneration would be capped at a maximum of 100% of base salary. RBS responded by stating that it 'acknowledge[d]' the decision taken by the majority shareholder but warned of the potential impact such a measures would have on the ability of RBS to 'remain competitive', warning of the 'commercial and prudential risk' which it must 'try to mitigate within the framework of a 1:1 fixed to variable compensation ratio' (RBS, 2014b).

Again, RBS' comments over the UKFI's intervention in how it would reward its employees suggests not only a failure to learn, with the input from institutional stakeholders being opposed by the bank, but also that this failure may be attributed to certain path dependencies concerning competitive pressures despite the introduction of CRD IV. Indeed, Marquis and Tilcsik (2013: 2) suggest that once a certain idea or notion has been imprinted on an organisation it 'will remain despite [a] changing external environment'. This may explain why in the decade that has followed the GFC, RBS has continued to cite structural competitive pressures as a mitigating factor when calculating bonus awards.

These competitive pressures would lead RBS to make further revisions to the LTIP award in 2017. Under the reformed LTIP scheme employees would be eligible, for the first time since the introduction of CRD IV, for a bonus of up to 200% of fixed salary (RBS, 2016, 2017). The new system would retain the caveat that awards be payable exclusively in shares vesting between three and eight years, but importantly, would remove the pro-rata performance stipulation[14] (ibid.). Instead, LTIP bonuses would be determined on an annual basis with awards being locked away for a prescribed period in keeping with 'regulatory requirements' (RBS, 2017: 104). Accordingly, while RBS has correctly pointed out that the group has removed all annual variable remuneration, the revised LTIP scheme

[14]The group would also retain its controversial fixed share award (discussed below).

has a distinctly short-term outlook with long-term awards being measured on a yearly basis.

Critics have argued that the elimination of the pro-rata measurement has given variable pay at the group a notably 'fixed' outlook with awards assuming a 'more guaranteed long-term offering' (Arnold & Croft, 2017). Likewise, the revised remuneration structure would also make it easier and more likely for the bank to make awards positioned at the upper threshold of regulatory allowances (Arnold & Croft, 2017; Macaskill & White, 2017). RBS admitted that changes to the LTIP were 'intended to carry a high degree of certainty' (RBS, 2016: 89) and lead to 'more predictable [pay] outcomes' for senior employees (RBS, 2017: 84). The motivation behind such changes were once again attributed to structural pressure with the bank claiming that the measures were aimed 'attracting and keeping the right people for RBS' (RBS, 2016: 89) by creating a remuneration package that would be 'more highly valued by executives' (RBS, 2018: 85).

Fixed Share Allowance

An overhaul of RBS' variable pay would also see the introduction of a new element of remuneration, the Fixed Share Allowance, or role-based allowance. The role-based allowance would provide employees with set pay awards reflective of their 'skills and experience' (RBS, 2018: 65). Under the entitlement, employees would be eligible for a share award of 100% of base salary, with awards vesting over a period of between one and eight years[15] (RBS, 2014a, 2018). However, City commentators have argued that the use of such 'role-based pay' has effectively allowed banks to circumvent CRD IV as awards, either cash or shares, can be adjusted year-on-year in accordance with an individual's fixed salary which is itself subject to revision (see Schafer & Arnold, 2014; Armitage, 2014; Allison, 2014). Announcing the introduction of the new fixed share allowance, Sandy Crombie, then chairman of the group performance and remuneration committee, told shareholders that the use of role-based fixed allowances were

[15] It should be noted that like RBS, Lloyds, Barclays and HSBC are also utilising so-called role-based allowances with Lloyds and HSBC similarly rewarding employees in shares exclusively. Barclays are the exception paying staff in both cash and shares.

> in line with market practice…[and that RBS had] a duty to reward our people fairly, and [a] responsibility to ensure that we are running a commercial business with the best available talent.
>
> (Crombie in RBS, 2014a: 73)

Thus, while we can see that RBS has complied with the letter of tougher new regulations concerning variable pay, it appears that the bank's remuneration practices are not necessarily in keeping with the spirit of CRD IV. As such, RBS has failed to demonstrate substantive evidence of learning with the group, like many of its competitors, seeking to circumvent regulatory powers aimed at tempering variable pay. This is particularly salient when we consider the fact that both exuberant bonuses and attempts to undermine, erode and rollback regulatory frontiers were both key causes of the GFC. Indeed, this evidence would suggest that in the decade that has followed the crisis, RBS has struggled against the tide of regulatory controls with those institutional path dependencies surrounding competition and pay again appearing to be a determining factor in how remuneration is structured and bonuses are awarded. These ideas have subsequently impacted negatively upon RBS' ability to learn and change by inhibiting the search for and application of new information with the group instead adhering to previously held beliefs and underlying theories-in-use.

RBS' approach to remuneration post-2008, along with those overriding ideas concerning competition, may likewise offer us insight into the how the group has interpreted the costs associated with learning and change. The evidence examined in this section appears to suggest that the perceived costs of learning—measured in terms of RBS' ability to 'attract and retain talent'—remains high and is viewed as having the potential to harm and negatively impact the group. While RBS has indeed changed the way in which employees are remunerated following the GFC—resulting in a reduction in the overall bonus pool—these changes have come largely in response to exogenous regulatory constraints, namely CRD IV. With little endogenously originated change, the group has failed to present evidence of a substantive self-reflexive learning process as associated with the double-loop theory.

Though I have not attempted to refute the claim that there remains a level of competition between banks to recruit and retain staff, we should keep in mind that while competition may be a structural factor in learning, institutions, and the agents that embody organisations, are key drivers of structural change (Archer, 2003, 2007). As such, the citing of competition as a mitigating factor in RBS' remuneration policies indicates that the group has failed to learn one of the key lessons of the GFC, namely, that excessive competition between institutions, and the proliferation of this competition by organisations, can harm the structural environment in which subjects operate. This may lead us to conclude that structures, and the way in which agents interpret the structural environment, will and do play an important role in learning.

Balance Sheet

We will now turn our attention to the balance sheet element at RBS that again, upon first reading, appears to present some evidence of positive change and potential learning. However, deeper analysis of the bank's position will reveal that, much like remuneration at the group, the majority of this change has come in response to exogenous structural factors. As such, this section will argue that while RBS' balance sheet has undergone a significant reshaping following the GFC, with the group exiting a number of markets and divesting its business, these changes have largely come as a result of domestic and European provisions concerning the group's 2008 bailout. What is more, RBS appears to lack the endogenously self-evaluative process associated with double-loop learning and which ultimately is indicative of the absence of learning.

In 2008, RBS would be forced to accept the first of several tranches of state aid from the UK Government after the bank announced catastrophic losses of more £24 billion (Werdigier, 2009). Matters were further complicated when it was revealed that the group were holding more than £325 billion of toxic assets on its balance sheet and as a result would be the first British bank to enter the UK Government's assets protection scheme (ibid.). RBS would go on to receive more than £45 billion in state aid—leaving the UK taxpayer as the majority shareholder. As a result, the group would be forced to accept the conditions set forth by the European Commission on state aid and which would require RBS to divest several businesses and reduce its balance sheet from £2.4 trillion to a more conservative £1 trillion (Quinn, 2013; *BBC News Online*, 2015). Accordingly, any changes to the nature and composition of the balance sheet must be considered in the light of these structural factors and the conditions attached to the group's 2008 bailout.

Group Funding

In 2008, RBS' total liabilities and equity were £2.4 trillion with total customer deposits accounting for £639 billion or approximately 26% of RBS' total funding. Comparative figures for 2018 show that total liabilities and equity had fallen to £694 billion with customer deposits accounting for £360 billion or 51% of total funding. This demonstrates that in the years following the GFC, RBS has increased total customer deposits, which as we already know is a much more stable funding source, as a percentage of total liabilities and equity by 25 percentage points (Fig. 4.1).

Moreover, in 2008 short-term funding—including short-term borrowings, money markets and other short-term funding—was worth £433 billion or 18% of total liabilities and equity. However, by 2018 short-term funding as a percentage of total liabilities and equity had decreased to 11%—being worth £78 billion. Thus, we can see that between 2008 and 2018, RBS significantly decreased its reliance on short-term borrowing while increasing total customer deposits substantially (Fig. 4.2).[16]

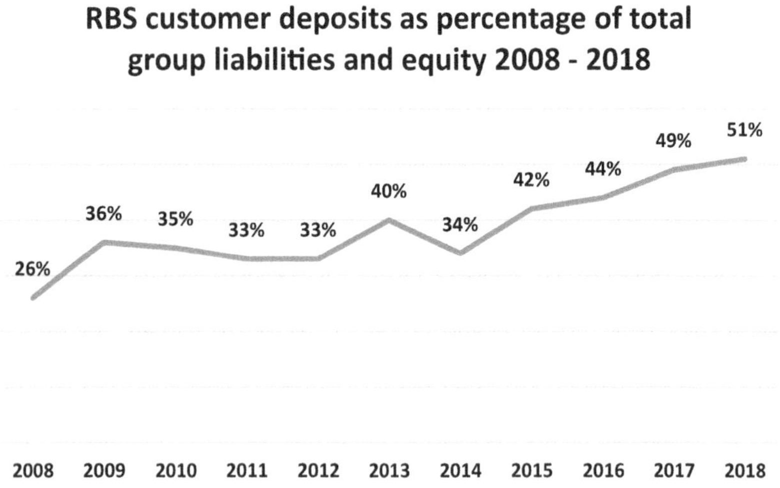

Fig. 4.1 Customer deposits as percentage of total group liabilities and equity 2008–2018

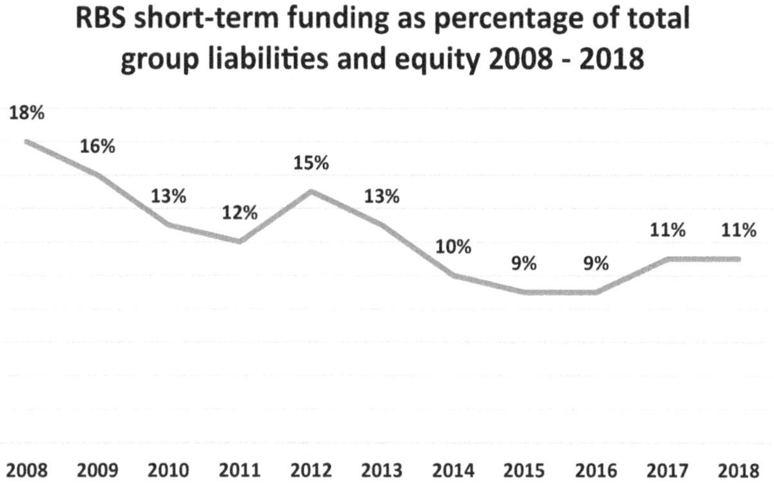

Fig. 4.2 Short-term funding as percentage of total group liabilities and equity 2008–2018

Regulatory Capital

When the crisis hit in 2008, RBS' regulatory tier 1 capital was £69 billion with a tier 1 regulatory capital ratio of 10%. Meanwhile, the group's total regulatory capital was approximately £98 billion with a total regulatory capital ratio of 14%. Figures for 2018 show that regulatory tier 1 capital was approximately £34 billion and total regulatory capital £41 billion. The tier 1 regulatory capital ratio was 18.4% with the total regulatory capital ratio being 21.8%.

However, we must be cautious in drawing conclusion from these figures due to the changing regulatory landscape which has seen regulatory capital requirements increase significantly. For example, rules set out by the Basel III Accord—introduced by the Basel Committee on Banking Standards in 2011—changed both the amount of regulatory capital which must be held by institutions and how tier 1 regulatory

[16] However, we should note that changes to minimum capital standards introduced by Basel III, along with the definition of tier 1 capital, may have affected the efficiency of borrowing on wholesale markets. As such, we should not consider these figures in isolation. For further discussion see Agur (2013).

capital is defined—which subsequently changed the definition of total regulatory capital (James & Quaglia, 2020; McDonald, 2019). El Radi (2014: 8) has highlighted the most prominent changes to the definition of tier 1 capital, noting that

> The elements/instruments to be included in Tier 1 capital should be sufficiently loss absorbent on a going-concern basis; i.e.: (i) subordinated; (ii) have fully optional non-cumulative dividends or coupons; and (iii) neither have a maturity date nor an incentive to redeem. Innovative instruments which was limited to 15% of Tier 1 capital [have been] phased out.

Essentially, these changes look to introduce stricter capital requirements by limiting what assets can be used by banks in the building of tier 1 capital, with an explicit focus upon the holding of more long-term instruments. Likewise, under new rules introduced by Basel III, certain financial instruments no longer qualify as regulatory capital.[17] Furthermore, Basel III also dictates that banks must have a minimum regulatory tier 1 capital ratio of 6% and a total regulatory capital of 8% (BIS, 2010, 2018). While definitions of tier 1 and total regulatory capital have changed post-GFC, making a like-for-like comparison difficult, analysis of such figures still make an important contribution to the current discussion as we able to draw conclusions about the spirit with which regulatory requirements have been met by the banks.

In the case of RBS, the group's regulatory capital allocation in relation to Basel III demonstrates that for the financial year ending 2018, the bank's tier 1 capital ratio exceeded minimum requirements by 206%. Likewise, the total regulatory capital ratio surpassed minimum standards, set forth by Basel III, by 172%. As such, these figures may be indicative of learning with RBS going beyond regulatory minimum standards. Moreover, in 2018 RBS had greatest capital ratios of our comparator group (Fig. 4.3).

While we can see that RBS has, in the decade since the crisis, operated within guidelines and gone beyond minimum regulatory standards—outperforming its peers in terms of capital requirements—we should not lose sight of the fact that a great deal of the bank's restructuring has come as a result of stipulations attached to its state-backed bailout. As noted above, EU mandated rules on state aid has required RBS to disinvest over

[17] For further discussion see: El Radi (2014) and James and Quaglia (2020).

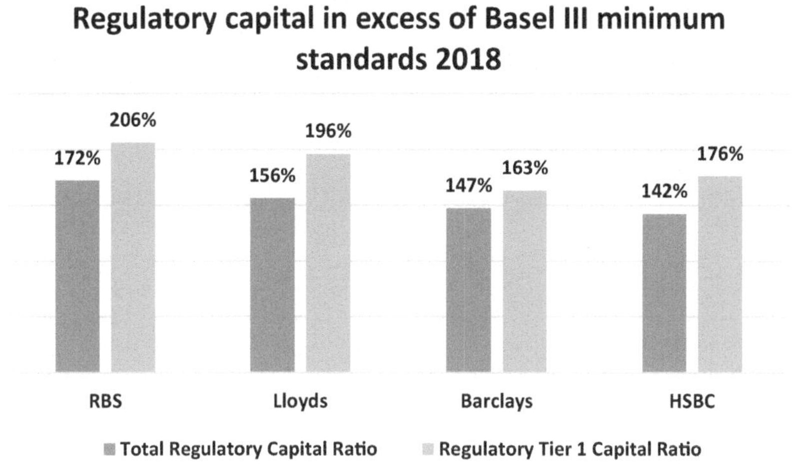

Fig. 4.3 Regulatory capital percentage in excess of Basel III minimum standards 2018

a £1 trillion worth of assets from its balance sheet and shed a number of business in order to meet rules on competition. This has undoubtedly had a positive effect on capital holdings, and subsequently leverage,[18] thereby calling into question any correlation between a reduction in leverage and learning. Instead, it may be argued that changes to the group's leverage are merely a by-product of the disinvestment project[19] that has been driven by exogenous regulatory conditions. Moreover, RBS has been rather resistant to such change, frequently clashing with regulators over plans to shrink the bank and failing to meet successive deadlines.[20] This stands in stark opposition to RBS' counterparts at Lloyds that have similarly been subject to regulatory requirements to shrink its business and is discussed in more detail in the coming chapter.

[18] Leverage is the inverse of the capital ratio - if capital levels are down leverage ratios will be up by definition.

[19] Discussed in more detail below.

[20] Discussed in more detail below.

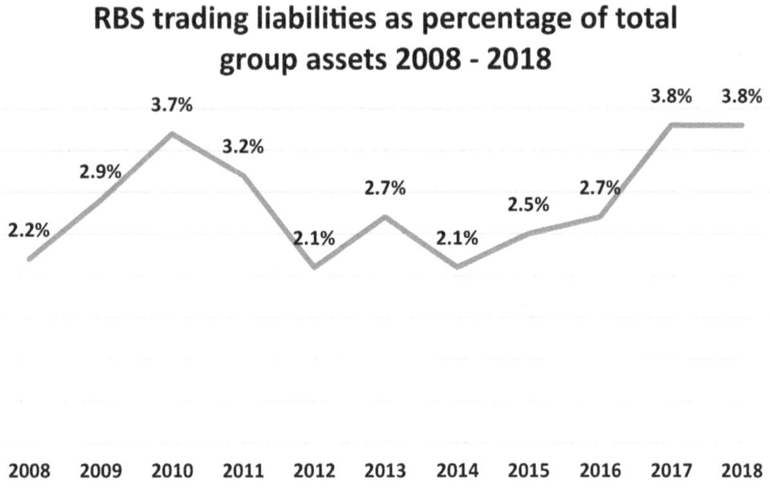

Fig. 4.4 Trading liabilities as percentage of total assets 2008–2018

Trading Liabilities

Indeed, these changes have been accompanied by an increase in trading liabilities as percentage of total group assets and which may undermine the progress made to date. For example, in 2008 trading liabilities at RBS were £54 billion or 2.25% of total assets. Comparable figures show that in 2018, trading liabilities were worth £26 billion or approximately 3.8% of total group assets, an increase of around 72%. This shows that while RBS has significantly reduced the size of its balance sheet, trading exposures carried by the newly streamlined group have increased as financial trading continues to play an important role in the group's portfolio (Fig. 4.4).

Loan/Deposit Ratio

Despite this, an examination of the group's loan-to-deposit ratio reveals further evidence of progress post-GFC. For example, in 2008 RBS' gross loans totalled £885 billion, with total deposits being worth £639 billion. These figures demonstrate that in 2008 gross loans extended by the group was the equivalent of approximately 138% of total customer deposits. However, figures for 2018 show that gross loans were worth approximately £308 billion, or 85% of total customer deposits which totalled

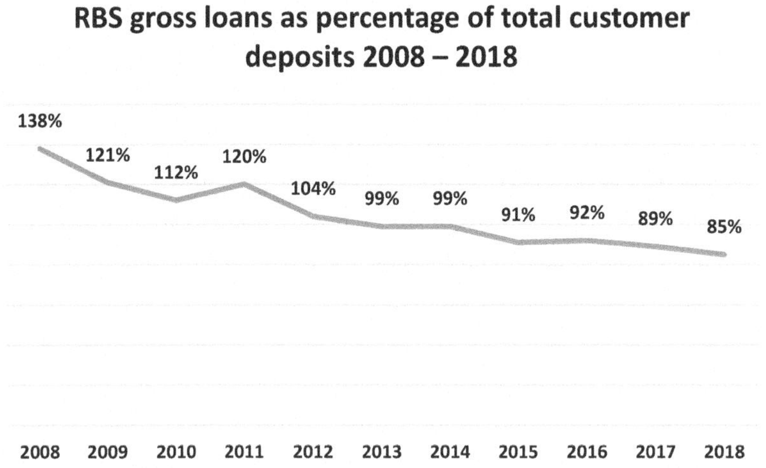

Fig. 4.5 Gross loans as percentage of total customer deposits 2008–2018

£360 billion. This suggests that in the years following the crisis RBS' lending, as a proportion of deposits taken, decreased by approximately 53 percentage points and may be indicative of learning. For example, we know that the loan-to-deposit ratio has a corresponding effect on a bank's liquidity, the higher the ratio the greater the chance that a bank could become illiquid if depositors simultaneously withdrew their cash. These figures demonstrate that since the GFC, RBS has operated with a much more conservative loan-to-deposit ratio. However, such numbers should not be considered in isolation and must instead take account of the broader regulatory environment. In particular, increased minimum capital standards set out by Basel III has undoubtedly had an effect upon the ratio (Fig. 4.5).

Loan Quality/Impairments

In addition to the loan-to-deposit ratio being reduced, the quality and type of loans extended by RBS also appear, upon first reading, to be of a much safer asset class. For instance, in 2008 gross loans were worth £885 billion with £139 billion of these loans being allocated towards residential mortgages, which as we already know are a particularly stable asset-backed

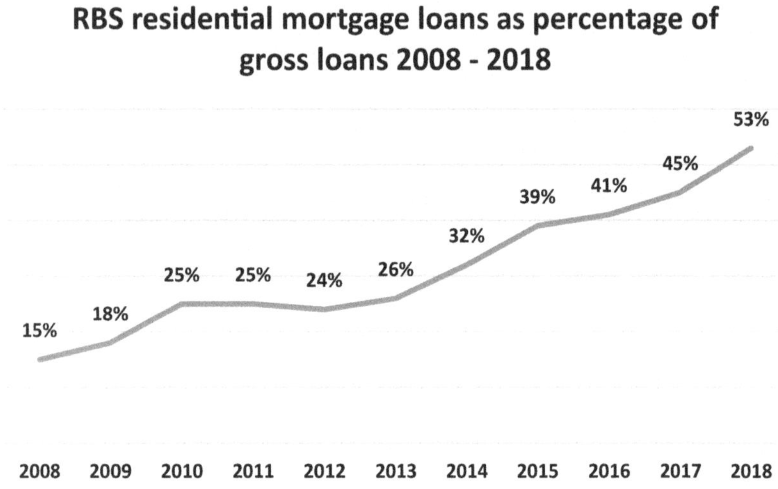

Fig. 4.6 Residential mortgage loan as percentage of gross loans 2008–2018

loan and carry a much lower risk to the lender.[21] As such, we know that in 2008 residential mortgage loans at RBS' were worth 15.7% of gross loans made. Equivalent figures for 2018 likewise demonstrate that gross loans extended were worth £308 billion with £163 billion or approximately 53% of gross loans being dedicated towards residential mortgage lending (Fig. 4.6).

However, while the number of residential mortgage loans made by RBS has increased exponentially in the post-crisis period, this has not been accompanied by a reduction in impairments. Indeed, the group has experienced a slight rise in the percentage of impairments between 2008 and 2018, calling into question the quality of lending. For instance, in 2008 total impaired loans were worth approximately £21 billion or 2.4% of gross loans extended. In 2018, this figure stood at £7.7 billion or 2.5%. The average yearly impairment rate across the post-GFC decade stood at approximately 6%. In contrast to our comparator group over the same period, Lloyds recorded and impairment rate of 4.6%, Barclays

[21] The exception being so-called subprime mortgages most closely associated with US markets and which as we have previously seen were laden with a plethora of risk and uncertainty.

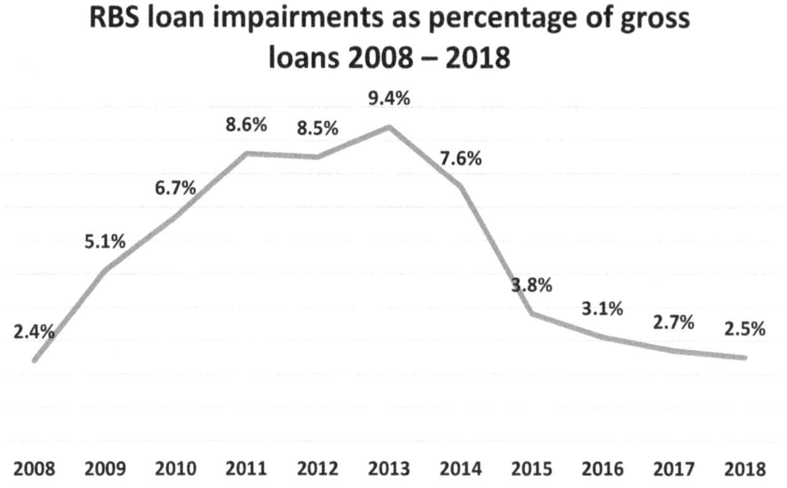

Fig. 4.7 Loan impairments as percentage of gross loans 2008–2018

2.6% and HSBC 0.8%. While we should exercise caution in drawing conclusions about impairment rates, which may reflect more adverse economic conditions post-crisis, we can see that though impairments have increased marginally at RBS, the group did perform broadly in-line with its competitors and outpaced Lloyds on this metric (Fig. 4.7).

Derivatives

The use of derivatives by banks and other financial actors is a controversial issue. On the one hand, derivatives can allow a bank to significantly ramp up its leverage ratio and place undue demands for liquidity upon both institutions and markets. As such, derivatives are considered in some quarters as potentially harmful particularly when used for investment purposes (Mayer, 1999). Conversely, derivatives can allow an institution to 'hedge' its exposure to price fluctuations that may be contained elsewhere within the trading book (Tuckman, 2016: 65).

In 2008, RBS held £971 billion in derivatives that accounted for approximately 40% of the group's total balance sheet. However, by 2018 this figure had been reduced to approximately £131 billion or approximately 19% of the total balance sheet, a reduction of 21 percentage

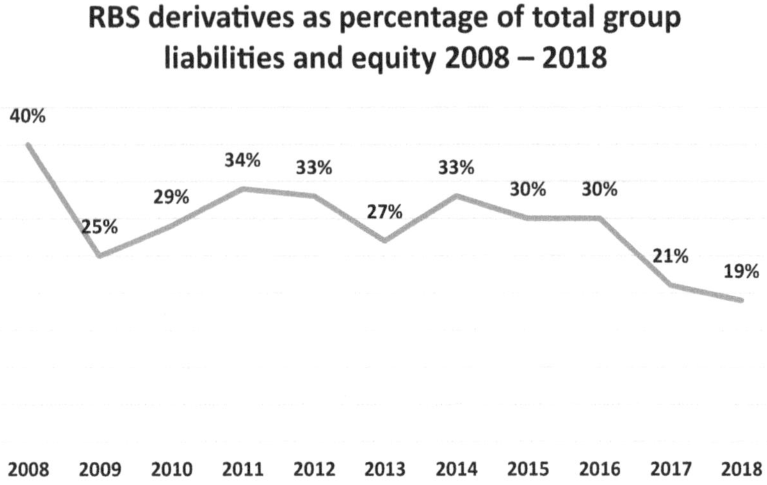

Fig. 4.8 Derivatives as percentage of total liabilities and equity 2008–2018

points. Consequently, these numbers are indicative of a scaling back in the extent to which RBS has engaged in this potentially harmful form of financial trading. However, comparable figures show that RBS had the joint highest percentage of derivatives of our comparator group along with Barclays (19%), with Lloyds (2.9%) and HSBC (8%) outperforming RBS (Fig. 4.8).

Off Balance Sheet Vehicles

Though RBS' use of derivatives has decreased following the GFC, the group has broadly maintained its utilisation of off-balance-sheet vehicles in the post-crisis decade. Off-balance-sheet vehicles are particularly problematic because, by their very nature, such instruments conceal the true contents and origin of the products held within them. As such, the task of accurately identifying counterparty risk can be extremely difficult. Moreover, off-balance-sheet products allow banks and other institutions to circumvent regulatory stipulations that would typically apply to 'on balance sheet' items (Erturk, 2017). In 2008 off-balance-sheet vehicles at RBS were worth £433 billion or approximately 18% of total group assets. Yet, comparative figures for 2018 show that the group maintained its use of these instruments with off-balance-sheet items being worth 18.7% of total group assets or £124 billion. While RBS were outperformed on this metric by Lloyds (17%), they did outstrip both Barclays (30%) and HSBC (34%) (Fig. 4.9).

Thus far, this section of the chapter does indeed appear to suggest a degree of positive change to the structure and composition of the balance sheet. While some elements of the balance sheet, such as loan quality/impairments, trading liabilities and off balance sheet items show little improvement, RBS has diversified its funding base, reduced reliance on wholesale markets, grown regulatory capital in excess of minimum standards and delivered a more conservative loan-to-deposit ratio. On the face of this evidence, the hypothesis put forwards in this chapter—that RBS has failed to demonstrate substantive evidence of learning and change—would appear to be erroneous when applied to the balance sheet element.

However, such progress must take account of the wider structural environment in which change has occurred, in particular the group's EU

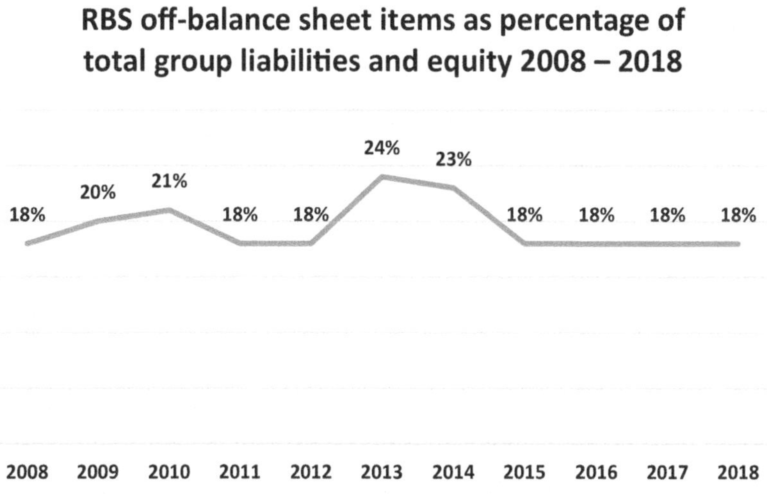

Fig. 4.9 Off-balance-sheet items as percentage of total group liabilities and equity 2008–2018

mandated disinvestment.[22] Indeed, though RBS has complied, for the most part, to the letter of the law concerning exogenous stipulations attached to its bailout, the bank has been less than enthusiastic about the disinvestment process. This failure to engage positively with regulatory stipulations and embrace the conditions attached to its recapitalisation may be telling of the relationship between RBS and regulators, with regulatory constraints viewed by the bank as a hindrance to its competitive advantage. As such, I suggest that RBS' disinvestment, and the associated positive effect on the group's balance sheet, is not representative of the self-reflexive process associated learning, accordingly, we should conclude that learning is absent in this instance.

Disinvestments

To illustrate, in 2012 RBS announced that it would be going ahead with the sale of its insurance business, Direct Line, which incorporated several household names such as Churchill and Green Flag (*BBC News*, 2012). The sale was subsequently completed in February 2014 with RBS selling off its remaining 28% stake in the business (Knight & Dunkley, 2014). However, Jill Treanor of the *Guardian* newspaper highlights the fact that RBS had little desire to shed itself of Direct Line and did so only because of those stipulations imposed by the EU (Treanor, 2012b). Indeed, commenting on the sale, RBS stated that the disinvestment of Direct Line was motivated 'exclusively' by a need to 'comply with the European Commission State Aid' requirements (RBS, 2014a: 97). Likewise, Joe Rundle of ETX Capital also highlighted the fact that though the sale of Direct Line was completed in a timely manner, it came against the backdrop of mounting political pressure (Rundle cited Kollewe, 2014).

While the initial disinvestment of Direct Line would come at a relatively early stage in RBS' learning journey, the pertinence of this issue in relation to the overarching narrative presented in this chapter remains so. In particular, this event, along with those detailed below, establishes a clear timeline of events and behavioural patterns that cumulatively question the extent to which changes in the balance sheet demonstrate endogenously originated learning and change. Instead, the events detailed

[22] To reiterate, as part of its 2008 bailout deal RBS would be forced to shed over £1 trillion of assets from its balance sheet and disinvest a number of businesses in order to increase competition within banking markets.

here suggest that the restructuring of the balance sheet has occurred independently of learning and primarily because of structural regulatory considerations. Moreover, RBS has failed to embrace the spirit of change, resisting, openly challenging and deriding regulatory attempts to shrink the group's balance sheet.

In September 2013, and again owing to the stipulations attached to the state aid received in 2008, came the announcement that RBS would be selling more than 300 of its branches to a consortium of investors that would see the revival of the redundant Williams and Glyn brand (*BBC News Online*, 2015). The sell-off would offer the buyers a preferential bond that would later convert to shares worth an approximate 30–40% stake in the newly created bank (Treanor, 2013). In 2015, Emma Dunkley and Martin Arnold of the *Financial Times* reported that RBS had been approached by a number of investors interested in buying Williams and Glyn, and that RBS would sell the bank in early 2016 (Dunkley & Arnold, 2015a). However, in April 2016 RBS announced that it was doubtful that the sale would be completed before the December 2017 deadline set by the European Commission (Dunkley, 2016a). Though interested parties including the Clydesdale and Yorkshire Banking Group, Santander and Virgin Money all submitted bids to buy Williams and Glyn, RBS ultimately failed to find a buyer (Dunkley, 2016b), admitting that it could take until 2021 before a standalone entity was ready for sale (Dunkley, 2016c).

In July 2017, with losses mounting, multiple missed deadlines and a looming investigation by the PRA over the failed disinvestment, RBS submitted a proposal to deliver £835 million of funding to its rivals in order to boost competition (Dunkley, 2017c). Under the proposed plans, RBS would provide finance to a number of UK institutions in the form of a 'capability and innovation' fund, while also funding a scheme designed to incentivise some of its small business customers to switch accounts to its rivals—thereby increasing competition and meeting the conditions set out by the European Commission (Dunkley, 2017d). The plan would mean that RBS would no longer be forced to sell its 300 Williams and Glynn branches, with the European Commission agreeing to RBS' proposal in September 2017[23] (ibid.).

[23] RBS' disinvestment experience stand in stark opposition to that of Lloyds, which, like RBS, has also been forced to shed parts of its business due to its receipt of state aid. However, in contrast to RBS, Lloyds has completed its disinvestment projects in a timely

Similarly, in early 2014, and again as part of the group's £1 trillion retrenchment, RBS announced that it would be jettisoning a significant part of its investment bank (Scuffham, 2015). Under the plans, RBS would shrink operations in the division by approximately two-thirds and reduce risk-weighted assets by approximately £107 billion (Arnold, 2015). The move would see RBS cease investment-banking operations in twenty-five of the thirty-eight jurisdictions where it once operated and reduce staff numbers by around two-thirds (Lewin, 2016; RBS, 2016, 2017; Treanor, 2015).

However, despite ultimately complying with regulatory stipulations that would necessitate a retrenchment of the group's operations, the process of streamlining the investment bank does not appear to have been a wholly endogenous process. For example, Matt Scuffham of *Reuters* reported that during his tenure as GCE Stephen Hester and the RBS board of directors clashed with politicians and UKFI on several occasions over plans to shrink the investment bank (Scuffham, 2014). On one such occasion, Mr Hester was reported as telling officials that reducing the size and geographical footprint of the investment banking division would hurt the group's share price and leave RBS as a 'second best Lloyds' (Hester cited in Scuffham, 2014).

Moreover, while the size of the investment bank has been reduced and operations retrenched in the post-crisis decade, RBS has remained dependent upon the division as a key driver of group profitability. To illustrate, in 2007 the investment bank generated £3.8 billion or 30% of group profit. In 2008, this figure was £28 million or approximately 35% of overall group profit before tax and write-downs. In 2018, the investment banking division of RBS recorded a healthy pre-tax profit of £1 billion or 30% of group pre-tax profits. In addition, between 2014—the year that the group announced a shrinking of the division—and 2018, the average yearly contribution of the investment bank to group pre-tax profit stood at around 37%. Consequently, we can see that following the GFC, the strategic importance of the investment bank, and the operations carried out by the division, have continued to play an important role at RBS.

In 2015, RBS would complete the sale of its US subsidiary Citizens Finance. RBS' disposal of Citizens had begun a year earlier in September 2014 when the group sold a 25% stake in the bank, subsequently selling

manner and in many cases before the imposed deadline (discussed in more detail in the coming chapter).

a further 50% in March 2015 (Trotman, 2015). In October 2015, RBS confirmed that it had sold its final share in the bank through a public offering, with RBS group CEO Ross McEwan announcing on the bank's website that

> the sale of Citizens is a critical part of our capital plan and further improves our CET1 capital ratio. A strong capital position is the essential platform on which we will continue to build a simpler, stronger and more efficient UK focussed bank that can better serve the needs of its customers.
>
> (McEwan, 2015a)

However, while the disposal of Citizens came fourteen months earlier than originally expected, Ben McLannahan of the *Financial Times* highlighted that the sale, while completed in a timely fashion, was once again done so in order to meet the conditions set forth by the European Commission (McLannahan, 2015). Moreover, though Mr McEwan recognised the positive effect that the disposal had on the group's capital ratio, neither the group's CEO nor RBS acknowledged that the disinvestment had been largely motivated by the conditions attached to the group's state-sponsored bailout.

Also in 2015, RBS announced that it would be selling part of its private banking firm Coutts International to Swiss bank UBP (Matthew, 2015). RBS confirmed that the sale would see it jettison that part of the bank that dealt with client relationships outside of the UK, although it would retain the UK centred arm of Coutts, effectively splitting the bank (Arnold, 2015). Alison Rose,[24] CEO of Commercial and Private Banking at RBS, commented that the move was part of RBS' strategy to 'become a more UK focused business' (Rose cited in Matthew, 2015). However, *Forbes* duly noted that as late as 2011 RBS had been desperately trying to grow Coutts bank with plans to 'double the size of the business within several years' (*Forbes.com*, 2015). Instead, *Forbes* believed that the sale of Coutts had been the brainchild of former Chancellor George Osborne as part of the UK Government's plans to shed RBS of some of its international business (ibid.).

These disinvestment projects, and the related shrinking of the group's balance sheet, would subsequently allow the UK Government to begin

[24] Ms Rose would succeed Ross McEwan as GCE in November 2019 making her the first women to lead a major UK bank (Megaw, 2019b).

the sell-down of its stake in the bank. In 2015, Chancellor George Osborne announced that the Government would be selling a 5% share in RBS at a loss of approximately £1 billion (Dunkley & Arnold, 2015b). Then in June 2017, the Government sold a further 7.7% stake of the business, this time at a loss of around £2.1 billion and which would reduce the UK taxpayers' share in the business to 62.4% (Megaw, 2018b). In contrast, the sell-down of the Government's 43% stake in Lloyds, discussed in the coming chapter, has returned the UK Treasury a small profit of around £900 million (National Audit Office, 2018).

The downsizing of the investment bank, along with other notable disinvestment projects undertaken by RBS following its 2008 bailout, appear to have not only been largely motivated by structural constraints imposed by EU rules concerning state aid, but have also failed to be realised in a timely fashion or remain incomplete. Indeed, while RBS has clearly overhauled the structure and composition of the balance sheet post-GFC, there is little evidence to suggest that this shift has been accompanied by a corresponding change in the group's underlying theories-in-use. For example, regulatory stipulations that have mandated a shrinking of the business have been a source of conflict between RBS and its institutional stakeholders—the UKFI and government officials—with such rules appearing to have been interpreted by RBS and key agents within the bank, as hampering the group's economic performance. Consequently, we should remain sceptical of the extent to which changes at RBS following the GFC are reflective of learning as in keeping with conceptualisation set out in Chapter 2.

Conclusion

The analysis carried out in this chapter suggests that, despite some tentative evidence of change, RBS has ultimately failed to learn lessons from the GFC. Moreover, the most substantial changes to the group's operating procedures have come in response to exogenous structural factors—that along with the interpretation of structures by key agents—clearly matter in the learning process. Resultantly, such changes cannot be considered reflective of the double-loop, self-reflexive, process inherent in learning.

This lack of learning can be attributed to a catalogue of events linked to internal governance breaches and a failure to apply sufficient institutional resources—learning space—towards the search for, evaluation of and application of new information. This also suggests that, while dissatisfaction is clearly important in the learning trajectory of institutions, the orientation of learning space is equally important. Not only have RBS failed to learn from successive failures but these incidents highlight the distortionary impact such events can have upon learning if learning space is not applied effectively towards the self-reflexive process. As a result of this failure, RBS has reverted to and fallen back upon already established underlying theories-in-use. Indeed, in the decade that has followed the GFC, there appears to be the distinct lack of change to the group's normative preferences and institutional frames that have persisted beyond their natural life span and in the face of contending information.

The lack of learning experienced by RBS would suggest that the group is still exposed to many of the institutional weakness highlighted by the GFC. This in turn has potential ramifications for the financial stability of the domestic economy, and beyond, due to the systemically important nature of the bank. Moreover, there is a certain irony to RBS' failure to learn. While the group experienced perhaps the greatest losses of all the banks in this study, RBS has demonstrated the least reform of the banks surveyed. Indeed, in 2008 RBS learned to fail, yet in the decade since the GFC, the group has failed to learn.

References

Agur, I. (2013, January). *Wholesale bank funding, capital requirements and credit rationing* (IMF Working Paper No. 13/30). Available at: https://www.imf.org/en/Publications/WP/Issues/2016/12/31/Wholesale-Bank-Funding-Capital-Requirements-and-Credit-Rationing-40285.

Aldrick, P. (2009, October 19). RBS pays £5m for 11 bankers. *The Telegraph*. Available at: https://www.telegraph.co.uk/finance/newsbysector/banksandfinance/6379051/RBS-pays-5m-for-11-bankers.html.

Allison, I. (2014, October 15). European banking authority tightens rules on 'fixed pay' bonus cap dodge. *International Business Times*. Available at: https://www.ibtimes.co.uk/european-banking-authority-tightens-rules-fixed-pay-bonus-cap-dodge-1470171.

Archer, M. (2003). *Structure agency and the internal conversation*. Cambridge: Cambridge University Press.

Archer, M. (2007). *Making our way through the world*. Cambridge: Cambridge University Press.

Armitage, J. (2014, March 6). Banks could be wiped out by the 'role-based allowances'. *The Independent*. Available at: https://www.independent.co.uk/

news/business/comment/banks-could-be-wiped-out-by-the-rolebased-allowances-9172081.html.

Arnold, M. (2015, March 26). RBS agrees to sell Coutts International to Swiss bank UBP. *Financial Times*. Available at: https://www.ft.com/cms/s/0/a2f7e3ea-d3c3-11e4-99bd-00144feab7de.html#axzz41C1UVFL5.

Arnold, M. (2017, October 26). RBS settles DoJ fraud claims over mortgage-backed securities. *Financial Times*. Available at: https://www.ft.com/content/2231f092-f991-3eef-9ebe-4a46ed6ddf9f.

Arnold, M., & Croft, J. (2017, May 3). RBS investors advised to vote against pay policy. *Financial Times*. Available at: https://www.ft.com/content/fa35e1ca-3023-11e7-9555-23ef563ecf9a.

Bank of England [bankofengland.co.uk]. *Remuneration code—About*. Available at: https://www.bankofengland.co.uk/pra/Pages/supervision/activities/aboutremuneration.aspx.

BBC News. (2012, September 14). RBS confirms it will sell off Direct Line Insurance. *BBC News*. Available at: https://www.bbc.co.uk/news/business-19596192.

BBC News. (2013, February 6). RBS: The embarrassing transcripts. *BBC News*. Available at: https://www.bbc.co.uk/news/business-21358362.

BBC News. (2014, August 27). RBS fined £14.5m over mortgage advice by FCA. *BBC News*. Available at: https://www.bbc.co.uk/news/business-28948518.

BBC News Online. (2013, December 11). RBS fined $100m by US for Iran sanctions violations. *BBC News*. Available at: https://www.bbc.co.uk/news/business-25341882.

BBC News Online. (2015, December 16). RBS outlines Williams & Glyn sale plans. *BBC News*. Available at: https://www.bbc.co.uk/news/uk-scotland-scotland-business-35111705.

Bell, S. (2011). Do we really need a new 'constructivist institutionalism' to explain institutional change? *British Journal of Political Science, 41*, 883–906.

Bell, S., & Hindmoor, A. (2015). *Masters of the universe slaves of the market*. Cambridge, MA: Harvard University Press.

Binham, C. (2018a, January 17). Rogue RBS unit told to 'let customers hang themselves'. *Financial Times*. Available at: https://www.ft.com/content/ecbca106-fbab-11e7-a492-2c9be7f3120a.

Binham, C. (2018b, January 30). RBS drops challenge to scathing report about restructuring unit. *Financial Times*. Available at: https://www.ft.com/content/c1b36dbc-05d0-11e8-9650-9c0ad2d7c5b5.

Binham, C. (2018c, February 8). RBS chair hits back against allegations of misleading UK parliament. *Financial Times*. Available at: https://www.ft.com/content/0116c31e-0cc5-11e8-8eb7-42f857ea9f09.

Binham, C., Arnold, M., Noonan, L., & Chon, G. (2015, May 15). Forex rigging settlement: 10 things you need to know. *Financial Times*. Available at: https://www.ft.com/cms/s/0/a9c85836-fb09-11e4-9aed-00144feab7de.html#axzz41YViGO3G.

Binham, C., & Dunkley, E. (2017, October 16). RBS excludes thousands of small businesses from compensation. *Financial Times*. Available at: https://www.ft.com/content/351172aa-b035-11e7-aab9-abaa44b1e130.

BIS [Bank for International Settlements]. (2010, December). *Basel III: A global regulatory framework for more resilient banks and banking systems* (rev June 2011). Available at: https://www.bis.org/publ/bcbs189.htm.

BIS [Bank for International Settlements]. (2018). *Basel III monitoring report March 2018*. Available at: https://www.bis.org/bcbs/publ/d433.pdf.

Brinded, L. (2013, November 1). Mis-selling PPI scandal: RBS compensation pot hits £2.6bn. *International Business Times*. Available at: https://www.ibtimes.co.uk/rbs-mis-selling-ppi-results-ross-mcewan-518833.

Brinded, L. (2014, August 8). RBS scraps controversial GRG unit criticised in Tomlinson report. *International Business Times*. Available at: https://www.ibtimes.co.uk/rbs-scraps-controversial-grg-unit-criticised-tomlinson-report-1460346.

Cameron, G. (2014, January 27). RBS sets aside £3.1bn for new mortgage and PPI claims. *The Herald Scotland*. Available at: https://www.heraldscotland.com/news/13142627.RBS_sets_aside___3_1bn_for_new_mortgage_and_PPI_claims/.

Dunkley, E. (2016a, February 26). RBS piles up £50bn in losses since crisis. *Financial Times*. Available at: https://www.ft.com/cms/s/0/2b9428ec-dc58-11e5-a72f-1e7744c66818.html#axzz41YViGO3G.

Dunkley, E. (2016b, December 28). Williams & Glyn sale faces Bank of England review. *Financial Times*. Available at: https://www.ft.com/content/739cfc9e-cd17-11e6-864f-20dcb35cede2.

Dunkley, E. (2016c, April 30). RBS sale of Williams & Glyn among most prolonged in history. *Financial Times*. Available at: https://www.ft.com/content/c842fc72-0e08-11e6-ad80-67655613c2d6.

Dunkley, E. (2017a, July 12). RBS to pay £4.2bn for mis-sold US mortgage-backed securities. *Financial Times*. Available at: https://www.ft.com/content/49872ce2-6702-11e7-8526-7b38dcaef614.

Dunkley, E. (2017b, October 23). UK watchdog publishes review of alleged abuses by RBS unit. *Financial Times*. Available at: https://www.ft.com/content/68b3d138-b7fc-11e7-8c12-5661783e5589.

Dunkley, E. (2017c, July 26). RBS deal with EU pushes UK closer to selling stake. *Financial Times*. Available at: https://www.ft.com/content/ac6fe344-721f-11e7-aca6-c6bd07df1a3c.

Dunkley, E. (2017d, September 18). Brussels approves RBS plan for boosting competition. *Financial Times*. Available at: https://www.ft.com/content/95eb931d-680f-3141-90c1-9ee8b1019911.
Dunkley, E., & Arnold, M. (2015a). RBS plans to sell Williams & Glyn next year. *Financial Times*. https://www.ft.com/cms/s/0/87cc4f28-a3c7-11e5-873f-68411a84f346.html#axzz41C1UVFL5.
Dunkley, E., & Arnold, M. (2015b, August 4). Sale of RBS stake marks start of the UK's biggest privatisation. *Financial Times*. Available at: https://www.ft.com/content/8a09333a-39e3-11e5-8613-07d16aad2152.
Edmondson, A., & Moingeon, B. (1999). Learning, trust and organizational change. In M. Easterby-Smith, J. Burgoyne, & L. Araujo (Eds.), *Organizational learning and the learning organization: Developments in theory and practice* (Chapter 9, pp. 157–176). London: Sage.
El Radi, A. (2014, August). *Enhancing quality of capital under Basel III. Ahmad El Radi METAC banking supervision advisor*. Beirut, Lebanon. Available at: https://www.imfmetac.org/Upload/Link3_753_105.pdf.
Erturk, I. (2017, November 16). Shadow banking: A story of the Doppelganger (the Double) in science of finance. *Journal of Cultural Economy, 10*, 377–392.
FCA [Financial Conduct Authority]. (2013, July 24). *Royal Bank of Scotland fined £5.6m for failing to properly report over a third of transactions*. Press Release. Available at: https://www.fca.org.uk/news/rbs-fined.
FCA [Financial Conduct Authority]. (2014, August 27). *FCA fines RBS and NatWest for failures in mortgage advice process*. Press Release. Available at: https://fca.org.uk/news/fca-fines-rbs-and-natwest-for-failures-in-mortgage-advice-process.
FCA [Financial Conduct Authority]. (2017). FCA Handbook: SYSC 19C.3 Remuneration principles. Available at: https://www.handbook.fca.org.uk/handbook/SYSC/19C/3.html?date=2017-09-01.
FINMA [Financial Market Supervisory Authority]. (2017, February 2). *FINMA sanctions Coutts for 1MDB breaches*. FINMA. Available at: https://www.finma.ch/en/news/2017/02/20170202-mm-coutts/.
Forbes.com. (2015, March 19). RBS close to a deal with UBP for sale of Coutts International. *Forbes*. Available at: https://www.forbes.com/sites/greatspeculations/2015/03/19/rbs-close-to-a-deal-with-ubp-for-sale-of-coutts-international/#4eb822d7104c.
Fraser, I. (2014). *Shredded: Inside RBS: The bank that broke Britain*. Edinburgh: Birlin.
FSA [Financial Services Authority]. (2011). *FSA fines RBS and NatWest £2.8m for poor complaint handling*. Press Release. Available at: https://www.fsa.gov.uk/pages/Library/Communication/PR/2011/003.shtml.

FSA [Financial Services Authority]. (2012). *Coutts fined £8.75 million for anti-money laundering control failings*. Press Release. Available at: https://www.fsa.gov.uk/library/communication/pr/2012/032.shtml.

Immelmann, K. (1975). Ecological significance of imprinting and early learning. *Annual Review of Ecology & Systematics, 6*, 15–37.

Inman, P. (2009, December 2). RBS warns cap on bonuses will lead to exodus of top staff. *The Guardian*. Available at: https://www.theguardian.com/business/2009/dec/02/rbs-warns-over-bonus-cap.

Insley, J. (2011, January 11). NatWest and RBS fined £2.8m over complaint handling failures. *The Guardian*. Available at: https://www.theguardian.com/money/2011/jan/11/natwest-rbs-fined-complaint-handling-failures.

James, S., & Quaglia, L. (2020). *The UK & multi-level financial regulation: From post-crisis reform to Brexit*. Oxford: Oxford University Press.

Jenkins, P. (2018, June 1). UKFI goes out without any RBS bang. *Financial Times*. Available at: https://www.ft.com/content/f1f03cb6-64ef-11e8-a39d-4df188287fff.

Kar-Gupta, S. (2012, March 26). Coutts fined 8.75 million pounds for money laundering failures. *Reuters UK*. Available at: https://uk.reuters.com/article/2012/03/26/uk-coutts-fine-idUKBRE82P0BL20120326.

King, M. (2016). *The end of alchemy: Money banking and the future of the global economy*. London: Little Brown.

Knight, J., & Dunkley, J. (2014, February 27). RBS sells Direct Line stake on eve of revealing losses. *The Independent*. Available at: https://www.independent.co.uk/news/business/news/rbs-sells-direct-line-stake-on-eve-of-revealing-losses-9155966.html.

Kollewe, J. (2014, February 26). Royal Bank of Scotland plans to sell remaining 28% stake in Direct Line. *The Guardian*. Available at: https://www.theguardian.com/business/2014/feb/26/royal-bank-scotland-sell-stake-direct-line.

Lambert, R. (2011, December 12). Unchecked excess: the lessons of RBS failure. *Financial Times*. Available at: https://www.ft.com/cms/s/0/c91ca412-24b6-11e1-ac4b-00144feabdc0.html#axzz40R7UIlfX.

Lewin, J. (2016, March 15). RBS slashing 448 investment banking jobs. *Financial Times*. Available at: https://www.ft.com/content/86aaa6da-d176-3b8e-95d6-322067f0a66d.

Macartney, H., & Calcagno, P. (2019). All bark and no bite: The political economy of bank fines in Anglo-America. *Review of International Political Economy, 26*(4), 630–665.

Macaskill, A., & White, L. (2017, May 11). RBS defends directors' bonuses in response to criticism. *Reuters*. Available at: https://www.reuters.com/article/us-rbs-agm/rbs-defends-directors-bonuses-in-response-to-criticism-idUSKBN1871RP.

Martin, I. (2014). *Making it happened: Fred Goodwin and the men who blew up the British economy*. London: Simon & Schuster.
Marquis, C., & Tilcsik, A. (2013, January 9). *Imprinting: Toward a multilevel theory* (Harvard Business School Working Paper. No. 13-061).
Matthew, J. (2015, March 27). RBS confirms sale of Coutts International to Swiss bank UBP. *International Business Times*. Available at: https://www.ibtimes.co.uk/rbs-confirms-sale-coutts-international-swiss-bank-ubp-1493780.
Mayer, M. (1999, May 20, Thursday). *The dangers of derivatives*. The Brookings Institute. Available at: https://www.brookings.edu/opinions/the-dangers-of-derivatives/.
McDonald, O. (2019). *Holding bankers to account: A decade of market manipulation, regulatory failure and regulatory reforms*. Manchester: Manchester University Press.
McEwan, R. (2015a, October 30). *RBS News 2015: RBS completes sale of Citizens Financial Group Inc.* stake. RBS. Available at: https://www.rbs.com/news/2015/october/rbs-completes-sale-of-Citizens-Financial-Group.html.
McEwan, R. (2015b, May 20). *Royal Bank of Scotland plc reaches Foreign Exchange settlements*. RBS. Available at: https://www.rbs.com/news/2015/may/rbs-plc-reaches-foreign-exchange-settlements.html.
McEwan, R. (2018, August 14). The Royal Bank of Scotland Group plc—Declaration of interim dividend. *RBS News and Opinion*. Available at: https://www.rbs.com/rbs/news/2018/08/the-royal-bank-of-scotland-group-plc--declaration-of-interim-div.html.
McLannahan, B. (2015, October 30). Citizens Financial breaks free of Royal Bank of Scotland shackles. *Financial Times*. Available at: https://www.ft.com/cms/s/0/7be28b06-7f18-11e5-93c6-bba4b4b36134.html#axzz41C1UVFL5.
Megaw, N. (2018a, August 15). US investigation highlights extent of wrongdoing at RBS. *Financial Times*. Available at: https://www.ft.com/content/614f9b4c-a07d-11e8-85da-eeb7a9ce36e4.
Megaw, N. (2018b, June 5). UK government takes £2.1bn loss with RBS stake sale. *Financial Times*. Available at: https://www.ft.com/content/5d8eab1e-6889-11e8-b6eb-4acfcfb08c11.
Megaw, N. (2019a, September 4). RBS to take hit of up to £900m from late PPI claims. *Financial Times*. Available at: https://www.ft.com/content/0c8d4e84-cede-11e9-99a4-b5ded7a7fe3f.
Megaw, N. (2019b, September 20). UK lender RBS appoints Alison Rose as chief executive. *Financial Times*. Available at: https://www.ft.com/content/26229e04-db6c-11e9-8f9b-77216ebe1f17.
National Audit Office. (2018). *The return of Lloyds Banking Group to private ownership*. Report by the Comptroller and Auditor General Ordered by the House of Commons to be printed on 21 June 2018. Available

at: https://www.nao.org.uk/wp-content/uploads/2018/06/The-return-of-Lloyds-Banking-Group-to-private-ownership.pdf.

Parker, G., & Jenkins, P. (2013, February 2). RBS to cut bonuses to pay US Libor fine. *Financial Times*. Available at: https://www.ft.com/content/a0dc728a-6d2f-11e2-889d-00144feab49a.

Pickford, J. (2014, August 29). RBS fine over mortgage advice failures 'might not be last'. *Financial Times*. Available at: https://www.ft.com/cms/s/0/55a1f8b2-2ecb-11e4-a054-00144feabdc0.html#axzz3in2bVkIS.

Press Association. (2014, August 27). RBS fined £14.5m over mortgage advice. Press Association *Guardian*. Available at: https://www.theguardian.com/business/2014/aug/27/rbs-fined-mortgage-advice.

Prudential Regulation Authority [Bank of England]. (2011). *Remuneration code—About*. Available at: https://www.bankofengland.co.uk/pra/Pages/supervision/activities/aboutremuneration.aspx.

Prudential Regulation Authority [Bank of England]. (2017, April). *Supervisory Statement | SS2/17 Remuneration*. Available at: https://www.bankofengland.co.uk/-/media/boe/files/prudential-regulation/supervisory-statement/2017/ss217.

PwC [Pricewaterhouse Coopers]. (2013, July). *Regulatory Brief: EU bonus cap to take effect January 1st 2014*. Available at: https://www.pwc.com/us/en/financial-services/regulatory-services/publications/assets/fs-reg-brief-eu-bonus-cap.pdf.

Quinn, J. (2013, September 27). RBS to create new challenger bank under revived 'Williams & Glyn's' brand. *The Telegraph*. Available at: https://www.telegraph.co.uk/finance/newsbysector/banksandfinance/10322675/RBS-to-create-new-challenger-bank-under-revived-Williams-and-Glyns-brand.html.

Quinn, J., & Wilson, H. (2011, January 8). RBS chief Stephen Hester awarded a £2.5m bonus. *The Telegraph*. Available at: https://www.telegraph.co.uk/finance/newsbysector/banksandfinance/8248374/RBS-chief-Stephen-Hester-awarded-a-2.5m-bonus.html.

Rankin, J. (2013, July 24). RBS fined £5.6m by FCA for 'pervasive' reporting failures. *The Guardian*. Available at: https://www.theguardian.com/business/2013/jul/24/rbs-fined-fca-share-dealing-reporting-failure.

Rayner, G. (2009, January 20). Banking bailout: The rise and fall of RBS. *The Telegraph*. Available at: https://www.telegraph.co.uk/finance/newsbysector/banksandfinance/4291807/Banking-bailout-The-rise-and-fall-of-RBS.html.

RBS [Royal Bank of Scotland]. (2007). *Annual report and accounts 2007*. Available at: https://www.investors.rbs.com/~/media/Files/R/RBS-IR/annual-reports/rbs-group-accounts-2007.pdf.

RBS [Royal Bank of Scotland]. (2008). *Annual report and accounts 2008*. Available at: https://www.investors.rbs.com/~/media/Files/R/RBS-IR/annual-reports/rbs-group-accounts-2008.pdf.

RBS [Royal Bank of Scotland]. (2009a). *Annual report and accounts 2009.* Available at: https://investors.rbs.com/~/media/Files/R/RBS-IR/annual-reports/rbs-group-accounts-2009.pdf.
RBS [Royal Bank of Scotland]. (2009b, November 27). *Proposed accession to the Asset Protection Scheme and B Share and Dividend Access Share issues.* RBS Investor Relation. Available at: https://investors.natwestgroup.com/~/media/Files/R/RBS-IR-V2/corporate-actions/asset-protection-scheme-and-b-share-issuance/asset-protection-scheme-and-b-share-issuance-1.pdf.
RBS [Royal Bank of Scotland]. (2010). *Annual report and accounts 2010.* Available at: https://www.investors.rbs.com/~/media/Files/R/RBS-IR/annual-reports/rbs-group-annual-report-and-accounts-10.pdf.
RBS [Royal Bank of Scotland]. (2012). *Annual report and accounts 2012.* Available at: https://www.investors.rbs.com/~/media/Files/R/RBS-IR/annual-reports/annual-report-2012.pdf.
RBS [Royal Bank of Scotland]. (2013). *Annual report and accounts 2013: Serve customers well. This is our purpose.* Available at: https://www.investors.rbs.com/~/media/Files/R/RBS-IR/2013-reports/annual-report-and-accounts-2013.pdf.
RBS [Royal Bank of Scotland]. (2014a). *Annual report and accounts 2014: Earning our customers' trust.* Available at: https://investors.rbs.com/~/media/Files/R/RBS-IR/2014-reports/annual-report-2014.pdf.
RBS [Royal Bank of Scotland]. (2014b, April 25). *The Royal Bank of Scotland Group plc, 25th April, 2014 annual report and accounts 2013, Strategic report 2013, Pillar 3 Disclosure 2013.* Available at: https://hsprod.investis.com/ir/rbsl/ir.jsp?page=news item&item=1745474709094400.
RBS [Royal Bank of Scotland]. (2015). *Annual report and accounts 2015: Building a strong, simple, fair bank.* Available at: http://www.investors.rbs.com/~/media/Files/R/RBS-IR/resultscenter/annual-report-2015.pdf.
RBS [Royal Bank of Scotland]. (2016). *Annual report and accounts 2016: Creating a simple, safe, customer-focused bank.* Available at: https://investors.natwestgroup.com/~/media/Files/R/RBS-IR-V2/results-center/annual-report-2016.pdf.
RBS [Royal Bank of Scotland]. (2017). *Annual report and accounts 2017: Becoming simple, safe and customer focused.* Available at: https://investors.natwestgroup.com/~/media/Files/R/RBS-IR-V2/results-center/annual-report-2017.pdf.
RBS [Royal Bank of Scotland]. (2018). *Annual report and accounts 2018: Building a simple, safe and more customer focused bank.* Available at: https://investors.natwestgroup.com/~/media/Files/R/RBS-IR-V2/results-center/annual-report-2018.pdf.
RBS [Royal Bank of Scotland]. (2019). *Annual report and accounts 2019: We champion potential, helping people, families and businesses to thrive.* Available

at: https://investors.rbs.com/~/media/Files/R/RBS-IR/results-center/annual-report-2019.pdf.

RBS.com [Royal Bank of Scotland]. (2015, May 20). Royal Bank of Scotland plc reaches Foreign Exchange settlements. RBS. Available at: https://www.rbs.com/news/2015/may/rbs-plc-reaches-foreign-exchange-settlements.html.

RBS Online. (2013, December 4). *RBS reaches settlement with the European Commission*. Available at: https://www.rbs.com/news/2013/12/rbs-reaches-settlement-with-the-european-commission.html.

Rose, R. (1991). What is lesson-drawing? *Journal of Public Policy, 11*(1), 3–30.

Rose, R. (1993). *Lesson-drawing in public policy: A guide to learning across time and space*. Chatham, NJ: Chatham House Publishers.

Rose, R. (2005). *Learning from comparative public policy: A practical guide*. London: Routledge.

Ross, A. (2017, February 2). Coutts sanctioned by Swiss regulator over 1MDB. *Financial Times*. Available at: https://www.ft.com/content/27e0771d-b086-37a4-bb09-a5c54b8a880d.

Royal Bank of Scotland. (1998). *Royal Bank of Scotland annual report and accounts 1998*. Available at: https://investors.natwestgroup.com/reports-archive/archived.

Samuels, B. (2019). *FCA remuneration code guide*. Kervin & Barnes Solicitors Online Resources. Available at: https://www.kervinandbarnes.co.uk/resources/fca-remuneration-code-guide/.

Scannell, K. (2013, December 11). RBS settles US sanctions case with $100m pact. *Financial Times*. Available at: https://www.ft.com/cms/s/0/a28f9064-6291-11e3-bba5-00144feabdc0.html#axzz41YViGO3G.

Schafer, D., & Arnold, M. (2014, April 13). City bankers to evade EU bonus cap with 'role-based' allowances. *Financial Times*. Available at: https://www.ft.com/cms/s/0/02213446-c19d-11e3-b95f-00144feabdc0.html#axzz3hlYESIG9.

Scuffham, M. (2014, February 12). RBS to shrink investment bank and cut 30,000 jobs—Sources. *Reuters UK*. Available at: https://uk.reuters.com/article/2014/02/21/uk-rbs-restructuring-idUKBREA1K0FR20140221.

Scuffham, M. (2015, February 27). RBS shrinks investment bank, posts 3.5 billion-pound loss. *Reuters UK*. Available at: https://uk.reuters.com/article/2015/02/27/uk-rbs-results-idUKKBN0LU0HO20150227.

Selznick, P. (1957). *Leadership in administration: A sociological interpretation*. New York: Harper & Row.

Shubber, K. (2018, March 6). RBS in $500m mis-selling settlement with New York State. *Financial Times*. Available at: https://www.ft.com/content/fb30c9c8-2181-11e8-a895-1ba1f72c2c11.

Simon. H. A. (1983/1999). *Reason in human affairs*. Stanford, CA: Stanford University Press.

Simon. H. A. (1995, March). Rationality in political behaviour. *Political Psychology 16*(1) (Special Issue: Political Economy and Political Psychology), 45–61

Simon, H. A. (1957). *Models of man*. New York: Wiley.

Simon, H. A. (1998). *The sciences of the artificial* (3rd ed.). Cambridge: MIT Press.

Smith, M. K. (2011, 2013). *Chris Argyris: Theories of action, double-loop learning and organizational learning*. The Encyclopaedia of Informal Education. Available at: https://infed.org/mobi/chris-argyris-theories-of-action-double-loop-learning-and-organizational-learning/. Accessed 11 April 2014.

Stinchcombe, A. L. (1965). Social structure and organizations. In J. G. March (Ed.), *Handbook of organizations* (pp. 142–193). Chicago: Rand McNally & Co.

The Telegraph. (2009, August 13). RBS spends more than £10m hiring two bankers. *The Telegraph*. Available at: https://www.telegraph.co.uk/finance/newsbysector/banksandfinance/6020004/RBS-spends-more-than-10m-hiring-two-bankers.html.

Tomlinson, L. (2013). Banks' lending practices: Treatment of businesses in distress. Available at: https://www.tomlinsonreport.com/docs/tomlinsonReport.pdf.

Treanor, J. (2009, December 15). RBS chief blasts 'politicisation' of bank. *The Guardian*. Available at: https://www.theguardian.com/business/2009/dec/15/rbs-bank-bonuses.

Treanor, J. (2010a, February 26). Bonuses: RBS admits that more than 100 bankers awarded over £1m each. *The Guardian*. Available at: https://www.theguardian.com/business/2010/feb/25/bonus-rbs-bankers.

Treanor, J. (2010b, February 25). Analysis: Royal Bank of Scotland and bankers' bonuses. *The Guardian*. Available at: https://www.theguardian.com/business/2010/feb/25/royal-bank-of-scotland-bonuses-analysis.

Treanor, J. (2012a, March 26). Queen's banker fined for poor money laundering checks. *The Guardian*. Available at: https://www.theguardian.com/business/2012/mar/26/coutts-fined-money-laundering-checks.

Treanor, J. (2012b). RBS unveils Direct Line insurance IPO. *The Guardian*. Available at: https://www.theguardian.com/business/2012/sep/14/rbs-direct-line-insurance-ipo.

Treanor, J. (2013, September 27). RBS sells 314 branches to church-backed Corsair consortium. *The Guardian*. Available at: https://www.theguardian.com/business/2013/sep/27/rbs-branches-church-corsair-consortium.

Treanor, J. (2015, March 3). RBS could cut 14,000 staff in retreat from US and Asia. *The Guardian*. Available at: https://www.theguardian.com/business/2015/mar/03/rbs-could-cut-14000-staff-us-asia-ross-mcewan.

Treanor, J. (2016, November 7). RBS to set up compensation fund for small businesses. *The Guardian*. Available at: https://www.theguardian.com/business/2016/nov/07/rbs-to-set-up-compensation-fund-for-small-businesses.

Treasury Select Committee [House of Commons Treasury Committee]. (2018). *Ross McEwan RBS GRG—Correspondence between Ross McEwan and Rt Hon Nicky Morgan MP 9th January 2018*. Available Online at: https://www.parliament.uk/documents/commons-committees/treasury/Ross-McEwan-RBS-GRG-090118.pdf.

Trotman, A. (2015, October 29). RBS to sell off final stake in US bank Citizens. *The Telegraph*. Available at: https://www.telegraph.co.uk/finance/newsbysector/banksandfinance/11964598/RBS-to-sell-off-final-stake-in-US-bank-Citizens.html.

Tuckman, B. (2016). Derivatives: Understanding their usefulness and their role in the financial crisis. *Journal of Applied Corporate Finance, 28*(1), 62–71.

US Department of the Treasury. (2013, December 11). *Treasury department reaches $33 million settlement with the Royal Bank of Scotland plc*. Available at: https://www.treasury.gov/press-center/press-releases/Pages/jl2239.aspx.

Wearden, G. (2011, May 5). How the PPI scandal unfolded. *The Guardian*. Available at: https://www.theguardian.com/business/2011/may/05/how-ppi-scandal-unfolded.

Werdigier, J. (2009, February 26). Record Loss at Royal Bank of Scotland. *The New York Times*. Available at: https://www.nytimes.com/2009/02/27/business/worldbusiness/27rbos.html?_r=0.

Wilson, H. (2013, July 24). RBS fined £5.6m over reporting failures. *The Telegraph*. Available at: https://www.telegraph.co.uk/finance/newsbysector/banksandfinance/10199474/RBS-fined-5.6m-over-reporting-failures.html.

Wilson, H., Aldrick, P., & Ahmed, K. (2011, May 6). Royal Bank of Scotland investigation: The full story of how the 'world's biggest bank' went bust. *The Telegraph*. Available at: https://www.telegraph.co.uk/finance/newsbysector/banksandfinance/8496654/Royal-Bank-of-Scotland-investigation-the-full-story-of-how-the-worlds-biggest-bank-went-bust.html.

CHAPTER 5

Lloyds: To the Brink and Back

Introduction

Lloyds Banking Group was formed in 2009[1] when Lloyds TSB successfully acquired Halifax Bank of Scotland (HBOS) in a takeover bid worth an estimated £12 billion (LloydsBankingGroup.com, 2016). Lloyds TSB had entered the GFC in good health, recording pre-tax profits of £4 billion and £2.2 billion in 2007 and 2008, respectively. The bank had always enjoyed a reputation as being a well-run, conservative, even boring, institution with its conservatism often making it the butt of jokes amongst City highfliers. Lloyds TSB had largely avoided the lucrative trappings of the US subprime market and its investment bank was modest when compared to its peers (Bell and Hindmoor, 2015). Instead, Lloyds TSB had grown its business organically, focusing upon more traditional activities such residential mortgage lending and wealth management (Fallon, 2015). When HBOS ran into trouble in late 2008, Lloyds TSB were one of the few banks in a strong position to take over the failing institution. However, the merger would prove to be a disaster as the newly formed Lloyds Banking Group (Lloyds hereafter) was quickly overcome by the number of bad exposures contained, primarily, within the HBOS book and which left the bank on the verge of

[1] Because Lloyds was formed in January 2009, the analysis in this chapter will cover the period 2009–2018.

A. Barber, *UK Banks and the Lessons of the Great Financial Crisis*, Building a Sustainable Political Economy: SPERI Research & Policy, https://doi.org/10.1007/978-3-030-70254-0_5

collapse. Following a series of failed attempts to raise capital, and with legacy losses mounting, Lloyds had little option but to accept financial assistance from the UK Government that, in February 2009, would become a 43% stakeholder in the bank (Bell and Hindmoor, 2015).

Chapter Overview

In this chapter, I argue that despite Lloyds' catastrophic failure and subsequent bailout, the bank has learned lessons from the GFC and has taken tangible steps towards regaining its former reputation as a well-run and cautious institution. Indeed, in 2011, just two years after its rescue by the UK taxpayer, Lloyds would embark upon a group-wide evaluation of its business model and overall strategic direction. The result of this appraisal would culminate in the publication of the Strategic Review 2011 (the Review hereafter). While now rather dated, the Review has been a key conduit for change at the group and the defining moment in Lloyds' post-crash recovery, ushering in a series of policies that have fundamentally changed the bank, its business model and strategic orientation.

For example, policies introduced by the Review have significantly strengthened the group's internal governance framework by delayering the management structure and devolving power and authority away from any one person or committee. The group's new governance framework also has a much flatter structure whereby specialist sub-committees, previously held outside the upper echelons of senior management, are able to make direct challenges to the board; the audit committee; board risk committee; and group chief executive, thereby encouraging cross-divisional appraisals and increasing oversight and accountability.

The way in which Lloyds rewards employees has also undergone significant change post-crisis. The primary focus of this change has been to place much greater emphasis upon long-term growth by aligning employee remuneration with sustainable shareholder value creation. In particular, Lloyds has restructured its variable pay to include the use of more long-term bonuses such as options and share awards as well as introducing a £2000 cap on all cash bonuses. Variable remuneration for executive directors is now paid exclusively in shares.

Similarly, the group's balance sheet has also seen substantive change following the GFC and the publication of the Review. Lloyds' reliance upon short-term funding has decreased while customer deposits have increased, trading liabilities have been cut by more than half and the group has reduced its oversees presence from thirty to just six countries and shed more than £250 billion from the balance sheet. As such, the Review represents not only the search for and evaluation of new information but, importantly, the application of lessons learned. Consequently, in this section of the book I argue that Lloyds has been to the brink and back.

Factors Explaining Lloyds' Ability to Learn

Lloyds' ability to learn lessons from the GFC can be explained by two central concepts drawn from the account of learning presented in Chapter 2. In particular, ideas associated with the learning space theory (see, e.g., Edmondson, 1996; Edmondson and Monigeon, 1999; Simon, 1957, 1983, 1995, 1998; Smith, 2011, 2013) and Rose's (1991, 1993, 2005) policy learning framework—specifically synthesis learning—may best explain how and, importantly, why the bank has been a successful learner.

Learning space theory is associated with the field of behavioural economics (see, e.g., Simon, 1957; 1983, 1995, 1998), organisational studies (see, e.g., Edmondson, 1996; Edmondson and Monigeon, 1999) and education science (see, e.g., Smith, 2011, 2013). The learning space theory contends that in order for an organisation to learn it must first have the space necessary to undertake a thorough evaluation of its institutional underlying theories-in-use—these being an organisation's guiding principles, philosophies and standard operating procedures (Argyris et al., 1985; Argyris and Schon, 1996). In this context, space is understood as being the dedication of both time and resources—human and fiscal capital—towards the self-reflective process inherent in learning (Smith, 2011, 2013).

In the wake of the GFC, Lloyds has deployed its learning space efficiently by undertaking a group-wide evaluation of its business model and standard operating procedures in light of the lessons of the crisis—as is encapsulated by the Review. In doing so, the bank has protected its precious time and resources that may have otherwise been lost on firefighting missions. For example, Lloyds, like its counterparts at RBS, has suffered a number of post-crash regulatory scandals and governance breaches that have threatened to undermine learning by eroding the group's time and resources. However, what sets Lloyds apart from its rivals is that when confronted with failures, either contemporary or historical, the bank has not dealt with these matters on a case-by-case basis, as is common with firefighting. Instead, the bank has treated problems holistically by examining the underlying theories-in-use that allowed such incidents to occur. Moreover, when matters with the potential to hamper learning have arisen, Lloyds has dealt with these issues quickly and decisively, thus further freeing-up and preserving the learning space. This effective management and protection of space may explain why the group has demonstrated a greater propensity for learning. Indeed, the learning space literature suggests that the more space applied to the introspective process, the greater the likelihood of learning (Smith, 2011, 2013).

The creation and preservation of learning space has then allowed Lloyds to utilise factors associated with the synthesis policy-learning framework. Synthesis learning is synonymous with the work of the political scientist Richard Rose (1991, 1993, 2005) and suggests that an organisation will increase its propensity to learn when policies drawn from either endogenous or exogenous sources, and that have a proven track record—either positive or negative—are synthesised to create new policies (Rose, 1991: 22). Rose (ibid) submits that in order to ensure successful implementation, newly formed policies ought to be accompanied by a very specific set of operating procedures and performance metrics that should be used to evaluate and ensure that new policies are both efficient and adhered to.

The commissioning and subsequent application of the findings of the Review highlights Lloyds' utilisation of the synthesis-learning framework. The group has made use of 'adjacent information' (Rose, 1991: 13) gathered from its own internal practices, rival organisations and other exogenous sources to evaluate its underlying theories-in-use. Consequently, this new information has been synthesised into a series policy responses that have in-turn been instilled by a number of key performance indicators as a means of ensuring the implementation and uptake of new ideas.

Thus, this chapter argues that Lloyds' ability to learn can be attributed to these two non-exclusive concepts of learning with evidence of both the learning space theory and policy-learning framework featuring strongly in Lloyds post-crash recovery. Moreover, changes to Lloyds' business model and standard operating procedures following the GFC are representative of a bank that is now safer and poses a significantly reduced threat to the wider system of globalised financial markets.

The Strategic Review 2011

Following the GFC Lloyds were quick to realise that a more 'sustainable' and 'resilient' business model was needed to avert further disaster and regain 'customers' trust' (Lloyds 2011a: 1). Consequently, Lloyds would promise major reform and subsequently announced a group-wide evaluation of its underlying business model, standard operating procedures and overall strategic orientation. The Strategic Review 2011 would have three immediate objectives: *first*, increase customer expectations by transforming the group into a more open and transparent organisation; *second*, increase capital and liquidity; *third*, deleverage the balance sheet and increase cost efficiency (Lloyds, 2011a: 9).

The Review would also contain a number of specific initiatives particular to individual facets of the business that would align the lessons of the GFC to Lloyds' new business model more broadly.[2] As such, while the Strategic Review 2011 now seems like a rather dated document given the speed at which banking and financial markets move, the importance of the Review remains so due to this key document being a catalyst for the group's post-crash recovery and subsequent learning experience. I argue in the coming sections that transformations stemming from the Review provide us with a number of tangible examples of a fundamental reappraisal of the group's underlying theories-in-use that is indicative of double-loop learning and change.

Governance and Regulation

In the immediate aftermath of the GFC Lloyds were quick to recognise the role that banks' internal governance and risk oversight and control functions had played in the global meltdown (Lloyds, 2009). In 2009, Lloyds told investors that the absence of a robust internal regulatory framework had been a key contributor to the 2008 crisis and had greatly compromised institutions (ibid). Then in 2011, Antonio Horta-Osorio, the newly appointed group chief executive, told delegates at the Bank of America Merrill Lynch Conference that what had separated banks that navigated the crisis successfully from those that had failed, was the presence of effective internal oversight and strong institutional governance controls (Horta-Osorio in Lloyds, 2011b). Furthermore, Horta-Osorio

[2] These will be outlined for the reader throughout the chapter accordingly.

added that those banks that had mitigated the worst effects of the crisis had been more risk-aware than their counterparts that had experienced the greatest difficulties and sustained the largest losses (ibid).

As such, we can see that in the years following the GFC Lloyds, along with key agents at the bank, acknowledged the role that defunct institutional governance and risk controls functions had played in the crash. These observations thus suggest the presence of single-loop learning with Lloyds correctly identifying a central cause of the crisis—as highlighted in Chapter 3. Importantly however, Lloyds has moved beyond the single-loop learning process by enshrining lessons learned with a number of tangible policy initiatives that are indicative of more substantive double-loop learning. Indeed, one of the central tenants of Lloyds' restructuring following the GFC, and which is set out in the Review, is a commitment to 'strengthen' both the bank's management team and governance structure (Lloyds, 2011a: 1). Specifically, this would include making new additions to the executive as part of the group's commitment to deliver 'improved control' (ibid, p. 6). Likewise, Lloyds would also announce a 'delayering' of the group's governance structure to create a 'flatter' and more simplified organisation (Lloyds, 2011a: 3). The objective of this initiative was to make senior management more accessible to both customers and frontline staff thus eliminating barriers between different facets of the business (ibid)—a factor that has also been synonymous with the silo effect discussed in Chapter 3.

New Additions to Management Team

On this first promise—strengthening the management team—Lloyds certainly appear to have delivered results. A simple survey of the membership and composition of the group's board shows that no non-executive or executive director who sat on the Lloyds TSB and HBOS boards in 2008 held a position on the Lloyds board of directors as of 2018 (Lloyds, 2009, 2018). These departures, including two chairman—Sir Victor Blank who left in September 2009 and his replacement Sir Winfried Bischoff who retired in April 2014—and one group chief executive—Eric Daniels, who parted ways with Lloyds in February 2011—are by no means exceptional and are characteristic of the kind of turnover of personnel we would expect to see from a large organisation such as Lloyds. However, what is of particular interest to the current discussion of post-crash bank learning is both the recruitment process behind new appointments and the individuals selected by Lloyds to fill its most senior roles. Indeed, an examination of these procedures may be indicative of the group's ability to harness 'adjacent information', as detailed by the work of Richard Rose (1991, 1993, 2005), and consequently evidence of peer-to-peer learning.

When Victor Blank, Winfried Bischoff and Eric Daniels announced that they would be leaving Lloyds, the group established specialist sub-committees made up of both independent and non-executive directors to oversee the selection and appointment of suitable replacements (Lloyds, 2009, 2013). Meetings to discuss potential candidates were open to all non-executive directors who were actively encouraged to attend these specialist sessions (ibid, 2009, 2013). On each occasion, the committees met several times throughout the succession periods to discuss fine-grain details concerning shortlists, role specifications and the proposed terms and conditions of potential candidates. In all instances, institutional stake-holders, including the UKFI, were consulted throughout and gave their full confidence to final decisions made (Lloyds, 2009, 2013).

While the succession process usedto appoint Norman Blackwell as chairman and Antonio Horta-Osorio as GCE, may not upon first reading appear exceptional, and is perhaps in-keeping with what we would expect from a major bank or business, what sets Lloyds' process apart is the engagement with, and involvement of, institutional stakeholders in the decision-making process. For instance, throughout the recruitment of the aforementioned executives, the input and approval of UKFI was expressly sought and went beyond a simple shareholder vote on candidates.[3] Literature taken from the field of strategic management, set out in Chapter 2, suggests that an organisation may be more prone to learning when key decisions are taken out of the hands of any one individual (Brackenet al., 2005). The work of Bracken et al. (2005) argues that an organisation will have a greater propensity to learn when institutional stakeholders are consulted and are directly involved in the decision-making process. In this instance, Lloyds deliberately sought the input of UKFI on the recruitment and appointment of key agents at the bank.[4] As such, the role of

[3] Moreover, the active participation of UKFI and Lloyds' encouragement of such, stands in stark opposition to that of RBS which, as we have seen in the previous chapter, has been somewhat of a confrontational relationship.

[4] Beyond this, UKFI has also backed and voted in favour of all suggested resolutions at the bank's annual general meetings between 2011 and 2017 (UKFI online).

UKFI in the selection of senior executives—which goes beyond what we would typically expect from a majority shareholder—may be indicative of learning as in keeping with the strategic management literature, with this important institutional stakeholder being an active participant in the decision-making process at Lloyds.

The appointment of Antonio Horta-Osorio in March 2011 along with other prominent senior executives, including Juan Colombas (appointed November 2013), may likewise suggest the presence of learning as described by Rose's (1991, 1993, 2005) policy-learning framework and particularly synthesis and hybrid theories of learning. According to the author, both synthesis and hybrid learning occur when an organisation draws upon 'adjacent information' from its peers[5] (ibid). In this case, Lloyds has recruited senior executives from rival organisations that not only bring with them a wealth of knowledge and banking practice but, importantly, possess very specific experience particular to Lloyds' own circumstances. This expertise, or adjacent information, has then been imparted upon the group with these key agents influencing policy and driving strategic decisions.[6]

For instance, upon his arrival at Lloyds, Mr Colombas had over thirty years' experience within the banking and finance sector and previously served at Santander UK operations as chief risk officer (CRO) under Antonio Horta-Osorio. Moreover, prior to joining Santander Mr Colombas held a number of senior risk and control positions at various banks and financial intermediaries across the globe (Lloyds, 2015a). Equally, before joining Lloyds, Mr Horta-Osorio likewise worked for some of the world's biggest banks, including CitiBank, Goldman Sachs and Santander where he ran a number of operations (Kollewe, 2010).[7] Importantly however, during his time at Santander, Mr Horta-Osorio, with Juan Colombas as his CRO, oversaw the successful integration of the Bradford and Bingley and Alliance and Leicester brands into the

[5] See Chapter 2 page 39–40 for further discussion.

[6] Moreover the recruitment of senior managers and the strengthening of the management team was key objective of the *Review* (Lloyds, 2011a: 6) which, as argued above, has been instrumental in Lloyds' post-crisis recovery.

[7] Furthermore, Antonio has also held positions at the highest level including; chief executive officer at Alliance & Leicester plc, chief executive officer of Santander UK, executive vice president at Banco Santander and head of capital markets at CitiBank (BloombergBusiness.com, 2015).

Santander group (ibid). Intrinsically, Mr Horta-Osorio and Mr Colombas have an intimate knowledge of managing the successful incorporation of an already established banking brand into a larger group—a particularly salient factor given Lloyds' position.

The takeover of Bradford and Bingley and Alliance and Leicester by Santander would also mean that Antonio Horta-Osorio and Juan Colombas would bring with them to Lloyds valuable experience of working closely with the UK Government—an important element given the UKFI's position as a majority shareholder. During their tenure at Santander, Mr Horta-Osorio and Mr Colombas worked tirelessly with government officials and regulators at a time of heightened instability to assimilate Bradford and Bingley and Alliance and Leicester into the Santander organisation (Dunkley and Jenkins, 2017). The timely and effective merger of the institutions would win Antonio Horta-Osorio and Juan Colombas admiration from both the UK Government and the banking fraternity, with the takeover deemed as a huge success for all parties involved (ibid).

Furthermore, Mr Horta-Osorio has a proven track record of prioritising long-term economic value over, potentially harmful, short-term gains. During his tenure at Santander, Antonio Horta-Osorio was charged with achieving a combined 10% market share for the Abbey National, Alliance and Leicester and Bradford and Bingley brands (Kollewe, 2010). However, realising that the targeted 10% within the timescale set by Santander was both unsustainable and could potentially expose the group to undue risk, Mr Horta-Osorio, under advisement from his close college and CRO, Juan Colombas, re-negotiated the deadline set by the Santander board of directors. After successfully incorporating the three brands into the Santander group, Mr Horta-Osorio and his team would then go-on to return a consistent market share of approximately 14% thus surpassing the board's original targets (ibid).

Inappointing Antonio Horta-Osorio as GCE and Juan Colombas as CRO,[8] Lloyds appear to have selected candidates that have demonstrated both a willingness and ability to resist structural competitive pressures and direct the group clear of riskier, yet higher rewarding, business strategies.[9]

[8] In 2017, Mr Colombas would go on to become Lloyds' chief operating officer.

[9] Indeed, upon the announcement of his retirement in 2019, Lloyds noted that Mr Colombas had played a 'critical role' in Lloyds' post-crash recovery and the restructuring of the balance sheet towards a more long-term, sustainable foundation (Lloyds, 2019a).

This is particularly important because, as established above, powerful and authoritative agents, both in the run up to the crisis and today, possess the ability to steer and shape institutions. Moreover, Mr Horta-Osorio's and Mr Colombas' experience of successfully integrating several businesses into one organisation and building a working relationship with the UK Government and regulators, is a key example of Lloyds ability to transport information across time and space and which has informed the bank's own learning journey. Likewise, as detailed below, Mr Horta-Osorio has not simply been a passive CEO but has instead initiated a number of strategic decisions that have enhanced learning by defending the group's learning space. As such, it may be possible to conclude that the selection of Antonio Horta-Osorio and Juan Colombas is indicative of peer-to-peer learning with Lloyds harnessing the adjacent information of its newly appointed senior executives.

Delayering of Management and Risk Governance Structure

Another key element of Lloyds' post-crash recovery plan has been the restructuring of the group's managerial and risk governance framework. In particular, the Review would identify the need to 'delayer' the bank's governance structure in order to make senior management more accountable to customers and frontline staff while also reducing barriers between departments (Lloyds, 2011a: 1). Lloyds consequently introduced a number of reforms that has resulted in a more robust control framework with increased oversight and integration between departments across the business. For example, in 2009, the governance structure at Lloyds was divided along three distinct lines, namely, *the first line of defence*; *the second line of defence* and *the third line of defence* (Lloyds, 2009). The most senior feature of the first line of defence was the group board with whom sole operational authority resided (ibid). However, by 2018 responsibility for the most senior branch of group risk governance and oversight had been divided amongst ten separate bodies as opposed to just one as was the case in 2009 (Lloyds, 2009, 2018).

As discussed in Chapter 3, one of the central causes of the GFC was that the authority of the most senior figures within banks often went unchallenged,[10] thereby allowing managers to ride roughshod over

[10] See Chapter 3 page 74–76 for further discussion.

junior colleges even when strategic decisions were erroneous (Davies, 2010; Bank of England, 2015). However, the devolvement of power and authority away from one, to ten separate committees suggest greater accountability at the most senior level. The revised governance structure places each committee, which has specialist knowledge of its designated business area, in a strong position to challenge, guide and temper the strategic decisions of one another and the group's board. Similarly, this new decentralised structure should allow expertise within specific areas of the bank to flourish by removing the unchecked authority of senior management thus, reducing the possibility of staff with expert knowledge being coerced into endorsing or pursuing business strategies that they believe to be flawed.

In 2009, the second line of defence consisted of a number of committees and divisional risk officers. By 2018, the second line of defence had been upgraded with the inclusion of a number of additional committees covering eight key areas of risk. Yet, what is of particular significance is how the structure and role of the second line of defence have been strengthened post-crisis. In 2009, the main function of the second line of defence was to report to, and support, committees located within the first line of defence (Lloyds, 2009). An important feature of the updated 2018 model is the addition of powers that allow the second line of defence to launch independent challenges on the first line of defence, thereby adding a further layer of oversight and accountability. Similarly, from 2014 onwards, executive and non-executive directors upon leaving the group would be compelled to provide the chairman and board with a written statement addressing any concerns that they may have regarding the bank's governance and overall strategic direction (Lloyds, 2015a, 2018).

The revision of Lloyds' governance and internal risk framework post-GFC suggests that the bank has achieved its goal of 'delayering' the management structure as set out by the Review. Importantly, this delayering has increased accountability by encouraging cross-divisional appraisals and the use of independent challenges that collectively have the potential to increase internal oversight. Additionally, the reshaping of the first and second lines of defence suggests that managerial networks have been strengthened by directly linking senior figures located across all departments to one another and the group board. The upgrading and restructuring of the governance framework suggest that oversight at Lloyds is now stronger than in 2009 as the performance of different departments and business areas are subject to enhanced scrutiny and internal critique. This has been made possible by a risk governance framework that is clearly more self-reflexive, joined-up and flatter post-crisis and which should also address the silo effect with greater permeation between departments. Such changes bring with them the potential to increase top-down/bottom-up learning by allowing information to flow more freely from one source to another. This, according to the work of Bracken et al. (2005), will increase an organisation's propensity for learning by smoothing the exchange of information and allowing organisations to overcome pre-existing cognitive biases. Accordingly, Lloyds' post-crisis governance structure represents a number of substantive structural and cultural changes at the group, in keeping with the objectives of the Review, that are indicative of learning and change.

Controversies

Though Lloyds has demonstrated evidence of learning in relation to the composition of the management team and structure of the group's risk governance framework, the bank has also come under a great deal of scrutiny concerning its involvement in a number of high profile regulatory failures that have threatened to undermine the group's post-crisis recovery. However, while it is true that Lloyds, like its rivals, has faced a number of governance and regulatory issues that have threatened to erode learning, what sets the bank apart from its peers, such as RBS, is that the group has dealt with these challenges in a timely and decisive manner. Consequently, Lloyds has been able to protect and preserve its learning space—time and resources—from undue pressures and may explain why the bank has been a successful learner despite some regulatory breaches.

Trading Sanctions and 'Making the Sale'

In January 2009, the United States Department of Justice fined Lloyds £231 million after it was brought to light that Lloyds TSB had knowingly engaged in the transfer of funds to sanctioned countries including Iran, Libya and Sudan (Clark, 2009). A Report published by Global Witness details how Lloyds TSB had, for almost two decades, been involved in the so-called stripping of customer details from dollar wire transfers, with the bank dedicating specialist teams to removing customer account particulars in order to circumvent US stipulations (Global Witness, 2009).[11] By facilitating such flows, Lloyds TSB were found to be in direct violation of US law which forbade financial transactions with sanctioned countries (ibid).[12]

Then, in 2013 Lloyds would receive a record fine of approximately £28 million for 'serious' retail conduct failures following an investigation by the FCA (FCA, 2013). It was found that between 2010 and 2012 employees at Lloyds TSB, Bank of Scotland and Halifax came under immense pressure—known by frontline staff as the 'sell or be demoted' incentive plan—to sell to customers a raft of financial products including investments and insurance (Hawkes and Armstrong, 2013). While bonuses for meeting tough monthly targets included champagne and 'a grand in your hand', staff who failed to meet targets were lambasted in front of colleagues and faced the threat of demotion or termination (ibid). It was reported that confronted with such perverse incentives, employees had sold products to themselves, family members and other colleagues in order to avoid ridicule and loss of their position (Hawkes and Armstrong, 2013).

While these incidents may appear, upon first reading, to stand in contrast to the hypothesis extended so far in the chapter, evidence of lesson learning can still be observed despite such failures. For example, following these occurrences, the FCA noted that Lloyds had since made 'substantial changes' to its internal governance framework and had put in place policies that should 'right many of these wrongs' (FCA, 2013). The City regulator likewise concluded that it was confident that initiatives subsequently introduced by Lloyds had been adequate to address key gaps that had allowed such breaches to occur (ibid).

The literature on learning tells us that an organisation has a greater propensity to learn when changes in the learning subject's underlying theories-in-use are accompanied and upheld by specific policies initiatives

[11] We should note that all the banks in this study have been found guilty of similar breaches with RBS, Barclays and HSBC all having been investigated and subsequently fined by the United States Department of Justice.

[12] While it was Lloyds Banking Group that was ultimately held responsible for these actions, we should note that the incident in question predated the formation of Lloyds Banking Group and the Review 2011, which, it is argued in this chapter, represents the starting point of Lloyds learning journey.

(Rose, 1991: 22). In addition to making 'substantial changes' to its governance and regulatory oversight framework, Lloyds has similarly shifted how success is measured and rewarded at the bank. In the years that followed these regulatory failures, Lloyds moved its remunerative practices away from 'making the sale' to a strategy that prioritises improved customer satisfaction and service (Lloyds, 2013: 33), thereby suggesting a cultural shift in relation to performance-linked pay.[13] Consequently, while these incidents represent a failure of governance at Lloyds, such occurrences have also proved a positive learning experience causing sufficient dissatisfaction to seek alternatives. As a result, Lloyds has implemented tangible policy change that should guarantee the space needed to learn by preventing potential future breaches.

Libor, Rate Rigging and PPI

In July 2014, Lloyds' governance and business best-practice procedures would once again be called into question as it was handed a fine of £105 million by the FCA for its part in the rigging of Libor and other 'benchmark rates', most notably the Bank of England's REPO rate (FCA, 2014). Like its counterparts at RBS and Barclays, Lloyds became embroiled in the fixing of the Libor rate between 2006 and 2009 in order to profit a small bunch of insiders. However, in addition to Libor, the bank was also found guilty of trying to manipulate the Special Liquidity Scheme extended by the Bank of England between 2008 and 2009[14] (Goff and Scannell, 2014). The FCA commented that while the rigging of Libor by the bank was not unique given the gross misconduct of other UK banks in this area, Lloyds had gone to new lengths of rate-rigging by trying to defraud the British taxpayer of millions of pounds in fees (FCA, 2014).

While the rigging of Libor and other benchmark rates represents a gross failure in the internal governance model at Lloyds, we must note that the incidents detailed here predate the Review, which, as I have argued, is when Lloyds' learning journey essentially took hold and began. Commenting on the issue in July 2014, Lloyds stated that the actions

[13] Discussed in more detail in the following section.

[14] At the height of the GFC, struggling banks were extended cheap loans by the central bank with low fees (Goff and Scannell, 2014). Lloyds sought to profit from these loans by manipulating short-term rates in order to drive the value of the loans down and thus reduce what would be payable by the bank (ibid).

of those individuals involved in rate rigging was 'totally unacceptable and unrepresentative of the cultural changes that the Group [had since] implemented', with the persons involved having either left the bank or been sacked (Lloyds, 2014b). The scandal would eventually cost the bank more than £218 million in fines imposed by both UK and US authorities (FCA, 2014). Lloyds would go on to terminate eight members of staff and claw back more than £3 million in bonuses (Hosking, 2014).

Like the other banks in this study, Lloyds has also been heavily implicatedin the mis-selling of PPI. Claims against Lloyds over the mis-selling of PPI have cost the bank approximately £22 billion in compensation—the largest of any UK bank (Wallace, 2016; Makortoff and Kollewe, 2019). While the exact date of the mis-selling of PPI is unclear, Brummer (2015) notes that Lloyds, under its previous incarnation, had been fighting City regulators and consumer groups over the issue since 1998.[15] However, in 2011 Lloyds, thanks in no small part to the new group chief executive Antonio Horta-Osorio,[16] gave up its legal battle with the FSA and set aside an initial £3.2 billion to compensate customers who had been affected (Treanor, 2011). Commenting on the bank's decision to cease its PPI legal battle, António Horta-Osório said 'it is the sensible, prudent and right thing to do' and that 'we believe it draws a line under this issue' (Horta-Osório cited in Treanor, 2011).

The conceding of Lloyds' PPI legal battle, along with comments made by Antonio Horta-Osorio surrounding the group's capitulation, offers us valuable insight into why Lloyds has been a successful learner despite historical failures. For example, the group's wishes to 'draw a line under [the PPI] incident' by making compensation provisions and thus effectively bringing to a decisive end what had already become a lengthy legal affair, suggests that Lloyds has been able to defend its learning space from undue pressures despite the obvious short-term economic loses. As a result of this preservation of space—measured in terms of the dedication of time and resources—Lloyds has then been free to focus upon the

[15] Like the manipulation of Libor and REPO rates, much of the criticism levelled against Lloyds in relation to PPI predates the group's formation in 2009. Instead, this incident is the result of legacy issues that the bank's former businesses and brands were exposed to.

[16] Brummer (2015: 225) notes that Mr Horta-Osorio was instrumental in bringing about a close to the PPI saga despite some initial reservations from Lloyds. Ultimately, the group agreed with Antonio and decided that it would be in the long-term interests of Lloyds to surrender its legal battle and agree terms of compensation.

broader lessons of GFC, culminating in a reflective group-wide strategic evaluation—the Review. Consequently, Lloyds has avoided the mistakes of the some of its peers, such as RBS, that have been embroiled in a series of firefighting missions that have subsequently retarded the learning process by consuming precious time and resources.

Despite this, in a separate incident in 2014, it was revealed that the FCA and Serious Fraud Office was investigating a small number of former HBOS employees over allegations of fraud at the bank's corporate division headquarters in Reading (Verity, 2017). It became known that between 2002 and 2007 a handful of insiders had conspired to defraud hundreds of small business owners, including the TV personality Noel Edmonds, of millions of pounds worth of cash and assets (ibid). The scheme involved reclassifying otherwise healthy businesses as 'high-risk' resulting in them being moved into the bank's impaired assets division (Ford, 2019a). Once inside, the division's head, Lynden Scourfield, would insist that businesses employ the services of the turnaround consultants Quayside Corporate Services (QCS), run by David Mills and Michael Bancroft (ibid). QCS would then run-up huge consultancy fees and when businesses could not pay, QCS would take control of the now failing business and sell-off goods and assets leaving hundreds of businesses owners bankrupt (Ford and Binham, 2019). In exchange for his part in the scheme Mr Scourfield, who effectively 'sourced' businesses for asset stripping, received payments of cash, holidays, drugs and the use prostitutes (ibid). David Mills, Michael Bancroft and Lyden Scourfield, along with three others—including Mark Dobson a senior HBOS employee—were jailed in 2017 for a total of 47 years (Ford, 2018).

However, Lloyds has taken some positive steps and do appear to have at least tried to right many of the wrongs associated with its handling of the HBOS fraud and get back to the relationship-banking model that had served it so well in the past. For example in December 2019, Lloyds announced that it would make a number of *ex gratia* payments of £35,000 to 191 victims of the fraud in an attempt to rebuild trust (Ford, 2019b). The group would also spend £5million reimbursing the legal fees of its victims and offer all those affected by the incident the option of having their case reviewed by an independent body (Lloyds, 2019b). In addition, GCE Antonio Horta-Osorio has also announced possible plans to extend compensation payments to a number of individuals indirectly affected by the HBOS Reading case (ibid). The GCE has also agreed to meet with victims in an attempt to better understand, and garner ideas about, how Lloyds can help victims and their families recover from the fraud (Lloyds, 2019b). Commenting on Mr Horta-Osorio's offer to meet with victims Nikki Turner of the SME Alliance said, 'I think it's a positive step to have people at the top of the bank right up to the CEO being actively involved… and meeting the victims' (Turner cited in Ford, 2019b).

Despite some obvious regulatory failures, the evidence presented in this section of the chapter does indeed suggest that Lloyds has learned lessons from the GFC. Specifically, it appears that Lloyds has been a successful learner due to the management of dissatisfaction—which is evidently an important factor in learning. The level of dissatisfaction experienced by Lloyds has clearly been sufficient to prompt learning but, importantly, has not overwhelmed the bank, with Lloyds, unlike its counterparts at RBS, avoiding a series of firefighting missions that may have otherwise placed unnecessary pressure on the bank's learning space. Instead, when faced with large scale issues or challenges that have posed a significant threat to the group's time and resources, Lloyds has acted decisively and accepted short-term losses, drawing a line under issues and making substantive changes, thus preserving the learning space. The protection of the learning space has subsequently endowed the bank with the necessary time and resources needed to enter into an evaluative process concerning the strategic orientation of the group and the lessons of the GFC more broadly—as typified by the objectives set out in the Review. The bank has then dedicated its learning space towards upholding lesson learned with a series of policy initiatives that are indicative of learning in keeping with Rose's (1991, 1993, 2005) synthesis and hybrid theories of learning.

Remuneration and Bonuses

Another example of where the bank has learned lessons is in the area of remuneration. In the immediate aftermath of the GFC the then Lloyds' chairman Sir Victor Blank, explicitly recognised the role that 'perverse' remunerative practices had played in the crisis (Blank in Lloyds, 2008: 3). However, Sir Victor was keen to point out that the short-term high-risk and high-reward culture that had underwritten the GFC was confined, predominantly, to the investment banking divisions of Anglo-American institutions with Lloyds' exposure to these sectors—through both the HBOS and Lloyds TSB brands—being minimal (ibid).

Nonetheless, Lloyds assured shareholders and the public that the newly formed Lloyds Banking Group would instil prudence in its remuneration structures across all of its principal brands, despite pay within these businesses already being positioned at 'median, or below, levels offered by [its] competitors' (Lloyds, 2008: 74). Additionally, Lloyds would also pledge that the caution that had served the Lloyds TSB brand so well in the years preceding the crisis (Fallon, 2015), would continue to be the central feature of Lloyds' remuneration structure moving forwards (Lloyds, 2008).

While comments made in the immediate wake of the GFC by Lloyds and its former chairman may now appear somewhat dated, the pertinence of these statements to learning, the observations of this book and the argument presented in this chapter, remain so. This is because, ideas expressed by interpretive agents at Lloyds in the years following the crisis, along with the changes that these sentiments have given rise to, have subsequently being entrenched at the group with Lloyds maintaining its commitment to 'prudence' over pay in the decade that has followed the crisis. Moreover, ideas surrounding restraint over pay have been underpinned by a series of policy initiatives and revisions that have resulted in tangible policy change and suggest evidence of learning.

The Annual Incentive

In 2009, remuneration at Lloyds was divided along three distinct lines, namely: the annual incentive (AI); the long-term incentive plan (LTIP); and base salary. The AI award would allow executive directors to earn a bonus with a maximum potential of up to 200% of base salary, with the GCE eligible for an award of up to 225% of base salary (Lloyds, 2009). The AI would be measured equally against two objectives: profits before tax and economic profit and the balanced scorecard objectives (ibid). By 2018, the remuneration committee had revised down the maximum potential made available under the AI, which would now be limited to 100% of base salary for executive directors and 140% of base salary for the GCE, and would continue to be measured against the same objectives (Lloyds, 2018: 98).

As already established in previous chapters, the introduction of the EU CRD IV Directive dictates that all variable remuneration is subject to a maximum potential ratio of 1:2 of base salary (Prudential Regulation Authority, 2017: 28). As such, this may explain why Lloyds lowered the maximum award made available under the AI. However, while the bank would be permitted under CRD IV to extend the bonus to a potential 200% of base salary (with shareholder approval), Lloyds has opted to keep the AI award at just 50% of the upper threshold for executive directors and material risk-takers and 70% for the GCE (Lloyds, 2018). This suggests that Lloyds' remunerative practices, in relation to the AI, are well within the maximum limits set by the EU. Indeed, Lloyds is the only bank in this study that has not sought shareholder approval to extend variable remuneration to the full 1:2 ratio. This demonstrates that Lloyds has not only voluntarily exceeded minimum regulatory standards but has also maintained its commitment to prudence over pay in the post-crisis decade.

While the qualifying criteria and composition of the AI has remained broadly in-line with 2009 metrics, one area where we witness a definitive change is how awards are made to employees. For example, in 2009 all awards made under the AI were paid exclusively in cash (Lloyds, 2009). By 2018, payments were delivered in the form of both cash—made immediately available—and deferred payments of cash, shares, notes and similar debt instruments (Lloyds, 2018). The postponement of awards may be attributed to regulatory stipulations that require that at least 60% of variable pay above £500,000 to be deferred, while 50% of all variable remuneration should be payable in shares and other similar options[17] (bankofengland.co.uk). However, we should note that in 2011, Lloyds introduced provisions that would limit any cash payments made under the AI to a maximum of £2000 (Lloyds, 2011c). These changes would be applicable to all colleagues across the group with the exception of executive directors and the GCE, that would receive any variable remuneration in the form of deferred shares exclusively (Lloyds, 2011c, 2018).

Given that cash bonuses have been limited to a maximum of £2000 and have been totally eliminated for executive directors since 2013 (Lloyds, 2013), this would suggest that Lloyds has re-engineered its remuneration structures to be more risk-averse by 'building-in' incentives that reward long-term sustainable growth. These measures have consequently moved the bonus culture at the bank further away from the short-termism that proved so fatal in 2008. Therefore, it may be possible to conclude that

[17] We should note that such regulatory requirements were established before the UK's withdrawal from the EU. The UK has now entered into a transition period, due to end on 31 December 2020, during which EU law continues to apply.

Lloyds has learned lessons from the GFC, with such provisions not only exceeding regulatory minimum standards but also being more conservative than those in place at rival banks, as will be detailed in the coming chapters.

Long-Term Incentive Plan

In 2009, the maximum award made available to executive directors under the LTIP was 275% of base salary (Lloyds, 2009). However, in 2013 the remuneration committee raised the maximum potential of awards to 300% of base salary (Lloyds, 2013). By 2018, Lloyds had introduced provisions that would allow for discretionary awards of up to 400% of base salary to be made[18] (Lloyds, 2015a, 2018).

Despite these changes, further analysis reveals that while the maximum potential for bonuses has risen post-crisis, the qualifying criteria for awards, along with how bonuses are both calculated and paid, has undergone a fundamental reappraisal. Indeed, following the GFC, Lloyds has introduced a series of long-term risk-adjusted metrics that may yet demonstrate evidence of learning. In particular, the deferment and vesting of award made under the LTIP has consistently gone beyond minimum regulatory standards. For instance, new rules introduced by the bank's remuneration committee in 2010 would mean that following an initial vesting period of three years any shares awarded under the LTIP would be subject to a further holding period of two years, bringing the total deferment period to five years (Lloyds, 2009).

Though detractors may argue that these stipulations were simply in keeping with requirements set out by the PRA's Remuneration Code (2011), that, at the time, required a vesting period of three years, we can see that Lloyds had voluntarily chosen to hold awards for an additional two-year period. Likewise, while CRD IV would require awards to be deferred for a period of five years, we should note that Lloyds first announced such measures in 2010, taking effect from 2011 onwards. As a result, vesting stipulations introduced by the group significantly predated CRD IV, that only required similar measures to be in place by January 2017.

[18] Because the LTIP award is paid in deferred shares and not cash, it is subject to discount under CRD IV rules which allow banks to make awards in excess of the 1:2 ratio (Prudential Regulation Authority, 2017).

Similarly, when the PRA and FCA updated its remuneration codes in 2017, Lloyds would once again go beyond minimum requirements. Under new stipulations set out by the regulators, banks of a certain size would be required to defer vesting awards for a period of seven years (FCA, 2017; Prudential Regulation Authority, 2017). However, Lloyds would exceed these conditions by putting in place mechanisms that would allow the bank to defer awards made under the LTIP for a period of up to ten years (Lloyds, 2018). Consequently, it appears that deferral stipulations attached to the LTIP throughout the post-crisis decade have consistently been in excess of minimum regulatory standards and as such, suggest endogenously originated learning.

A second element of the LTIP that may also demonstrate evidence of learning can be seen in how awards are paid. The PRA and FCA remunerations codes, along with Article 94 of CRD IV, state that in addition to at least 60% of all bonuses being deferred, a minimum of 50% of variable remuneration must be paid in non cash options (bankofengland.co.uk; Eversheds Sutherland, 2016; FCA, 2017; Prudential Regulation Authority, 2017). Once again, Lloyds has gone beyond regulatory requirements with 100% of all LTIP awards made to executive directors and material risk-takers, namely those key agents that have the greatest potential impact upon the stability of the group, being subject to deferment (Lloyds, 2018). Likewise, all awards made under the LTIP are paid in the form of shares and other non-cash options (ibid). Consequently, while the potential for bonuses under the LTIP has remained broadly consistent in the years that have followed the GFC, there has been significant change in how awards are made.

Though Lloyds largely avoided the trappings ofexcessive remuneration that incentivised short-term risk-taking and which fatally compromised so many institutions in 2008, changes made to the LTIP suggests that Lloyds has sought to build into the award added measures that ensure bonuses are aligned with the long-term risk-adjusted performance of the group.[19] These changes likewise demonstrate that sentiments expressed by the group, and its former chairman, in relation to prudence over pay, have been upheld with specific policy initiatives. Moreover, such changes

[19] However, we should note that while the LTIP does indeed encourage a more risk-averse long-term approach to business, it is still possible for employees, particularly the most senior members, to earn exuberant bonuses that have attracted the attention and criticism of commentators (see, e.g., Partington [2015]; Salmon [2015]; Treanor [2014]).

may be symptomatic of learning and greater risk aversion with remuneration practices encouraging and ensuring a commitment to a sound long-term growth strategy recognised in the Review.

Equally, it has already been established above that banks operate within highly competitive structures, namely globalised financial markets (see Introduction). Consequently, institutions continue to face pressure, in particular from shareholders, to maximise returns. However, while it would appear that Lloyds recognise the importance of economic measures, including shareholder return, when determining awards made under the LTIP, the evidence suggests that post-crisis economic measures of performance have been somewhat subordinated. For example, in 2009 the LTIP was measured by three equally weighted metrics, namely, earnings per share; economic profit; and absolute share price growth (Lloyds, 2009). Yet, in 2018 LTIP awards would be judged on eight separate factors including: cost: income ratio (10%); total shareholder return (30%); economic profit (25%); customer satisfaction (10%); digital active customer growth (7.5%); customer complaints (5%); colleague engagement (7.5%); customer complaints FOS change rate (5%) (Lloyds, 2018: 85).

As we can see, in 2009, 100% of the LTIP award was determined by economic measures. In contrast, 2018 saw economic factors account for just 65% of the award with the remaining 35% being judged by non-financial metrics. Again, this demonstrates that though economic measures are still an important factor of both group and individual performance, something that is representative of the wider competitive structures that banks operate within, Lloyds has removed some of the significance of economic performance. Instead, post-GFC Lloyds has included a number of non-fiscal metrics when calculating awards.

Lloyds' apparent ability to learn lessons in relation to remuneration may have been assisted by the fact that the group has retrenched operations on domestic markets.[20] As such, while still exposed to a degree of competition over pay, the group has not been subject to the same competitive pressures as its peers with larger international exposures. As we shall see in the coming chapters, one of the biggest determinants in relation to learning and remuneration has been structural competitive pressures. Banks such as Barclays and HSBC that have maintained

[20] Discussed below.

or increased their international presence post-2008 seem to have been exposed to greater competition over the recruitment and retention of banking talent, particularly from overseas institutions that are not subject to the same regulatory constraints. This, I argue, has adversely affected the ability of banks to learn with institutions that have maintained their international position post-GFC failing to learn in relation pay.[21] Lloyds' retrenchment of the business on UK markets post-2008 may have assisted its learning journey in this respect.

Fixed Share Award and CRD IV

I have argued thus far that Lloyds has taken a number of positive steps in relation to remuneration that are indicative of learning and change. However, there are certain elements of the group's pay structure that do not necessarily fit the hypothesis extended in this section of the chapter. For example, in 2013 Lloyds announced that it would be introducing an annual 'fixed share award' for executive directors and material risk-takers (Lloyds, 2013: 100). As discussed in the previous chapter, in response to regulatory changes such as CRD IV, and later the PRA and FCA remuneration codes, many of the UK's largest banks including RBS, Lloyds, Barclays and HSBC, have introduced 'role-based allowances'. Yet, as noted above, many financial commentators have argued that such mechanisms effectively allow banks to circumvent and outmanoeuvre the maximum ratio for variable pay set out by legislators. Therefore, the introduction of fixed share awards by Lloyds may leave the group open to the charge that while complying with the letter of the law, some elements of its pay structure are not necessarily in keeping with the 'spirit' of tougher new regulations.

While the introduction of new role-based allowances by Lloyds does not necessarily fit with hypothesis extended in this section of the chapter, we should not lose sight of the wider changes around remuneration that the bank has made post-GFC. Indeed, the analysis above suggests that not only has Lloyds exercised prudence in relation to remuneration, with

[21] An exception to this hypothesis would be RBS that while retrenching operations on UK markets continue to cite competitive pressures over talent and pay as being a key driver of remuneration. However, I suggest that RBS is an outlier in this respect with the group's failure to learn being attributable to a series of institutional path dependencies that have negatively affected learning.

a number of tangible changes and policy initiatives being evidence of this conservatism, but that risk and pay have been deliberately aligned with the wider long-term interests of shareholders. Such policies have led to a more risk-averse and conservative organisation. Moreover, Lloyds has continued to operate well within the regulatory maximum pay levels, despite the actions of its peers. This suggests not only the presence of learning within this facet of the bank but also a more amenable relationship with regulators than some of its contemporaries examined in this study.

Balance Sheet

In 2009, Lloyds would require a state-sponsored bailout worth approximately £21 billion that would make the UK taxpayer a 43% stakeholder in the bank (National Audit Office, 2010: 3). In the same year, the group would also fail an FSA stress test that simulated further economic upheavals within financial markets (Fallon, 2015). The group's balance sheet, in particular its funding and liquidity position, was then further called into question when Lloyds announced that it would be recording a year-end loss for 2009 of £6.3 billion.

However just one year later Lloyds had begun to transform itself, announcing that it would be recording a year end pre-tax profit of £2.2 billion for the first time since the group's conception (Lloyds, 2010). Commenting on Lloyds' apparent turnaround, Eric Daniels, group chief executive at that time, told reporters that the return to profitability was a direct result of the group's efforts to solidify income growth, reduce the number of impairments within the wholesale business and rundown and restructure the group's existing book along with improving risk measures in the new business (Daniels cited in Treanor, 2010c).

While the return to profit in 2010 is now somewhat of a dated reference, it is nonetheless important to the narrative of this chapter. This is because while the former group chief executive's statement does not explicitly address the issue of learning at the bank, Mr Daniels' comments do point towards the ability of the group to recognise past failures and areas of weakness, a key component of learning. This aptitude for engagement with the learning process demonstrated by Lloyds following the GFC would result in the Review that, as discussed below, has subsequently overhauled the bank's balance sheet.

Group Funding

In 2009,[22] Lloyds' total liabilities and equity was approximately £1 trillion, with customer deposits, made up of both current and savings accounts, being worth £406 billion or 39% of total liabilities and equity. By 2018, total liabilities and equity had decreased to £797 billion with customer deposits increasing to £416 billion or 52% of total liabilities and equity. Importantly however, the most significant increase in customer deposits, measured as a percentage of total group liabilities and equity, came between 2010 and 2013 before the EU mandated sale of Intelligent Finance and TSB in 2014 and 2015, respectively.[23] For example, by 2013 the customer deposit base had increased to £436 billion and accounted for approximately 51% of group liabilities and equity (Fig. 5.1).

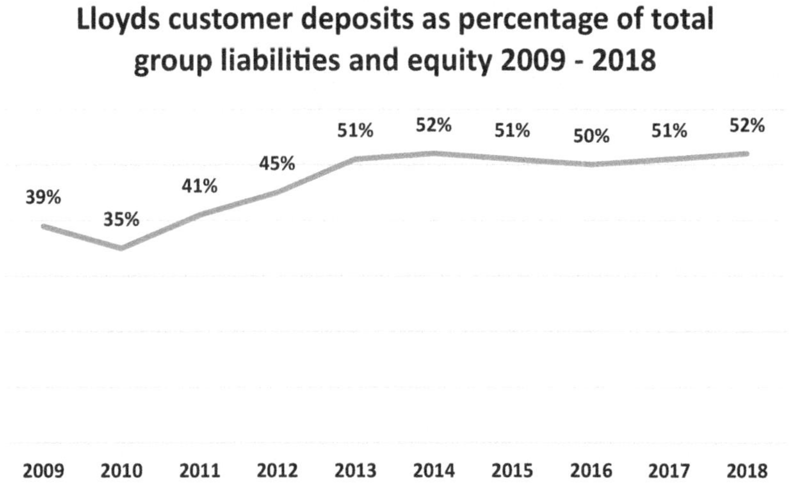

Fig. 5.1 Customer deposits as percentage of total group liabilities and equity 2009–2018

[22] Lloyds Banking Group was formed in January 2009. As such, the balance sheet analysis will take the year ending 31st December 2009 as its starting point.

[23] Following Lloyds bailout in 2009, EU rules on state aid would require the bank to divest a portion of the business as a key measure to limit distortions of competition created by the aid.

Thus, in the period 2009–2018, Lloyds significantly strengthened its funding position by increasing total customer deposits as a percentage of group liabilities and equity by approximately 13 percentage points. Moreover, these figures demonstrate that the re-engineering of this particular facet of the balance sheet witnessed the greatest changes before the EU mandated sale of Intelligent Finance and TSB. As such, the increase of customer deposits should not be considered the result of exogenous factors but is instead indicative of the presence of learning. In comparison, in 2018 total customer deposits at RBS were worth 51% of total liabilities and equity with Barclays being 33% and HSBC 53%.

Likewise, short-term funding including 'other deposits', short-term borrowings, money markets and 'other short-term funding' decreased between 2009 and 2018. In 2009, short-term funding was worth £190 billion or 18% of group liabilities and equity. In 2018, this figure had decreased to £79 billion or around 9% of total liabilities and equity.[24] These figures demonstrate that short-term funding at Lloyds has decreased by approximately 9 percentage points over a nine-year period following the GFC (Fig. 5.2).

Once again, these figures indicate the presence of learning at Lloyds. Moreover, such changes are particularly important when we consider the 2009 takeover of HBOS and specifically the shortfall of customer deposits and the over-reliance on wholesale funding that Lloyds inherited through the HBOS book (Bell and Hindmoor, 2015; Fallon, 2015; Perman, 2013). Moreover, when presenting the findings of the Review at a KPMG conference in 2011, GCE Antonio Horta-Osorio explicitly recognised the inherent vulnerabilities that an over-reliance on wholesale markets can place upon a bank (Horta-Osorio in Perrin, 2014). Mr Horta-Osorio told delegates that a dependence upon wholesale markets had been ruinous for Lloyds and had left the bank close to 'running out of money' (ibid). The GCE added that moving forwards this was just one of the key changes that would be implemented at the bank (Horta-Osorio in Perrin, 2014).

The Review also identified the need to 'strengthen the Group's balance sheet, funding and liquidity position' and specified that Lloyds would reduce its reliance upon wholesale funding (Lloyds, 2011a: 28). This

[24] However, as discussed in the previous chapter, when considering short-term funding, in particular wholesale funding, we should take account of changes to capital standards and the definition of tier 1 capital.

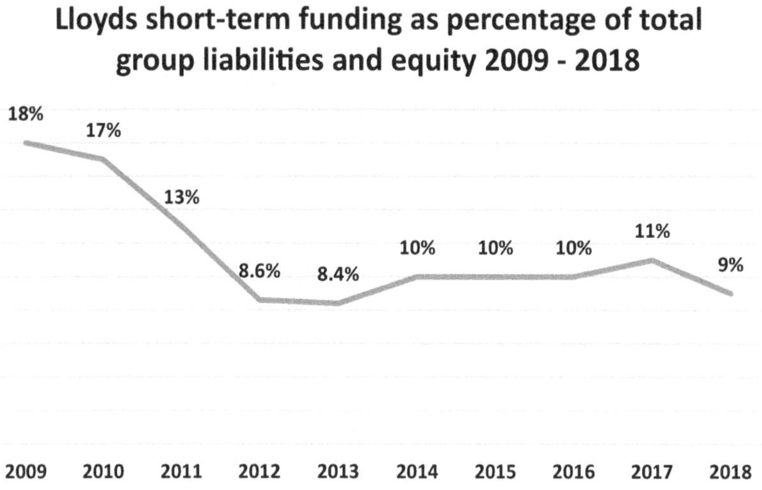

Fig. 5.2 Short-term funding as percentage of total group liabilities and equity 2009–2018

demonstrates that not only has Lloyds recognised the vulnerabilities synonymous with the inter-bank markets but, importantly, have addressed such shortcomings within its business model. As a result, in the post-crash period we witness a reduction in the reliance on short-term funding and especially so-called overnight money markets. Similarly, evidence suggests that the comments made by the GCE pertaining to this issue have been upheld by a series of policy initiatives that are in keeping with Rose's (1991, 1993, 2005) synthesis learning framework detailed above.

Regulatory Capital

If we consider thegroup's capital resources, we can see once more that Lloyds has made significant gains in strengthening its capital position and increasing its loss-absorbing capacity.[25] For example, in 2009 the group were holding a total sum of regulatory tier 1 capital of £47 billion which

[25] As established in previous chapters, a comparative analysis of the amount of regulatory capital held by the banks post-crisis is complicated due to the regulatory landscape which was substantially different pre-2008—including how tier and total capital is defined.

carried a tier 1 regulatory capital ratio of 9.6%. Likewise, the bank's total regulatory capital in 2009 was £61 billion and equated to a total regulatory capital ratio of 12.4%. In contrast, 2018 saw the group report regulatory tier 1 capital of £36 billion, which converted to a regulatory tier 1 capital ratio of 17.8%. Similarly, in 2018 Lloyds had a total regulatory capital of £42 billion, which accounted for a total regulatory capital ratio of 20.5%. In 2018, the group's total regulatory capital stood at 156% higher than minimum requirements[26] with regulatory tier 1 capital being 196% above Basel III standards and which is the second highest rate, behind that of RBS,[27] of the banks in this study.

Furthermore, the Review 2011 would identify the need for a 'robust' regulatory capital ratio (Lloyds, 2011a: 8), with Antonio Horta-Osorio telling investors that 'higher capital and higher liquidity' were key lessons which the group had drawn from the crisis (Horta-Osorio cited in Lloyds, 2011b: slide 12). Given Mr Horta-Osorio's comments, along with the fact that the bank has made changes to its capital structure which have exceeded both the minimum regulatory requirements and the deadline for the implementation of such provisions, it may be possible to conclude that Lloyds has indeed learned lessons from the GFC.

Firstly, given the large excess reserves of capital that have been built-up by Lloyds, the second largest of any bank in our study, we may conclude that the group has recognised that more stringent capital allowances are needed to preserve the health of the bank during times of crisis. Indeed, the Review would pledged that Lloyds would 'always maintain prudent levels of capital in excess of regulatory requirements' (Lloyds, 2011a: 33). *Secondly*, by building a capital buffer which is far in excess of regulatory stipulations, it may be suggested that the group has recognised that compliance with regulatory minimum standards alone is insufficient to guarantee the long-term well-being of the bank. As such, Lloyds has implemented capital ratios that go beyond the minimum requirements and consequently is indicative of learning. Furthermore, we can see that those sentiments expressed in the Review have been upheld by a series of policy initiatives which likewise point towards lesson learning as detailed by Rose (2005). The author states that learning associated with the

[26] The Base III framework stipulates a minimum regulatory tier 1 capital ratio of 6% and a total regulatory capital of 8% (BIS, 2010).

[27] See Chapter 4, page 119, Fig. 4.3 for comparison.

'synthesis' thesis will generally see lessons learned upheld by a series of guidelines, standard operating procedures and institutional policy norms (ibid).

Trading Liabilities

In 2009, the newly formed Lloyds had total group assets of approximately £1 trillion and trading liabilities of £28 billion, or 2.8% of total assets. In contrast, by 2018 the group had reduced its total assets to £797 billion with trading liabilities being worth £8 billion, or 1.1% of total assets. However, while critics may argue that such a reduction could be attributed to the 2014 EU mandated disinvestment of TSB and Intelligent Finance, figures from as early as 2010 demonstrate that Lloyds had already begun the long process of reducing the percentage of trading liabilities. For example, Fig. 5.3 shows that by 2013 trading liabilities had been reduced to approximately 1.6% of total assets. As such, while a reduction in trading liabilities and the overall balance sheet may indeed have been motivated by disinvestment stipulations put in place by the EU, we can clearly see that Lloyds has embraced both the letter and spirit of EU regulations on state aid. Indeed trading liabilities have been reduced

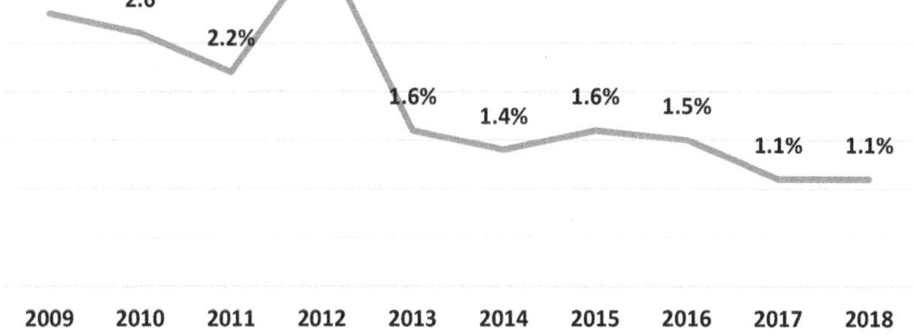

Fig. 5.3 Trading liabilities as percentage of total assets 2009–2018

in timely fashion—a trend that has continued despite Lloyds return to private ownership—and suggests the presence of learning. Moreover, in 2018 the group also had the smallest percentage of trading liabilities of the banks surveyed here, outperforming RBS (3.8%), Barclays (10.2%) and HSBC (8.5%) on this metric.

Loan/Deposit Ratio

Analysis of the loan-to-deposit ratio may further support the hypothesis that following the GFC Lloyds has exhibited behaviour that is indicative of learning. Post-crash, the group has adopted a more conservative balance sheet and reduced its exposure to the turbulence of financial markets. For example, the Review stated that Lloyds would target a 'lower loan to deposit ratio'[28] by increasing 'the number of commercial and retail deposits' (Lloyds, 2011a: 43). In 2009, gross loans totalled £660 billion, with total customer deposits being £406 billion. These figures demonstrate that in 2009 gross loans were worth 162% of total customer deposits. Comparable figures for 2018 show that gross loans were worth £456 billion, or 109% of total customer deposits which stood at £416 billion.[29] These figures demonstrate significant restructuring of the balance sheet, in keeping with targets set out in the Review, with gross loans as a percentage of total deposits decreasing by 53 percentage points post-crash. However, we should note that in 2018 Lloyds did have the highest loan-to-deposit ratio of the banks in this study, with RBS (85%), Barclays (84%) and HSBC (73%) all out performing the bank on this measure (Fig. 5.4).

Loan Quality/Impairments

Not only has Lloyds reduced the number of loans being extended as a percentage of total customer deposits but, the quality of these loans has also improved. For example, in 2009 residential mortgage loans totalled £362 billion, with 54% of gross loans being dedicated towards this kind of lending (Fig. 5.5). In 2018, residential mortgage loans totalled £296

[28] Although we should note that a specific value was not given to this target.

[29] However, we should exercise caution here as a lower loan-to-deposit ratio may be reflective of increased minimum capital standards discussed in Chapter 4.

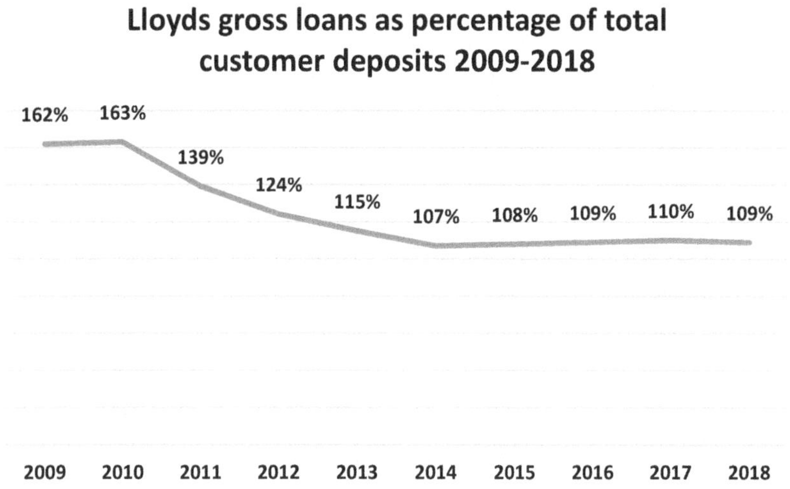

Fig. 5.4 Gross loans as percentage of total customer deposits 2009–2018

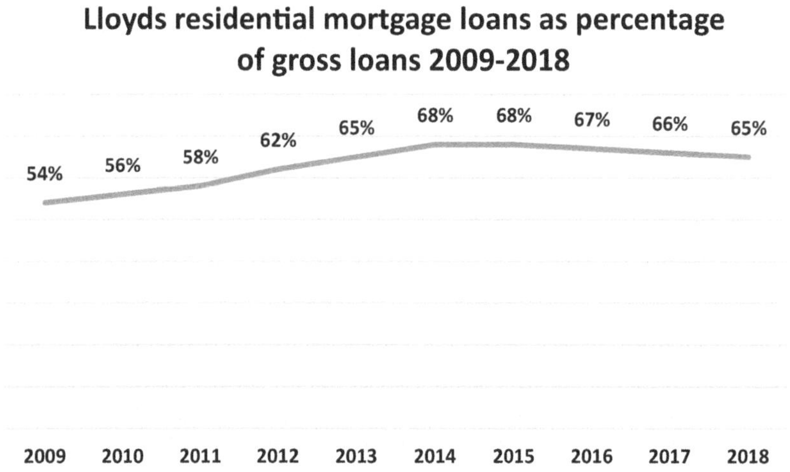

Fig. 5.5 Residential mortgage loan as percentage of gross loans 2009–2018

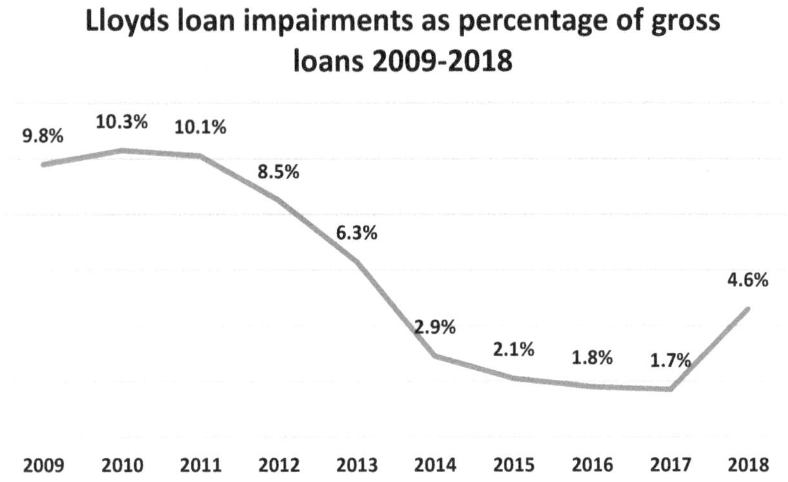

Fig. 5.6 Loan impairments as percentage of gross loans 2009–2018

billion or 65% of gross loans. These figures show that post-crash, Lloyds has committed a greater percentage of lending towards safer residential mortgage loans.

Similarly, in 2009 Lloyds incurred £65 billion worth of impairment charges against its loan book. This equated to an impairment rate 9.8% of gross loans. However, by 2018 impaired loans had fallen and represented just 4.6% of gross loans extended at £21 billion.[30] These figures indicate that the quality of loans made by Lloyds post-GFC are of a much higher worth, with a lower rate of total impairments against the loan book. In comparison, impairment rates at RBS were 2.5%, Barclays 2.6% and HSBC 0.8% for the financial year ending 2018. Despite this, we should note that Lloyds has decreased its impairment rate by approximately 53% across the post-GFC period and though still comparatively high these figures may yet indicate evidence of learning (Fig. 5.6).

Moreover, the Review specifically stated that the group would target lower impairment rates as part of the bank's plans to 'reshape the business

[30] We should note that these comparative figures for the year 2009 and 2018 do not account for wider structural factors and in particular fluctuations in both the domestic and global economy which may impact impairment rates.

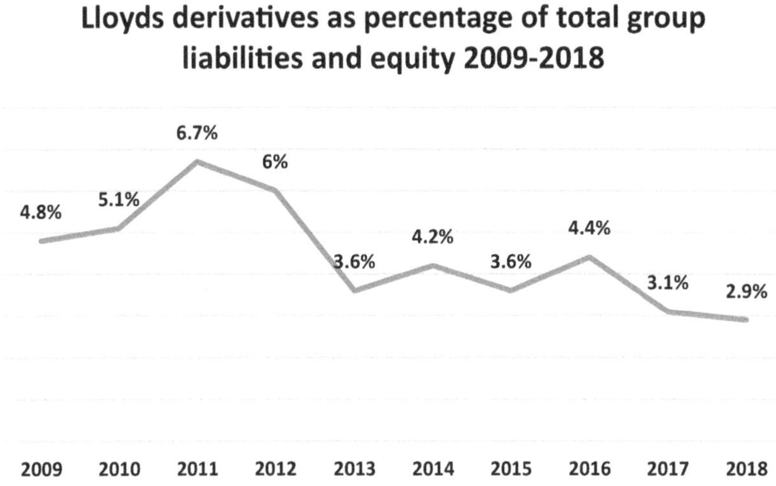

Fig. 5.7 Derivatives as percentage of total liabilities and equity 2009–2018

portfolio to fit asset capabilities and risk appetite' (Lloyds, 2011a: 28). Once more, this appears to suggest the presence of learning in keeping with the synthesis-learning framework as key strategic initiatives have been underpinned by specific policies[31] that uphold lessons learned. Likewise, Fig. 5.6. demonstrates that, for the most part, the fall in impairments once again predates the 2014 EU mandated disinvestment of the balance sheet and reveals that change has occurred in response to endogenously, as opposed to exogenously, originated factors.

Derivatives

Post-GFC Lloyds has also decreased its exposure to derivatives as a percentage of total group liabilities and equity. In 2009, derivatives were worth approximately 4.8% of group liabilities and equity. This figure would then grow slowly until reaching a peak in 2011 at 6.7%. From 2012 onwards, we witness a progressive decline in the group's exposure

[31] However, once again we should note that while Lloyds would explicitly target lower impairments as part of its initiative to reshape the business portfolio in keeping with the group's wider risk appetite, the bank failed to quantify a specific target impairment rate.

to derivatives, reaching a yearly average low of 2.9% in 2018. Once more, this may be indicative of learning, with Lloyds working to reduce the number of derivatives held on its balance sheet post-GFC. Moreover, in 2018 the group had a significantly lower exposure to derivatives than any other bank in this study with its closest rival being HSBC at 8%.[32]

Off-Balance-Sheet Vehicles

Despite this, off-balance-sheet vehicles, as a percentage of total group liabilities and equity, have increased post-GFC. For example, in 2009 off-balance sheet items were worth 13% of total group liabilities and equity. This figure would fall between 2010 and 2013, before rising again in 2014 and peaking at 17% in 2018. However, we should once again note that despite this increase, the group outperformed its peers with RBS (18.%), Barclays (30%) and HSBC (34%) all operating with much higher exposures to these potentially volatile entities (Fig. 5.8).

An analysis of Lloyds' balance sheet demonstrates a changing structure and composition of the key financial indicators towards a stronger and more robust business. Such change is indicative of the presence of learning in keeping with the double-loop theory. For instance, not only does the Review represent a fundamental re-evaluation of the group's underlying theories-in-use, but, importantly, details specific policies, objectives and benchmarks that uphold lesson learned on the balance sheet. In this respect, Lloyds has sought, evaluated and implemented new information—factors that are synonymous with Rose's (1991, 1993, 2005) policy learning framework—and may explain why the group has learned. Indeed, post-GFC, Lloyds appear to have advanced a more sustainable business model that subsequently poses a diminished risk to financial stability.

Return to Private Ownership

Given Lloyds commitment to re-engineering the group balance sheet, which is in-line with a more cautious and robust underlying business model, there is little surprise that the bank has been returned to private

[32] However, as noted in the previous chapter we should exercise caution in drawing conclusions surround derivatives, which while increasing leverage may also be used as an effective tool for hedging certain exposures.

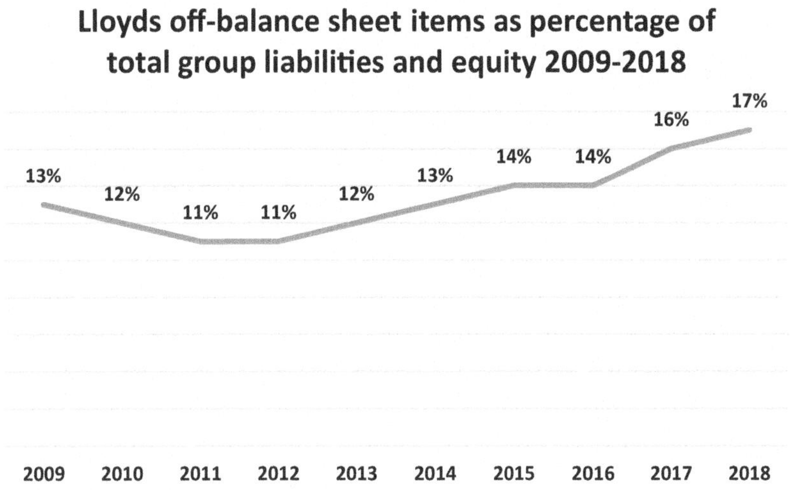

Fig. 5.8 Off-balance sheet items as percentage of total group liabilities and equity 2009–2018

ownership. Shortly after its formation in 2009, Lloyds would be forced to accept £20.3 billion in state aid that would see the UK Government take a 43% stake in the business (Bell and Hindmoor, 2015). In September 2013, the UKFI began selling down its stake in Lloyds, successfully completing the sale of a 6% share in the bank and raising approximately £61 million in profit for the Treasury (Farrell, 2015). Over the next four years, the UK Government would go on to 'drip-feed' its remaining shares into the market and in May 2017 Lloyds was fully returned to private ownership (Dunkley, 2017e). The sale of Lloyds would net the Treasury over £16 billion in revenue and return the UK Government a profit of approximately £900 million (National Audit Office, 2018).

Commenting on the completion of the UK Government's sell-down in the business and Lloyds' successful return to private ownership, Lord Blackwell, Lloyds chairman, said:

> Today marks the final step in the rescue and rejuvenation of Lloyds Banking Group...The sale marks the successful delivery of the Group's strategy to transform itself into a simple, low risk, UK focused retail and commercial bank...However, we are not complacent. While we are proud of the progress we have made over the last few years, we recognise there

is still a lot to do to transform Lloyds Banking Group into the best bank for customers and play our full role in helping Britain prosper. (Blackwell in Lloyds, 2017)

Disinvestment

This return to private ownership along with the re-engineering of the group's balance sheet should not be considered in isolation. Importantly, Lloyds' 2009 state-sponsored bailout would mean that the group would be required by EU mandate to disinvest a part of its business in order to meet competition rules (Treasury Select Committee, 2014: 10). Under the disinvestment plan—known as project 'Verde'—the bank identified approximately 600 branches that would be carved out of the existing business and be rebranded and sold off under the TSB name (ibid).

In 2011 Lloyds began negotiations with the Co-operative Group over the possible sale of its newly resurrected TSB brand. However, these negotiations ultimately proved unsuccessful and in June 2014 Lloyds opted to make an initial public offering of TSB shares which would see the group shed more than a 38% stake in the bank (Salmon, 2015). In June 2015, the sale of TSB was finally realised when the Lloyds' remaining shares were sold to the Spanish bank, Banco de Sabadell for around £680 million (Lloyds, 2015b). Commenting on the sale, Lloyds' group CEO, Antonio Horta-Osorio, highlighted the fact that not only did this represent a 'significant and positive step for the group', but stressed that the sale had been realised ahead of the EU deadline[33] and further demonstrated the group's turnaround since its 2009 bailout (Horta-Osorio cited in Goodway, 2015). The accelerated sale of TSB was one of the principle objectives set out in the Review (Lloyds, 2011a: 2) and suggests that Lloyds not only exceeded regulatory stipulations concerning the disinvestment of the TSB brand but that sentiments expressed in the Review concerning the sale of TSB have been reinforced by direct policy action.

While it is true that the sale of TSB was largely motivated by exogenous structural factors, namely EU rules regarding state aid, it would be inaccurate to describe the re-engineering of Lloyds' balance sheet as being motivated solely by outside forces. Instead, the origins of Lloyds' restructuring, and the subsequent stability that this recomposition has

[33] This stands in stark opposition to RBS' own EU mandated sale of Williams and Glynn.

delivered, predate the 2015 EU mandated sale of TSB, as demonstrated by the key financial metrics examined above. Indeed, the re-engineering of the balance sheet has been accompanied and underpinned by a series of endogenously originated 'capital assertive' disinvestment projects outlined by the Review (Lloyds, 2011a: 1). This has included the sale of several subsidiaries and non-principal businesses, particularly within international private banking.

In March 2013, for example, Lloyds announced that it would be selling-off a 20% stake in St James's Place, a wealth management business (Coates, 2013). The group had inherited a 60% share in the company through the HBOS book, and it was estimated that the initial sale of its 20% stake would be worth approximately £400 million and contribute significantly to strengthening the Lloyds' capital position (Treanor, 2013). The disposal of St James's Place from the group's balance sheet would continue throughout 2013, until December of that year when Lloyds announced that it would be selling its remaining 21% stake in the company for £670 million, and which would mark the bank's exit from the firm entirely (Gray, 2013). Though it is true that under the Basel III Capital Adequacy Framework banks and other financial institutions holding an equity share of greater than 10% in another financial firm are subject to stringent rules and certain fiscal burdens (James and Quaglia, 2020), the selling-down of Lloyds' entire stake in the wealth management business goes beyond regulatory requirements.

Moreover, in October 2013 the group completed the sale of its international private bank, headquartered in Geneva, to Union Bancaire Privée, UBP (Lloydsbank.com. 2014). The deal would be worth a reported £100 million and would see Lloyds exit markets in Geneva, Zurich, Monaco, Gibraltar and Uruguay (Wilson, 2013). In the same year, it was also announced that Lloyds would be selling its Miami-based private bank to Banco de Sabadell for £8 million (Lloydsbank.com. 2014). The sale of both the Swiss- and Miami-based private banks would see Lloyds shed more than £8 billion of combined assets and over £764 million from the group's overall balance sheet (Wilson, 2013). The sale would also see Lloyds exit the private banking sector in Dubai and South Africa. However, it would retain those businesses oriented towards the 'mass affluent' and 'affluent' customers within the UK and Channel Islands (Lloydsbankinggroup.com. 2013). To date Lloyds has reduced its international presence from 30 to just 6 countries (Lloyds, 2014a: 5, 2015b, 2018).

Conclusion

Following the GFC, Lloyds does appear to have learned lessons with the bank recognising and identifying many of the causes of the crisis within both its own institution and the wider banking industry. Importantly, Lloyds has consistently implemented policies aimed at upholding lesson learned. In particular, the Review has been central in this process acting as a key conduit for learning by ushering in a series of policy changes that have fundamentally shifted the strategic orientation of the bank. Indeed, Lloyds has constantly met and surpassed the goals and objectives set out in the Review. Likewise, many of the policy and strategic changes implemented post-GFC have been in excess of regulatory minimum standards and are in keeping with the double-loop learning theory. Likewise, the Review has not only equipped Lloyds with a series of benchmarks or metrics against which success can be measured, in keeping with the synthesis learning theory, but is also indicative of the group's willingness and ability to engage and learn from adjacent information.

This propensity towards learning may be explained by the learning space theory. For example, when confronted with moments of dissatisfaction with the potential to erode learning space, Lloyds has deployed its resources in an efficient and effective manner thus preserving space. This space has then been applied to a broader examination of the group's underlying theories-in-use in the light of the lessons of the GFC. Similarly, when challenged with incidents that have threatened to undermine space, Lloyds has acted swiftly and decisively to rectify issues, even when this has meant incurring short-term losses, thus preserving the learning space further. The surrendering of the PPI legal battle is a case in point. The group accepted short-term penalties, in the form of customer compensation, but in doing so were able to free-up time and resources that may have otherwise have been lost fighting a lengthy legal battle. Consequently, lesson learning and change is observable across the group. As such, it is possible to conclude that space, and specifically how institutional resources are utilised, is an important factor in institutional learning.

Lloyds' decision to capitulate its legal battle over the PPI case also highlights a second important feature of post-crash bank learning, namely, that agency as well as structures matter. For example, we know that the ending of Lloyds' PPI dispute was largely motivated by the newly appointed Antonio Horta-Osorio. In doing so, the GCE was responsible for freeing-up the necessary resources crucial to learning—time and human and fiscal capital. Lloyds were then free to apply these resources, or learning space, towards a self-reflexive examination in light of the challenges stressed by the GFC. Lessons drawn from this evaluative process have subsequently been underpinned by factors synonymous with Rose's (1991, 1993, 2005) thesis on policy learning. Specifically, Lloyds has effectively instilled and implemented lessons learned with a number of targeted policy responses. This demonstrates that while structural constraints, such as regulatory stipulations, do indeed have a role in learning, agency and the individual choice of key agents clearly still matter in shaping institutions. Put simply, Lloyds has been a successful learner because it has actively sought to learn. The group has oriented institutional resources towards seeking, evaluating and, importantly, applying new information to create new institutional underlying theories-in-use, improved policy actions, behavioural patterns and normative preferences.

References

Argyris, C., Putnam, R., & Smith, D. (1985). *Action science*. San Francisco: Jossey-Bass.

Arygris, C., & Schon, D. A. (1996). *Organizational learning II: Theory, method, and practice*. Reading, MA: Addison-Wesley Publishing.

Bank of England [bankofengland.co.uk]. *Remuneration code—About*. Available at: http://www.bankofengland.co.uk/pra/Pages/supervision/activities/aboutremuneration.aspx#.

Bank of England. (2015, November). *The failure of HBOS plc (HBOS) a report by the Financial Conduct Authority (FCA) and the Prudential Regulation Authority (PRA)*. Bank of England. Available at: http://www.bankofengland.co.uk/pra/Documents/publications/reports/hbos.pdf.

Bell, S., & Hindmoor, A. (2015). *Masters of the universe, slaves of the market*. Cambridge, MA: Harvard University Press.

BIS [Bank for International Settlements]. (2010, December). *Basel III: A global regulatory framework for more resilient banks and banking systems* (rev June 2011). Available at: http://www.bis.org/publ/bcbs189.htm.

BloombergBusiness.com. (2015, February 27). *Lloyds banking group PLC: 'People'*. At: http://www.bloomberg.com/research/stocks/people/person.asp?personId=2461671&ticker=LLOY:LN.

Bracken, P., Bremmer, I., & Gordon, D. (2005). *Managing strategic surprise: Lessons from risk management and risk assessment*. Cambridge: Cambridge University Press.

Brummer, A. (2015). *Bad banks: Greed, incompetence and the next global crisis*. Random House Business: London.

Clark. A. (2009, January 10). Lloyds forfeits $350m for disguising origin of funds from Iran and Sudan. *The Guardian*. Available at: https://www.theguardian.com/business/2009/jan/10/lloyds-forfeits-350m-to-us.

Coates, S. (2013, March 12). Lloyds plays it simple with St James's place sale. *The Times*. Available at: http://www.thetimes.co.uk/tto/business/industries/banking/article3711088.ece.

Davies, H. (2010). *The financial crisis: Who is to blame?*. Cambridge: Polity Press.

Dunkley, E. (2017e). UK Government No Longer Largest Shareholder in Lloyds. *Financial Times Online*. Available at: https://www.ft.com/content/9cc4c9e6-d64d-11e6-944b-e7eb37a6aa8e.

Dunkley, E., & Jenkins, P. (2017, May 18). How Lloyds came back from the brink. *Financial Times*. Available at: https://www.ft.com/content/34e57e76-3a87-11e7-821a-6027b8a20f23?myftTopics=TnN0ZWluX09OX0ZvcnR1bmVDb21wYW55X0xMT1k%3D-T04%3D#myft:my-news:grid.

Edmondson, A. (1996). Learning from mistakes is easier said than done: Group and organizational influences on the detection and correction of human error. *The Journal of Applied Behavioural Science, 32*(1): 5–28.

Edmondson, A., & Moingeon, B. (1999). Learning, trust and organizational change. In M. Easterby-Smith, J. Burgoyne & L. Araujo (Eds.), *Organizational learning and the learning organization: Developments in theory and practice* (Chapter 9, pp. 157–176). London: Sage Publications.

Eversheds Sutherland. (2016, January 28). Remuneration and the EBA final guidelines on sound remuneration policies. *Eversheds Sutherland International. Online Report*. Available at: http://www.eversheds-sutherland.com/global/en/what/articles/index.page?ArticleID=en/Employment_and_labour_law/BA_Final_Guidelines_on_sound_remuneration_policies.

Fallon, I. (2015). *Black horse ride: The inside story of Lloyds and the banking crisis*. London: The Robson Press.

Farrell, S. (2015, September 25). Government reduces stake in Lloyds banking group. *The Guardian*. Available at: http://www.theguardian.com/business/2015/sep/25/government-sells-further-stake-lloyds-banking-group-share.

FCA [Financial Conduct Authority]. (2013, December 11). *FCA fines Lloyds banking group firms a total of £28,038,800 for serious sales incentive failings*. FCA News/Press Release. Available at: http://www.fca.org.uk/news/press-releases/fca-fines-lloyds-banking-group-firms-for-serious-sales-incentive-failings.

FCA [Financial Conduct Authority]. (2014, July 28). *Lloyds banking group fined £105m for serious LIBOR and other benchmark failings*. Available at: https://www.fca.org.uk/news/lloyds-banking-group-fined-105m-libor-benchmark-failings.

FCA [Financial Conduct Authority]. (2017). *FCA handbook: SYSC 19C.3 remuneration principles*. Online. Available at: https://www.handbook.fca.org.uk/handbook/SYSC/19C/3.html?date=2017-09-01.

Ford. J. (2018). 'Lloyds accused of ignoring police whistleblower request in HBOS probe'. Financial Times. 26th September 2018. Available at: https://www.ft.com/content/28ae208a-c0d8-11e8-8d55-54197280d3f7

Ford, J. (2019a, December 10). Business victims of HBOS fraud in line for bigger payout. *Financial Times*. Available at: https://www.ft.com/content/918d9c1a-1b64-11ea-97df-cc63de1d73f4.

Ford, J. (2019b, December 20). HBOS fraud victims to receive £35,000 special payout. *Financial Times*. Available at: https://www.ft.com/content/c1061c40-2273-11ea-92da-f0c92e957a96.

Ford. J. and Binham. C. (2019). 'Lloyds bows to pressure from watchdog by reviewing HBOS redress'. Financial Times. 3rd May 2019. Available at: https://www.ft.com/content/6768de62-6dbe-11e9-80c7-60ee53e6681d

Global Witness. (2009, March). *Undue diligence how banks do business with corrupt regimes*. A report by global witness. Available at: https://www.globalwitness.org/documents/14621/undue_diligence_lowres.pdf.

Goff, S., & Scannell, K. (2014, July 28). 'Reprehensible' Lloyds under fire from carney. *The Financial Times*. Available at: https://www.ft.com/content/f0d55584-1640-11e4-93ec-00144feabdc0.

Goodway, N. (2015, March 21). Lloyds sells 50% of TSB to sabadell for £1.7bn. *Independent*. Available at: http://www.independent.co.uk/news/business/news/lloyds-sells-50-of-tsb-to-sabadell-for-17bn-10124603.html.

Gray, A. (2013, December 9). Lloyds sells St. James's place stake for £670m. *The Financial Times*. Available at: http://www.ft.com/cms/s/0/835c1dee-60f1-11e3-916e-00144feabdc0.html#axzz47ItLdg1G.

Hawkes, S., & Armstrong, A. (2013, December 11). Lloyds fined £28m for 'sell or be demoted' incentive plan. *The Telegraph*. Available at: http://www.telegraph.co.uk/finance/newsbysector/banksandfinance/10510228/Lloyds-fined-28m-for-sell-or-be-demoted-incentive-plan.html.

Hosking, P. (2014, September 29). Lloyds sacks staff and claws back bonuses over rate-rigging. *The Times*. Available at: http://www.thetimes.co.uk/tto/business/industries/banking/article4221170.ece.

James, S., & Quaglia, L. (2020). *The UK & multi-level financial regulation: From post-crisis reform to Brexit*. Oxford: Oxford University Press.

Kollewe, J. (2010, Wednesday 3 November). Profile: New Lloyds chief antónio horta-osório. *The Guardian*. http://www.theguardian.com/business/2010/nov/03/profile-lloyds-chief-antonio-horta-osorio.

Lloyds [Lloyds Banking Group]. (2008). Annual Report and Accounts 'Creating the UK's Best Financial Services Provider'. Available at: https://www.lloydsbankinggroup.com/globalassets/documents/investors/2009/2009_lbg_ra.pdf

Lloyds [Lloyds Banking Group]. (2009). *Annual report and accounts 2009 'creating the UK's best financial services provider'*. Available at: http://www.lloydsbankinggroup.com/globalassets/documents/investors/2009/2009_lbg_ra.pdf.

Lloyds [Lloyds Banking Group]. (2010). *Annual report and accounts 2010 'creating the UK's best financial services provider'*. Available at: http://www.lloydsbankinggroup.com/globalassets/documents/investors/2010/2010_lbg_ra.pdf.

Lloyds [Lloyds Banking Group]. (2011a, June 30). *Lloyds banking group plc outcome of strategic review*. Available at: http://www.lloydsbankinggroup.com/globalassets/documents/investors/2011/2011jun30_lbg_strategic_review_transcript.pdf.

Lloyds [Lloyds Banking Group]. (2011b, October 4). *Presentation given by António Horta-Osório group chief executive at bank of America Merrill Lynch conference*, 'The Financial Crisis: Key Questions, Reality and Responses'. London. Available at: http://www.lloydsbankinggroup.com/globalassets/documents/investors/2011/2011oct4_lbg_boamlconf_london.pdf.

Lloyds [Lloyds Banking Group]. (2011c). *Annual report and accounts 2011 'becoming the best bank for customers'*. Available at: http://www.lloydsbankinggroup.com/globalassets/documents/investors/2011/2011_lbg_randa.pdf.

Lloyds [Lloyds Banking Group]. (2013). *Annual report and accounts 'becoming the best bank for customers'*. Available at: http://www.lloydsbankinggroup.com/globalassets/documents/investors/2014/2013_lbg_interactive_annual_report.pdf.

Lloyds [Lloyds Banking Group]. (2014a). *Annual report and accounts 2014: Becoming the best bank for customers*. Available at: http://www.lloydsbankinggroup.com/globalassets/documents/investors/2014/2014_lbg_annual_report.pdf.

Lloyds [Lloyds Banking Group]. (2014b, July 28). *Settlements reached on legacy LIBOR and BBA Repo rate issues*. Press Release. Available at: http://www.lloydsbankinggroup.com/Media/Press-Releases/2014/lloyds-banking-group/settlements-reached-on-legacy-libor-and-bba-repo-rate-issues/.

Lloyds [Lloyds Banking Group]. (2015a). *Annual report and accounts 2015 'becoming the best bank for customers'*. Available at: http://www.lloydsbankin

ggroup.com/globalassets/documents/investors/2015/2015_lbg_annual_report_v3.pdf.

Lloyds [Lloyds Banking Group]. (2015b, June 30). *Sale of TSB banking group PLC*. Available at: http://www.lloydsbankinggroup.com/globalassets/documents/investors/2015/2015jun30_tsb_sale.pdf.

Lloyds [Lloyds Banking Group]. (2017, May 17). *2017 Press releases: Lloyds banking group returns to full private ownership*. Lloyds Press Release. Available at: https://www.lloydsbankinggroup.com/Media/Press-Releases/press-releases-2017/lloyds-banking-group/lloyds-banking-group-returns-to-full-private-ownership/.

Lloyds [Lloyds Banking Group]. (2018). *Annual report and accounts 2018, helping Britain prosper*. Available at: https://www.lloydsbankinggroup.com/globalassets/documents/investors/2018/2018_lbg_annual_report_v2.pdf.

Lloyds [Lloyds Banking Group]. (2019a, October 31). *2019 press releases: Juan colombas to retire during Q3 2020*. Lloyds Press Release. Available at: https://www.lloydsbankinggroup.com/globalassets/documents/investors/2019/2019oct31_lbg_board_change.pdf.

Lloyds [Lloyds Banking Group]. (2019b, December 10). *2019 Press releases: Lloyds banking group responds to the outcome of assurance review*. Lloyds Press Release. Available at: https://www.lloydsbankinggroup.com/Media/Press-Releases/2019-press-releases/lloyds-banking-group/lloyds-banking-group-responds-to-the-outcome-of-assurance-review/.

Lloydsbank.com. (2014). *Lloyds bank Switzerland—Post-closure contact details April 2014 update*. LloydsBankingGroup.com. Available at: https://international.lloydsbank.com/LloydsBankSwitzerland/.

Lloydsbankinggroup.com [Lloyds Banking Group]. (2013, May 29). *LLOYDS banking group announces the sale of its international private banking operations*. Press Release Full Transcript. Available at: http://www.lloydsbankinggroup.com/globalassets/documents/media/press-releases/lloyds-banking-group/2013/2905_pb_sale.pdf.

LloydsBankingGroup.com. (2016). *Our history LloydsBankingGroup.com*. Available at: http://www.lloydsbankinggroup.com/our-group/our-heritage/our-history/.

Makortoff, K., & Julia Kollewe, J. (2019, September 9). PPI claims: Lloyds and Barclays face billions of pounds in extra charges. *The Guardian*. Available at: https://www.theguardian.com/business/2019/sep/09/lloyds-ppi-claims.

National Audit Office. (2010). *Maintaining the financial stability of UK banks: Update on the support schemes*. Available online at: https://www.nao.org.uk/wp-content/uploads/2010/12/1011676es.pdf.

National Audit Office. (2018). *The return of Lloyds banking group to private ownership*. Report by the Comptroller and Auditor General Ordered by the House of Commons to be printed on 21 June 2018. Available online at: https://www.nao.org.uk/wp-content/uploads/2018/06/The-return-of-Lloyds-Banking-Group-to-private-ownership.pdf.

Partington, R. (2015, March 6). Lloyds's Horta-Osorio tops HSBC boss as best-paid bank CEO. *Bloomberg*. Available at: http://www.bloomberg.com/news/articles/2015-03-06/lloyds-s-horta-osorio-tops-hsbc-boss-as-best-paid-u-k-bank-ceo.

Perman, R. (2013). *HUBRIS, How HBOS wrecked the best bank in Britain*. Birlinn Limited: Edinburgh.

Perrin, S. (2014, December 2). Rebuilding lloyds banking group: Interview with Antonio Horta-Osorio. *ICAS*. Available at: http://icas.org.uk/News/Latest-News/Rebuilding-Lloyds-Banking-Group-Interview-with-Antonio-Horta-Osorio/.

Prudential Regulation Authority [Bank of England]. (2017, April). *Supervisory statement|SS2/17 remuneration*. Available at: https://www.bankofengland.co.uk/-/media/boe/files/prudential-regulation/supervisory-statement/2017/ss217.

Prudential Regulation Authority [Bank of England]. *Remuneration code—About*. Available at: http://www.bankofengland.co.uk/pra/Pages/supervision/activities/aboutremuneration.aspx.

Rose, R. (1991). What is lesson-drawing? *Journal of Public Policy, 11*(1), 3–30.

Rose, R. (1993). *Lesson-drawing in public policy: A guide to learning across time and space*. Chatham, New Jersey: Chatham House Publishers.

Rose, R. (2005). *Learning from comparative public policy: A practical guide*. London: Routledge.

Salmon, J. (2015, May 1). *Lloyds sells TSB to Spanish bank sabadell—And loses a staggering £2.5bn*. Thisismoney.co.uk. Available at: http://www.thisismoney.co.uk/money/markets/article-3064784/Lloyds-sells-TSB-Spanish-bank-Sabadell-loses-staggering-2-5billion.html.

Simon, H. A. (1957). *Models of man*. New York: John Wiley and Sons.

Simon, H. A. (1983). *Reason in human affairs*. California: Stanford University Press.

Simon, H. A. (1995). Rationality in political behaviour. *Political Psychology, 16*(1) Special Issue: Political economy and political psychology (March), 45–61.

Simon, H. A. (1998). *The sciences of the artificial* (3rd ed.). Cambridge, MA: MIT Press.

Smith, M. K. (2011, 2013). Chris argyris: Theories of action, double-loop learning and organizational learning. *The encyclopaedia of informal education*. Available at: http://infed.org/mobi/chris-argyris-theories-of-action-double-loop-learning-and-organizational-learning/. Accessed 11 April 2014.

Treanor, J. (2010, April 27). Lloyds banking group returns to profit. *The Guardian*. Available at: http://www.theguardian.com/business/2010/apr/27/lloyds-banking-group-returns-to-profit.

Treanor, J. (2011, May 5). Lloyds U-turn on £3bn payment protection bill drags it into the red. *The Guardian*. Available at: https://www.theguardian.com/business/2011/may/05/lloyds-loss-payment-protection-costs.

Treanor, J. (2013, March 11). Lloyds to raise £400m selling part of St. James's place stake. *The Guardian*. Available at: http://www.theguardian.com/business/2013/mar/11/lloyds-bank-sell-stake-st-james-place.

Treanor, J. (2014, May 8). Barclays to cut 19,000 jobs as it scales back investment arm. *The Guardian*. Available at: https://www.theguardian.com/business/2014/may/08/barclays-to-cut-19000-jobs-scale-back-investment-bank-antony-jenkins.

Treasury Select Committee [House of Commons Treasury Committee]. (2014). *Project verde: Sixth report of session 2014–2015 volume I*. London: The Stationery Office.

UKFI [UK Financial Investments Ltd]. [Online]. Press Release Archives 2011–2015. Available at: http://www.ukfi.co.uk/index.php?URL_link=press-releases&Year=2015.

Verity, A. (2017, January 30). HBOS: A highly unusual fraud case. *BBC News*. Available at: https://www.bbc.co.uk/news/business-38796087.

Wallace, T. (2016, January 28). George osborne delays final sell-off of Lloyds shares due to market turmoil. *Telegraph*. Available at: http://www.telegraph.co.uk/finance/newsbysector/banksandfinance/12127179/George-Osborne-delays-final-sell-off-of-Lloyds-shares-due-to-market-turmoil.html.

Wilson, H. (2013, May 29). Lloyds continues sale of private banks. *Telegraph*. Available at: http://www.telegraph.co.uk/finance/newsbysector/banksandfinance/10087830/Lloyds-continues-sale-of-private-banks.html.

CHAPTER 6

Barclays: Lessons Lost?

Introduction

Barclays navigated the GFC with a reasonable amount of success. The group reported pre-tax profits throughout 2007, 2008 and 2009. In September 2008, Barclays were one of the few banks in a strong enough position to take over the failing US giant Lehman Brothers. In a move that has since been dubbed 'the deal of the century', Barclays acquired £73.5 billion of Lehman's assets for a mere £168 million (Bell & Hindmoor, 2015: 117). However, this initial success led to a certain degree of complacency within the bank as the immediate lessons of the GFC went largely unrecognised—something that I argue in this chapter may be attributed to Barclays lacking the necessary dissatisfaction to seek new information and propel the group from a state of inertia towards the progress of learning.

Yet, in July 2012 following a series of misconduct cases, most prominently brought to light in the Libor and Euribor rate-fixing scandals, Barclays commissioned the Salz Review (Salz hereafter), an independent evaluation of the group. The objective of Salz was to undertake a 'deep dive' into all facets of the business and come up with a series of policy initiatives that would help Barclays 'recapture the trust' of its customers and peers and make the bank a 'market leader' (Salz, 2013: 2). Following the report, Barclays promised major reform and set about enshrining the lessons of Salz by launching a new group-wide strategic plan named the

A. Barber, *UK Banks and the Lessons of the Great Financial Crisis*, Building a Sustainable Political Economy: SPERI Research & Policy, https://doi.org/10.1007/978-3-030-70254-0_6

Transform Programme (Transform hereafter). Transform would see the 'majority' of those recommendations set out by Salz aligned to a series of financial and non-financial metrics that would look to remedy the shortcomings highlighted by the review (Barclays, 2013a: 58).

Chapter Overview

While the publication of Salz and the subsequent commissioning of Transform would, upon first reading, appear to suggest the presence of learning—being a fundamental reappraisal of the group's underlying theories-in-use successively upheld by policy initiatives—the story of learning at Barclays has been rather mixed. Post-crisis, regulatory scandals including: the fixing of Forex rates, events pertaining to money laundering, tax evasion, allegations of fraud, the mistreatment of whistleblowers and reporting compliance issues have all questioned the extent to which Barclays has truly undergone a fundamental reappraisal of its normative frames, policy preferences and institutional biases and truly learned lesson from the GFC.

Similarly, though remuneration has been reduced by approximately 53% at the group level and 63% within the investment bank between 2010 and 2018, the most fundamental shifts appear to have come in response to tougher new regulatory standards, namely CRD IV. Likewise, the group has utilised role-based allowances to circumvent the regulation of pay and has been vehemently opposed to such rules. Comments made by leading figures within the group appear to suggest that structural competitive pressures and Barclays' ability to 'attract and retain' the best banking talent may explain these shortcomings.

Equally, while the group has made some progress on the structure and composition of the balance sheet—increasing customers deposits and residential mortgage lending, reducing impaired loans and derivatives and recoding strong capital ratios—more recently there has been a degree of backsliding on the reform agenda. Reports in the financial media, along with statements by key agents at Barclays, suggest that the investment bank may once again become the bedrock of the group's business strategy and which questions the extent of learning. Discussions around structural competitive pressures, the primacy of shareholder value and the agency of the group chief executive are used to explain Barclays' learning journey and how lessons learned may become lessons lost.

Factors Explaining Barclays' Learning Journey

The story of learning at Barclays in the post-crisis decade is a rather complicated and nuanced phenomenon. For this reason, I argue that in order to fully understand the learning trajectory of Barclays, we must analyse individual facets of the business on a case-by-case basis and consider the relevant structural, institutional and agency-based factors that have determined the group's ability to learn.

One such contingent factor that may explain Barclays' learning trajectory, particularly in relation to the investment bank, is Margaret Archer's (2003, 2007, 2012) work on the 'internal conversation' (discussed in Chapter 2). According to Archer (2003, 2007, 2012), all human behaviour is determined by a series of internal conversations. When faced with complex decisions, agents will enter into an unconscious self-reflexive internal dialogue whereby the individual will carefully consider their position against a number of structural constraints including social norms, expectations of the self and of one's peers and the potential of the immediate operating environment (ibid.: 2003). This internal deliberative process subsequently leads an agent to become 'meta-reflexive' whereby an individual becomes aware of their 'situational logic of opportunity', that being, a greater understanding of both the possibilities and limitations of their own agency and the structures which surround them (Archer, 2012). In the case of Barclays, I argue that while change has been desired by the bank, and has to some extent been achieved, Barclays' internal conversation and situational logic of opportunity has determined the associated costs of learning, encapsulated by perceived structural competitive pressures, as being too high. As such, we witness an unravelling of the reform agenda set out in Salz and Transform.

Libor, Euribor, Salz and Transform

Barclays navigated the GFC with a degree of success and came through the crisis in much better health than some of its rivals; growing the business when others were retrenching, avoiding state-sponsored bailouts and continuing to record profits at a time when rivals were making record losses. As such, Barclays' experience of the GFC appears to have resulted in the group suffering insufficient dissatisfaction to prompt the bank to seek new information and learn. Instead, in the immediate aftermath of the crisis Barclays continued to operate in a 'business-as-usual' manner with any changes at the bank being confined to the very fringes of pre-existing structures and institutional norms. Indeed, between 2008 and 2012, we witness little change in the overall structure and composition of the business.

However, in 2012 Barclays became embroiled in a series of rate-rigging scandals. Following an investigation by both UK and US regulators that would last almost 4 years, it was revealed that a significant number of the group's employees had been complicit in the rigging of the London Inter-Bank Rate (Libor) and the Euro Interbank Offered Rate (Euribor) (McBride et al., 2015; Reuters, 2016a). A Financial Services Authority (FSA) report concluded that Barclays' involvement in the rate-rigging scandals stretched back as early as 2003 (FCA, 2012). Damning email conversations between Barclays traders and colleagues at rival institutions were subsequently published. In one such exchange, a Barclays trader was reported as saying 'If you aint cheating, you aint trying' (anonymous cited in Titcomb, 2015). Regulators including the FSA in the UK and the Department of Justice and the Commodity Futures Trading Commission in the United States would subsequently fine Barclays with the bank paying a total of £290 million in penalties (Binham, 2015; Treanor, 2012). Civil and criminal hearings would follow (Binham & Thompson, 2017) with a number of employees being sacked and sentenced to prison terms of between two and six years (Reuters, 2016b; Ridley, 2016).[1]

It would appear that Barclays' involvement in the Libor and Euribor scandals would result in sufficient dissatisfaction to prompt learning as shortly thereafter, the group commissioned Anthony Salz to undertake an independent review of the bank's 'values, principles and standards of operation' with a view to providing a 'comprehensive roadmap for cultural change at the bank' (Salz, 2013: 1). However, while Salz and the resulting Transform Programme initially suggest evidence of learning, deeper analysis of the group's performance across the areas of governance and regulation, remuneration and bonuses, and the balance sheet suggests that learning and change is still absent in some areas of the business. In this respect, while Salz and Transform represent a search for, and evaluation of, new information, Barclays, importantly, has failed to apply lessons learned. This is despite the dedication of institutional resources—learning

[1] Barclays would later claim that during the GFC, it had come under great pressure from the UK Government and the Bank of England to submit false Libor rates, something that the Bank and officials vehemently denied (Noonan et al., 2017a).

space—towards the self-reflexive process. The failure to execute the *application* phase of the learning process has meant that in many cases learning at the group is either absent or incomplete.

Governance and Regulation

In this section of the chapter, I argue that despite Salz and Transform Barclays has failed to present evidence of learning and change. The examples examined below suggests that there is present at Barclays the distinct lack of tangible change to the group's underlying theories-in-use, ideational frames and policy preferences. It will be posited that this failure to learn may be attributed to Transform lacking substantial reforms and policy initiatives aimed at remedying those failures highlighted by Salz. On a wider scale, these shortcomings can be tied to how structural competitive pressures in relation to remuneration and bonuses have been perceived post-GFC.

PPI and Mis-Selling

Like the other banks in this study, Barclays would become embroiled in the PPI scandal when in 2011, a court ruling concluded that banks had been aggressively selling PPI on loans and credit cards for over a decade (Weardon, 2011). By 2018, the PPI scandal had cost Barclays approximately £11 billion in compensation claims (Barclays, 2018; Dunkley, 2016). Barclays would also face further litigation and costs relating to the mis-selling of products. For instance, the US Department of Justice (DoJ) has sued the bank over claims that it had mis-sold residential mortgage-backed securities before the GFC (Arnold & Shubber, 2018). In 2018, following a three-year investigation by the DoJ, Barclays agreed to pay £1.5 billion in penalties for the mis-selling of products between 2005 and 2007 (DoJ, 2018). We should of course note that these two incidents predate the GFC and the subsequent publication of Salz and Transform and as such do not necessarily represent a failure to learn or otherwise. Yet, these events remain pertinent to the argument set out in this chapter as in many respects, they epitomise the wider setting against which Barclays' learning journey has occurred.

Benchmark Rigging: Libor, Euribor and Forex

Salz (2013: 8) concluded that remuneration structures in place at Barclays at the time of the GFC had created a results-driven culture that paid little attention as to how targets were achieved. The review went on to suggest that this lack of oversight, coupled with an inherently skewed bonus culture, had meant that individuals had been incentivised to operate in questionable ways (ibid.). The result of which had culminated in the manipulation of Libor and Euribor with Salz (2013: 8) noting that 'pay [had been] the primary tool [that had] shaped behaviour' at Barclays.

In late 2012, the then GCE Bob Diamond wrote to Andrew Tyrie MP, Chairman of the Treasury Select Committee, to assure Mr Tyrie that Barclays had taken 'decisive action' to guarantee that future Libor submissions would be 'protected from inappropriate pressure' and that new measures would prevent further abuses (Diamond, 2012). However, Mr Diamond failed to recognise the inherent dangers of the group's remuneration structures and the role that these institutional arrangements had played in the rate-rigging scandals as identified by Salz (2013: 8). Moreover, while Barclays promised 'decisive action' to ensure such breaches would not happen again, Harry Bradford of the *Huffington Post* noted that the culmination of this action resulted in employees being made to watch a 12-minute video on the subject of values, ethics and transparency (Bradford, 2012). Similarly, Salz reported that:

> Following the LIBOR event, Barclays initiated a review of all of its business activity involving benchmark rates or indices. Lessons learned studies were also conducted after other loss events...However, it is not evident that they were carried out consistently, promptly or following the same approach.
> (Salz, 2013: 158)

This failure to recognise the role that skewed remuneration structures had played in the Libor and Euribor scandals, along with insufficient policy initiatives aimed at remedying institutional flaws concerning the group's bonus culture, would later give rise to further benchmark abuses as Barclays were found guilty of rigging the Forex rate. In 2015, Barclays agreed to pay the FCA £284 million and US regulators £99 million following an investigation which revealed that the bank had conspired to fix Forex rates between 2009 and 2014—over two years after the original Libor and Euribor scandals had come to light and over a year after Transform had been launched (Barclays, 2015c; Bourke, 2015). Investigators on both sides of the Atlantic found that Barclays' staff would deliberately 'hold' a customer's Forex trade in an attempt to better their own position. If markets then moved in a direction that would benefit Barclays, and subsequently the trader by way of a bonus, the trade would be executed (Chon & Martin, 2015). However, if the trade meant that the customer would benefit, but not Barclays, traders would disregard the transaction blaming a computer error with senior managers instructing staff that 'if you get enquiries [about rejected trades] just obfuscate and stonewall' (anonymous cited in Chon & Martin, 2015).

In a statement issued by Antony Jenkins, the group chief executive said:

> The misconduct at the core of these investigations is wholly incompatible with Barclays' purpose and values and...[t]his demonstrates again the importance of our continuing work to build a values-based culture and strengthen our control environment. We remain completely committed to that effort.
>
> (Jenkins, 2015)

However, Mr Jenkins and Barclays failed once again to implement specific policy initiatives in keeping with those sentiments expressed which, as established in Chapter 2, is a key determinant in the learning process. Instead, the GCE cited the importance of Transform in changing Barclays' culture. Yet, as discussed below, Transform lacks tangible policy initiatives and instead relies upon a single subjective measure of good governance. Moreover, while the GCE noted that it had been individuals that had committed the infractions, the account of learning presented in Chapter 2 stresses that organisations learn when agents that embody institution learn.[2] As such, the failure of individual agents to learn lessons from Salz and Transform, and the GFC more broadly, may also be indicative of a wider institutional failure to learn.

Elephant Deal

In 2015 Barclays were once again in the crosshairs of the FCA, this time for failing to carry out the proper due diligence on a huge private transaction worth a reported £1.9 billion (Binham & Dunkley, 2015).

[2] See Sabatier (1988) and Bell and Hindmoor (2015) for further discussion.

Known in the banking industry as an 'elephant deal' because of its colossal size, the transaction involved Barclays transferring the funds of politically exposed persons without completing the necessary checks and balances and which would reportedly earn the bank more than £50 million in fees (Treanor, 2015c). The FCA concluded that in its eagerness to complete the deal, Barclays failed to carry out crucial checks on clients and ignored its own protocols on the handling of large transactions, even going so far as to offer clients £37.7 million in compensation if their identity was ever revealed (ibid.). The deal was principally carried out by the Wealth & Investment division, which has subsequently been retrenched into the retail bank,[3] and landed the group a fine of £72 million, which included a £52.3 million disgorgement of commission earned on the deal (Treanor, 2015b).

Like previous regulatory failures that occurred in the aftermath of Salz and Transform, Barclays has failed to demonstrate tangible evidence of change with the distinct lack of improved policy action aimed at preventing potential future abuses. Likewise, following the incident, Barclays has refused to comment on the specifics of the case such as the number of staff involved and whether those responsible for the deal have ever been reprimanded (Salmon, 2015). Similarly, there is no evidence to suggest that Barclays has reneged or backed out of the deal that is set to last several decades with plans for similar transactions to be carried out over a number of years.

Dark Pool Trading

In January 2016, Barclays was hit with further penalties and reputational damage when it was fined approximately £50 million by the US Securities Exchange Commission (SEC) over its use of so-called trading 'dark pools'. Dark pools were devised as means of protecting investors by allowing certain trades to be made in private and thus sheltering actors from market reactions to the purchase of stock (Treanor & Rushe, 2014). The SEC concluded that Barclays had led investors to believe that their trades would be carried out in secret and thus protecting the client from

[3] Although we should note that the retrenchment of the division is in no way connected to the deal in question.

high frequency predatory trading[4] (Rennison, 2016). However, Barclays failed to carry out the proper due diligence on its dark pools meaning that the secret trades could be identified by algorithms and stock purchased by rival investors before the dark pool trade could be executed (Treanor & Rushe, 2014). As Andrew Verity of the BBC described, '[t]he problem with [Barclays'] dark pools was that they were too damn light' (Verity, 2016).

Money Laundering and Whistle-Blowing

In 2016, an internal whistle-blower would once again call into question Barclays' due diligence when it emerged that the chief risk officer of Barclays France, Philippe Hebert, had raised serious concerns over anti-money laundering procedures and selling practices at certain Barclays France branches. In a letter obtained by the *Financial Times* addressed to Barclays France CEO Tony Blanco, Mr Hebert claimed that he had increasing worries about the implementation of anti-money laundering controls and good governance best practice (Hebert cited in Arnold and Jenkins, 2016). Mr Hebert went on to state that he believed there to be:

> serious mismanagement at cashier level and…particularly poor handling of this situation by the various control services and lines of defence, even though it carries serious risks of money laundering, especially at branches already known to be at risk (such as Biarritz).
>
> (Hebert cited in Arnold & Jenkins, 2016)

The letter would detail several incidents in which internal regulatory oversight and good governance was lacking. Specifically, Mr Hebert claimed that Barclays staff had failed to identify wealthy clients as 'politically exposed persons'; allowed customers to make multiple and successive large-scale withdrawals under the €10,000 threshold[5]; failed to adequately investigate the detention of staff by police over the suspicion of money laundering and had mis-sold costly investment and insurance

[4] Predatory trading is particularly harmful as it has the potential to significantly push up the value of stock before a 'buy' can be executed, thus diminishing an investor's return (Rennison, 2016).

[5] In one case, a client was permitted to make 38 sequential transactions (Grandhi, 2016).

products that were inappropriate for clients (Grandhi, 2016). In written response to the *Financial Times* Barclays stated that:

> [w]e were already aware of these allegations. We are satisfied that the concerns were already identified and under investigation and action being taken in accordance with our standard processes.
>
> (Barclays cited in Arnold & Jenkins, 2016)

However, in his letter Mr Hebert noted that while his concerns had indeed been raised previously, the issues highlighted had not been 'taken seriously enough' (Hebert cited in Arnold & Jenkins, 2016). The chief risk officer likewise referred to the fact that following the incident, Barclays had failed to take a single disciplinary action against any of the accused (ibid.).

Barclays would face further reputational damage when in April 2017 it came to light that the GCE, Jes Staley, had attempted to uncover the identity of an anonymous whistle-blower (Noonan et al., 2017b). It was revealed that following several letters written by an unidentified Barclays' employee, which criticised the recent appointment of a senior manager, Mr Staley approached the group's head of compliance in an effort to discover the details of the author (Arnold, 2017a). The compliance team informed Mr Staley that the anonymity of the source was protected and that the GCE should abandon his investigation (ibid.). Yet, Mr Staley took it upon himself to pursue the culprit, this time employing the services of the Barclays' security team and a US law enforcement agency (Arnold, 2017b). Mr Staley's efforts ultimately proved unsuccessful but the GCE's actions led to multiple investigations by authorities in both the UK and United States.

In the UK, the FCA and PRA would each launch its own investigation into the matter and which culminated in Mr Staley being fined a total of £642,430 (Binham, 2018). Barclays would also reprimand Mr Staley and disgorge £500,000 from the GCE's 2016 bonus (Barclays, 2018). In the United States, The New York Department of Financial Services would fine Barclays £11.2 million after it concluded that:

> shortcomings in governance, controls and corporate culture relating to Barclays' whistleblowing function permitted a sequence of events that potentially could have had a detrimental impact on the efficacy of Barclays' whistleblowing program.

(Department of Financial Services, 2018)

Despite this, in 2017 Barclays' internal audit committee concluded that the bank was still not doing enough to ensure that it met its control and compliance obligations. In its annual address to shareholders, the committee challenged the 'application' of Barclays' 'lessons learned process' noting the 'low level of coverage of significant control incidents' (Barclays, 2017: 59). However, a year later the committee would once again raise concerns over Barclays' control functions and the remediation of associated risk, noting that:

> issues arising from unsatisfactory audits indicated that there was still work to do in embedding the required level of control consciousness across the Barclays Group and ensuring that control exceptions were highlighted clearly in management reporting.
>
> (Barclays, 2018: 64)

Misconduct Over Capital Raising

Barclays would face additional litigation and costs when in 2014, it emerged that the UK Serious Fraud Office (SFO) and FCA were investigating the bank over allegations that it had acted inappropriately when raising capital from investors located in the Middle East (Binham & Jenkins, 2014). In 2008, at the height of the GFC and in a desperate attempt to shore up its balance sheet and avoid government intervention, Barclays sought to raise more than £11 billion in capital from overseas investors. The group successfully raised £4.5 billion via a non-traditional rights issue and then secured a further £7 billion of private capital from investors in Qatar and Abu Dhabi (Bell & Hindmoor, 2015). However, the deal later became the subject of a criminal investigation after it was alleged that Barclays had secretly agreed to pay investors a total of £322 million in 'fees' and other 'commission' in order to gain support for the deal (Schäfer et al., 2013). Barclays was then accused of loaning investors from Qatar its own money that would be reinvested in the bank at a later date. In an effort to protect the group's share price, Barclays failed to disclose the particulars of the deal meaning that the group would breach market rules on competition and reporting (Binham, 2017a).

The FCA concluded that the bank's reporting of the fees and commission paid on the deal were insufficient, subsequently fining Barclays £50 million (Schäfer et al., 2013). The SFO's investigation into Barclays would last over five years. However, in 2018 the Crown Court would dismiss charges of conspiracy to commit fraud and unlawful financial activity and discharge the case (Arnold et al., 2018). The SFO subsequently pursued four former Barclays' executives, including ex group CEO John Varley, who would each face separate criminal prosecutions. In 2020, despite a seven-year investigation costing around £10 million, all four men were cleared of any wrongdoing (Croft & Binham, 2020; Serious Fraud Office, 2020).

This notwithstanding, the 2008 Qatari funding call would continue to plague the bank when in 2016, PCP Capital Partners, an investment group run by businesswoman Amanda Staveley, filed a lawsuit against Barclays worth £1.6 billion for unpaid fees and damages (Binham, 2016). In 2008, Ms Staveley's business was recruited by Barclays to put together a parallel Abu Dhabi investment in the bank. It is alleged that Ms Staveley's client, Sheikh Mansour bin Zayed al-Nahyan—who would invest £3.25 billion in Barclays as part of its 2008 capital raising—was led to invest on 'manifestly worse terms than Qatari investors' (Binham, 2017b). PCP Capital Partners claimed that were it not for Barclays' deceit over alleged 'side deals' with its Qatari investors, the business would have secured an agreement that would have netted it and Ms Staveley £1.6 billion in fees and commission (Makortoff, 2020).[6]

These incidents along with a lack of substantive reform to the group's underlying theories-in-use, institutional preferences and policy actions, suggest that Barclays has failed to learn despite the promise of Transform to implement a 'cultural revolution'. Moreover, the events detailed above indicate that while Salz and Transform may, upon first reading, appear to present evidence of learning and change, there remains an obvious lack of tangible policy initiatives aimed at upholding those sentiments expressed in Salz and Transform. Indeed, despite having the dissatisfaction needed to learn, Barclays has failed to address post-crisis regulatory and governance breaches. As such, we may conclude that in the post-crisis decade, Barclays has failed to learn and change in keeping with the double-loop theory described in Chapter 2. Given the role that systemically important institutions like Barclays can and have played in the transfer of risk to the real economy, this failure to learn could mean that Barclays may yet prove to be a threat to the wider stability of financial markets.

[6]At the time writing (October 2020) the case in ongoing.

The Failure of Transform

This apparent lack of learning and change in relation to group governance and regulatory oversight can be attributed to the failure of Transform to implement detailed policies aimed at upholding lesson learned. Instead, Transform relies upon just a single measure of good governance and best practice, namely, the balanced scorecard. Transform, for example, asserts that at the heart of its 'cultural revolution' is the balanced scorecard that sets out the group's key performance indicators and which is a 'crucial piece' of the restructuring plan (Barclays, 2013c: 10). In relation to culture and conduct, the balanced scorecard has just one specific key performance indicator; 'to consistently achieve a score of 6.5/10 in the YouGov survey by 2018' (Barclays, 2013c: 44; Barclays, 2018: 117). This measure is essentially a 'conduct reputation survey' that includes input from:

> MPs, business and political stakeholders, media, non-governmental organisations, charities, think tanks and other general opinion formers (drawn from academia, public sector, arts/leisure, professionals and religion).
>
> (Barclays, 2013c: 44)

However, a simple review of the group's balanced scorecard reveals that in 2013 Barclays achieved 5.2/10 on the YouGov survey (Barclays, 2014b: 11). In 2014, this figure rose to 5.3/10 and then 5.4/10 in 2015 (Barclays, 2015a). Yet despite this incremental progress, between 2015 and 2018 the group failed to improve its YouGov survey score entirely. Moreover, between 2013—the year that the measure was introduced—and 2018, Barclays recoded an average score of just 5.3/10 (Barclays, 2014b, 2015a, 2016, 2017, 2018). As such, Barclays not only missed its desired target of achieving a consistent score of 6.5/10 by 2018, but also, based on the group's year-on-year progression, will not achieve its target until the year 2029.

The failure of the balanced scorecard, and relatedly Transform, to achieve its desired outcome can be attributed to the scorecard's objectives and application being directly tied to employee remuneration. Specifically, the significance of the balanced scorecard in determining the bonus pool at Barclays has over time been eroded and diluted, particularly at senior levels, with the metric coming to playing an increasingly smaller role in the calculation of awards. For example, when the scorecard was launched in 2013, it would have a maximum weighting of 35% in calculating each the annual and long-term bonuses[7] (Barclays, 2013c). However, data shows that in practice the balanced scorecard would in fact determine just 20% of the long-term incentive's overall value for executive directors between 2013 and 2015 (Barclays, 2013c, 2014b, 2015a). In 2015, Barclays announced that it would be lowering the official weighting of the scorecard which, from 2016 onwards, would contribute to just 15% of the long-term bonus' value (Barclays, 2015a). In 2018, the allowance of the balanced scorecard in calculating the annual incentive would similarly be reduced to 20% (Barclays, 2018).

Given the diminished role that the balanced scorecard—heralded by Barclays as a 'crucial' part of its plan to overhaul culture at the group—has played in determining employee remuneration, it is of little surprise that Barclays has failed to realise its targets in relation to group governance and compliance. Moreover, as discuss below, post-GFC Barclays' remuneration has continued to emphasise economic measures as a key determinant for bonuses at the bank. Indeed, in the post-crisis decade, Barclays has continued stress a result-based culture with a dwindling regard for how such outcomes are delivered. Such factors may explain why the group has continued to suffer from governance and regulatory breaches despite the presence of Salz and Transform.

The evidence presented in this section indicates that while Barclays has dedicated institutional resources towards the search for and evaluation of new information, the group has failed to *apply* lessons learned. The events detailed above demonstrate that post-GFC there is present at Barclays a distinct lack of improved policy action and change. This failure to uphold lessons learned with targeted policy initiatives may explain why Salz and Transform have failed despite Barclays orienting learning space—institutional resources—towards the self-reflexive process. Put simply, though Barclays has sought and evaluated new information, the group has failed to apply this information. As such, it may be possible to conclude that learning is absent within the facet of governance and regulation with a lack of change to pre-crisis structures and culture at the bank.

[7] Discussed in more detail below.

Remuneration and Bonuses

Following the GFC Barclays, like many of its competitors, sought to address the issue of remuneration which, as discussed in Chapter 3, played a significant role in the events of 2008. However, this rebalancing of executive pay has taken place, like the balance sheet element below, against the backdrop of structural constraints. Most notably, competition over talent and increased regulatory requirements has determined the extent of reform. While Barclays has made some impressive strides in relation to pay, with total remuneration at the bank falling by 53% between 2010 and 2018 and 63% within the investment bank over the same period (Barclays, 2015a, 2018), we must recognise that the most significant change has come in the light of tougher new regulatory standards. Specifically, CRD IV has largely determined the structure and composition of pay post-crisis and as such may be indicative of a failure to learn in keeping with the double-loop theory.

In this section, I argue that Barclays' failure to learn in relation to remuneration and bonuses may be attributed to the structural environment. Specifically, I posit that the perceived threat posed by international rivals to Barclays' ability to attract and retain talent has determined the learning trajectory of the group. Exposure to these pressures can be attributed to Barclays' overall strategic direction, which, post-crisis, has seen the group maintain a large international presence that according to GCE Jes Staley is now 'very focused... on both sides of the Atlantic' (Staley, 2016).[8] I suggest that the group's repositioning following the GFC has maintained Barclays' exposure to international markets and hence competition for talent. In particular, Barclays' focus upon US markets has meant that the group has been pitted against rival institutions located in North America[9] that are not subject to the same regulatory stipulations and can explain why we witness little evidence of

[8] Since the GFC, we have seen Barclays' business model shift towards a two-pronged attack. On the one hand, we have Barclays UK—the ring-fenced UK bank focused on UK consumer and business banking—and on the other, Barclays International—with an emphasis upon transatlantic wholesale and consumer banking across the United States, Germany, Tokyo, Hong Kong, Singapore and Mumbai (Staley, 2016).

[9] For a discussion of regulatory changes to pay and compensation in the United States following the GFC, see Ferrarini and Ungureanu (2011).

learning and change.[10] Similarly, much like RBS and HSBC—discussed in the coming chapter—the capacity to recruit and retain talent may also shed light on the associated costs of learning with a perceived diminished ability to compete for staff being viewed as a huge penalty to the bank and subsequently an obstacle to change. It will be demonstrated that competitive emulation, along with responses to shifting regulatory requirements, has been the underlying feature of Barclays' remuneration structure post-crisis.

Annual Incentive

When the GFC hit in 2008, Barclays' remuneration structure was very much 'performance based' with the group using bonuses to 'drive a high performance culture' (Barclays, 2007: 144–145). In 2008, variable group remuneration consisted of two main elements, the annual incentive and long-term incentive (Barclays, 2007). In 2008, the annual incentive carried a maximum of up to 250% of base salary with awards paid in both cash and shares (ibid.). However, awards made for the financial year 2007–2008, demonstrate that cash bonuses for executive directors totalled £10.1 million, with the median award being £2 million (Barclays, 2007). This reveals that bonuses paid to executive directors at the height of the GFC were worth approximately 314% of the average base salary of an executive director and way in excess of 'typical' allowances under the annual incentive. Salz (2013: 7) concluded that such structures had encouraged excessive risk-taking, noting that 'there was an overemphasis on short-term financial performance, reinforced by remuneration systems that tended to reward revenue generation'.

[10] Indeed, evidence from the comparator group in this study appears to suggest that those banks that have maintained or transitioned into a more internationally focused business model, particularly outside of the EU, have been more sensitive to structural competitive pressures regarding employee remuneration. Both Barclays and HSBC have directly cited competitive pressures as being a key factor in determining remuneration. Lloyds, on the other hand, that have retrenched operations on domestic markets, appear to be the only bank that has shown substantial evidence of learning in relation to remuneration. While detractors may argue that the case of RBS does not fit with this hypothesis—with RBS also retrenching operations on domestic markets post-GFC—I suggest that RBS is unique insomuch as the failure to learn in relation to remuneration can be attributed to the failure to orient learning space towards the learning process. As a result, RBS has fallen back upon institutional path dependencies.

However, following the GFC Barclays reformed the annual incentive, which by 2018 was worth a maximum of 80% of fixed pay (Barclays, 2018). Awards in excess of £500,000 would be subject to a 60% deferment under the bank's share value plan, with bonuses below £500,000 also liable to a 40% deferment (Barclays, 2015a, 2018). In both cases, the holding period would total 3 years and 6 months (ibid.). These changes, for the most part, would be in keeping with rules on remuneration set out by the FCA, PRA and EU. Although, we should note that Barclays did extend the holding period by an additional six months beyond the regulatory minimum of three years set out by the authorities.

These figures demonstrate that in the post-crisis decade, Barclays reduced the maximum potential of the annual incentive as a percentage of base salary by 68%. However, it is worth noting that up until 2013—the final year before the EU mandated introduction of CDR IV—the award still carried an allowance of up to 250% of base salary (Barclays, 2013c). Additionally, like the other banks in this study, with the exception of Lloyds, Barclays would also seek shareholder consent to increase the variable pay ratio to its upper limit of 1:2 of base salary, as permitted under CRD IV (Barclays, 2013c, 2014b). Consequently, the limiting of awards may be directly tied to tougher new regulatory requirements and as a result would fail to present evidence of independent learning as associated with the double-loop thesis. Indeed, much of Barclays' rescaling of both the annual award and long-term incentive, discussed below, has by the bank's own admission been largely influenced by the introduction of both the Remuneration Code (2011) and the European Parliament's CRD IV legislation with Sir John Sunderland, former head of the remuneration committee, telling investors in 2014 that:

> our variable pay decisions were taken against a background of significant regulatory developments with Barclays being subject to both UK regulatory requirements… [and] CRD IV.
>
> (Sunderland in Barclays, 2014b: 78)

Similarly, in the group's 2013 strategic review, Barclays assured investors that it would 'continue to pay for performance – and [would] continue to pay competitively for the best talent' (Barclays, 2013b: 10). Then in the 2013 annual report, Sir John Sunderland noted that changes to the group's bonus structure had not been:

> matched by our peers, most notably the major US banks who are among our primary competitors. As a result, our lack of pay competitiveness [has caused] demonstrable damage to our business, especially outside the UK. The global resignation rate for senior staff in 2013 was significantly above that in 2012. This was particularly marked in the Investment Bank with a near doubling of resignations of senior staff in the US.
>
> (Sunderland in Barclays, 2013c: 89)

These comments suggest that the restructuring of Barclays' remuneration policies have come not just in the light of new regulatory requirements, but also in the face of structural competitive pressures concerning the recruitment and retention of staff. Post-GFC, the fear of losing talent to rival organisations appears to have been an underlying feature of Barclays' remuneration, having negatively affected the group's ability to learn. Similarly, staff resignations in relation to pay may be symptomatic of the associated costs of reform, with Barclays losing valuable talent to rival organisations that are not held to the same domestic and European regulatory standards.

When Salz (2013: 8) concluded that remuneration at the bank had incentivised short-term risk-taking, Barclays responded by stating that it would introduce policies that would look to align employee rewards not only with performance but with how such objectives were achieved (Barclays, 2013a: 8). As a result, it was determined that from 2013 onwards, group remuneration would include a series of non-financial benchmarks encapsulated in the 'balanced scorecard' and which would carry a weighting of 35% in calculating both the annual and long-term bonuses (ibid.: 3). Yet, as discussed above, in reality the balanced scorecard would play a much smaller role in determining the actual bonus pool. By 2018, the weighting of the balanced scorecard had been officailly revised down with non-financial metrics determining just 20% of the annual award and financial performance carrying a weighting of 60%, role dependent 'personal objectives' would account for the remaining 20% (Barclays, 2018).

This may lead us to conclude that while Barclays has reduced the overall value of its annual bonus in the post-crisis decade, the greatest changes have come in response to tougher regulatory standards. Moreover, the use of financial measures has continued to be the standard for the bank's remuneration policies and which is indicative of a lack of learning with Barclays failing to account for the potential of such metrics to incentivise risk-taking. Similarly, perceived structural competitive pressure surrounding the group's ability to retain its senior bankers has likewise being a key factor in Barclays' learning trajectory.

Long-Term Incentive Plan

Barclays' failure to learn in relation to remuneration can likewise be observed across the long-term incentive plan (LTIP). In 2008, Barclays' long-term element of variable pay was measured over a three-year period, paid entirely in shares and carried a maximum potential value of 150% of fixed salary (Barclays, 2007). The LTIP would be calculated based solely on financial metrics with *economic performance* and *total shareholder return* each accounting for 50% of the award's value (ibid.). While the bonus would have a distinctly long-term outlook utilising retention periods and share awards, a focus upon purely economic measures meant that the bonus paid little attention as to how results were delivered and consequently may have encouraged excessive risk-taking.

In contrast, by 2018 Barclays had updated the LTIP which was claimed by the group would:

> [reward] growth in shareholder value over a multi-year period...discourage excessive risk-taking and inappropriate behaviours and [foster] a long term view and align executive Directors' interests with those of shareholders. (Barclays, 2018: 110)

Under the reformed LTIP, financial performance would no longer be the sole measure of the bonus. Instead, the value of awards would be calculated using a combination of both financial and non-financial metrics, including the balanced scorecard. However, while the balanced scorecard would, by 2018, carry a weighting of 15%—revised down from 35% in 2013—in the determining awards, over 70% of the bonus would continue to be calculated using financial metrics, with personal objectives accounting for the remaining 15% (Barclays, 2018). Though the introduction of the balanced scorecard may represent some limited evidence of learning, we can see that, much like the annual incentive, financial measures have continued to dominate how LTIP awards have been calculated at Barclays in the post-crisis decade.

The maximum value of the LTIP would also witness a 20% decrease with the award being limited to 120% of base salary by 2018 (Barclays,

2014b, 2018). Though the upper value of the LTIP decreased between 2008 and 2018, it can be argued that such a reduction, once again, was largely motivated by structural factors, namely, CRD IV. For example, in 2013—the final year before the implementation of CRD VI—the award still carried a maximum potential of 400% of base salary (Barclays, 2011, 2012). While this does not necessarily represent an absence of learning in of itself, such details do cast doubt over the extent to which we may conclude that changes at the bank have been endogenously originated.

This apparent lack of learning and change may once again be attributed to competitive pressures that have been a constant feature of remuneration at Barclays post-GFC. Indeed, sentiments expressed by key agents at the bank appear to suggest that a fear of losing talent to rivals has factored heavily in the restructuring process. In his 2015 remuneration report Crawford Gillies, the newly appointed chairman of the remuneration committee, noted that the 'volume and pace of regulatory change' had accentuated the 'competitive disadvantages attributable to the lack of a global level regulatory playing field' and as such, it was necessary that Barclays revise the 'performance measures of the LTIP' (Giles in Barclays, 2015a: 84). Similarly, in 2017 Mr Giles once again commented that regulatory changes concerning remuneration introduced by the PRA, FCA and European Banking Association had 'compounded the competitive disadvantage for UK based global firms' (Giles in Barclays, 2017: 100).

Role-Based Pay

Like all the banks in this study, Barclays has also utilised role-based pay (RBP), with the group introducing this element of remuneration in 2014 as a 'key action' in response to CRD IV (Barclays, 2013c: 90). Under the RBP initiative, senior employees would be eligible to receive a monthly cash payment alongside their salary, that would reflect the 'seniority, breadth and depth' of their role (Barclays, 2018: 106). Though Barclays would be clear to stress that the RBP would not be 'adjusted for performance' (Barclays, 2013c: 95), the fact remains that the award would be reviewed annually and subject to both upwards and downward revisions in-line with fixed pay (Barclays, 2018) and would be reflective of the 'business and economic environment' (ibid., 2013c: 95).

The introduction of RBP indicates that Barclays though compliant with the letter of the law may not have truly embraced the spirit of new regulations on pay in the post-crisis decade. As discussed in previous chapters, the use of these controversial awards has allowed institutions to circumvent regulatory stipulations while remaining amenable with the 'letter of the law'. Accordingly, the inclusion of RBP may be further evidence of a lack of learning in relation to the role of regulators in the global financial order. Furthermore, Barclays appear to have failed to learn from its own evaluation carried out by Salz (2013: 10) which concluded that the group needed to move beyond the 'confrontational approach [to] regulators' that dominated the bank pre-crisis. However, the use of RBP clearly calls into question the spirit with which Barclays has met regulatory standards. Again, though Barclays has sought and evaluated new information in the form of Salz and Transform, the group has failed to *apply* lessons learned with the distinct lack of positive policy change.

Like the annual bonus and LTIP, the introduction of RBP and the subsequent failure to learn can be attributed to perceived structural pressures pertaining to competition over talent. For example, Barclays' 2013 remuneration report commented that the introduction of CRD IV would impact its 'competitiveness in the global market for talent' (Barclays, 2013c: 90). Consequently, the group would introduce RBP as a means to 'remain competitive for global talent' (Barclays, 2014b: 81). Moreover, when Jes Staley was appointed as GCE in December 2015, Barclays announced that it would be granting him RBP of £1.1 million in order to remain 'commensurate with market pay levels' (Barclays, 2015a: 83), adding that RBP for all employees would be determined by 'market practice and ability to recruit' (ibid.: 113).

These statements suggest that structural pressures have influenced Barclays' pay decisions post-GFC. Moreover, sentiments expressed by key agents at the bank support the assertion that lesson learning has been impeded by how Barclays has interpreted the structural environment and responded to competitive pressures. Indeed, regulatory constraints and competitive pressures have undoubtedly been an important in factor in the learning trajectory of the group, which has failed to make substantive changes to both the composition and culture fostered by remuneration post-2008. This indicates that structures and the meaning applied to the structural environment by 'interpretive agents' (Bell, 2011) are clearly a contingent factor in how institutions learn.

Balance Sheet

The balance sheet element at Barclays breaks with the above section, insomuch as we do indeed witness some evidence of learning and change post-crisis. However, this learning has been slow and has, on the whole, only emerged following the publication of Salz and Transform. As such, it would appear that Barclays' successful navigation of the crisis resulted in the group lacking the necessary motivation to seek new information—in-keeping with the dissatisfaction thesis explored in Chapter 2—and which subsequently led to some initial complacency. The analysis below suggests that between approximately 2008 and 2012, Barclays increased its exposure to risk with learning being either marginal or absent during this time. Yet, following the publication of Salz and Transform, we witness some positive behavioural shifts with learning either taking hold or accelerating markedly from 2013 onwards.

Despite this, a recent turnaround in the status and future of the investment bank has called into question the extent and longevity of these changes. Following the appointment of Jes Staley as GCE, the investment bank has witnessed something of a resurgence with many of the lessons learned from Salz and Transform having been eroded. Structural competitive pressures linked to the primacy of shareholder value and diminishing share price valuations, along with the individual agency of the GCE, will be used to explain why, despite some evidence of learning and change, we may yet witness a reversal of that learning.

Group Funding

In 2008, group liabilities and equity stood at approximately £2 trillion. Customer deposits totalled £335 billion or around 16% of total funding. In contrast, by 2018 total liabilities and equity was around £1.1 trillion[11]

[11] This reduction in group liabilities and equity has been driven by a number of disinvestment projects including: the 2009 sale of Barclays Global Investors (*The Economist*, 2009); the closure of the financial planning division (Steger, 2011); the 2011 sale of Barclays' Russian commercial and retail business (Treanor, 2011); the 2012 disposal of a 19.6% stake in BlackRock (Schäfer & McCrum, 2012). Likewise, between 2014 and 2018 Barclays would continue its sell-down of the business disposing of a number of non-core entities including: the group's United Arab Emirates retail bank (BBC News, 2014); the Spanish retail, wealth management and commercial bank in a deal worth £960 million (Buck & Sharman, 2014); the US wealth and investment management unit, which would see Barclays dispose of around £40 billion of assets (Wursthorn & Stynes, 2015); the

with customer deposits worth £380 billion or 33% of liabilities and equity. As we can see, Barclays significantly improved its funding position post-crisis with customer deposits, as a percentage of total group liabilities and equity, more than doubling.

An examination of the intervening years would also appear to support the hypothesis extended above. Figure 6.1 demonstrates that between 2009 and 2012 the percentage of customer deposits as a share of total group liabilities and equity remained broadly flat experiencing only a 2% rise. However, from 2012 onwards customer deposits would witness a sharp increase growing by 16 percentage points and peaking at 41% in 2015. Following this high, this figure has slowly decreased falling 8 percentage points between 2015 and 2018. Similar figures for our

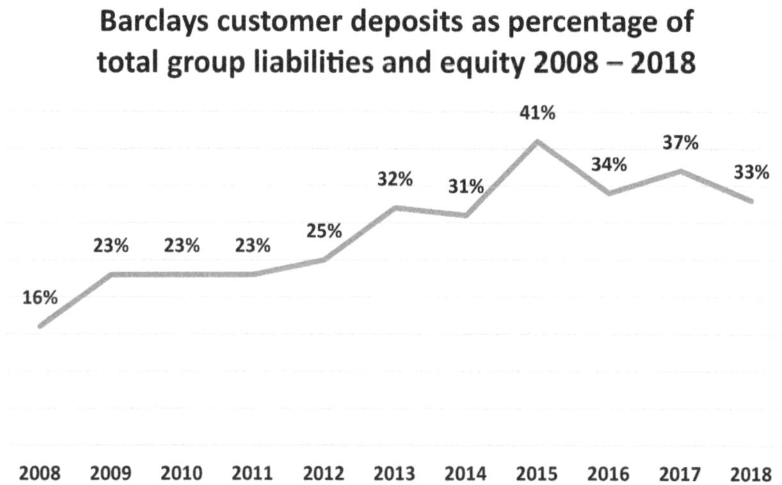

Fig. 6.1 Customer deposits as percentage of total group liabilities and equity 2008–2018

Barclaycard businesses in Portugal and Spain (Bray, 2016); the French retail and wealth management business to the private equity firm AnaCap, although Barclays would hive-off and retain its French investment bank (Moshinsky, 2016a); the Asian wealth management and investment business centred in Hong-Kong and Singapore for around £228 million—and which would see the disposal of around £13 billion of assets (Weinland, 2016); and the Barclays Africa division which was bought by a consortium headed by the former Barclays GCE Bob Diamond (Arnold & England, 2016; Cotterill, 2017).

comparator group reveal that RBS (51%), Lloyds (52%) and HSBC (53%) all outperformed Barclays on this metric.

Though Barclays did not specifically articulate a desire to increase customer deposits as a proportion of overall group funding, the group's 2013 strategic review[12] did address the issue of funding stating that Barclays would seek to:

> maintain a diversified funding base. Our expectation is that our wholesale unsecured funding volumes will come down and the mix will change over the next three years, in particular towards secured funding.
>
> (Barclays, 2013b: 9)

While Barclays would not implement specific policies that would target an increase in customer deposits, the group's 2013 strategic review clearly recognised that a more diversified funding base would be desirable. However, the downwards trend witnessed from 2015 onwards questions the longevity and extent of this positive change.

Given the increase in customer deposits, it is surprising that we find that Barclays' reliance on short-term funding including money markets and other deposits has increased by around 10 percentage points in the post-crisis decade. For example, in 2008 short-term funding was worth £298 billion or 14.5% of group liabilities and equity. However, figures for 2018 reveal that short-term funding was worth £271 billion or 24% of total group funding. This would appear to suggest that despite the conclusions of Salz (2013: 222), which identified short-term funding and an over-reliance on wholesale markets as being a key cause of the crisis, Barclays has failed to learn. Moreover, following a post-GFC low between 2014 and 2016, we witness a marked acceleration in the group's reliance upon short-term funding from 2016 onwards. Again, this may suggest that lesson learned may have begun to unravel (Fig. 6.2).

Trading Liabilities

Likewise, Fig. 6.3 shows that between 2008 and 2018 trading liabilities as a percentage of total assets grew by approximately 8 percentage points, reaching a ten-year high in 2018 of 10.2%. While the group began

[12] The strategic review is an annual review of the business that informs the annual report.

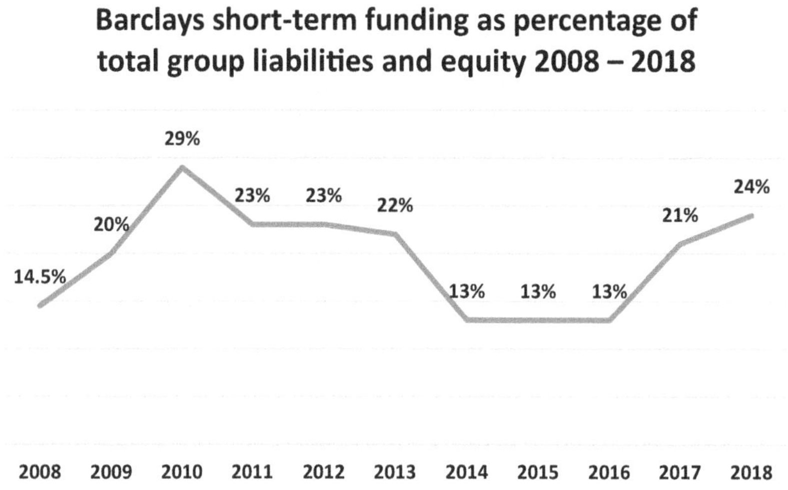

Fig. 6.2 Short-term funding as percentage of total group liabilities and equity 2008–2018

Fig. 6.3 Trading liabilities as percentage of total assets 2008–2018

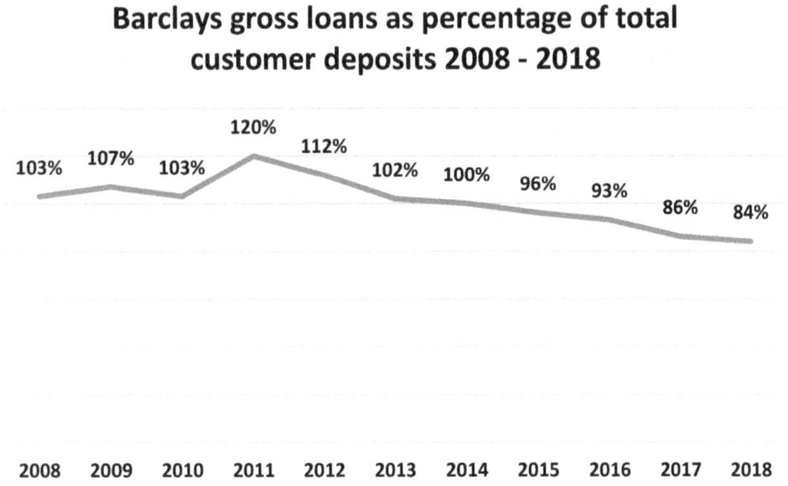

Fig. 6.4 Gross loans as percentage of total customer deposits 2008–2018

to show some positive progress between 2013 and 2016, Barclays once again experienced a sharp rise from 2016 onwards. In comparative terms, Barclays were significantly outperformed by RBS (3.8%), Lloyds (1.1%) and HSBC (8.5%) which in 2018 all recorded smaller trading liabilities as a percentage of total assets.

Loan/Deposit Ratio

However, an examination of the group's loan book breaks with the hypothesis extend thus far. For example, we can see that between 2008 and 2018, gross loans extended as a percentage of total customer deposits decreased by 19 percentage points. Moreover, from 2011 onwards, there was consistent year-on-years progress (Fig. 6.4).

Loan Quality/Impairments

This decrease in gross loans as a percentage of total customer deposits has likewise been accompanied by an increase in residential mortgage lending. Figure 6.5 shows that between 2008 and 2018, Barclays increased its residential mortgage lending as a percentage of gross loans by 18 percentage

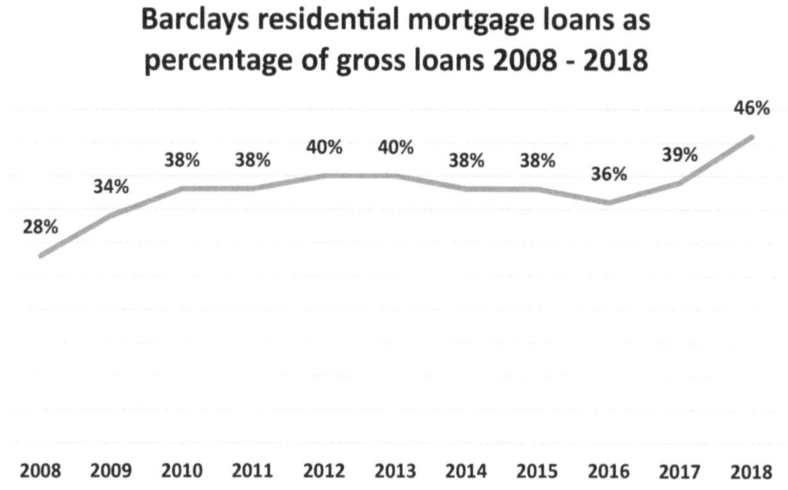

Fig. 6.5 Residential mortgage loans as percentage of gross loans 2008–2018

points. In contrast to the data examined above, these figure may indeed be indicative of learning in the post-crisis decade, with Barclays dedicating a greater percentage of its lending activity towards this comparatively safer asset class. Moreover, Transform would explicitly commit the group to this kind of lending telling investors that it would target 'high-return businesses such as UK mortgages' (Barclays, 2013d: 2). Consequently, an examination of Barclays' loan book in the decade that has followed the GFC appears to break with the hypothesis extended so far insomuch as the application of new information contained in Transform has led to tangible change.

Likewise, when we consider the quality of loans extended by Barclays, measured in terms of impaired loans as a percentage of gross loans, we once again witness evidence of learning. For example, while it is true that between 2008 and 2010 impaired loans increased significantly, data from 2011 onwards illustrates a sustained improvement. In the decade that has followed the crisis, Barclays has decreased impaired loans from 3.3% in 2008 to 2.6% in 2018—a reduction of 21% (Fig. 6.6). In contrast, Lloyds has witnessed a 53% decrease in impaired loans across the same period with HSBC reporting a 69% decrease. While RBS saw a marginal

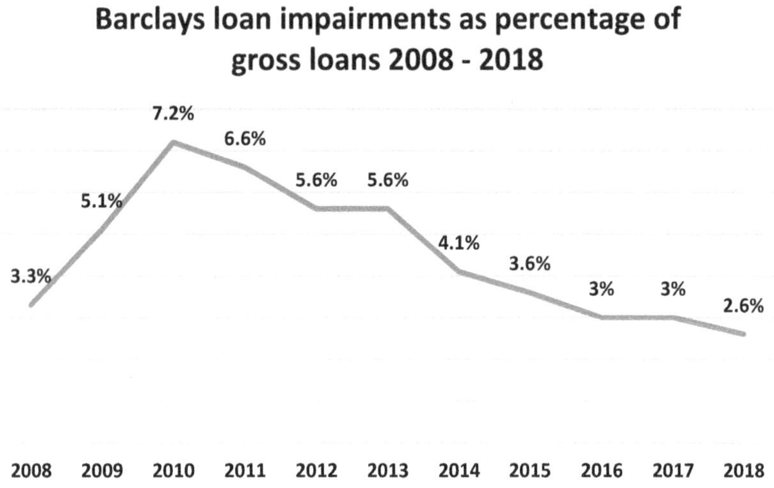

Fig. 6.6 Impaired loans as percentage of gross loans 2008–2018

increase of 4% over the same period, we should note that in 2018 RBS did have the lowest impairment rate of the comparator group at 2.5%.

Derivatives

Barclays has also made progress on the extent to which derivatives contribute to the balance sheet. In 2008, derivatives made up approximately 47% of total group assets. By 2018, this figure had declined by 28 percentage points to just 19% of total group liabilities and equity. The greatest improvement would come between the years 2008 and 2013 with the group reducing derivatives by 21 percentage points. Salz (2013: 59) concluded that in the run-up to the GFC, derivatives contracts had been sold to investors without the necessary 'attention to customer needs', which in itself may have been fuelled by the bonus culture at the bank. However, Salz (ibid.) went on to note that since the crisis Barclays had significantly improved its 'sales processes to ensure that risk is appropriately explained' and which may explain why we witness a reduction in the volume of such products (Fig. 6.7).

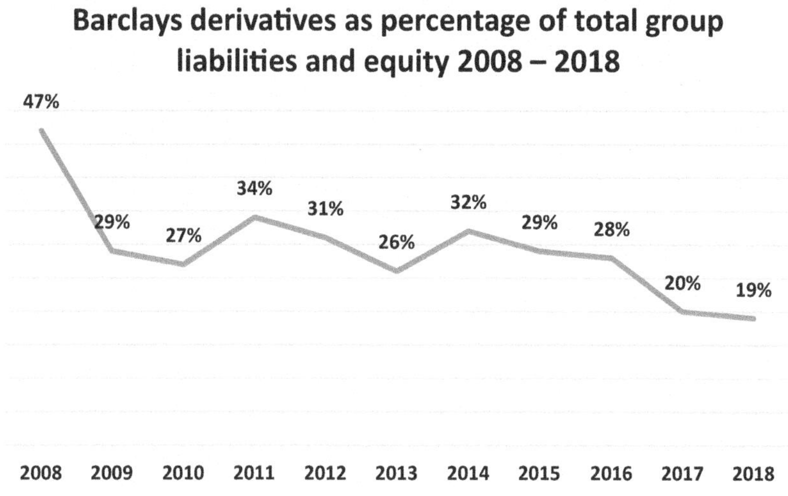

Fig. 6.7 Derivatives as percentage of total liabilities and equity 2008–2018

Regulatory Capital

In 2008, Barclays were holding £37 billion of regulatory tier 1 capital. This equated to a regulatory tier 1 capital ratio of 8.6%. For the year ending 2018, the group were holding £49 billion of regulatory tier 1 capital, which was equal to a tier 1 capital ratio of 15.8%.[13] As such, we can see that in 2018 Barclays exceeded regulatory tier 1 capital requirements by 163%. Likewise, in 2008, total regulatory capital stood at £58 billion or 13.6%. In 2018, total regulatory capital had increased to £61 billion or 19.8%. This means that in 2018, the group had a total regulatory capital ratio that was in excess of minimum standards by 147%. In the context of learning, this is important because by exceeding minimum capital requirement Barclays has greatly increased its loss absorbing capacity. Comparable figures show that in 2018 Barclays were outperformed by both RBS and Lloyds. Barclays would record a marginally

[13] As in previous chapters, we should note that the shifting nature of regulatory capital requirements post-crisis complicates the accuracy of making comparisons between 2008 and 2018.

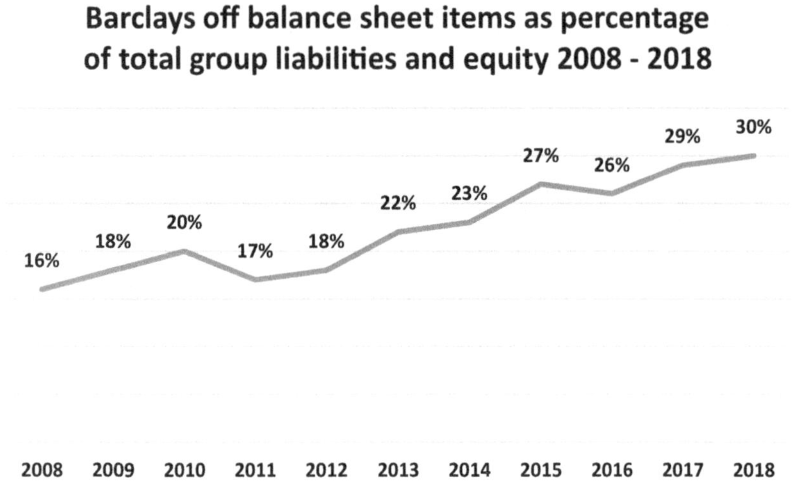

Fig. 6.8 Off-balance-sheet item as percentage of total group liabilities and equity 2008–2018

higher tier 1 capital ratio than HSBC but a lower total regulatory capital ratio.[14]

Off-Balance-Sheet Vehicles

One of the key lessons of the GFC, explored in Chapter 3, was the compounding effect that the shadow-banking sector had played in the crisis. While it can be difficult to measure the extent to which banks have engaged in shadow banking activities post-crisis due to the opaque nature of the industry, one widely accepted indicator of activity is the use of off-balance sheet vehicles (OBSV) (Erturk, 2017). In 2008 OBSV were worth 16% of total group assets. However, by 2018 this figure had almost doubled, rising to 30% of total group liabilities and equity. While data for the years 2008–2012 demonstrates a modest increase of just 2 points, the most dramatic shift occurred from 2012 onwards, rising 12 percentage points in just six years to almost one-third of total group assets (Fig. 6.8).

[14]See Chapter 4, page 119, Fig. 4.3.

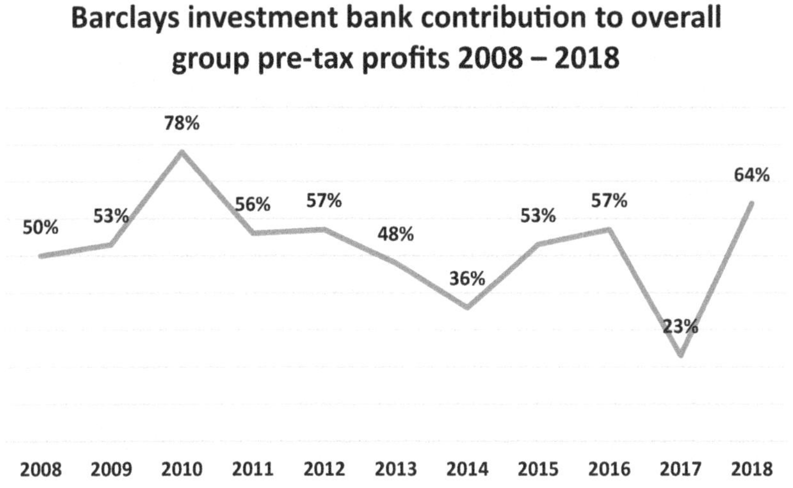

Fig. 6.9 Investment bank contribution to overall group pre-tax profits 2008–2018

Investment Bank

Barclays, like HSBC, record an annual pre-tax profit each year in the decade that followed the GFC. In 2008, the group reported pre-tax profits of £5.1 billion, with the investment bank contributing approximately £2.5 billion or 50% to this total.[15] Comparable figures for 2018 show that the investment bank recorded pre-tax profits of £2.4 billion and contributed to approximately 64% of group pre-tax profits. Moreover, we can see that between 2008 and 2018 Barclays has increasingly relied upon the investment bank as an engine for growth. This would indicate that, like many of the metrics already examined in this section, the loan book notwithstanding, lessons learned appear to have unravelled in the latter years of the post-crisis decade (Fig. 6.9).

[15] The substantial increase in income and profit contribution of the investment bank for the year 2010 can be attributed to the integration of the Lehman Brothers brand and the subsequent 'write up' of assets contained on the Lehman's book.

Learning in Retreat?

The evidence examined in this section of the chapter is rather mixed. On the one hand, Barclays has increased customers deposits and residential mortgage lending, reduced impaired loans and the use of derivatives and reported robust regulatory capital ratios. Conversely, the group has increased its reliance on short-term funding, increased trading liabilities and the use of OBSV and come to rely more heavily on the investment bank as generator of group profit. Moreover, many of the lessons learned from the GFC appear to be in retreat with much of the early progress made on the structure and composition of balance sheet unravelling in recent years, despite Barclays seeking and evaluating new information in the form of Salz and Transform. This is because in many instances new information has failed to be applied with the group lacking specific policies initiatives aimed at upholding lessons learned, a factor that can be attributed more broadly to the failure of Transform outlined above. Moreover, the future direction of the investment bank as a central piece of Barclays' post-crisis business model may further undermine and erode any progress made by the bank. The primacy of shareholder value, structural competitive pressures and the individual agency of the GCE all being contributory factors that may explain why learning may be in retreat.

We know from the data above that in 2008 Barclays' investment bank generated around 50% of group pre-tax profits. The division was not only institutionally important, with approximately three-quarters of total group assets held in the investment bank, but was also systemically significant being 'one of the largest investment banks in the world' (Salz, 2013: 4). While the investment bank had always been important to Barclays, Salz concluded that the division had also become a reputational and operational vulnerability with many of the central factors that contributed to the GFC, and the group's numerous regulatory failures stemming from the division, which 'set the tone' of group-wide behaviour (ibid.: 5).

Barclays' official response to Salz in 2013 simply stated that the group would address the 'underlying causes of issues' in the investment bank and 'apply lessons learned more broadly' (Barclays, 2013a: 10). In May 2014, and under the stewardship of GCE Antony Jenkins, Barclays announced that it would be looking to 'exit or run down' approximately £115 billion of risk weighted assets (RWA) (Barclays, 2014a). Almost 80% of which would consist of RWA located in the investment bank as Barclays sought to remove approximately £90 billion from the division's book (Barclays,

2014a). The group would also announce plans to reduce RWA within the division to less than 30% by 2016 (ibid.).

Commenting on the plans, GCE Antony Jenkins stated that the move would mean a 'significantly more balanced' group as Barclays sought to simplify its operations and concentrate on areas in which the group had:

> capability, scale and competitive advantage [and that i]n the future, Barclays will be leaner, stronger, much better balanced and well positioned to deliver lower volatility, higher returns, and growth.
>
> (Jenkins in Barclays, 2014a)

Barclays implemented a number of initiatives that would signal the group's intention to shift the focus of its business away from the investment bank. In May 2014 the bank announced that it would be shedding approximately 7,000 employees from the investment banking division over a two-year period with approximately 2,000 jobs going immediately (Treanor, 2014). In March 2015, disappointed by the investment bank's lacklustre performance, Mr Jenkins told reporters that he would make further cuts to the division if it did not improve its profitability (Slater & Scuffham, 2015). Mr Jenkins went on to say that 'every business within the group has to deliver the ROE that we require of it' adding that '[w]e won't hesitate to continue to optimise capital allocated to the investment bank, the cost base and revenues to generate those returns' (Jenkins cited in Slater & Scuffham, 2015). Then in July 2015, Barclays announced that it would be cutting a further 2,500 jobs from the investment bank including 150 senior roles (Slater, 2015). In October of the same year, Martin Arnold of the *Financial Times* reported that two bank insiders had told the FT that Barclays was planning to accelerate the rundown of the investment bank and deliver the restructured division ahead of Mr Jenkins 2016 schedule (Arnold, 2015a). By the 31st December 2015 the investment bank had exited nine countries, including operations in Russia, Brazil and Asia, retrenched cash equities trading to its London and New York markets and suspended local currency trading outside of the group's non-core regions (Barclays, 2015b: 2). Moreover, the group had essentially hit its 2016 target of reducing RWA within the investment bank to 30% almost a year early, with figures for 2015 showing RWA within the division to be worth £108 billion or 30.1% of group RWA.

Despite the investment bank making some impressive strides under the stewardship of Antony Jenkins, in July 2015 Barclays announced that it would be terminating Mr Jenkins' contract amid rumours that the GCE and the head of investment banking, Tom King, had clashed over the future of the division in a fiery exchange of words (Arnold, 2015b). It was reported that following a highly charged disagreement Mr King told members of the group's board that he intended to retire due to his exacerbation over Mr Jenkins' plans for the division (ibid.). Antony Jenkins' employment at Barclays was terminated shortly thereafter.

Mr Jenkins' dismissal sparked a series of rumours over the future of the investment bank and the extent to which the division would feature in Barclays' business model (Moore & Goodway, 2015). Indeed, shortly after his dismissal reports began to circulate that the group's board had moved against the former GCE following unannounced plans that Mr Jenkins intended to shrink the investment bank further still (Augar, 2018). Those close to the bank told reporters that the board was unhappy with Mr Jenkins' plans for the division, which was seen by the board as Barclays' flagship product, and that this was the true motive behind his dismissal (Moore & Goodway, 2015). Though Barclays would try spuriously to quash rumours, telling reporters that Antony Jenkins' dismissal would not 'signal a major change in strategy' for the group (Barclays cited in Arnold, 2015b), John McFarlane, group chairman, did admit that the investment bank was a crucial part of the Barclays brand (Treanor, 2015a). Speculation that the run-down of the investment bank would be halted or even reversed was given further credence when in October 2015, Barclays announced that it would be appointing Jes Staley a career investment banker as the new GCE (Arnold & Jenkins, 2015).

Shortly after joining Barclays, Mr Staley told staff that he remained committed to running down and managing RWA within the investment bank and would 'complete the necessary transformation and repositioning of the Investment Bank to a less capital intensive model' (Staley cited in Savage 2015). However, while Mr Staley's comments at the time indicated no radical divergence from the plans put in place by his predecessor, a series of events concerning the investment bank suggest a reversal of the learning that took place under Mr Jenkins. For example, in a 2016 speech given to investors on Wall Street Mr Staley commented that:

> [a]t the heart of Barclays' strategy is to build on our strength as a transatlantic Consumer, Corporate and Investment bank anchored in the two financial centres of the world, London and New York.
>
> (Staley cited in Gale, 2016)

In addition, in his first annual results presentation Mr Staley told investors that the group's investment bank was a 'bulge-bracket Investment Bank' adding that Barclays' was a 'top tier' player in the investment banking league (Staley cited in Moshinsky, 2016b). Sarah Butcher, a City analyst, noted that the language used by Mr Staley was a clear sign of where the future of the investment bank would lie, suggesting that both Mr Staley and Barclays clearly saw the group competing with other large investment banks such Goldman Sachs and J.P. Morgan (Butcher, 2016).

Likewise, though Barclays reduced RWA within the investment bank between 2014 and 2016, RWA in the division would rise exponentially under the stewardship of Jes Staley. As discussed above, by late 2015 RWA in the investment bank accounted for approximately 30% of total group RWA. However, just twelve months later this figure would rise to 59% (Barclays, 2016). In 2017, RWA in the investment bank contributed to 67% of total group RWA, and in 2018, this figure had risen again to 67.5% thereby greatly exceeding the 30% target set under Mr Jenkins' tenure as group CEO (Barclays, 2017, 2018). Commenting, Jes Staley noted that:

> to significantly reduce RWA further would reduce the investment bank's core functionality and ability to compete in the top tier.
>
> (Staley cited in Moshinsky, 2016b)

Similarly, a recruitment drive by the investment bank following the appointment of Jes Staley would further bolster the future prospects of the division and its central role in Barclays' business model. In February 2016, Barclays recruited 150 senior staff to strengthen its US investment banking operations (Wallace, 2016a). Just one month later in March 2016, and around the time that Mr Staley was outlining his future plans for the bank, the group announced that it had recruited nine senior mergers and acquisition specialists (Wallace, 2016b). Then in May 2017, the group would hire a further 100 investment bankers in order to 'keep pace with US rivals' (Arnold, 2017c). Commenting on the appointments Tim Thorsby, then head of Barclays International, noted that the appointment of 'the right talent [would allow Barclays] to execute on [its] ambitions and growth strategy' central to which was the 'ability to continually enhance our investment bank' (Thorsby in Barclays, 2018).

This apparent reversal in the strategic importance of the investment bank to Barclays' post-crisis business model, along with Mr Jenkins termination and the eroding of lessons learned surrounding the investment bank as a 'reputational' and 'operational' liability (Salz, 2013: 5), can be explained by how key agents at the bank have interpreted the structural environment. For example, competitive pressures and the primacy of shareholder value stressed by Barclays' most senior figures have factored heavily in the turnaround of the division. Indeed, shortly after Mr Jenkins was terminated rumours began to surface that both the group's board and senior management team had lost confidence in Antony Jenkins, telling reporters that the former GCE was 'under-ambitious' in his plans for the investment bank which was threatening Barclays' competitive position (anonymous cited in Arnold, 2015b). Commenting on Mr Jenkins' dismissal, former group deputy chairman Sir Michael Rake told members of the press that a significant number of board members had grown unhappy with Mr Jenkins' strategy adding that the prevailing sentiment was that the performance of the investment bank had become sub-standard (Rake cited in Brinded, 2015).

We may infer from such comments that the future of the investment bank, along with the division's 'sub-standard' performance, was clearly seen by the board as being explicitly linked to Mr Jenkins personally and appears to stress that the individual agency of the GCE has been an important factor in the group's learning trajectory. Similarly, the primacy of shareholder value and structural competitive pressures surrounding the performance of the group may also explain the apparent revival of the investment bank with Barclays' competitive position, in the face of the reform process, having grown untenable. Indeed, commenting on the termination of Antony Jenkins in 2015, John McFarlane, then group chairman, noted that:

> [i]t became clear that existing management plans had shareholder value creation too far out in the future. Barclays [sic] shares stand where they did six years ago and the dividend is flat.
>
> (McFarlane cited in Moore & Goodway 2015)

Moreover, since assuming control in 2016, Mr Jenkins predecessor, Jes Staley has stressed a commitment to increasing shareholder value through growing the investment bank. In 2016 Mr Staley told investors that in order to 'generate attractive, sustainable, and distributable, returns for… shareholders', management would increase its focus upon the investment bank (Staley in Barclays, 2016) adding that 'competing in the top tier of global investment banking' would be centrally 'important to Barclays' future returns' (Staley in Barclays, 2018).

Though an apparent reversal in the importance of the investment bank to Barclays' post-GFC business model may, upon first reading, suggest an erosion of the group's already limited learning, it can be argued that Barclays has not failed to learn or 'unlearned' lessons, but rather, has perceived the associated cost of learning to be too high. Once again, structural competitive pressures—including but not limited to shareholder value creation—have been the driving force behind this reluctance to implement and adhere to far-reaching reform. Archer's (2003, 2007, 2012) thesis on the meta-reflexives can be used to explain why it is possible that despite this apparent backsliding on the reform agenda, learning may yet be witnessed at the group in the post-crisis decade.

Archer (2003, 2007, 2012) for example suggests that following a period of reflection a learning agent will become aware of their 'situational logic of opportunity' whereby the subject recognises both the opportunities and constraints of the immediate structural environment. Though these structural constraints can indeed be overcome, the learning agent or organisation must make a decision based on all available information and carefully weigh-up the associated costs and benefits of potential choices. In this instance, Barclays has interpreted the reform of the investment bank to carry with it a number of costs including losing ground to competitors and an erosion of the group's ability to generate shareholder value. Put simply, the 'situational logic of opportunity' presented by the structural environment concerning a scaling back of the investment bank has led the group to turn its back on the reform agenda. Indeed, Archer herself concludes that the 'situational logic of opportunity is...predominant...The prizes go to those who can manipulate concomitant cultural compatibilities' (Archer, 2007: 54). In this example, Barclays has learned that substantive reform of the investment bank carries with it undesirable costs. As such, the price of learning in this case is simply too high with the 'situational logic of opportunity' being too narrow to pursue a reform agenda that sees the investment bank shrinking. Consequently, many of the changes implemented within the division under the tenure of Mr Jenkins have been eroded.

Conclusion

The evidence examined in this chapter suggests that there is no one-size-fits-all answer to the underlying research question posed in the introduction to this text. Indeed, lesson learning at Barclays in the post-crisis decade has been highly nuanced and as such, we should consider individual facets of the group and instances or pockets of learning on their own merit. For example, it may be possible to conclude that Barclays has failed to present strong evidence of learning in relation to governance and regulation with a series of events suggesting an absence of change. This can be attributed to Barclays having failed to enshrine lessons learned through specific policy initiatives. In this respect, though Barclays may have sought and evaluated new information in the form of a group wide strategic review, the bank has not applied lessons learned. As a result, the group's underlying theories-in-use has not undergone a fundamental change.

Structural competitive pressures and how Barclays' has interpreted its situational logic of opportunity have also been a mitigating factor in the group's learning trajectory. For example, in relation to remuneration, Barclays has concluded that the cost of learning, measured in terms of the group's ability to attract and retain staff, is simply too high with fear of losing talent to rival institutions clearly having been an important factor in why the group's remuneration structure has lacked more substantive reform.

Although Barclays has demonstrated some evidence of learning in relation to the structure and composition of the balance sheet, there are a number of areas where the group has remained exposed to the key vulnerabilities stressed by the GFC. For instance, an increase in trading liabilities and a greater reliance upon short-term funding as well as an increase in OBSV have all meant that the group has maintained and, in some cases, increased its risk exposure. Moreover, a resurgence in the structural importance of the investment bank may undermine the limited learning that has taken place in the decade since the crisis. Once again, the revival of the investment bank may be attributed to the group's situational logic of opportunity and the associated costs of learning. In this instance Barclays has concluded that the price of learning, seen in this case as being a diminished ability to create shareholder value and losing ground to competitors, has again been interpreted as being too high.

The agency of key individuals at the bank may similarly offer us insight into why Barclays has failed to learn. The shrinking of investment bank was clearly viewed by Barclays and the board as being the brainchild of Anthony Jenkins. When reform became untenable, Barclays removed Mr Jenkins and replaced him with the career investment banker Jes Staley.

Mr Staley immediately set out his plans for Barclays which would involve reorienting the business on the investment bank despite Salz's conclusion about the division being an institutional vulnerability.

These factors stress the importance of considering both structure and agency as well as the intricacies, ideational preferences and institutional beliefs of organisations in the learning process. In particular, how the structural environment is interpreted and how an institution understands its situational logic of opportunity, and the lesson that can be gathered from this, along with the preferences and beliefs of key situational agents is clearly a contingent factor in the post-crisis learning experience of Barclays. Moreover such explanations can help us to understand why, despite the presence of a group wide strategic evaluation, lessons have been lost at Barclays. As such, different theoretical explanations must be applied to the varying elements of organisations in order to understand how institutions learn and the impact of this learning or lack thereof upon financial stability.

References

Archer, M. (2003). *Structure, agency and the internal conversation*. Cambridge: Cambridge University Press.

Archer, M. (2007). *Making our way through the world*. Cambridge: Cambridge University Press.

Archer, M. (2012). *The reflexive imperative in late modernity*. Cambridge: Cambridge University Press.

Arnold, M. (2015a, October 16). Barclays to speed up investment bank cuts. *Financial Times Online*. Available at: https://next.ft.com/content/0b971e08-7418-11e5-bdb1-e6e4767162cc#myft:saved-articles:page_

Arnold, M. (2015b, July 8). Barclays fires Jenkins after clash over investment banking unit. *Financial Times Online*. Available at: https://next.ft.com/content/74fed7c6-2537-11e5-9c4e-a775d2b173ca#myft:saved-articles:page.

Arnold, M. (2017a, May 10). Barclays chief apologises to shareholders for trying to identify whistleblower. *Financial Times Online*. Available at: https://www.ft.com/content/a5f8caed-9677-326f-bd69-a1fe72155e40.

Arnold, M. (2017b, May 10). Barclays chief Jes Staley apologises for pursuit of whistleblower. *Financial Times Online*. Available at: https://www.ft.com/content/aa0fa830-3572-11e7-bce4-9023f8c0fd2e.

Arnold, M. (2017c, May 11). Barclays rejigs top management at investment banking arm. *Financial Time Online*. Available at: https://www.ft.com/content/47d37ce2-366b-11e7-bce4-9023f8c0fd2e.

Arnold, M., Croft, J., & Binham, C. (2018, May 21). UK court dismisses charges against Barclays over Qatar deal. *Financial Times Online*. Available at: https://www.ft.com/content/b1a78a9a-5ce0-11e8-ad91-e01af256df68.

Arnold, M., & England, A. (2016, May 5). Barclays makes £600m from stake sale in African subsidiary. *Financial Times Online*. Available at: https://www.ft.com/cms/s/0/109031b8-1212-11e6-91da-096d89bd2173.html#axzz4GA9DEhts.

Arnold, M., & Jenkins, P. (2015, October 13). Barclays set to pick Jes Staley as chief executive. *Financial Times Online*. Available at: https://next.ft.com/content/31fbe252-7122-11e5-9b9e-690fdae72044.

Arnold, M., & Jenkins, P. (2016, May 2). Barclays' risk officer in France alleges laundering and mis-selling failures. *Financial Times Online*. Available at: https://www.ft.com/cms/s/0/981b083e-1054-11e6-839f-2922947098f0.html#axzz4GpAcMw00.

Arnold, M. & Shubber, K. (2018, March 29). Barclays agrees to pay $2bn to settle US mis-selling claims. *Financial Times Online*. Available at: https://www.ft.com/content/358a35da-3359-11e8-ac48-10c6fdc22f03.

Augar, P. (2018). *The bank that lived a little: Barclays in the age of the very free market*. London: Allen Lane.

Barclays [Barclays Banking Group PLC]. (2007). *Annual report and accounts 2007*. Available at: https://www.home.barclays/content/dam/barclayspublic/docs/InvestorRelations/AnnualReports/AR2007/2007-barclays-plc-annual-report.pdf.

Barclays [Barclays Banking Group PLC]. (2011). *Annual report and accounts 2011*. Available at: https://www.home.barclays/content/dam/barclayspublic/docs/InvestorRelations/AnnualReports/AR2011/barclays-plc-annual-report-2011.pdf.

Barclays [Barclays Banking Group PLC]. (2012). *Annual report and accounts 2012: Building the 'Go-To' bank*. Available at: https://www.home.barclays/content/dam/barclayspublic/docs/InvestorRelations/AnnualReports/AR2012/2012-barclays-plc-annual-report.pdf.

Barclays [Barclays Banking Group PLC]. (2013a). *Integrity Barclays' response to the Salz review*. Available at: https://www.home.barclays/content/dam/barclayspublic/documents/news/471-392-250413-salz-response.pdf.

Barclays [Barclays Banking Group PLC]. (2013b, February 12). *Becoming the 'Go-To' bank Barclays strategic review executive summary*. Available at: https://www.home.barclays/content/dam/barclayspublic/docs/Microsites/Transform/barclays-strategic-review-executive-summary.pdf.

Barclays [Barclays Banking Group PLC]. (2013c). *Annual report and accounts 2013*. Available at: https://www.home.barclays/content/dam/barclayspublic/docs/InvestorRelations/AnnualReports/AR2013/2013-barclays-annual-report-final.pdf.

Barclays [Barclays Banking Group PLC]. (2013d, February 12). *Press Release: Barclays announces the outcome of its strategic review and sets out commitments for 2015*. Available at: https://www.home.barclays/content/dam/barclayspublic/docs/Microsites/Transform/barclays-strategic-review-announcement.pdf.

Barclays [Barclays Banking Group PLC]. (2014a, May 8). *Barclays PLC Barclays announces group strategy update*. Available at: https://www.home.barclays/content/dam/barclayspublic/docs/InvestorRelations/IRNewsPresentations/2014News/Barclays-group-strategy-update.pdf.

Barclays [Barclays Banking Group PLC]. (2014b). *Barclays PLC annual report and accounts: Helping people their ambitions—In the right way*. Available at: https://www.home.barclays/content/dam/barclayspublic/docs/InvestorRelations/AnnualReports/AR2014/Barclays_PLC_Annual_Report_%202014.pdf.

Barclays [Barclays Banking Group PLC]. (2015a). *Annual report and accounts 2015*. Available at: https://www.home.barclays/content/dam/barclayspublic/docs/InvestorRelations/AnnualReports/AR2015/Barclays_PLC_Annual_Report_%202015.pdf.

Barclays [Barclays Banking Group PLC]. (2015b). *Barclays PLC strategic report 2015*. Available at: https://www.home.barclays/content/dam/barclayspublic/docs/InvestorRelations/AnnualReports/AR2015/Barclays_PLC_Strategic_Report_2015.pdf.

Barclays [Barclays Banking Group PLC]. (2015c, November 26). *Press release: Barclays announces settlement with the FCA*. Available at: https://www.newsroom.barclays.co.uk/r/3272/barclays_announces_settlement_with_the_fca.

Barclays [Barclays Banking Group PLC]. (2016). *Annual report and accounts 2016: Building the bank of the future*. Available at: https://home.barclays/content/dam/home-barclays/documents/investor-relations/reports-and-events/annual-reports/Barclays-PLC-Annual-Report-2016.pdf.

Barclays [Barclays Banking Group PLC]. (2017). *Annual report and accounts 2017, positioned for growth, sharing and success*. Available at: https://www.home.barclays/content/dam/home-barclays/documents/investor-relations/annualreports/ar2017/Barclays%20PLC%20Annual%20Report%202017.pdf.

Barclays [Barclays Banking Group PLC]. (2018). *Annual report and accounts 2018: Creating opportunities to rise*. Available at: https://home.barclays/content/dam/home-barclays/documents/investor-relations/reports-and-events/annual-reports/2018/2018-barclays-plc-annual-report.pdf.

BBC News. (2014, April 6). Barclays sells its United Arab Emirates retail business. *BBC News Online*. Available at: https://www.bbc.co.uk/news/business-26915911

Bell, S. (2011). Do we really need a new 'constructivist institutionalism' to explain institutional change? *British Journal of Political Science, 41*, 883–906.

Bell, S., & Hindmoor, A. (2015). *Masters of the universe, slaves of the market*. Cambridge, MA: Harvard University Press.

Binham, C. (2015, September 30). Former trader challenges FCA forex investigation. *Financial Times Online*. Available at: https://www.ft.com/content/7ff80642-6778-11e5-a57f-21b88f7d973f.

Binham, C. (2016, February 19). Barclays Qatari deal turns into tale of two battles. *Financial Times Online*. Available at: https://www.ft.com/cms/s/0/18cc5926-d728-11e5-829b-8564e7528e54.html#axzz4GM2fIvfG.

Binham, C. (2017a, March 23). City watchdog relaunches probe into Barclays' cash call. *Financial Times Online*. Available at: https://www.ft.com/content/073efae2-0e2c-11e7-b030-768954394623.

Binham, C. (2017b, March 23). Qatari connection casts long shadow over Barclays. *Financial Times Online*. Available at: https://www.ft.com/content/dadda8fa-0d58-11e7-a88c-50ba212dce4d.

Binham, C. (2018, May 11). Barclays CEO Jes Staley fined £640,000 over whistleblowing scandal. *Financial Times Online*. Available at: https://www.ft.com/content/86089810-5502-11e8-b24e-cad6aa67e23e.

Binham, C., & Dunkley, E. (2015, November 26). Attempted 'elephant deal' costs Barclays £72m. *Financial Times Online*. Available at: https://www.ft.com/cms/s/0/9d77d27c-9461-11e5-bd82-c1fb87bef7af.html#axzz4GSlHG8s3.

Binham, C., & Jenkins, A. (2014, May 11). UK fraud office steps up probe into Barclays' dealings with Qatar. *Financial Times Online*. Available at: https://www.ft.com/cms/s/0/cda8004e-d7a1-11e3-80e0-00144fcabdc0.html#axzz31UZn5j85.

Binham, C., & Thompson, B. (2017, August 17). FDIC sues Barclays, RBS and other banks over Libor. *Financial Times Online*. Available at: https://www.ft.com/content/46d51cbe-8360-11e7-a4ce-15b2513cb3ff.

Bourke, J. (2015, November 19). Barclays fined another $150m over forex-rigging scandal. *The Independent Online*. Available at: https://www.independent.co.uk/news/business/news/barclays-fined-150m-more-over-forex-rigging-scandal-a6740011.html.

Bradford, H. (2012, July 27). Barclays makes employees watch video to ensure Libor rigging 'Never Happens Again'. *The Huffington Post Online*. Available at: https://www.huffingtonpost.com/2012/07/27/barclays-libor-video_n_1710895.html.

Bray, C. (2016, April 28). Barclays to sell credit card business in Portugal and Spain. *The New York Times Online*. Available at: https://www.nytimes.com/2016/04/29/business/dealbook/barclays-sell-credit-card-business-spain-portugal.html?_r=0.

Brinded, L. (2015, July 8). The fired Barclays CEO had two nicknames inside the bank that tell you why he was forced out. *Business Insider UK Online*.

Available at: https://uk.businessinsider.com/barclays-ceo-antony-jenkins-left-because-of-his-lack-of-investment-banking-understanding-2015-7.

Buck, T., & Sharman, A. (2014, September 1). Barclays loses £500m on sale of Spanish business. *Financial Times Online*. Available at: https://www.ft.com/cms/s/0/fae5d374-3147-11e4-8313-00144feabdc0.html#axzz4GA9DEhts.

Butcher, S. (2016, March 1). Jes Staley's rose-tinted vision for Barclays' investment bank. Efinancialcareer.com. Available at: https://news.efinancialcareers.com/uk-en/237824/jes-staleys-strategy-for-barclays-investment-bank/.

Chon, G., & Martin, K. (2015, November 18). Barclays fined $150m over electronic forex trading. *Financial Times Online*. Available at: https://www.ft.com/cms/s/0/4afc8ea6-8e09-11e5-a549-b89a1dfede9b.html#axzz4GSlHG8s3.

Cotterill, J. (2017, May 31). Barclays to sell £1.6bn stake in African unit. *Financial Times Online*. Available at: https://www.ft.com/content/5b67ec64-7fa8-389d-ac49-7c7c08aedee9.

Croft, J., & Binham, C. (2020, February 28). London jury clears 3 former Barclays bankers of fraud charges. *Financial Times Online*. Available at: https://www.ft.com/content/d0bc7fd4-5a19-11ea-a528-dd0f971febbc.

Department of Financial Services [New York State Department of Financial Services]. (2018, December 18). *DFS fines Barclays bank plc and New York branch $15 million following whistleblower investigation*. DFS Press Release. Available online at: https://www.dfs.ny.gov/reports_and_publications/press_releases/pr1812181_

Diamond, B. (2012, June 12). *Barclays press release 28th June 2012: Letter from Bob Diamond, Barclays Chief Executive*. Barclays Media Relations, Press Release. Available at: https://www.newsroom.barclays.co.uk/r/2306/letter_from_bob_diamond__barclays_chief_executive.

DoJ [United States Department of Justice]. (2018, March 29). Barclays agrees to pay $2 *billion in civil penalties to resolve claims for fraud in the sale of residential mortgage-backed securities*. Press Release. Available at: https://www.justice.gov/opa/pr/barclays-agrees-pay-2-billion-civil-penalties-resolve-claims-fraud-sale-residential-mortgage.

Dunkley, E. (2016, August 2). UK banks face more than £1bn in extra PPI costs. *Financial Times Online*. Available at: https://www.ft.com/cms/s/0/2e997baa-5886-11e6-9f70-badea1b336d4.html#axzz4GpAcMw00.

Erturk, I. (2017, November 16). Shadow banking: A story of the Doppelganger (the Double) in science of finance. *Journal of Cultural Economy*, 1–16.

FCA [Financial Conduct Authority]. (2012). Barclays fined £59.5 million for significant failings in relation to LIBOR and EURIBOR. FCA Press Release First published: 27 June 2012, Last updated: 22 March 2013. Available at: https://www.fca.org.uk/news/press-releases/barclays-fined-%C2%A3595-million-significant-failings-relation-libor-and-euribor.

Ferrarini, G., & Ungureanu, M. C. (2011, December 15). Bankers' pay after the 2008 Crisis: Regulatory reforms in the US and the EU. *Journal of Banking Law and Banking, 11*(6), 1–13. Available at: https://www.academia.edu/1630936/Bankers_Pay_after_the_2008_Crisis_Regulatory_Reforms_in_the_US_and_the_EU.

Gale, A. (2016, March 1). What is Jes Staley's strategy for Barclays? *Management Today Online*. Available at: https://www.managementtoday.co.uk/jes-staleys-strategy-barclays/article/1380329.

Grandhi, K. (2016, May 3). Barclays France alleged to be involved in money laundering and mis-selling. *International Business Times Online*. Available at: https://www.ibtimes.co.uk/barclays-france-alleged-be-involved-money-laundering-mis-selling-1557899.

Jenkins, A. (2015). *Barclays press release 20th May 2015: Barclays announces foreign exchange and ISDAfix settlements*. Statement by Barclays Group Chief Executive. Barclays Media Relations Press Release. Available at: https://www.newsroom.barclays.co.uk/r/3171/barclays_announces_foreign_exchange_and_isdafix_settlements_.

Makortoff, K. (2020, July 15). Claim Amanda Staveley in charge of Abu Dhabi Barclays deal 'a fantasy', court told'. *The Guardian Online*. Available at: https://www.theguardian.com/business/2020/jul/15/claim-amanda-staveley-in-charge-of-abu-dhabi-barclays-deal-a-fantasy-court-told.

McBride, J., Alessi, C., & Sergie, M. (2015, May 21). Understanding the Libor Scandal. CFR.org Online. Available at: https://www.cfr.org/united-kingdom/understanding-libor-scandal/p28729.

Moore, J., & Goodway, N. (2015, July 9). Antony Jenkins fired: Investors cheer Barclays' shock move to get rid of chief executive. *Independent Online*. Available at: https://www.independent.co.uk/news/business/news/antony-jenkins-fired-investors-cheer-barclays-shock-move-to-get-rid-of-chief-executive-10376705.html.

Moshinsky, B. (2016a, April 27). Barclays is selling off 74 French branches. *Business Insider UK Online*. Available at: https://uk.businessinsider.com/barclays-is-selling-off-74-french-branches-2016-4.

Moshinsky, B. (2016b, March 1). BARCLAYS INTERNAL MEMO: Here's CEO Jes Staley's message to staff. *Business Insider UK Online*. Available at: https://uk.businessinsider.com/barclays-internal-memo-heres-ceo-jes-staleys-message-to-staff-2016-3.

Noonan, L., Binham, C., & Giles, C. (2017a, April 10). Barclays blamed BoE over lowering of Libor rate, claims BBC. *Financial Times*. Available at: https://www.ft.com/content/f7b6b39a-1dcf-11e7-a454-ab04428977f9.

Noonan, L., Megaw, N., Binham, C., Thompson, J., Dunkley, E., & Jenkins, P. (2017b, April 10). Barclays chief censured for attempt to identify whistle-blower. *Financial Times Online*. Available at: https://www.ft.com/content/155df86c-1db8-11e7-b7d3-163f5a7f229c.

Rennison, J. (2016, January 31). Barclays and Credit Suisse to pay $154m over dark pools. *Financial Times Online*. Available at: https://www.ft.com/cms/s/0/d160fc2a-c84c-11e5-be0b-b7ece4e953a0.html#axzz4GSlHG8s3.

Reuters. (2016a, July 7). Libor-rigging trial: ex-Barclays traders jailed for two to six years. *The Guardian Online*. Available at: https://www.theguardian.com/business/2016/jul/07/libor-rigging-trial-ex-barclays-traders-jailed-merchant-pabon-mathew-johnson.

Reuters. (2016b, January 12). Six bankers charged: UK begins Euribor rigging case. *CNBC Online*. Available at: https://www.cnbc.com/2016/01/12/.

Ridley, K. (2016, January 13). Euribor 6 face 2017 trial in UK, charged with rate-rigging plot. *Reuters Online*. Available at: https://uk.reuters.com/article/uk-court-euribor-britain-idUKKCN0UR1GQ20160113.

Sabatier, P. A. (1988). An advocacy coalition framework of policy change and the role of policy-orientated learning therein. *Policy Sciences, 21*, 129–168.

Salmon, J. (2015, November 27). Barclays is fined £72m for secret deals with mega-rich: Bank shamed over no-questions-asked policy that left Britain vulnerable to financial crime. *The Daily Mail Online*. Available at: https://www.dailymail.co.uk/news/article-3335743/Barclays-fined-72m-secret-deals-mega-rich-Bank-shamed-no-questions-asked-policy-left-Britain-vulnerable-financial-crime.html.

Salz, A. (2013, April). Salz review: An independent review of Barclays' business practice. Available at: https://online.wsj.com/public/resources/documents/SalzReview04032013.pdf.

Savage, R. (2015, October 28). Jes Staley won't return Barclays to big, brash investment banking. *Management Today Online*. Available at: https://www.managementtoday.co.uk/jes-staley-wont-return-barclays-big-brash-investment-banking/article/1370451.

Schäfer, D., Jenkins, A., & Binham, C. (2013, September 16). Barclays contests £50m fine for breach of listing rules. Available at: https://www.ft.com/cms/s/0/2e565e1e-1ebf-11e3-b80b-00144feab7de.html#axzz4GM2flvfG.

Schäfer, D., & McCrum, D. (2012, May 21). Barclays to sell £3.8bn BlackRock stake. *Financial Times Online*. Available at: https://www.ft.com/cms/s/0/0422a6c0-a332-11e1-8f34-00144feabdc0.html#axzz4GA9DEhts.

SFO [Serious Fraud Office]. (2020, February 28). Former Barclays executives acquitted of conspiracy to commit fraud. SFO Press Release. Available online at: https://www.sfo.gov.uk/2020/02/28/former-barclays-executives-acquitted-of-conspiracy-to-commit-fraud/.

Slater, S. (2015, July 31). Barclays cuts 150 investment bank jobs under cost-cutting plan. *Reuters Online*. Available at: https://www.reuters.com/article/us-barclays-employment-investmentbank-idUSKCN0Q51ES20150731.

Slater, S., & Scuffham, M. (2015, March 3). Barclays will cut investment bank again if performance doesn't improve. *Reuters Online*. Available at: https://uk.reuters.com/article/uk-barclays-results-idUKKBN0LZ0H820150303.

Staley, J. (2016). Investor relations media centre: 'Accelerating the delivery of our strategy' Group Chief Executive Jes Staley. *Barclays Online*. Available at: https://www.media.barclays.co.uk/player-standalone/?id=167779-5153926&width=604&height=340.

Steger, A. (2011, January 26). Barclays financial planning arm to close. Citywire.co.uk. Available at: https://citywire.co.uk/new-model-adviser/news/barclays-financial-planning-arm-to-close/a466159.

The Economist. (2009, June 12). BlackRock and a hard place, Barclays sell BGI. *The Economist Online* Extra. Available at: https://www.economist.com/node/13848711.

Titcomb, J. (2015, May 20). Barclays handed biggest bank fine in UK history over 'brazen' currency rigging. *The Telegraph Online*. Available at: https://www.telegraph.co.uk/finance/newsbysector/banksandfinance/11619188/Barclays-handed-biggest-bank-fine-in-UK-history-over-brazen-currency-rigging.html.

Treanor, J. (2011, July 18). Barclays faces large loss in Russian exit. *The Guardian Online*. Available at: https://www.theguardian.com/business/2011/jul/18/barclays-faces-large-loss-russian-exit.

Treanor, J. (2012, June 28). Barclays fined £290m as bid to manipulate interest rates is exposed. *The Guardian Online*. Available at: https://www.theguardian.com/business/2012/jun/27/barclays-chief-bob-diamond-bonus-fine.

Treanor, J. (2014, May 8). Barclays to cut 19,000 jobs as it scales back investment arm. *The Guardian Online*. Available at: https://www.theguardian.com/business/2014/may/08/barclays-to-cut-19000-jobs-scale-back-investment-bank-antony-jenkins.

Treanor, J. (2015a, October 15). UK government waters down financial regulation regime. *The Guardian Online*. Available at: https://www.theguardian.com/business/2015/oct/15/financial-accountability-regime-will-not-be-fully-operational-until-2018.

Treanor, J. (2015b, December 1). Barclays faces higher recruitment bill for new boss Jes Staley. *The Guardian Online*. Available at: https://www.theguardian.com/business/2015/dec/01/barclays-higher-recruitment-bill-chief-executive-jes-staley-bonuses-jp-morgan.

Treanor, J. (2015c, November 26). Barclays fined £72m over 'elephant deal'. *The Guardian Online*. Available at: https://www.theguardian.com/business/2015/nov/26/barclays-fined-72m-elephant-deal-fca.

Treanor, J., & Rushe, D. (2014, June 26). Barclays investigated in US over 'dark pool' activities. *The Guardian Online*. Available at: https://www.theguardian.com/business/2014/jun/26/barclays-investigated-dark-pool-new-york-trading.

Verity, A. (2016, February 1). Barclays and credit Suisse are fined over US 'dark pools'. *BBC News Online*. Available at: https://www.bbc.co.uk/news/business-35456219.

Wallace, T. (2016a, February 27). Barclays' new boss to support US investment bank with more hiring. *The Telegraph*. Available at: https://www.telegraph.co.uk/business/2016/02/26/barclays-new-boss-to-support-us-investment-bank-with-more-hiring/.

Wallace, T. (2016b, March 7). Barclays hires nine M&A executives to bolster investment bank. *The Telegraph*. Available at: https://www.telegraph.co.uk/business/2016/03/07/barclays-hires-nine-ma-executives-to-bolster-investment-bank/.

Weardon, G. (2011, May 5). How the PPI scandal unfolded. *The Guardian Online*. Available at: https://www.theguardian.com/business/2011/may/05/how-ppi-scandal-unfolded.

Weinland, D. (2016, April 7). Barclays to sell Asia wealth division to OCBC for $320m. *Financial Times Online*. Available at: https://www.ft.com/cms/s/0/1e8923dc-fc74-11e5-b3f6-11d5706b613b.html?siteedition=uk#axzz4GA9DEhts.

Wursthorn, M., & Stynes, T. (2015, June 8). Stifel to buy Barclays's U.S. wealth management ops. *The Wall Street Journal Online*. Available at: https://www.wsj.com/articles/stifel-to-buy-barclays-u-s-wealth-management-ops-1433766107.

CHAPTER 7

HSBC: Learning Without Change?

Introduction

In comparative terms, HSBC had what can be considered a rather successful GFC. The group avoided state assistance, did not need to undertake private capital raising and was able to continue to report pre-tax profits throughout the immediate crisis period and beyond. While this successful navigation of the crisis endowed the group with the 'space' needed to learn, it also meant that HSBC lacked the necessary dissatisfaction that drives learning. As such, we witness little change to the overall structure and composition of HSBC's business model—group governance and regulation, remuneration and bonuses and the balance sheet—in the years following the crisis.

Despite this, subsequent moments of 'dissatisfaction' post-2008 would result in HSBC implementing a number of policy initiatives causing substantive change. As such, it is possible to conclude that HSBC has, on the whole, learned lessons from the GFC. However, the group appear to have learned different lessons in relation to different areas of the business. Moreover, this learning has taken place at a contrasting pace. Indeed, HSBC's strong position going into, and in the wake of, the GFC has resulted in contending typologies of learning at the bank in the post-crisis decade. Consequently, while it is possible to identify positive double-loop learning within certain areas of the group, there is no singular explanation

A. Barber, *UK Banks and the Lessons of the Great Financial Crisis*, Building a Sustainable Political Economy: SPERI Research & Policy, https://doi.org/10.1007/978-3-030-70254-0_7

for this change. Instead, and much like the preceding chapter, it is necessary to consider individual facets of the business upon their own merit in order to understand how and why learning has unfolded in such a way and why, in some areas of the business, learning remains incomplete.

Factors Explaining HSBC's Learning Journey

Though HSBC came through the GFC with little regulatory or reputational damage, a series of governance failures post-2008, including criminal proceedings over money laundering; the mis-selling of investments; exchange rate rigging; and the facilitation of tax avoidance, meant that the group would subsequently undergo the necessary dissatisfaction to prompt learning in relation to group governance and regulation. This learning resulted in a series of tangible policy outcomes in the post-crisis decade that has addressed many of these regulatory shortcomings. Ideas associated with the policy learning literature will be used to explain why the group may have learned in relation to this particular facet of the business. In particular, the evidence suggests that following moments of dissatisfaction, HSBC has sought, evaluated and applied new information with lessons learned being upheld by a series of improved policy actions resulting in a shift in the group's normative frames and institutional preferences.

Conversely, remunerative practices in the post-crisis decade paint a rather mixed picture. On the one hand, the group has recognised that in order to attract and retain the brightest banking talent it must be competitive on pay and that a failure to do so would put it at a strategical disadvantage. On the other hand, HSBC has overhauled how variable pay is calculated, shifting bonuses away from purely economic measures. As such, some elements of variable pay represent a substantive change to pre-crisis norms. Despite this, the group has also been a vocal critic of tougher new regulations aimed at tempering variable pay and, like other banks in this study, have utilised so-called fixed pay allowances in order to circumvent legislation. Theoretical explanations surrounding structural competitive pressures will be used to explore these variations in learning. For example, competitive pressures built-into banking markets and the fear of sanction—in this case losing talent to rival organisations—may explain why HSBC has adapted its behaviour in such a way that learning has not been optimal.

When we consider the balance sheet element at HSBC a different picture emerges with the group showing few signs of change. HSBC's balance sheet served it well throughout the GFC and in the immediate aftermath. However, in 2011 as the 'fog' of the crisis began to lift, HSBC undertook a strategic review that would look at how best to improve the group's capital allocation and cost accountability. The conclusion of this review determined that the business was in good health but would require minor modifications—including the retrenchment and exit of some business areas and an expansion of others. In particular, it was deemed that HSBC's overall strategic direction would require a reorientation of the business towards emerging markets, particularly in Asia, as a means of maintaining the bank's financial strength and position as a market leader.

Consequently, we witness relatively little change in the group's key financial metrics—which present limited divergence from pre-GFC figures. However, utilising the work of Margaret Archer (2003, 2007, 2012) on the meta-reflexives, I will explore how this apparent lack of change, which upon first reading appears to be more akin to the single-loop theory, may indeed present evidence of learning. It will be argued that HSBC has recognised that to deviate too far from the already established path would place the organisation at a strategical disadvantage. In this respect, the lesson learned from the GFC, and subsequent review of the balance sheet, is that radical change was not needed. As such, it may be possible in this instance to conclude that HSBC has learned without change.

Governance and Regulation

HSBC navigated the GFC without any serious regulatory or internal governance breaches or scandals. As such, in the immediate aftermath of the crisis we witness little change as the group continued to operate in a business-as-usual manner. This moment of quiet contentedness can be explained by the 'dissatisfaction thesis' which runs throughout the literature explored in Chapter 2 and argues that dissatisfaction is central to the learning process.[1] Thus, it appears that HSBC's successful

[1] It may be possible to conclude that a degree of 'dissatisfaction' is not only desirable in the learning process but is in fact a necessary condition of learning. Indeed, this study suggests that it is only after an organisation has undergone sufficient dissatisfaction that it will seek new information and learn.

navigation of the crisis, while endowing the group with the space—institutional resources—needed to learn, failed to promote the necessary dissatisfaction to seek alternatives.

Yet, a series of regulatory scandals brought to light in the post-crisis era, while highlighting serious shortcomings at HSBC, would prove to be a valuable experience and spurred learning at the group. For instance, in response to weaknesses in the group's governance framework, stressed by post-crisis regulatory failures, HSBC would introduce a series of ad hoc policy responses. Though at first these policies may appear to be more reactive than preventative, the prescriptions made by the bank would nonetheless result in tangible outcomes and improved policy actions aimed at remedying institutional flaws. Therefore, it may be possible to conclude that HSBC has demonstrated evidence of substantive double-loop learning in the post-crisis decade with failures in the group's governance and regulatory framework causing the necessary dissatisfaction to prompt learning.

Money Laundering and Trade Sanctions

One of the key events that would propel HSBC from a static state towards the progress of learning would come in 2012 when the US Senate Permanente Sub-Committee on Investigations revealed that HSBC had 'seriously breached' anti-money laundering controls (Roberts & Kynaston, 2014: 656). US prosecutors subsequently revealed that HSBC Mexico had failed to implement satisfactory anti-money laundering controls which had allowed a Mexican drug cartel to launder approximately £452 billion worth of wire transfers and £6 billion worth of currency purchases (Smythe, 2013). The group would suffer further embarrassment and reputational damage when it was revealed that Russian criminal gangs had also been using HSBC accounts to launder the proceeds of crimes including racketeering and the selling of illegal drugs and arms (Bernstein, 2019). The US Sub-Committee later noted that HSBC had become known in the criminal underworld as 'the best place to launder money' (Pachico, 2012).

During the investigation, HSBC also admitted to devising methods to circumvent trade sanctions with countries such as Iran, Cuba and Sudan. The group disclosed that it knowingly facilitated potentially questionable customers to move hundreds of millions of dollars between sanctioned countries and the United States (Mazur, 2013).[2] Proceedings subsequently revealed how HSBC staff had coached colleagues in Iran and other jurisdictions on how to disguise payment messages so that the nature and country of origin could be concealed thus avoiding detection by US authorities (ibid.).

In 2013, HBSC reached a settlement with US prosecutors, agreeing to pay more than £1.2 billion in fines and entering into a five-year deferred prosecution agreement (Smythe, 2013).[3] Commenting on the issue, Stuart Gulliver, GCE, told colleagues that it was right that HSBC should be held to account for what went wrong and that the group would prevent further breaches by ensuring that more stringent safeguards be implemented (Blackden, 2012). In a press release HSBC added that

> We have learned a great deal working with the Subcommittee on this case history and also working with US regulatory authorities, and recognize that our controls could and should have been stronger and more effective in order to spot and deal with unacceptable behaviour. We believe that this case history will provide important lessons for the whole industry in seeking to prevent illicit actors entering the global financial system...HSBC has already taken concrete steps to augment the framework to address these issues.
>
> (HSBC, 2012a)

Sentiments expressed by HSBC concerning the importance of this incident for lesson learning were subsequently upheld as the bank announced two extremely important and observable tangible changes to its' governance structure and which may be indicative of learning. For example, the policy learning literature suggests that learning may be present when an organisation utilises targeted policies aimed at closing the gap between 'aspirations' and 'achievements' with 'improved policy actions' being a key requisite of learning (May, 1992).

[2] We should also note that HSBC is not the only bank to be have been found guilty of such breaches with all the banks in this study being implicated in the transfer of funds to sanctioned countries.

[3] It is widely acknowledged that sanctions against the bank could have been much more severe were it not for former Chancellor George Osborne and the FSA intervening and negotiating a more favourable deal for the group (see Neate 2016; McLannahan, 2016 for further discussion).

Firstly, in 2012, the group announced that it would be introducing an additional board committee with the establishment of the Financial Systems Vulnerabilities Committee (FSVC) (HSBC, 2012b). The working remit of the FSVC would be to oversee and give guidance on the bank's procedures and control framework in relation to financial crime, including, but not limited to, money laundering and terrorist financing (*HSBC.com*). In particular, the FSVC would be responsible for safeguarding business best practice by ensuring that the group's policies were fit for purpose and that HSBC met all of its regulatory and legal requirements pertaining to the prevention of financial crime (ibid.).

The establishment of the FSVC would see HSBC remedy many of those issues highlighted by US investigators by creating a specialist committee aimed at addressing both structural and cultural weaknesses and which may be indicative of the self-reflexive learning process. Importantly however, this critical reflection did not simply end with the formation of the FSVC. Indeed, the committee has been proactive in identifying potential risks and devising policies aimed at tackling vulnerabilities. For instance, in 2014 the FSVC undertook a 'deep-dive' into the group's key regulatory compliance and control practices in order to ensure that polices were fit for purpose. The committee identified three key areas of weakness and subsequently devised and successfully implemented new policy initiatives that would address these strategical flaws including; ***developing an updated anti-money laundering framework, establishing new group-wide best practice policies for dealing with sanctioned countries;*** and ***enhancing the group's cyber security capabilities*** (HSBC, 2014: 282–283). Consequently, the formation of the FSVC is indicative of learning with the committee enjoying genuine powers to the extent that it has been instrumental in shaping policy outcomes at the group. What-is-more, the FSVC appears to have been engaged in an ongoing evaluative process that has produced targeted policies.

Secondly, HSBC would also spend approximately £800 million on compliance technology upgrades and increase its regulatory and control staff numbers by hiring more than 7000 additional new employees (Roberts & Kynaston, 2014; Arnold, 2017). Moreover, between 2012 and 2018, the group would also appointment a number of high-profile independent experts—all with extensive backgrounds in the detection and the prevention of financial crime—that would advise the board and FSVC on emerging threats and internal controls. This would include: Nick Fishwick—former senior official in security intelligence and counterterrorism at the Foreign and Commonwealth Office; Bill Hughes—former head of the UK's Serious Organised Crime Agency; Dave Hartnett—former head of HM Revenue & Customs; Sir Jonathan Evans—former head of MI5; Stuart Levey—former Under Secretary for Terrorism and Financial Intelligence in the US Department of the Treasury; Kathleen Casey—former Commissioner of the US Securities and Exchange Commission; and the Honourable Juan Zarate—former Deputy Assistant to the US President and Deputy National Security Advisor for Combating Terrorism (Thompson, 2013; Thompson & Kortekaas, 2013; Roberts & Kynaston, 2014; HSBC, 2016, 2018).

While breaches in anti-money laundering controls and sanction protocols brought to light post-GFC represent a gross failure of internal governance, HSBC's behaviour following these incidents indicates that the group has subsequently implemented significant change to its governance and regulatory control framework. These reforms suggest that despite initial shortcomings following the GFC, HSBC has indeed learned lessons post-crisis with the group closing the gap between 'aspiration's and 'achievements' in-keeping with Rose's (1991, 1993, 2005) policy learning framework. Indeed, in 2017, the Department of Justice announced that it would be dismissing the deferred criminal charges that it had brought against the group in late 2012 (Arnold, 2017). The DoJ had retained its right to extend the deferment period beyond the initial five years or proceed with the prosecution. However, HSBC noted that its commitment to ensuring 'US level standards across the entire bank' coupled with the group living up to 'all of its commitments' under the deferred agreement had led the DoJ to file for a dismissal of the case (HSBC, 2017a). Commenting on the dismissal Stuart Gulliver, GCE, stated that 'HSBC is able to combat financial crime much more effectively today as the result of the significant reforms… implemented over the last five years' adding that the group was committed to 'protect[ing] the integrity of the global financial system' (Gulliver in HSBC, 2017a). In this respect, HSBC has learned because it has not only sought and evaluated new information but, importantly, has upheld lessons learned with specific policy actions. Moreover, unlike its counterparts at RBS—that failed to orient sufficient institutional resources towards the application of new information, HSBC, like Lloyds, has applied and upheld lesson learned with a series of improved policy actions.

Mis-Selling and Rate Rigging

Despite HSBC taking tangible steps towards remedying deficiencies in its anti-money laundering controls post-GFC, the group has also been the subject of a number of civil and criminal proceedings pertaining to the mis-selling of products and the rigging of various benchmark rates. However, these incidents have, once again, proven to be a valuable learning experience, causing the necessary dissatisfaction to prompt learning. Indeed, following these moments of dissatisfaction HSBC appeared to orient its learning space towards rectifying institutional shortcomings and in doing so have addressed many of the wider cultural vulnerabilities that infected banks in the years leading up to the crisis and which may be indicative of learning.

To illustrate, in 2011 following an investigation by the FSA, it was revealed that one of HSBC's subsidiary companies, NHFA Limited, had knowingly sold investment products to elderly customers that were unsuitable (Wilson, 2011). As a result, HSBC was fined £10 million and ordered to pay a further £29.3 million in compensation to victims who had been mis-sold products between 2004 and 2010 (ibid.). Then in 2012, HSBC announced that it would be putting aside approximately £300 million to recompense customers that had been mis-sold interest payment protection products, better known as interest rate swaps (Brinded, 2014). While HSBC was not the only bank to be implicated in the ordeal—indeed all the banks in this study have been embroiled in the scandal to some extent—the group did have the largest exposure of any UK bank with estimates suggesting that HSBC customers accounted for approximately 27% of victims (ibid.). Further to this, and again like all the banks examined here, HSBC would also be implicated in the mis-selling of PPI and by 2018 had paid more than £3.8 billion in compensation (HSBC, 2018).[4] In 2018, the group would similarly agree to pay US authorities £590 million to settle claims brought against the bank over the mis-selling of mortgage-backed securities between 2005 and 2007 (Shubber, 2018).

HSBC would face additional governance and regulatory upheaval in 2012 when the group became embroiled in the manipulation of certain

[4]We should note that by 2007 HSBC had stopped selling PPI products and has the smallest exposure of the banks in this study (see Roberts & Kynaston, 2014; Farrell, 2016).

benchmarks including the Libor, Euribor and Forex rates (Treanor, 2012; Arnold et al., 2016). Following investigations by UK, United States and European regulators, it was discovered that HSBC employees had been conspiring to manipulate some of the most important interest rates in the global economy between 2007 and 2011 (Arnold et al., 2016). It was subsequently revealed that HSBC staff had been fixing rates at the request of colleagues in order to hedge markets for their own gain and receive the associated performance bonuses (*The Telegraph Online*, 2014; *BBC News*, 2015a; Arnold et al., 2016). In total, the bank would pay more than £300 million in fines levied by various domestic and international regulatory agencies (Treanor, 2012; FCA, 2014; Arnold et al., 2016; Arnold, 2018a).

Addressing the rate-rigging scandals specifically, and HSBC's post-crisis governance and regulatory failures in general, Douglas Flint—the group's then chairman—commented that HSBC was determined to hold itself and staff to the 'highest behavioural and compliance standards' and would implement mechanisms that would ensure and 'enforce the highest standards' (Flint cited in Jaeger, 2013). Likewise, Stuart Gulliver—GCE—noted that the bank 'had lost its way' and pledged that HSBC would 'take concrete steps to resolve issues' (Gulliver cited in Brinded, 2012). The GCE would go on to tell reporters that

> In response to this risk, we are progressing a number of initiatives which seek to address the issues identified, including creating our new global management structure, enhancing our governance and oversight, increasing our compliance function resource, emphasising our values and designing and implementing new global standards as outlined elsewhere.
>
> (ibid.)

This emphasis placed upon the highest behavioural and compliance standards by HSBC's most senior agents led, in 2013 and 2014, respectively, to the establishment of two additional board committees; the Philanthropic and Community Investment Oversight Committee (PCIOC) and the Conduct and Values Committee (CVC) (HSBC, 2013a: 2014). The PCIOC was established in December 2014 and would be given responsibility for overseeing HSBC's philanthropic and community investment projects, including ensuring that the appropriate procedures were followed when approving charitable donations (HSBC, 2014). The PCIOC would operate in conjunction with, and support, the group's corporate sustainability objectives (HBSC, 2017b).[5] Conversely, the CVC would be tasked with supervising the design, implementation and monitoring of the group's key policies and control framework and ensuring that HSBC 'consistently adheres' to the highest corporate and ethical values (HSBC, 2013a: 330). Moreover, the CVC would also be charged with responsibility for ensuring that business at the bank was conducted in a way that enhances the HSBC brand (HSBC, 2013a, 2016). Specifically, the CVC would make certain that the group dealt 'openly' and 'fairly' with its customers (HSBC, 2013a: 330), choose the right customers to do business with and conduct that business in such a way as to not harm or cause distress to the communities in which the bank operates (HSBC, 2018: 138).[6]

Much like the FSVC discussed above, the CVC has not simply been a passive actor. Instead, the committee has been proactive in its duties implementing a series of reforms that have sought tangible cultural change. For example, in 2014 the CVC would undertake a series of 'deep-dives' which involved interviews with leadership teams and functional specialists, focus groups with line managers and staff, and reviews of management information handling (HSBC, 2014). The objective of these measures was to better understand the bank's culture and employee attitudes towards conduct, along with the drivers of staff behaviour (ibid.). One of the key policies resulting from the evaluations would be that from 2015 onwards the CVC would take responsibility for managing whistle-blowing facilities at the group. Specifically, the CVC would pledge to protect whistle-blowers by guaranteeing anonymity and voluntarily adopting the recommendations and principles on whistle-blowing set out by the Parliamentary Commission on Banking Standards and the Banking Standards Board (HSBC, 2014). The Committee would likewise recommend and oversee the implementation of a new and improved whistle-blowing framework based on these recommendations (HSBC, 2015a). The enhanced group-wide reporting platform would include a confidential telephone, email, web and mail options for those wishing to raise concerns and would require all staff undergo annual whistle-blowing awareness training (HSBC, 2016, 2018).

[5] In 2018 the PCIOC would be subsumed into the Group Risk Committee (HSBC, 2018: 158).

[6] In 2018, the CVC would be renamed the Group People Committee (HSBC, 2017b: 138).

The formation of supplementary committees along with policies introduced by these newly established collectives in the post-crisis decade, is indicative of learning at HSBC. Indeed, the group has implemented improved policy actions aimed at addressing the institutional and cultural weakness that gave rise to the mis-selling and rate-rigging scandals. Moreover, the CVC has played an instrumental role in shaping institutional norms and shifting the group's underlying theories-in-use to the extent that new organisational policy preferences ought to mitigate against potential future abuses. Such changes appear to have corrected many of the weaknesses that precipitated governance and regulatory failures at the group in the post-crisis period, thereby ensuring the 'highest behavioural and compliance standards' by adding specialist oversight to the bank's governance structure. In this instance, HSBC's ability to identify flaws, seek out solutions and rectify areas of weakness, which posed a threat to both the reputation of the group and the wider stability of financial markets, is clearly identifiable. Again, this suggests that in relation to governance and regulation, following some initial complacency linked to the group's successful navigation of the GFC, HSBC has indeed demonstrated an ability and willingness to seek, evaluate and apply new information and learn, with sentiments expressed by the group having been upheld by specific policy actions.

Tax Evasion

Further evidence of learning can be witnessed by HSBC's response to a high-profile tax evasion scheme that was operated through its Swiss subsidiary between 2000 and 2010. In December 2008, Swiss authorities arrested HSBC IT expert Herve Falciani, over claims that Mr Falciani had stolen files from the bank containing the details of some of the group's global private bank clients. The computer files in question included the names of customers that, it is alleged, HSBC had helped to avoid taxes (Dunkley, 2015). Data found in Mr Falciani's possession was then passed to French, American, Greek, British and European authorities who immediately launched investigations into HSBC (ibid.). Subsequent civil and criminal litigation would follow when it was revealed that not only had HSBC helped its customers to evade taxes but had actively encouraged clients to do so by promoting various HSBC products and accounts to assist in the task (*BBC News*, 2015b).[7]

HSBC suffered further embarrassment when investigations into its Swiss subsidiary consequently revealed that the GCE, Stuart Gulliver, had used the group's Geneva-based bank to transfer millions of pounds worth of bonuses to a business in Panama in an apparent attempt to conceal the extent of his salary[8] (Arnold, 2015; Obermaier & Obermayer, 2017). HSBC would eventually pay more than £350 million in penalties to tax authorities and regulators across the globe for the actions of the Swiss bank with a number of investigations still pending (Keohane & Arnold, 2017; Megaw, 2017; Armstrong, 2019).

Speaking before a Parliamentary Select Committee in 2015, GCE Stuart Gulliver described the practices of HSBC's Swiss private bank as being 'unacceptable' and apologised for the group's actions (Gulliver cited in Arnold, 2015). Mr Gulliver went on to reassure politicians that HSBC had since put in place robust 'controls systems' and 'compliance functions' that would reduce the risk posed by the group's private banking operations 'to an absolute minimum' (ibid.). In response to the Swiss scandal, the group would release a statement noting that

> [HSBC has] implemented numerous initiatives designed to prevent its banking services being used to evade taxes or launder money. In the past, the Swiss private banking industry operated very differently to the way it does today...We have taken significant steps over the past several years to implement reforms and exit clients who did not meet strict new HSBC standards...Under the tax transparency initiative, we also enhanced both our 'know your customer' (KYC) procedures, including an independent validation by auditors, and our anti-money laundering (AML) procedures to ensure a more complete consideration of a new client's source of wealth.
> (HSBC, 2015b)

[7] For example, HSBC supplied one wealthy client with a foreign cash card so that untaxed monies could be withdrawn abroad and avoid the attention of domestic revenue inspectors (Evans, 2015). In another case, HSBC wrote to clients advising them how to evade the European Savings Directive, offering them products that were specifically designed to circumvent the European initiative aimed reducing tax evasion (Evans, 2015).

[8] We should note that Mr Gulliver's actions were by no means criminal and were well within the boundaries of the law. The use of the Panamanian conduit by Mr Gulliver was instead an attempt to shield the true nature of his salary from predatory bank insiders that may have used such information against the GCE or HSBC. This incident did not represent an attempt by Mr Gulliver to circumvent his tax responsibilities nor was Mr Gulliver ever accused of attempting to avoid any taxes.

As is the case above, the Swiss private banking scandal would produce a number of tangible policy changes at the group that are indicative of learning, with HSBC once again appearing to close the gap between aspirations and achievements. For example, in 2012—during the wake of scandal—the group's global private banking arm implemented a new 'tax transparency policy'. Under new provisions, the group would close or refuse accounts to customers that it determined were using, or intended to use, HSBC accounts for the evasion and avoidance of tax (HSBC, 2013a). HSBC would also go on to review all accounts held in its private bank against a series of benchmarks intended to identify tax non-compliance (HSBC, 2015b). Accounts that failed to meet the new strict criteria, or were judged by HSBC to pose a risk, were either closed immediately or put into special measures to exist customers from the division as soon as possible (ibid.).

This de-risking exercise would inadvertently sweep-up and close the accounts of a number of customers including a series of charities, individuals, Mosques and even the Vatican's UK ambassadorial office—which clearly posed no risk to the bank or the tax systems of states, and was perhaps a sign of HSBC's overzealousness (Tims & Collinson, 2015). Yet, the result of reforms implemented by HSBC in the wake of the tax evasion scandal is evident. For instance, HSBC would close almost two-thirds of its private bank accounts between 2012 and 2018 as part of the group's tax transparency initiative with HSBC reducing customer numbers in the unit from 30,412 in 2012 to just 10,343 in 2018 (HSBC, 2013a, 2018). Likewise, in 2007 the group's private banking operation held assets worth approximately £103 billion, by 2018 this figure had been reduced to approximately £51 billion, representing a reduction of around 50% (ibid.). Between 2012 and 2018, the group would also retrench its private banking operations from 150 countries to just 34 (Arnold, 2018b).

Following the scandal surrounding its Swiss-based operations, HSBC has implemented a number of reforms across its entire private banking division that suggest the presence of learning. Moreover, sentiments expressed by the group surrounding the division and lesson learning have been upheld by a series of improved policy actions. Such changes are also symptomatic of a wider post-crisis institutional shift in the group's underlying theories-in-use concerning group governance and regulation. Though HSBC has been plagued by a number of failures relating to its governance and regulatory control framework post-GFC, such incidents appear to have been the impetus for change. Indeed, while in the immediate aftermath of the crisis HSBC lacked the motivation to learn, which may be attributed to its successful navigation of the GFC, subsequent litigation and reputational damage appears to have caused the necessary dissatisfaction to seek alternatives and learn. What is more, the group have been successful 'learners' because, unlike its counterparts at RBS and Barclays, HSBC has oriented its learning space not only towards the seeking and evaluation of new information but, critically, has applied lessons learned by implementing a series of targeted policy initiatives designed to implement and uphold this new information.

Remuneration and Bonuses

Learning in relation to remuneration and bonuses in the post-crisis decade at HSBC breaks with the above section insomuch as the group has presented little evidence of learning and change. For example, HSBC has frequently clashed with shareholders over pay and has openly objected to and derided regulatory stipulations aimed at tempering remuneration—although ultimately complying with the letter, if not the spirit, of the law. Despite this, HSBC has shown some evidence of learning with reforms aimed at aligning employee remuneration to long-term shareholder value. However, the most significant change to group remuneration in the post-crisis decade has come in response to tougher regulatory stipulations concerning pay and bonuses. In this respect, though HSBC has demonstrated some learning, changes have been confined to the fringes of pre-existing structures. One factor that may explain why HSBC has, on the whole, failed to learn lessons is that fact that the group has been fearful of losing ground—the ability to attract and retain talent—to rivals. The literature on structure and agency, along with competitive pressures that appear inherent to the structures within which banks continue to operate, will be used to broaden our understanding of learning at HSBC in the post-crisis decade.

Annual Incentive

In 2008, variable remuneration at HSBC was divided between the annual incentive (AI) and long-term incentive plan (LTIP). The AI would carry a maximum potential of up to 400% of base salary with 40% of any award being deferred into shares, the remaining 60% would be paid as a cash bonus immediately (HSBC, 2007). After the GFC, the AI would remain broadly unchanged until 2014 when the award would undergo a restructuring in the light of new regulatory standards, specifically CRD IV. Under the new remuneration structure, the AI would have an upper limit of 67% of base salary[9] and would be paid in any combination of both cash and shares (HSBC, 2014). However, cash payments would be capped at a maximum of 50% of the total bonus awarded (HSBC, 2014, 2016, 2018). Share awards granted under the AI would be deferred for a vesting period of 12 months and subject to malus and clawback provisions for a period of not less than seven years from the date of the award (ibid.).[10]

While the AI has undoubtedly undergone reform following the GFC, with a reduction in the maximum potential of awards and the application of retention and clawback stipulations, these changes appear to have come in response to a shifting structural environment. Specifically, tougher regulatory requirements and perceived competitive pressures concerning the recruitment of talent have been a key determinant in HSBC's post-crisis remuneration policies. For example, commenting on the introduction of CRD IV, and the group's related reform of its remuneration structure, Simon Robertson, then chairman of the remuneration committee, noted that

> The main drivers of change in remuneration policy and practice within the financial services industry are the new regulations under CRD IV... This situation has necessitated a review of our remuneration policy.
>
> (Robertson in HSBC, 2013a: 378)

The remuneration committee's 2014 address to shareholders—the first year following the implementation of CRD IV—would similarly address the issue of regulatory reform and the extent to which changes in the group's immediate operating environment had influenced the pace and scale of institutional change. The committee would conclude that

[9] This being 1/3 of the maximum variable pay opportunity of 200% of fixed pay under CRD IV.

[10] Once again, this is in-keeping with the requirements set out by the PRA, FCA and CRD IV remuneration codes.

> consequential changes to...remuneration rules...have influenced how we pay our senior executives and those of our employees identified by the PRA as having a material impact on the institution's risk profile... The number and volume of regulatory changes that have been and are being proposed in connection with remuneration are, in the Committee's view, excessive.
>
> (HSBC, 2014: 300–302)

Though HSBC has untimely complied with the letter of the law—limiting cash payments, introducing malus stipulations and revising upper thresholds of bonuses—the group, and key agents within the bank, have clearly been uncomfortable with the role that regulators have played in shaping post-crisis remuneration structures, having labelled changes as 'excessive'. Such sentiments may be symptomatic of the absence of learning as it pertains to the relationship between the banks and regulators. As previously established in Chapter 3, resistance to regulatory change and sustained efforts by the banks to 'roll-back' supervisory frontiers were one of the causes of the GFC. Indeed, a denigration of supervisory interventions, along with a disregard for regulatory expertise, proved costly in 2008 for both banks and the wider system of globalised financial markets. Institutional attitudes and ideas expressed by HSBC in regard to the shifting nature of the regulatory landscape in the post-crisis decade suggest the absence of a fundamental reappraisal of the group's ideational preferences and beliefs in the light of new information concerning the role of the supervisor in protecting financial stability. As such, policies introduced as part of the AI fail to present substantive evidence of lesson learning in keeping with account of learning presented in Chapter 2. Instead, reform of the group's AI appears to have been motivated by structural factors, namely tougher regulatory requirements.

Long-Term Incentive

Although reform of the AI suggests little evidence of endogenously originated learning, changes to the second element of variable remuneration—the LTIP—may yet indicate learning. In 2008, the LTIP was worth a potential maximum of up to seven-times base salary (HSBC, 2008). This figure was subsequently revised down to six-times of annual salary in 2011 (HSBC, 2011a). The allowance of the LTIP would then remain unchanged until 2014 when HSBC once again restructured the award in the light of the European Parliament's CRD IV directive (HSBC, 2014). Under provisions set out in 2014, the LTIP would carry a maximum upper-threshold of 133% of base salary—this being two-thirds of the maximum opportunity of 200% of fixed pay allowed under CRD IV (HSBC, 2014, 2018). Likewise, in 2008 awards made under the LTIP were paid in the form of performance shares measured over a three-year vesting period (HSBC, 2008). However, as part of the restructuring of the LTIP in 2014—in the light of CRD IV, the group announced that the vesting period for awards would be extended to five years—increasing to seven years in 2016 in accordance with requirements set out by the PRA, FCA and CRD IV remuneration rules (HSBC, 2014, 2016, 2018; PwC, 2015). These changes suggest that in the wake of the GFC, the long-term element of variable remuneration underwent minimal endogenously originated change. Indeed, a revision of the upper limit of awards granted under the LTIP, along with an increase in retention periods, appears to have once again come in the light of exogenous structural factors, specifically the evolving regulatory landscape.

However, an examination of how the LTIP has been calculated, along with the qualifying criteria, following the introduction of CRD IV may yet demonstrate some evidence of learning. In 2008, the LTIP was calculated using three key metrics: *total shareholder return* (40%); *economic profit* (40%); and *growth in earnings per share* (20%) (HSBC, 2008: 318). Thus, we can see that in 2008 the LTIP was calculated solely on economic metrics. However, in 2011 HSBC announced that it would be introducing a series of non-financial measures when determining awards (HSBC, 2011a). These new metrics would take consideration of factors such as *conduct and reputation* and *risk and compliance* and account for 30% of the LTIP's overall value (HSBC, 2011a, 2014, 2018). HSBC stated that it had introduced non-financial performance measures as a means of 'incentivis[ing] senior executives to deliver sustainable long-term business performance' (HSBC, 2011a: 256). This structure would remain broadly in-line until 2014 when HSBC announced that going forwards 40% of the LTIP's weighting would be determined by these non-financial metrics (HSBC, 2014, 2018).

The use of non-financial measures in determining the employee bonus pool was absent from HSBC's pre-crisis remunerative practices. However, reform of the LTIP in the decade that has followed the GFC has moved the group's remuneration structure away from a bonus culture that may have incentivised short-term risk-taking. Moreover, changes to the

LTIP in the post-GFC decade have resulted in a more sustainable, risk averse long-term bonus that places a greater emphasis upon the means and manner in which results are delivered. The inclusion of these new measures marks a substantive shift from pre-crisis norms and underlying theories-in-use, as they pertain to the LTIP. As such, reforms announced under the revised LTIP appear to suggest the presence of learning at HSBC with the introduction of a series of improved policy actions upholding lessons learned concerning the harmful impact of remuneration structures that fail to consider how results are delivered. Indeed, commenting on the changes delivered in 2014 the group's remuneration committee noted that

> Performance should be judged not only on what is achieved over the short and long-term but also, importantly, on how it is achieved, as we believe the latter contributes to the long-term sustainability of the business.
> (HSBC, 2014: 300)

Changes to the way that HSBC has calculated the LTIP in the post-GFC decade has undoubtedly tied shareholder value creation and the long-term sustainability of the group to employee remuneration. As such, the group appears, to some extent, to have offset the short-term high risk/high reward culture that pervaded institutions pre-crisis and may be indicative of lesson learning. However, other areas of reform—including reductions in the maximum potential of bonuses and the extension of malus and clawback periods—appear to have come in response to tougher new regulatory requirements. Intrinsically, reform of the LTIP in the decade that has followed the GFC suggests a rather mixed picture of learning in relation to this element of variable pay.

Role-Base Pay

The measures discussed above in relation to the LTIP demonstrate some alignment between employee remuneration and the long-term sustainability of the group and as such may present a degree of learning. However, HSBC's decision to utilise role-based pay suggests that despite some evidence of learning and change, learning in the post-crisis decade in many instances has remained incomplete. Complacency towards the role played by shareholders along with structural competitive pressures concerning the group's ability to recruit and retain the best banking talent may explain why despite some positive steps HSBC has largely failed to learn in relation to this facet of the business.

The literature on single- and double-loop learning, accounted for in Chapter 2, tells us that learning is most likely to occur following a thorough examination of an organisation's underlying theories-in-use. Central to this evaluative process is the engagement with certain institutional stakeholders, for instance shareholders and regulators. However, post-2008 HSBC has openly stated its opposition to tougher regulatory standards over pay and has frequently clashed with its shareholders over the group's remuneration practices—particularly the introduction of role-base pay allowances.

At its annual general meeting in 2013, HSBC faced shareholder backlash after the group proposed changes to its remuneration policy to be implemented in 2014. In particular, shareholders voiced strong opposition to the planned introduction of a new role-based pay for executives and material risk takers (Neate, 2013). The new role-based pay would see certain employees entitled to a yearly fixed award reflective of their role and responsibility (HSBC, 2013a, 2014, 2018). The award would be paid in the form immediately vested shares and be subject to a five year retention period with shares released annually on a pro-rata basis (HSBC, 2014, 2018). However, a significant number of shareholders rejected the remuneration committee's report and recommendations and voted against the proposal (Neate, 2013). Further unrest would hit HSBC in 2014 when one-in-five shareholders voted against the remuneration committee's report and recommendations. According to Martin Arnold of the *Financial Times*, shareholders were keen to voice their concerns that the bank's implementation of role-based pay, in response to CRD IV, would effectively introduce a system of annual targets based upon each preceding year's financial performance rather than the long-term outlook of the group[11] (Arnold, 2014a). Likewise, investors accused the group of using these controversial allowances to 'effectively sidestep' bonus caps by making such payments unfixed and sensitive to the overall bonus pool, something which HSBC has denied (ibid.).

HSBC's failure to engage with institutional stakeholders, namely shareholders and regulators, thereby subordinating the input of these key

[11] Fixed pay allowances and their controversial use as means of circumventing regulatory stipulations have been discussed in the preceding chapters. Likewise, we should note that all the banks in this study have utilised such awards.

actors, may be indicative of a failure to learn in keeping with the account of learning presented in Chapter 2. Moreover, despite mounting pressure from shareholders and regulators, the introduction of role-based pay suggests that in the post-crisis decade, HSBC has continued to favour remuneration polices that place a strong emphasis upon short-term economic performance that may incentivise excessive risk-taking. The use of role-based pay by institutions has likewise been accused of undermining the role of the regulatory by circumventing tougher stipulations concerning pay and performance. As such, the utilisation of these policy instruments by HSBC in the post-crisis decade may be a further indicator of a failure to learn lessons from the GFC.

Structural competitive pressures can help to explain HSBC's apparent lack of learning and a reluctance to temper its remuneration policies. In the post-GFC decade, HSBC has been fearful of losing its best employees to competitors and resultantly, has been keen to defend its agency and determine its own remuneration policies. What is more, HSBC's strategical positioning following the GFC[12] may have exacerbated structural pressures by exposing the group to additional competition over the recruitment of talent. As hypothesised in Chapter 6, structural competitive pressures concerning the recruitment and retention of the best banking talent may have been more acute at institutions that maintained or increased an international exposure post-2008.[13] Indeed, following the GFC, and as part of HSBC's Strategic Review 2011, the group announced a 'pivot into Asia'. This strategic repositioning would see HSBC maintain its large international exposure by reorienting some areas of business on emerging markets in South East Asia. With this move, HSBC has undoubtedly come into greater competition with rival institutions that are not subject to the same domestic and European regulatory stipulations. This can explain why HSBC has been more sensitive to pressures over pay in the post-crisis decade than some of its counterparts, for example Lloyds, that have retrenched operations on UK and European markets.

For example, following the clash between the remuneration committee and shareholders over the introduction of role-based allowances at the

[12] Discussed in more detail in the coming section.

[13] See Chapter 6, page 204, footnote 10.

2013 annual general meeting, chairman Douglas Flint told those in attendance that 'we have to be competitive' and that new legislation on performance related pay 'could have a highly damaging impact on our competitive position' (Flint cited in Aldrick, 2013). Mr Flint would go on to question HSBC's ability to compete for talent in the light of new rules, adding that 'we will comply with the law, but will we be able to make ourselves competitive' (ibid.). Sentiments of this kind were then reiterated by the chairman of the remuneration committee, Sir Simon Robertson, who commented that

> changes in the rules on remuneration and the application of a cap on variable pay...presents significant challenges for the HSBC Group...most of our international peers and domestic competitors do not have to comply with similar restrictions. This situation has necessitated a review of our remuneration to ensure that HSBC can remain competitive.
>
> (Robertson in HSBC, 2013a: 378)

Again, in 2014 following the introduction of the EU's hard-cap on bonuses Sir Simon Robertson commented that CRD IV would

> present challenges for HSBC in ensuring that the total compensation package for our employees in all of the markets in which we operate remains competitive, in particular, relative to other banks not subject to these requirements... HSBC must continue to retain and attract talent in key non-EU markets where our international peers and their domestic competitors do not have to comply with the CRD IV pay cap.
>
> (Robertson in HSBC, 2014: 300–301)

In 2015, Sam Laidlaw, the newly appointed chairman of the remuneration committee, addressed the issue of regulation and HSBC's international presence—this time in relation to new rules due to be implemented by the PRA—commenting that

> The new PRA Remuneration Rules are more stringent than the rules in force in the EU, US and Asia-Pacific, making it challenging for UK banks to attract talent with transferable skills or from other industries. We believe more regulator co-ordination is required to ensure there are globally consistent remuneration standards and a level playing...There is still a wide divergence in local regulations governing remuneration structures globally. This presents significant challenges to HSBC.
>
> (Laidlaw in HSBC, 2015a: 287–288)

More recently, HSBC has described the use of role-based pay as key to ensuring that employee remuneration was 'commensurate with the individual's role, experience and responsibility and the local market' thereby allowing the group to 'maint[ain]... a competitive total remuneration package for the retention of key talent' (HSBC, 2018: 176).

These statements made by HSBC and its executive team demonstrate that, much like Barclays discussed previously, structural competitive pressures interpreted by key agents have been a crucial determinant in post-crisis remuneration. While all the banks in this study have expressed some concerns about their competitive position in the post-crisis decade, HSBC along with Barclays has been particularly vocal on the issue, as demonstrated above. This can be attributed to both HSBC's and Barclays' large international exposures that, along with the banks' strategical repositioning towards markets located in Asia and North America, respectively, may explain why these institutions have felt the fear of losing talent more acutely than their rivals such as Lloyds. In this respect, HSBC's vast globalised banking model has increasingly brought it into contact with other institutions that not held to the same regulatory regime and may explain why reform of the group's remuneration has not been more radical.

The literature on structure and agency accounted for in Chapter 2 notes that agents are capable of overcoming powerful structures (King, 2000, 2005). However, HSBC and interpretive agents (Bell, 2011) within the bank, much like Barclays, have failed to subjugate competitive structural pressures. In this instance, the cost of learning—a perceived diminished ability to recruit and retain talent—has been interpreted to be too high and has presented itself as a significant barrier to learning. While the group has demonstrated some evidence of change, introducing a series of non-financial metrics to its long-term element of remuneration, learning in relation to remuneration at HSBC in the post-crisis decade appears to be largely absent. Instead, the most significant change to group pay and bonuses has come in response to a shifting structural environment, namely tougher regulatory requirements, that have impacted how employees are rewarded at the bank. Indeed, the structural environment within which institutions operate post-GFC has clearly been an important mitigating factor in the learning process.

Balance Sheet

Despite HSBC failing to demonstrate substantive evidence of learning and change in relation to remuneration and bonuses, the balance sheet element may yet prove evidential of learning in the post-crisis decade. HSBC's successful navigation of the GFC appeared to validated the bank's overall business strategy. As a result, we witness little change in the structure and composition of the balance sheet in the years that immediately followed the crisis. Indeed, in 2008 just months after the devastating events that left markets on the brink of collapse Stephen Green, then HSBC chairman, noted that while the bank had not been immune to the GFC, it had to a large extent avoided the most devastating effects (Green in HSBC, 2008). This successful navigation of the crisis was attributed to the group's robust balance sheet and funding structure with the former chairman noting that

> we have built our business on very strong foundations...which demonstrate our ability to withstand the storm...our strategy has been tested and remains intact...If anything, the current crisis validates our renewed focus over the last few years...Our strategy has served HSBC well and positions it for long-term growth with attractive returns.
>
> (Green in HSBC, 2008: 8–11)

In 2010 incoming chairman, DJ Flint, expressed similar sentiments commenting that HSBC had a certain 'continued success [in] many of the markets in which [it] operated' (Flint in HSBC, 2010: 4–6). The chairman emphasised that HSBC's strategic position had meant that it had 'neither sought nor received support from any government' (ibid.). Meanwhile, GCE Stuart Gulliver noted that 'shareholders [would] continue to benefit from HSBC's universal banking model' and that 'conservative management of the balance sheet' had meant that the group had 'remained strongly profitable', stressing that 'HSBC's financial performance [had] not been materially affected by events to date' (Gulliver in HSBC, 2010: 7–9).

Yet in late 2010, as markets began to recover and return to a degree of normality, HSBC announced that it would be undertaking a review of the group's business model and strategic direction with a particular focus upon the structure and composition of the balance sheet. According to HSBC, the 2011 Strategic Review (the Review hereafter) was motivated by a stalling share price and an acute awareness of being overtaken by 'more agile competitors' (HSBC, 2011b: 1). In this respect, the fear of losing ground to competitors appeared to cause sufficient dissatisfaction to seek new information and propel the group towards leaning. The Review would not announce any radical plans or a major strategical reform. Instead, it was concluded that the group's business model and exposure to certain key markets and sectors, which had served it so well throughout the GFC, ought to be broadly maintained (HSBC, 2011b). HSBC would however look to reposition itself in order to capture the 'flow between the developed world and emerging markets', establishing a 'credible presence' in both regions (HSBC, 2011b: 2–3). In particular, the Review announced a 'pivot into Asia', motivated by strong macroeconomic indicators suggesting that South East Asia and specifically China would become 'the most important region for HSBC over the next thirty years' (ibid.: 9). This reorientation inevitably resulted in the retrenchment and disposal of some areas of the business[14] while expanding others. Yet, HSBC maintained that it would preserve its position on a capital, liquidity and a diversified funding and customer base stating that 'we are not going to change that' (HSBC, 2011b: 4).

As a result of HSBC's adherence to its business model following the Review, many of the key financial metrics examined in this section of the chapter have undergone very little change between 2008 and 2018. Moreover, this lack of divergence is particularly pronounced when we compare the years 2011—the year of the Review—and 2018. However,

[14] In July 2011, HSBC announced that it would selling almost 200 of its New York based branches to First Niagara in a deal worth approximately £670 million (Thomas & Braithwaite, 2011). In August of the same year HSBC agreed to sell its US credit card business to Capital One Financial in a deal worth approximately £1.7 billion (Goff and Thomas, 2011) and would see the group shed approximately £19 billion of its credit card loans (Rushe, 2011). Further disposals also included: the sale of the group's Japanese private banking arm, with assets of £1.9 billion (Simonian, 2011); the 2012 sale of its insurance businesses in Hong Kong, Singapore, Argentina and Mexico with assets worth approximately £830 million (Wilson, 2012); the disposal of HSBC Shipping Services Ltd with assets of £4.5 million (Arnason, 2012); the 2012 sale of its property advise service (CityAm); the 2012 sell-off of the bank's entire 15.6% share in the Chinese insurance company Ping An for approximately £6.3 million (Davies et al., 2012); the 2012 disinvestment of parts of HSBC's businesses located across Latin America to Banco GNB Sudameris, thereby disposing of £2.9 billion worth of assets (*BBC News*, 2012); the 2013 sale of HSBC's entire 8% stake in the Bank of Shanghai to Banco Santander SA which would see the group dispose of £334 million of non-core assets (HSBC, 2013b); the 2014 sale approximately £8.4 billion of its Swiss private banking portfolio to investors in Liechtenstein (Arnold, 2014b).

the narrowness of this change should not be considered as a failure to learn. When considered in the light of the literature on the meta-reflexives (Archer, 2003, 2007, 2012) the evidence examined in this section may indeed be indicative of learning despite the absence of radical reform.

Archer's (2003, 2007, 2012) thesis on the meta-reflexives, accounted for in Chapter 2, suggests that a learning subject—either an individual or organisation—following a deliberative internal process, may conclude that it is of a greater benefit to not undergo dramatic change. The 'situational logic of opportunity' put forwards by Archer (2007, 2012) proposes that learning may indeed be present within an institution despite the absence of substantive change. I argue that HSBC has become meta-reflexive in the post-crisis decade, and having a greater awareness of the possibilities and limitations of its own agency and the structural environment—or situational logic of opportunity (ibid.), has determined that change is unnecessary and of little benefit. In this respect, HSBC has learned however, the key lesson learned by the group is that to deviate too far from the business model that served it so well throughout the crisis period would in fact be harmful. As such, radical reform is unwarranted and may explain why we witness the lack of a substantive shift in the structure and composition of the balance in the post-GFC decade despite the presence of learning in the form of the meta-reflexive process.

Group Funding

In 2008, total liabilities and equity at HSBC were worth approximately £1.9 trillion. Customer deposits totalled £860 billion or 44% of total group funding. In 2018, total liabilities and equity had been maintained at around £1.9 trillion, with total customer deposits having increased to £1 trillion or 53% of total group funding.[15] From these figures we can see that in the decade that has followed the GFC, HSBC has increased customer deposits—which were already the highest amongst our comparator group—significantly. Moreover, in 2018 HSBC had the highest customer deposit ratio of all the banks in this study. While this does not necessarily fit with hypothesis extended above, this data

[15] Because HSBC reports its financial data in US Dollars, all figures have been converted to GBP using the Bank of England's 'daily spot exchange rates against Sterling' as of 31st December 2018. Available online at: https://www.bankofengland.co.uk/boeapps/database/Rates.asp?TD=31&TM=Dec&TY=2018&into=GBP&rateview=D.

nonetheless demonstrates evidence of learning with HSBC growing this particularly stable source of funding post-crisis (Fig. 7.1).

Likewise, in 2008 short-term funding, inclusive of short-term borrowing, money market funds and other deposits was worth approximately £200 billion or around 10% of group liabilities and equity. In 2018, short-term funding stood at £237 billion, which accounted for around 12% of total group funding. As such, we can see that in the ten years that has followed the GFC, short-term funding has remained broadly in line with pre-crisis levels, only deviating two percentage points across the entire post-GFC decade. Indeed, in 2011 as part of the Review, HSBC asserted its commitment to prudence on short-term funding—an overreliance on which the group identified as a key cause of the GFC—telling investors that 'if you're reliant on the wholesale market, you're reliant on a...shift that can take place very, very quickly' (HSBC, 2011b: 4). Though HSBC has grown its reliance upon short-term funding in the post-crisis decade, this increase has been minimal and does not represent a significant or radical divergence from the pre-established path, as in keeping with meta-reflexives thesis extended in this section. Moreover,

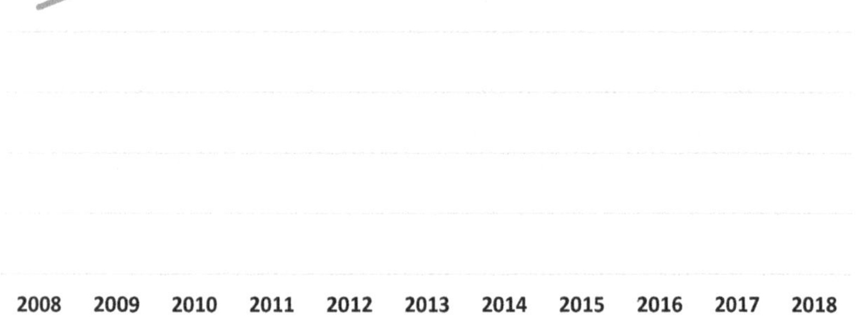

Fig. 7.1 Customer deposits as percentage of total group liabilities and equity 2008–2018

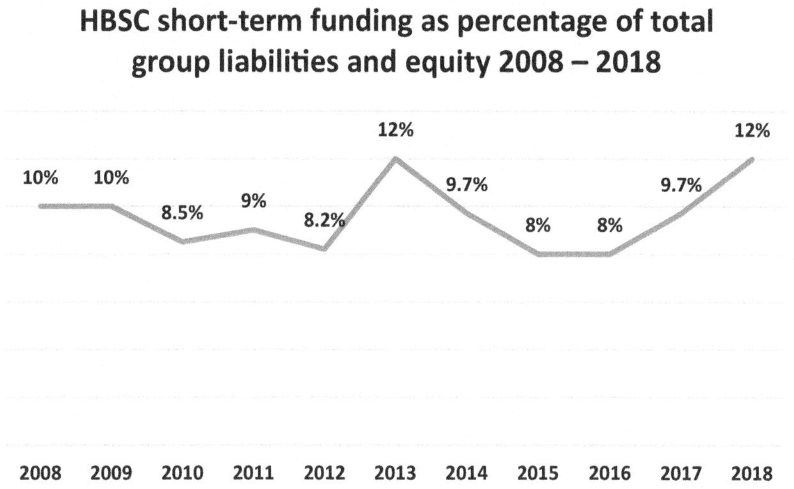

Fig. 7.2 Short-term funding as percentage of total group liabilities and equity 2008–2018

comparative figures show that in 2018 HSBC was marginally outperformed by Lloyds (9%) and RBS (11%) but reported a significantly lower ratio than Barclays (24%) on this metric (Fig. 7.2).[16]

Trading Liabilities

Data collated on trading liabilities as a percentage of total group liabilities and equity shows that in 2008 HSBC had trading liabilities worth £190 billion or 9.7% of total assets. In comparison, figures for 2018 demonstrate that trading liabilities were worth £168 billion or 8.5% of total liabilities and equity. This demonstrates that over the course of the post-crisis decade, trading liabilities as a percentage of total group funding fell just 1.2 percentage points. Again, these figures suggest that HSBC has largely maintained its trading exposures across the post-crisis decade. Moreover, though these figures do not rival the prudence of Lloyds (1.1%) or RBS (3.8%), HSBC did outperform the only other bank in this study to not receive a state-sponsored bailout, Barclays, that in 2018 had trading liabilities of 10.2% (Fig. 7.3).

[16] Tougher regulations on minimum capital standards and the definition of tier 1 capital may have had an effect on wholesale borrowings.

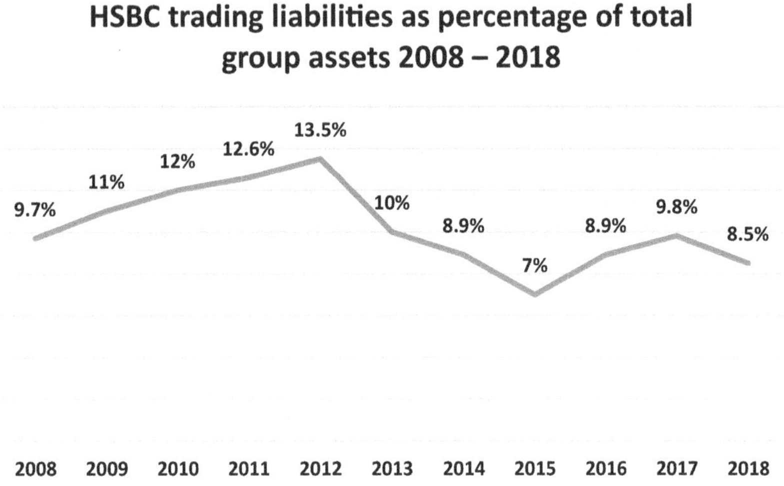

Fig. 7.3 Trading liabilities as percentage of total assets 2008–2018

Loan/Deposit Ratio

In 2008, gross loans totalled £736 billion or the equivalent of around 85% of total customer deposits. In contrast, figures for 2018 show a significant decrease in the number of loans extended as a percentage of customer deposits. In 2018, gross loan totalled £768 billion or around 73% of total customer deposits, a decrease of 12 percentage points. However, data for the intervening years may yet support the supposition presented in this section of the chapter. For example, in 2011—the year of the Review—HSBC's gross loans totalled £706 billion or 75% of total customer deposits. Consequently, we can see that between 2011 and 2018 gross loans as percentage of total customer deposits fell by just two percentage points. Moreover, the Review clearly stated HSBC's commitment to preserve the loan-to-deposit ratio telling investors that 'we continue to have a substantial surplus of deposits over loans and that will remain the case' (HSBC, 2011b: 4). This appears to support the meta-reflexives thesis concerning the structure and composition of the balance sheet. In contrast with our comparator group, we can see that in 2018 HSBC had by far the most conservative loan-to-deposit ratio at outperforming Barclays (84%), RBS (85%) and Lloyds (109%).

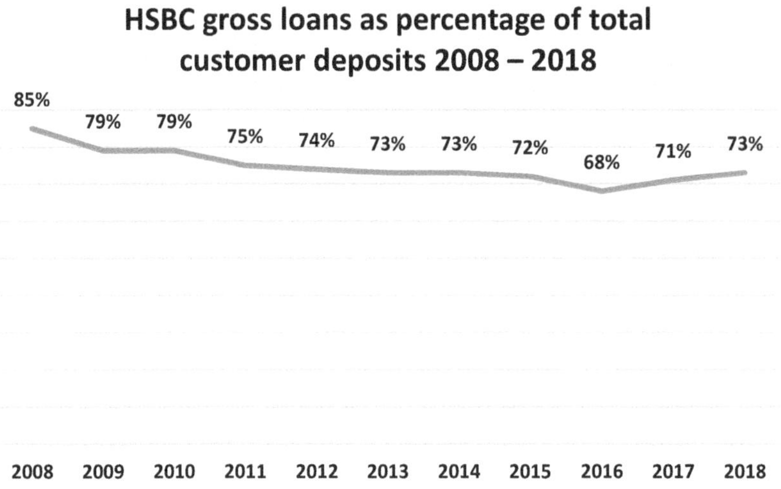

Fig. 7.4 Gross loans as percentage of total customer deposits 2008–2018

Similarly, the percentage of loans extended towards residential mortgage lending, which we know is a much safer loan, has also remained largely the same across the post-crisis decade, with this lack of divergence from the pre-established path more pronounced between 2011 and 2018. For example, in 2008 residential mortgages at HSBC were worth £184 billion or approximately 25% of gross loans. In 2018, residential mortgage lending totalled £222 billion or 29% of gross loans, a small increase of four percentage points. However, once again if we contrast figures for 2018 with those of 2011 we can see that HSBC maintained its level of exposure on this metric.

Given the shift towards increased residential mortgage lending in the post-crisis decade, it is unsurprising that we find that the number of impairments at the group as a percentage of gross loans has decreased. Figures for 2008 show that total impaired loans were worth approximately £17 billion or 2.6% of gross loans. Meanwhile, data for 2018 demonstrates that total impaired loans were equivalent to 0.8% of gross loans extended being worth £6 billion. Though these figures demonstrate the smallest reduction in the percentage value of impaired loans post-crisis, we must note that HSBC had the lowest number of impairments in

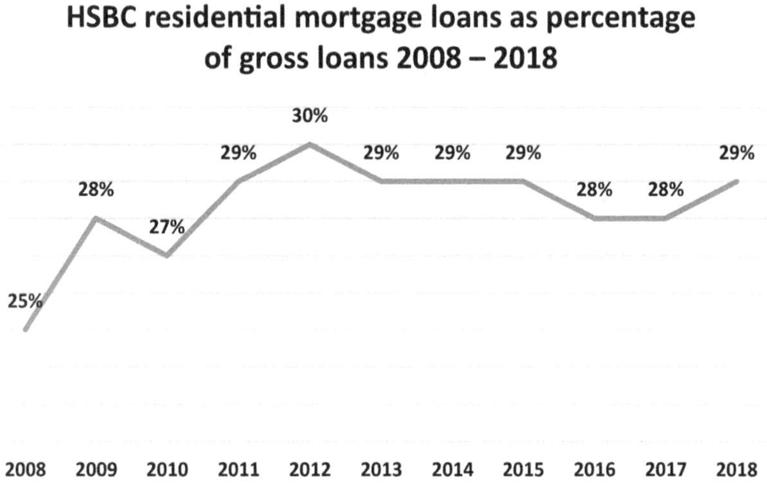

Fig. 7.5 Residential mortgage loans as percentage of gross loans 2008–2018

2018 with the data showing the bank to be ahead of RBS (2.5%), Barclays (2.6%) and Lloyds (4.6%).

While the data above demonstrates some movement following the GFC, we can see from Figs. 7.4, 7.5, and 7.6 that these shifts are far from radical, particularly when we compare data from 2011—the year of the Review—with that of 2018. Consequently, these figures do not suggest sweeping reform but rather incremental positive change to previously established underlying theories-in-use. As a result, it may be the case that HSBC, following a self-reflexive process encapsulated by the Review, learned that radical change was unwarranted. Indeed, sentiments expressed by the bank in the Review, concerning key facets of the balance sheet, suggest that in the wake of the GFC, HSBC sought and evaluated new information. However, after considering its situational logic of opportunity, the bank became meta-reflexive and concluded that the application of new information in this instance meant not deviating too far from its normative frames and preferences.

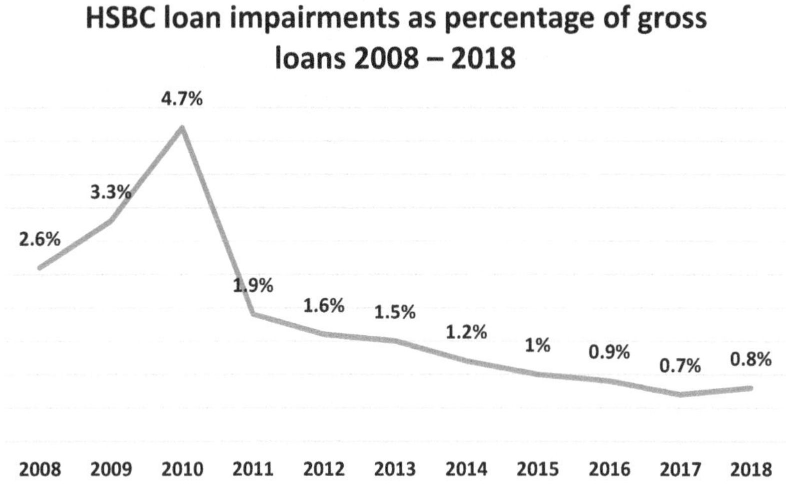

Fig. 7.6 Impaired loans as percentage of gross loans 2008–2018

Derivatives

In 2008 derivatives at HSBC were worth £369 billion, or as proportion of total group liabilities and equity, 19%. In 2009, derivatives fell significantly to 10% of total liabilities and equity before then rising slightly to 13% in 2011. In 2018, derivatives at HSBC were worth £155 billion or approximately 8% of group liabilities and equity. Figures for the comparator group demonstrate that in 2018 HSBC had the second lowest proportion of derivatives on its balance sheet behind Lloyds (2.9%) but significantly outperformed RBS (19%) and Barclays (19%). Moreover, these figures may be indicative of learning in accordance with the meta-reflexives thesis with HSBC, following a substantial decrease between 2008 and 2009, broadly maintaining derivatives as percentage of the balance sheet (Fig. 7.7).

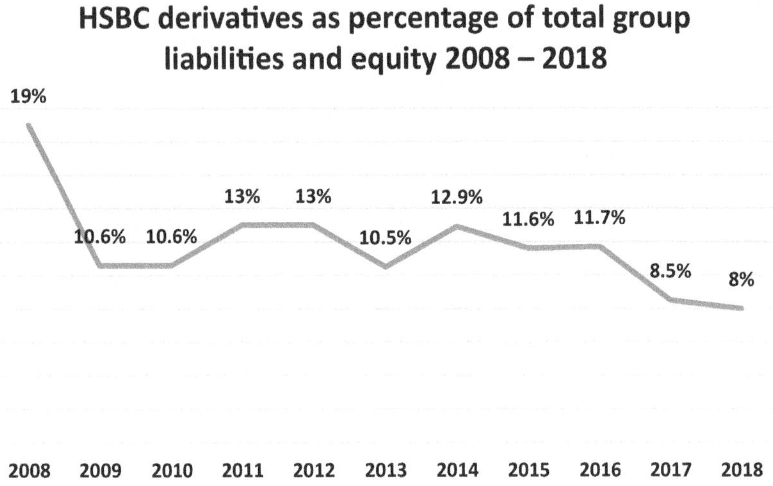

Fig. 7.7 Derivatives as percentage of total liabilities and equity 2008–2018

Regulatory Capital

In 2008,[17] HSBC held regulatory tier 1 capital of £64 billion which equated to a regulatory tier 1 capital ratio of 8.3%. In 2018, the group's regulatory tier 1 capital was £113 billion and carried a tier 1 regulatory capital ratio of 16.6%. Thus, we can see that in 2018 HSBC was operating with a tier 1 regulatory capital ratio that was in excess of regulatory standards by 176%. Likewise, in 2008 the group's total regulatory capital was approximately £88 billion with a total regulatory capital ratio of 11.4%. In 2018, total regulatory capital was £130 billion with a total regulatory capital ratio of £19.4%. Again, here we can see that in 2018 HSBC had a total regulatory capital ratio that was 142% higher than minimum regulatory standards. However, with the exception of Barclays, HSBC was outperformed by all the banks in this study in terms of the total regulator and tier 1 capital ratios. HSBC did have a higher tier 1 capital ratio

[17] Like our previous chapters measuring any potential changes in the amount of regulatory capital held by institutions both pre and post-crisis is difficult due to the shifting regulatory landscape. As such, we will discuss the application of regulatory capital against 2018 stipulations, namely Basel III.

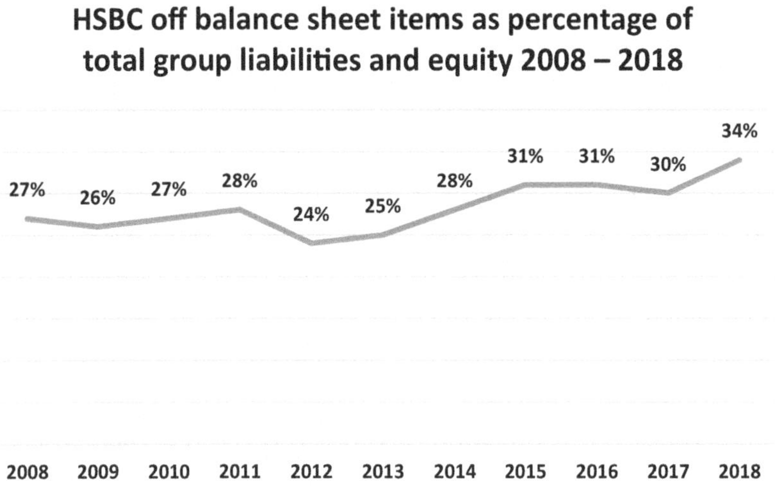

Fig. 7.8 Off-balance-sheet item as percentage of total group liabilities and equity 2008–2018

than Barclays, but recorded a lower total regulatory capital ratio.[18] These figures demonstrate that one of the key changes that appear to have been identified by all the banks in this study is the desire to carry regulatory capital that is in excess of minimum standards with the comparator group all holding reserves beyond minimum requirements.

Off-Balance-Sheet Vehicles

HSBC's use of OBSV in the post-crisis decade breaks with the hypothesis extended so far insomuch as we observe a marked increase. For example, the data presented in Fig. 7.8. demonstrates that in 2008 OBSV were worth £470 billion or 27% of total group liabilities and equity. However, from 2013 onwards we witness an upward trend with HSBC slowly increasing its use of OBSV. By 2018, OBSV were worth £679 billion or 34% of group liabilities and equity. Similarly, in 2018 HSBC had the highest exposure to OBSV of the comparator group with Lloyds (17%), RBS (18%) and Barclays (30%) all outperforming HSBC.

[18] See Chapter 4, page 119, Fig. 4.3.

Investment Bank

Despite a general rise in the use of OBSV by HSBC in the post-crisis decade, this data, when considered alongside the other metrics examined in this section, is not sufficient to undermine the hypothesis extended thus far. Indeed, an analysis of the contribution of HSBC's investment bank to overall group profit may yet prove positive the meta-reflexives hypothesis. For example, in 2008 the investment bank managed assets of £627 billion and made a pre-tax profit of £2.3 billion, contributing approximately 37% to overall group pre-tax profits.[19] By 2018, this figure had shrunk with the investment bank recording pre-tax profits of £4.6 billion and which accounted for 30% of group pre-tax profits. As such, we can see that between 2008 and 2018, the contribution of the investment bank to group pre-tax profits fell by seven percentage points.[20] However, if we compare data from 2011—the year of the Review—this decrease is marginal at just two percentage points. This appears to support the meta-reflexives hypothesis with HSBC broadly maintaining the role of its investment bank as a generator of group profit (Fig. 7.9).

The evidence examined above suggests that despite HSBC having a relatively stable and robust balance sheet in 2008, as evidenced by its successful navigation of the GFC, the group do appear to have learned lessons in the wake of the crisis. However, while HSBC has indeed learned from the GFC, the key lesson learned has been that sweeping reform to the structure and composition of the balance sheet in this instance was undesirable. Instead, following the Review, HSBC concluded that it should not stray too far from the business model and strategic orientation that served it so well previously. Consequently, this learning appears to be largely been in-keeping with the meta-reflexives thesis, with the metrics outlined above demonstrating a great deal of convergence with the pre-existing underlying theories-in-use, something that is particularly evident from 2011—the year of the Review—onwards.

[19] In comparison Barclays' investment bank contributed approximately 50% to overall group pre-tax profit in 2008.

[20] Comparatively, Barclays' investment bank contributed approximately 64% to overall group pre-tax profit in 2018.

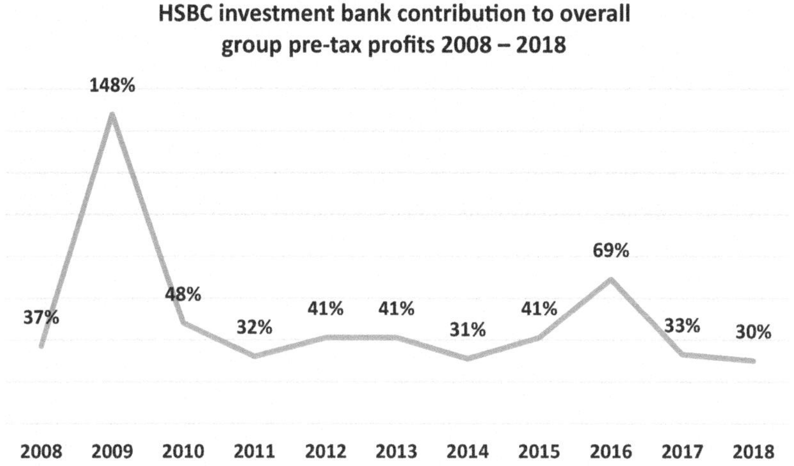

Fig. 7.9 Investment bank contribution to overall group pre-tax profits 2008–2018

Conclusion

Overall, HSBC do appear to have learned lessons in the post-crisis decade. However, different lessons have been learned in relation to contending areas of the business with this learning taking place at dissimilar speeds and in some cases, such as remuneration, remains incomplete. Despite this, following the GFC HSBC has, on the whole, demonstrated a series of improved policy actions that have subsequently given rise to tangible changes in the group's underlying theories-in-use. Theoretical descriptions drawn from the account of learning presented in Chapter 2 have been used to explain these variations in the group's learning trajectory.

In particular, dissatisfaction has been a key driver of group behaviour and learning. HSBC's successful navigation of the crisis meant that the group failed to suffer the necessary dissatisfaction to prompt learning and which resulted in some initial complacency with little evidence of change. However, after suffering a series of secondary internal crises, linked to the group's governance and regulatory framework, HSBC appeared to undergo the necessary dissatisfaction to seek, evaluate and apply lesson learned. Though lessons learned in this respect were not explicitly linked to the GFC, learning at HSBC has been representative of wider lessons concerning the stability of institutions and the sound functioning of financial markets.

Conversely, structural competitive pressures, interpreted by key agents at the bank, and a related perceived diminished ability to attract and retain the best banking talent can explain why, in relation to remuneration, learning is for the most part absent. In particular, the group's commitment to being an international facing bank, typified by its 'pivot into Asian', may explain why these competitive pressures have been felt far more acutely than at other institutions in this study that have retrenched operations on domestic and European markets subject to regulatory equivalents.

Finally, while the balance sheet presents little divergence from pre-crisis models, with the structure and composition of the balance sheet remaining broadly unchanged, the literature on meta-reflexives suggests that learning may be present despite the absence of radical change. In this instance, following an evaluative process—encapsulated by the Review—and aware of its own situational logic of opportunity, HSBC concluded that far-reaching reform was neither necessary nor desirable. As such, an adherence to those models that served it so well through the GFC is indicative of learning in keeping with the meta-reflexives theory. Consequently, over the course of the post-crisis decade HSBC has reoriented it business towards a more stable and risk averse banking model.

References

Aldrick, P. (2013, August 5). HSBC vows to limit impact of EU bonus cap. *The Telegraph Online*. Available at: http://www.telegraph.co.uk/finance/newsbysector/banksandfinance/10222839/HSBC-vows-to-limit-impact-of-EU-bonus-cap.html.

Archer, M. (2003). *Structure, agency and the internal conversation*. Cambridge: Cambridge University Press.

Archer, M. (2007). *Making our way through the world*. Cambridge: Cambridge University Press.

Archer, M. (2012). *The reflexive imperative in late modernity*. Cambridge: Cambridge University Press.

Armstrong, R. (2019, December 10). HSBC to pay $192m penalty in US tax evasion case. *Financial Times Online*. Available at: https://www.ft.com/content/e7d51ec4-1b99-11ea-97df-cc63de1d73f4.

Arnason, G. (2012, August 6). *HSBC sells ship brokerage and consultancy arm to management*. Financialnews.co.uk. Available at: http://www.financial-news.

co.uk/6752/2012/08/hsbc-sells-ship-brokerage-and-consultancy-arm-to-management/.

Arnold, M. (2014a, May 14). HSBC cuts chairman's bonus with £1m cap. *The Financial Times Online*. Available at: http://www.ft.com/cms/s/0/53f928e0-db7f-11e3-a460-00144feabdc0.html?siteedition=uk#axzz3alh4vVZ7.

Arnold, M. (2014b, June 24). HSBC continues banking retreat with sale of Swiss assets to LGT. *Financial Times Online*. Available at: http://www.ft.com/cms/s/0/cd4ab6de-fbb7-11e3-ad9b-00144feab7de.html#axzz4Bjy08QER.

Arnold, M. (2015, February 25). HSBC chiefs grilled by MPs over tax scandal. *Financial Times Online*. Available at: https://www.ft.com/content/0ee7112c-bd1a-11e4-b523-00144feab7de.

Arnold, M. (2017, December 11). US lifts threat of prosecution against HSBC. *Financial Times Online*. Available at: https://www.ft.com/content/58775414-de5a-11e7-a8a4-0a1e63a52f9c.

Arnold, M. (2018a, January 18). HSBC agrees to $101.5m US forex settlement. *Financial Times Online*. Available at: https://www.ft.com/content/5c7223ca-fca8-11e7-9b32-d7d59aace167.

Arnold, M. (2018b, April 16). HSBC announces private banking shake-up. *Financial Times Online*. Available at: https://www.ft.com/content/c5556682-418f-11e8-803a-295c97e6fd0b.

Arnold, M., Barker, A., & Toplensky, R. (2016, December 7). Trio of big banks hit back at EU's Euribor-rigging fine. *Financial Times Online*. Available at: https://www.ft.com/content/372aacae-bc71-11e6-8b45-b8b81dd5d080.

BBC News. (2012, May 11). HSBC sells South American units to Banco GNB Sudameris. BBC News Online. Available at: http://www.bbc.co.uk/news/business-18043315.

BBC News. (2015a, May 27). Libor: What is it and why does it matter? BBC News Online. Available at: http://www.bbc.co.uk/news/business-19199683.

BBC News. (2015b, February 10). HSBC bank 'helped clients dodge millions in tax'. BBC News Online. Available at: http://www.bbc.co.uk/news/business-31248913.

Bell, S. (2011). Do we really need a new 'constructivist institutionalism' to explain institutional change? *British Journal of Political Science, 41*, 883–906.

Bernstein, J. (2019). *The Laundromat: Inside the Panama papers investigation of illicit money networks and the global elite*. New York: Macmillan.

Blackden, R. (2012, July 12). HSBC's 'money-laundering' apology. *The Telegraph Online*. Available at: http://www.telegraph.co.uk/finance/newsbysector/banksandfinance/9393874/HSBCs-money-laundering-apology.html.

Brinded, L. (2012, July 30). Libor fixing scandal: HSBC faces six rate probes as CEO admits bank's failures. *International Business Times Online*. Available at: http://www.ibtimes.co.uk/hsbc-libor-fixing-scandal-euribor-money-laundering-368151.

Brinded, L. (2014, June 12). Mis-selling derivatives scandal: HSBC compensates victims £139,000 on average. *International Business Times Online*. Available at: http://www.ibtimes.co.uk/mis-selling-derivatives-scandal-hsbc-compensates-victims-139000-average-1452403.
CityAm. (2012, October 2). HSBC sells property advice unit. *CityAm Online*. Available at: http://www.cityam.com/article/hsbc-sells-property-advice-unit.
Davies, P., Rabinovitch, S., & Robinson, G. (2012, December 5). HSBC sells ping an stake to Thai group. *Financial Times Online*. Available at: http://www.ft.com/cms/s/0/e193282a-3e7a-11e2-829d-00144feabdc0.html#axzz4APxrj9ee.
Dunkley, J. (2015, February 18). HSBC tax avoidance scandal: Timeline of Britain's biggest banking leak. *The Independent Online*. Available at: http://www.independent.co.uk/news/business/comment/hsbc-tax-avoidance-scandal-timeline-of-britains-biggest-banking-leak-10054442.html.
Evans, M. (2015, February 9). HSBC 'helped wealthy clients evade millions in tax'. *The Express*. At: http://www.express.co.uk/news/uk/557025/HSBC-accused-evade-tax-millions-wealthy-clients.
Farrell, S. (2016, February 3). The price of PPI: What the banks have set aside to pay for mis-selling. *The Guardian Online*. Available at: https://www.theguardian.com/money/2014/feb/03/ppi-banks-misselling.
FCA [Financial Conduct Authority]. (2014, November 11). Final notice from FCA to HSBC Bank plc, Reference Number: 114216. *FCA Online*. Available at: https://www.fca.org.uk/publication/final-notices/final-notice-hsbc.pdf.
Goff, S., & Thomas, H. (2011, August 10). HSBC agrees to sell $30bn credit card business. *The Financial Times Online*. Available at: https://www.ft.com/content/55b34b1c-c254-11e0-9ede-00144feabdc0.
HSBC [HSBC Holdings PLC]. (2007). *Annual Report and Accounts 2007*. Available at: http://www.hsbc.com/investor-relations/financial-and-regulatory-reports#page-3.
HSBC [HSBC Holdings PLC]. (2008). *Annual Report and Accounts 2008*. Available at: http://www.hsbc.com/investor-relations/financial-and-regulatory-reports#page-3.
HSBC [HSBC Holdings PLC]. (2009). *Annual Report and Accounts 2009*. Available at: www.hsbc.com/-/media/hsbc-com/.../financialresults/2009/hsbc2009ara0.pdf.
HSBC [HSBC Holdings PLC]. (2010). *Annual Report and Accounts 2010*. Available at: https://www.hsbc.co.uk/1/PA_esf-ca-app-content/.../annual_results2010_full.pdf.
HSBC [HSBC Holdings PLC]. (2011a). *Annual Report and Accounts 2011*. Available At: http://www.hsbc.com/investor-relations/financial-and-regula tory-reports#page-2.

HSBC [HSBC Holdings PLC]. (2011b, May 10). *HSBC 2011 investor day: Group strategy presentation*. Available at: http://www.hsbc.com/investor-relations/events-and-presentations/investor-day-2011.
HSBC [HSBC Holdings PLC]. (2012a, July 16). *HSBC statement on testimony before the United States Senate Permanent Subcommittee on Investigations*. HSBC Media Release. Available at: http://www.hsbc.com/news-and-insight/media-resources/media-releases/2012/statement-psi-hearing.
HSBC [HSBC Holdings PLC]. (2012b). *Annual Report and Accounts 2012*. Available at: http://www.hsbc.com/investor-relations/financial-and-regulatory-reports#page-2.
HSBC [HSBC Holdings PLC]. (2013a). *Annual Report and Accounts 2013*. Available at: http://www.hsbc.com/investor-relations/financial-and-regulatory-reports#page-1.
HSBC [HSBC Holdings PLC]. (2013b, December 10) *HSBC news release: HSBC to sell minority stake in Bank of Shanghai*. Available at: http://www.hsbc.com/~/media/HSBC-com/InvestorRelationsAssets/StockExchangeAnnouncements/2013/december/sea-131210-hsbc-to-sell-minority-stake-in-bank-of-shanghai.
HSBC [HSBC Holdings PLC]. (2014). *Annual Report and Accounts 2014*. Available at: http://www.hsbc.com/investor-relations/financial-and-regulatory-reports#page-1.
HSBC [HSBC Holdings PLC]. (2015a). *Annual Report and Accounts 2015: Value of the network connecting customers to opportunities*. Available at: https://www.hsbc.com/-/files/hsbc/investors/investing-in-hsbc/all-reporting/subsidiaries/2015/annual-results/hsbc-bank-plc/hsbc-bank-plc-annual-report-and-accounts-2015.pdf.
HSBC [HSBC Holdings PLC]. (2015b). *HSBC's Swiss Private Bank progress update—January 2015, press release*. Available at: http://www.hsbcprivatebank.com/~/media/pdf/update-on-the-swiss-private-bank.
HSBC [HSBC Holdings PLC]. (2016). *Annual Report and Accounts 2016: Connecting customers to opportunities*. Available at: https://www.hsbc.com/-/files/hsbc/investors/investing-in-hsbc/all-reporting/group/2016/annual-results/hsbc-holdings-plc/170221-annual-report-and-accounts-2016.pdf.
HSBC [HSBC Holdings PLC]. (2017a, December 11). *HSBC holdings PLC expiration of 2012 deferred prosecution agreement*. Available at: https://www.hsbc.com/media/media-releases/2017/hsbc-holdings-plc-expiration-of-2012-deferred-prosecution-agreement.
HSBC [HSBC Holdings PLC]. (2017b). *Annual Reports and Accounts 2017: Connecting customers to opportunities*. Available at: https://www.hsbc.com/-/files/hsbc/investors/hsbc-results/2017/annual/hsbc-holdings-plc/180220-annual-report-and-accounts-2017.pdf.

HSBC [HSBC Holdings PLC]. (2018). *Annual Report and Accounts 2018: Connecting customers to opportunities*. Available at: https://www.hsbc.com/-/files/hsbc/investors/hsbc-results/2018/annual/hsbc-holdings-plc/190219-annual-report-and-accounts-2018.pdf.

HSBC [Online]. *About HSBC: Leadership: Kathleen Casey Profile*. Available at: http://www.hsbc.com/about-hsbc/leadership/kathleen-casey.

HSBC.com. [HSBC Holdings PLC—Online]. *HSBC home—Our approach—Corporate governance—Board committees*. Available at: http://www.hsbc.com/investor-relations/governance/board-committees.

Jaeger, J. (2013, February 4). *HSBC creates financial system vulnerabilities committee, appoints new director*. Available at: https://www.complianceweek.com/blogs/scuttlebutt/hsbc-creates-financial-system-vulnerabilities-committee-appoints-new-director#.VZ_M67fbKM8.

Keohane, D., & Arnold, M. (2017, November 14). HSBC agrees to pay €300m to settle probe into tax evasion. *Financial Times Online*. Available at: https://www.ft.com/content/7d228060-c959-11e7-ab18-7a9fb7d6163e.

King, A. (2000). The accidental derogation of the lay actor a critique of Giddens's concept of structure. *Philosophy of the Social Sciences, 30*(3), 362–383.

King, A. (2005). Structure and agency. In A. Harrington (Ed.), *Modern social theory* (pp. 215–232). Oxford: Oxford University Press.

May, P. J. (1992). Policy learning and failure. *Journal of Public Policy, 12*(4), 331–354.

Mazur, R. (2013, January 2). *How to halt the terrorist money train*'. NYTimes.com. Available at: http://www.nytimes.com/2013/01/03/opinion/how-bankers-help-drug-traffickers-and-terrorists.html?_r=4.

McLannahan, B. (2016, July 12). Osborne intervened in US HSBC money-laundering probe, report says. *Financial Times Online*. Available at: https://www.ft.com/content/2be49f84-47c9-11e6-b387-64ab0a67014c.

Megaw, N. (2017, November 21). HSBC fined record $51m by Hong Kong authorities over Lehman-linked products. *Financial Times Online*. Available at: https://www.ft.com/content/48dd91ce-0efd-37e7-8747-893f3c028d43.

Neate, R. (2013, May 24). HSBC suffers investor revolt over pay. *The Guardian Online*. Available at: https://www.theguardian.com/business/2013/may/24/hsbc-chairman-apologises-scandals.

Neate, R. (2016, July 11). HSBC escaped US money-laundering charges after Osborne's intervention. *The Guardian Online*. Available at: https://www.theguardian.com/business/2016/jul/11/hsbc-us-money-laundering-george-osborne-report.

Obermaier, F., & Obermayer, B. (2017). *The Panama papers: Breaking the story of how the rich and powerful hide their money*. London: Oneworld Publications.

Pachico, E. (2012, December 14, Friday). *Sinaloa Cartel bought narco plane via HSBC Bank*. InsightCrime.org. Available at: http://www.insightcrime.org/news-briefs/sinaloa-cartel-bought-narco-plane-via-hsbc-bank.

PwC [Pricewaterhouse Coopers]. (2015, June 26). *First take: A publication of PwC's financial services regulatory practice*. Available at: https://www.pwc.com/us/en/financial-services/regulatory-services/publications/assets/eu-final-bonus-compensation-rule.pdf.

Roberts, R., & Kynaston, D. (2014). *The lion wakes: A modern history of HSBC*. London: Profile Books.

Rose, R. (1991). What is lesson-drawing? *Journal of Public Policy, 11*(1), 3–30.

Rose, R. (1993). *Lesson-drawing in public policy: A guide to learning across time and space*. Chatham, NJ: Chatham House Publishers.

Rose, R. (2005). *Learning from comparative public policy: A practical guide*. London: Routledge.

Rushe, D. (2011, August 10). HSBC sells US credit cards to Capital One. *The Guardian Online*. Available at: https://www.theguardian.com/business/2011/aug/10/hsbc-sells-us-credit-card-business-to-capitalone.

Shubber, K. (2018, October 9). HSBC finalises $765m settlement over securities sales. *Financial Times Online*. Available at: https://www.ft.com/content/0d73cd4c-cbe6-11e8-b276-b9069bde0956.

Simonian, H. (2011, December 21). Credit Suisse buys HSBC's Japan private bank. *Financial Times Online*. Available at: http://www.ft.com/cms/s/0/bd7670b8-2bad-11e1-b194-00144feabdc0.html#axzz4BSfOfq71.

Smythe, C. (2013, July 3). HSBC Judge approves $1.9B drug-money laundering accord. Bloomberg.com. Available at: http://www.bloomberg.com/news/articles/2013-07-02/hsbc-judge-approves-1-9b-drug-money-laundering-accord.

Telegraph.co.uk. (2014, March 12). *Libor: FDIC sues Barclays, RBS, HSBC, Lloyds and BBA*. Available at: http://www.telegraph.co.uk/finance/libor-scandal/10699359/Libor-FDIC-sues-Barclays-RBS-HSBC-Lloyds-and-BBA.html.

Thompson, J. (2013, January 30). HSBC sets up crime-fighting unit. *Financial Times Online*. Available at: http://www.ft.com/cms/s/0/270cc020-6ade-11e2-9871-00144feab49a.html#axzz3fUZNGgJ5.

Thomas, H., & Braithwaite, T. (2011, July 31). HSBC will sell 195 US branches. *Financial Times Online*. Available at: http://www.ft.com/cms/s/0/199e0fc8-bbb9-11e0-a7c8-00144feabdc0.html#axzz4APxrj9ee.

Thompson, J., & Kortekaas, V. (2013, May 31). HSBC recruits ex-head of MI5 to shore up financial crime defence. *Financial Times Online*. Available at: http://www.ft.com/cms/s/0/e337b62a-c9dd-11e2-8f55-00144feab7de.html#axzz3fUZNGgJ5.

Tims, A., & Collinson, P. (2015, October 3). HSBC has wrecked our lives, say customers frozen out and unable to switch. *The Guardian Online*. Available at: https://www.theguardian.com/money/2015/oct/03/hsbc-derisking-account-frozen-marie-shaun-langley.

Treanor, J. (2012, December 11). Bleak day for British banking as Libor arrests follow record fine for HSBC. *The Guardian Online*. Available at: https://www.theguardian.com/business/2012/dec/11/banking-libor-fine-hsbc.

Wilson, H. (2011, December 5). HSBC hit with record fine over investment mis-selling. *The Telegraph Online*. Available at: http://www.telegraph.co.uk/finance/newsbysector/banksandfinance/8936729/HSBC-hit-with-record-fine-over-investment-mis-selling.html.

Wilson, H. (2012, March 7). HSBC sells insurance businesses for $914m. *The Telegraph Online*. Available at: http://www.telegraph.co.uk/finance/newsbysector/banksandfinance/9128234/HSBC-sells-insurance-businesses-for-914m.html.

CHAPTER 8

Conclusion

Overview

The central role that banks played in the Great Financial Crisis has been well documented with the crisis producing a plethora of scholarly literature. Academic inquiry into the causes of the GFC and its aftermath has similarly been matched and even eclipsed by media reports, with journalists and bank insiders all offering their own account of what went wrong and how problems stemming from the crisis might be addressed. Even Hollywood seems to have become obsessed with the GFC, creating a number of films telling the factual, and sometimes not-so-factual, stories of bankers and regulators and their role in the crisis and its immediate aftermath (notable highlights include Michael Moore's *Capitalism: A Love Story* (2009); *Margin Call* (2011) and the 2015 adaption of the Michael Lewis international bestseller *The Big Short*). However, while these various contributions have chartered the origins and regulatory answers to the 'biggest financial crisis in 80 years' (Turner, 2016: xi) these accounts fail to ask how the banks have responded to the GFC, if lessons have been learned and what, if any, these lessons mean for financial stability, the sound functioning of markets and growth.

Equally, following the GFC there has been an absence by state managers and policy-makers to implement far-reaching structural reform within bank markets. Instead, regulatory attempts to better manage financial markets have rested upon a rather narrow set of institutional processes

A. Barber, *UK Banks and the Lessons of the Great Financial Crisis*, Building a Sustainable Political Economy: SPERI Research & Policy,
https://doi.org/10.1007/978-3-030-70254-0_8

concerning bank capital and liquidity, culture and remuneration. While important, these reforms fail to address the systemically important nature of banks as regulatory stakeholders with the ability to trigger and amplify stresses within the real economy. Such failures reveal important insights about the nature of the UK's financialised growth model—with banks at the centre of this regime—that both engenders problems and constrains policy responses. Put simply, more radical reform has been curtailed by the inherent conditions of a highly financialised economic structure whereby the political and economic interests of state managers are intimately bound to those of big finance. Indeed, reform in the UK since the GFC has been characterised by somewhat of a balancing act. On the one hand, state managers and policy-makers have sought to mitigate the systemic risks posed by banks while at the same time not damaging the international competitiveness of institutions and their ability to attract the mobile capital upon which the UK's financialised growth model relies.

Given the role of banks in the GFC and the inherent risk posed by institutions, it is surprising that bank behaviour has not received more attention in the political economy literature. This book has attempted to address this shortcoming by adopting a bank-centric approach that examines post-crisis reform through the lens of bank learning. Such an account is important as it recognises banks as both rule takers but also regulatory stakeholders capable of being agenda setters. By applying a learning framework to the behaviour and performance of banks, this manuscript has sought to draw conclusions about the institutional capacity of banks to learn and change in the aftermath of the GFC.

In this chapter, I summarise the key arguments of the book. These are that: (i) following the GFC, different banks have taken very different paths. While some institutions, such as Lloyds and HSBC, have become more risk averse and display positive signs of learning others, for example RBS and Barclays, show little evidence of change; (ii) changes in culture, business models, balance sheets and institutional preferences may be set but they are not permanent; (iii) dissatisfaction is crucial in the learning trajectory of institutions with too little dissatisfaction failing to provide enough motivation to learn. However, dissatisfaction as a learning tool also appears to work in consonant with learning space; (iv) learning space—being the dedication of both time and resources towards the critical self-reflexive learning process—is largely dependent upon institutional interpretations and responses to internal failures and crises; (v) structure and agency matter. Constraints mediated through the structural environment and interpreted by key agents determine, to a great extent, the learning trajectory of banks; (vi) the banks' relationship with regulators, the costs of regulatory compliance and the ability of institutions to utilise adjacent information are potential threats to learning. As such, there remains a great deal of uncertainty about the level of systemic risk posed by the banks to financial stability and the integrity of markets.

The Research Questions and Key Arguments of the Book

Bank learning in the UK after the GFC is something we need to know more about. Whether banks are now safer and more likely to aid rather than disrupt the economy are important questions of social relevance. The aim of this book was to chart a clear account of what has happened inside the UK's largest banks following the GFC and evaluate whether and to what extent banks have learned and changed. The research has sought to establish what these changes, if any, tell us about the institutional capacity of banks to learn, the veracity of these approaches and the impact of learning, or otherwise, upon financial stability and the sound functioning of markets. In order to do this, the book had one central research question: *have banks in the UK learned lessons from the Great Financial Crisis?* In addition to addressing the overarching research question, the empirical puzzle posed by this book has also sought to interrogate and answer a number of important underlying questions. This section of the chapter will address these questions and draw a series of conclusions that will inform our understanding of current debates surrounding post-crisis reform and bank learning.

I would remind the reader that I am not presuming that the extent to which banks have learned lessons from the GFC will prevent or insulate financial markets from future crises. Indeed, as discussed in earlier chapters global markets face a number of emerging challenges. Post-crisis tax reforms in the United States; debt fuelled growth; global imbalances; Brexit trade negotiations; the emerging ecological crisis; and the ensuing health and economic crisis resulting from the COVID-19 global pandemic, all pose a threat to global economic stability and which banks have little or no control over. Likewise, the book has only surveyed one set of actors in the GFC (the banks and more precisely the UK 'big four' banks) and one set of causes. Yet, the question posed by this research remains important because of the systemically important role of the banks within both the UK and the global economy. Furthermore, many of those factors that contributed to the GFC, and are accounted for in Chapter 3, have played a role in previous crises too. As such, while the next financial crisis may not involve the banks directly, if the causes of the GFC have been addressed by the banks, and if these institutions have learned lessons and are now safer, we would expect them to be much more resilient if faced with future crises. This may in turn lead us to hypothesise that bank learning in the UK may make for a more robust and sound functioning financial system.

Have Banks in the UK Learned Lessons from the GFC?

The GFC affected the banks accounted for in this study in very different ways. For some institutions such as RBS and Lloyds, the crisis proved devastating and left the banks close to ruin. Conversely, Barclays and HSBC navigated the crisis with a degree of success and can even be considered to have had a 'good' crisis—growing their operations when others were retrenching and continuing to report pre-tax profits. Given the unique position of individual institutions following the GFC, it is of little surprise that we find a great deal of variation in the lesson learning experience of UK banks in the decade that has followed the crisis, with different banks taking very different paths. For example, the analysis reveals that institutions, such as Lloyds and HSBC, have become more risk-averse and display positive signs of learning (although the extent of this learning can be questioned within some areas of the respective businesses). Others, for example RBS and Barclays, demonstrate little evidence of learning and change (though both banks do present limited 'pockets' of change). As such, there is no single or uniform answer to the question *have banks in the UK learned lessons from the Great Financial Crisis*. Instead, we find that different banks have learned different lessons in relation to contending areas of both their own businesses and the banking industry in general. As such, the post-crisis learning experience of UK banks reveals a great deal of institutional variation.

While several of the causes of the crisis have been addressed by the banks in this study, many of the precursors to the GFC have failed to be adequately tackled by institutions. Inter-bank variations—the kind of assets banks are now holding, how institutions reward employees and the spirit within which banks have responded to the legacy of the crisis—mean that there is still a great deal of uncertainty about the level of systemic risk posed by the banks. Given the systemically important nature of institutions, such conclusions reveal important insights about the relationship between finance and society, financial stability and the wider capitalist economy and the politics and process of financialisation. Consequently, future research needs to consider the privileged position of banks and bankers as regulatory stakeholders and their unique ability to shape the structural environment in which they operate.

What Lessons Have Been Learned?

We should note that many of the examples and conclusions discussed in this section cannot be neatly compartmentalised into a fixed business area with several factors overlapping. Such considerations stress the interconnected yet nuanced nature of institutions and the banking sector more generally. Indeed, the issues discussed in this chapter should not be considered on their own merit but, should take in to account how contextual factors have interacted and shaped broader structural, institutional and agential changes that have taken place.

Governance, Regulation and Managerial Frameworks
The restructuring of internal governance and managerial frameworks, in response to a number of institutional regulatory breaches, by the selected banks has been a key determinant in the learning trajectory of institutions. However, we must exercise caution in drawing general inferences about the extent of learning with varying institutional responses, ideas and interpretations of the GFC meaning that there is present a great deal of disparity between the banks surveyed.

For example, those institutions with the greatest propensity for learning, such as Lloyds and HSBC, have generally made substantial changes to their internal governance and managerial frameworks by implementing a number of mechanisms aimed at strengthening regulatory oversight. Prominent examples include the delayering of governance structures at Lloyds. This has had the effect of making the organisation 'flatter' by building in instruments that allow information to flow in both a top-down and bottom-up manner—thereby addressing problems associated with the silo effect. At HSBC, we witness the establishment of additional specialist board committees tasked with addressing specific areas of weakness and the appointment of expert individuals that enjoy substantive powers to affect and shape change at the group.

In contrast, RBS and Barclays have displayed little evidence of learning and change, with pre-existing governance and managerial frameworks in place at the time of the GFC undergoing limited reform despite the presence of dissatisfaction (discussed below). In the case of RBS, this lack of learning may be attributed to the group failing to orient sufficient learning space to the reflexive process inherent in learning. On the other hand, Barclays' attempts at reform have been impeded by the group's interpretation of structural competitive pressures surrounding employee remuneration. As noted in Chapter 6, the Transform programme, heralded by Barclays as a 'roadmap for cultural change', has been directly tied to employee remuneration. However, overtime as the group has succumbed to perceived structural pressures over the bank's ability to attract and retain talent, the strategical importance of Transform has been eroded.

Remuneration and the Long-Term Outlook of Bonuses

This brings us to a second key change at the banks in the post-crisis decade, namely, that variable remuneration has taken on a distinctly long-term outlook, thereby addressing the short-termism that pervade institutions pre-crisis. However, and much like the above, these changes cannot be applied at a general level with differing institutional approaches to remuneration being evident, thus further reinforcing the notion that different banks appear to have learned different lessons.

Institutions such as Lloyds and, to a lesser extent, HSBC have restructured remuneration to include the use of more long-term options such as shares and other non-cash alternatives and have extended retention periods. In doing so, these banks appear to have addressed the high-risk/high-reward bonus culture that was evident before the crisis. Accordingly, key agents within the banks—whose actions have the ability to materially impact the business—have been incentivised to seek out decisions and behaviours that are in the long-term interest of institutions and, consequently, is indicative of learning and endogenously originated change.

However, both RBS and Barclays appear to lack change and which in turn suggests the absence of learning. Instead, the greatest shift at these banks appears to have come in response to tougher regulatory standards, particularly CRD IV and the PRA's and FCA's remuneration codes, respectively. As such, we are able to conclude that not only have these banks failed to learn, with already established institutional norms and preferences persisting beyond their natural lifespan, but, importantly, the post-crisis learning experience of banks presents a great deal of institutional divergence. These inter-bank variations can be attributed, much like the point above, to how institutions have responded to dissatisfaction, the orientation of institutional resources to the learning process and the interpretation of structures by key agents (explored in more detail below).

Changes to the Balance Sheet

Chapter 3 of the book outlined the key causes of the GFC. In particular, it was noted that in the years preceding the crisis, banks increasingly came to rely upon short-term wholesale markets as a funding source while significantly increasing their leverage ratios. In the decade that has followed the crisis, all the banks surveyed in this research have significantly increased their customer deposit base. Similarly, RBS and Lloyds have decreased their reliance upon wholesale funding. Though HSBC has slightly increased its use of short-term funding post-crisis, we should note that the group's reliance upon wholesale markets was already very conservative and, even in 2018, was still in-line with that of RBS and Lloyds. Barclays on the other hand has increased its use of wholesale markets with this potentially volatile source of funding coming to play a progressively more important role in the bank's business model. While Lloyds and HSBC have specifically cited the increase of customer deposits and exercising prudence when borrowing from wholesale markets as being key objectives of the groups' business models post-GFC, RBS has failed to address group funding specifically. Indeed, we must exercise caution when drawing conclusions about RBS' restructuring of the balance sheet and consider the group's mandated retrenchment of the business associated with its state-sponsored bailout.

Nonetheless, the banks surveyed here are all operating with much more conservative capital and leverage ratios than in the years preceding the crisis. As a result, individual institutions and banking markets in general should have a greater loss absorbing capacity in the event of a downturn and as such present a significantly reduced threat to the real economy.

Likewise, the loan-to-deposit ratio of all banks in the comparator group has been reduced with the number of loans being dedicated towards residential mortgage lending increasing across the post-crisis decade. Given the reorientation of bank lending towards residential mortgages, it is not surprising to find that the percentage of impaired loans at Lloyds, Barclays and HSBC has also decreased. Though RBS did witness a marginal increase in its impaired loans of 0.1 percentage points, the group did have the second lowest rate of impairments behind that of HSBC.

However, the prudence shown by banks towards lending and reducing the loan-to-deposit ratio has not been met with a similar conservatism in the trading activities of some institutions. For example, and once again, Lloyds and HSBC appear to have learned lessons from the GFC, with both institutions reducing their trading liabilities as a percentage of total group assets. Yet, RBS and Barclays have both increased their trading liabilities across the post-crisis decade and as such present little evidence of learning. While the use of derivatives has been reduced across all the banks in this study, the use of off-balance-sheet vehicles has generally increased.

It has been noted, however, that these changes have occurred against a shifting regulatory and economic context that has undergone substantial change following the GFC. For example, Bessis (2015) has discussed the impact of higher capital requirements, tighter lending controls and the increasing cost of liquidity. Consequently, banks no longer operate under the same structural conditions as they did in 2008 and as such, we must take account of these changes and the extent to which they may have affected the balance sheets of our chosen institutions. Nonetheless, and despite these regulatory and economic variations, a comparative balance sheet analysis reveals important insights about the level of systemic risk posed by institutions post-crisis and the spirit and extent to which banks have responded to the changes and challenges of a shifting economic and regulatory context.

While these key financial metrics generally point towards more robust balance sheets amongst our comparator group and which may prove for a more stable financial system with reduced systemic risk, there remains a great deal of institutional variation in the extent and pace of learning. While we may conclude that Lloyds and HSBC have generally learned lesson from the crisis, this learning is not necessarily applicable to all facets of the balance sheet and in some instances remains incomplete. Similarly, though RBS and Barclays fail to present substantive evidence of learning and change there are some limited pockets of lesson drawing. Therefore, we must consider institutional nuances when contemplating the extent to which learning has taken place in relation to the balance sheet element.

Investment Banking
While it is important that we do not lose sight of inter-bank variations when drawing conclusions about the extent to which institutions have or have not learned lessons about the role of investment banking, there is present a certain institutional path dependency amongst our comparator group. For example, institutions, such as Lloyds and HSBC, where the investment bank played a relatively modest role in profit generation pre-crisis, have rolled back their respective investment banking divisions, thus mitigating many of the harmful effects associated with the predominance of pre-crisis business models centred upon investment banking—explored in Chapter 3. Lloyds and HSBC are also now less reliant upon the investment bank as a generator of group profit. Meanwhile at RBS and Barclays where investment banking operations played a central role in the respective businesses pre-2008, the shrinking of the investment bank has been met with a degree of hostility and scepticism. In the case of Barclays, this would eventually lead to a revival of the division. Moreover, in the post-crisis decade both RBS and Barclays have become more reliant upon their investment banking divisions as a key driver of group profit.

As such, we can see that, to some extent, all the banks surveyed have solidified their pre-crisis position by returning to those models that were predominant in the years preceding the crisis. In the case of Lloyds and HSBC, this has resulted in the investment bank being retrenched or continuing to play a relatively small role at the banks. Yet, RBS and Barclays have continued to place a great importance upon their respective investment banking operations which remain an integral part of their business models post-GFC.

How Have Lessons Been Drawn?

The empirical analysis of post-crisis bank learning in the UK reveals important insights about how institutions learn, the veracity of these approaches and those conditions most conducive to lesson drawing. By examining the literature on learning drawn from across the social sciences, and applying these ideas to the behaviour and performance of banks, we are able to explain inter-bank variations in the learning trajectory of institutions. With this in mind, the analysis reveals two major factors that have determined the rate of reform at the banks in question, namely, the 'dissatisfaction thesis' and the 'learning space' theory.

The Dissatisfaction Thesis
The dissatisfaction thesis—explored in Chapter 2—contends that learning takes place when results no longer keep pace with desired outcomes. The ensuing void between that which is desirable and that which is achievable subsequently leads to dissatisfaction which itself determines the impetus for learning and change as the learning subject seeks to close this gap. While the dissatisfaction thesis may upon first reading appear to be a rather obvious precursor to learning, dissatisfaction and the level therein experienced by institutions has proven be vital in the lesson learning experience of banks.

While we might have expected the GFC and the huge reputational and financial losses sustained by the banks to have caused sufficient dissatisfaction to prompt learning, the GFC alone does not appear to have caused adequate dissatisfaction to propel institutions to seek new information and learn. Indeed, with the exception of Lloyds, it is only after suffering a series of secondary internal crises that the banks appear to have sought alternative information and close the gap between aspiration and achievements—although the extent to which learning and change has occured has differed between banks.

For example, both Barclays and HSBC navigated the GFC with a degree of success. Both institutions continued to grow their respective businesses at a time when others were retrenching and report pre-tax profits when their peers were recording substantial losses. As such, in the immediate aftermath of the crisis neither bank showed substantive evidence of learning and change with a successful navigation of the crisis appearing to confirm the banks' respective business models and strategic direction. Indeed, it was only after suffering a succession of secondary internal crises epitomised by the rigging of Libor (Barclays) and charges of money laundering (HSBC) that these institutions underwent the necessary dissatisfaction to seek alternatives.[1]

In contrast, the GFC devastated Lloyds that would require a state-sponsored bailout in order to continue operating. In this instance, the crisis alone appears to have caused the necessary dissatisfaction to prompt learning as shortly thereafter, the bank underwent a self-reflexive group wide strategic evaluation, with lessons learned being implemented shortly afterwards. RBS on the other hand, while undoubtedly suffering the

[1] Although ultimately Barclays would fail to implement lessons learned.

required dissatisfaction to learn, failed to orient sufficient learning space (discussed below) to the learning process and has ultimately failed to learn.

Consequently, the analysis suggests that while dissatisfaction is a condition that is conducive to learning, the level and degree to which dissatisfaction is experienced by institutions clearly matters. In this respect, too little dissatisfaction—the case of Barclays and HSBC immediately following the crisis—failed to provide enough motivation to learn. Moreover, the desired level of dissatisfaction, enough to propel learning while not overwhelming the subject, appears to be specific to each institution. Contrary to the policy learning framework accounted for in Chapter 2, the empirical analysis shows that institutions that suffered the greatest losses and most dissatisfaction did not demonstrate a greater propensity for learning. Indeed, the case of RBS stresses that the learning trajectory of institutions is dependent upon the ability of organisations to effectively deploy resources and utilise the learning space.

The Learning Space Theory

Learning space theory suggests that in order for an organisation to learn, the learning subject, in our case banks, must apply space—this being institutional resources—fiscal and human capital—towards the reflexive process inherent in learning. Indeed, the empirical analysis demonstrates that what separates successful learners from those that have failed to present substantive evidence of lesson learning and change is the application of institutional resources towards the seeking, evaluation and application of new information that results in a series of improved policy actions that shift an institution's normative frames, preferences and underlying theories-in-use.

The importance of space in the learning process is evidenced by all the banks in this study. Successful learners such as Lloyds and HSBC have in the post-crisis decade dedicated institutional resources towards the critical self-reflexive process by seeking new information in the form of reviews. Importantly however, these reviews have not only sought and evaluated new information but, would introduce tangible policy outcomes that have created new institutional preferences and policy norms. Though Barclays would likewise undergo a group-wide strategic review in the form of Salz and Transform—being representative of both the seeking and evaluation of new information—the bank would ultimately fail to uphold lessons learned with a distinct lack of improved policy actions aimed at implementing newly acquired theories-in-use.

Conversely, in the post-GFC decade RBS has failed to sufficiently orient its learning space towards the reflexive process. Instead, the group has been pre-occupied by a series or regulatory and governance failures that have led the bank on a number of firefighting missions. In this respect, the group has focused its precious learning space rather narrowly upon the minutiae of distinct failures. This has had the effect of diverting institutional resources away from a self-reflexive examination of the group's underlying theories-in-use in the light of those deficiencies highlighted by the GFC. Consequently, institutions that have used their learning space to implement improved policy actions that target specific areas of weakness and close potential gaps for future abuses have demonstrated the greatest propensity for learning.

Structure and Agency

This brings us to a third conclusion concerning bank learning in the post-crisis decade: structure and agency matter. However, while the force of structures and agents, like dissatisfaction and learning space explored above, has evoked powerful change at some institutions—for example the appointment of António Horta-Osório at Lloyds—for others, structural and agential forms of power have proven impossible to overcome and have impeded learning Barclays' revival of its investment bank being a case in point. Nonetheless, structure and agency has been a mitigating factor in how institutions have learned lessons.

Constraints mediated through the structural environment and interpreted by key agents within institutions have been shown to impact and determine the learning trajectory of our chosen banks. For example, structural competitive pressures interpreted by Barclays' board of directors concerning an erosion of the bank's status as top tier global institution following the shrinking of the investment bank ultimately led to the dismissal of GCE Anthony Jenkins. Mr Jenkins was replaced by career investment banker, Jes Staley, who quickly set about rebuilding the investment bank and which has subsequently become a central part of Barclays' post-crisis business model.

Similarly, institutions that have maintained a large international presence post-GFC, such as Barclays and HSBC, have frequently cited regulatory changes concerning how banks reward employees, ideas around competition for talent and the lack of a level international regulatory playing field as all being significant structural factors that have had a material impact upon institutions. In response to these perceived structural pressures, again interpreted by key agents, banks have come up with novel instruments that have allowed them to match remuneration packages being offered by their peers and which calls into question the extent of learning in relation to this facet of the business and the banking sector more generally.

However expanded historical institutionalism, upon which my research is centred, and the constructivist tradition in which historical institutionalism is rooted, stresses that in times of crisis we should move beyond a purely structural approach and consider the ideas and behaviour of key agents. Agential explanations of post-crisis bank learning are important as 'interpretive agents' (Bell, 2011) have the ability to both directly and indirectly generate 'new institutional blueprints' and 'new institutional arrangements' (Baker, 2015: 3). As we have seen, key agents have impacted the learning experience of banks by determining how institutions have interpreted, constructed and problematised certain structural factors. For example, in the case of Lloyds, the appointment of António Horta-Osório had an almost immediate impact upon the learning trajectory of the group. Lloyds had been fighting a legal battle against the FSA over the mis-selling of PPI for over a decade (Brummer, 2015). However, one of Mr Horta-Osório's first actions as GCE was to drop Lloyds' case and to set aside a compensation pot for victims. In doing so, the newly appointed GCE, while incurring some sort-term losses, was able to preserve the group's learning space that was subsequently applied to the reflexive learning process embodied in a group wide strategic review (the Review). As such, it is possible to conclude that agents, along with structures, are equally important in shaping and driving institutional learning and change.

While dissatisfaction, learning space and the role of structures and agents have all played important role in how institutions learn in the post-crisis decade, these factors have, in some instances, also impeded lessons drawing. As such, the ideas presented here transcend and overlap many of the research questions presented in the introductory chapter. Indeed, the conclusions drawn in this section of the book cannot be neatly compartmentalised into a single or definitive conclusion about post-crisis bank learning in the UK. Instead, when drawing conclusions about the lesson learning experience of UK banks it is imperative to take into account how contextual factors have interacted and shaped broader structural, institutional and agential responses to the GFC.

What Has Impeded Lesson Learning?

Banks' Relationship with Regulators

The analysis likewise finds variance in the relationships between the banks and regulators following the GFC and which in some cases has impeded lesson learning. Like many of the factors already discussed in this chapter, different banks have adopted very different stances on certain regulatory issues with a great deal of inter-bank variation in the post-crisis decade. Though banks have not necessarily or explicitly addressed their relationship with regulators post-crisis, sentiments expressed by key agents within banks concerning regulatory change, and the subsequent behavioural reactions by institutions, may shed light upon how banks view the role of regulators post-GFC.

Regulatory stipulations concerning variable remuneration have in some cases been met with a degree of scepticism and even hostility by certain banks. As noted above, those institutions such as Barclays and HSBC that have maintained a large international presence post-crisis appear to have been more reticent to regulatory changes concerning employee remuneration. These institutions have stressed a diminished ability to attract and retain banking talent within international markets owing to the lack of a regulatory level playing field. As such, the relationship between Barclays, HSBC and the regulators appears to have impeded lesson learning. On the other hand, Lloyds that retrenched its operations on UK markets has been more welcoming of regulatory changes concerning pay and in some cases has gone beyond minimum requirements.

Equally, regulatory requirements concerning the disinvestment and retrenchment of institutions that were recipients of state-aid have also produced varying results. For instance, Lloyds has complied with requirements, running down its business in a timely manner and in many cases before the required deadline. Meanwhile, RBS has viewed such requirements as an intrusion, has failed to meet deadlines and has generally had a more confrontational relationship with regulators and which generally suggest an absence of learning.

Regulatory Compliance Costs

Though the banks have failed to quantify the associated compliance costs associated with regulatory change, Parker and Gupta (2015) suggest that a potential loss of banking talent and a possible diminished ability by institutions to recruit the 'brightest minds' could be an impediment to learning. The author's argue that one of the associated costs of tougher regulatory stipulations on employee remuneration has been that senior talent have left banks for more 'lightly regulated markets' (ibid.). Similarly, *Thomson Reuters Regulatory Intelligence Services* (2016) has posited that changes to remuneration has led to a mass exodus of bank talent—that may be best situated to deal with an evolving regulatory landscape and the increasing complexity of markets—for institutions that operate in a more 'risk-friendly' environment not subject to the same stipulations on pay as banks.

Yet, we must exercise caution here as many banks do not disclose information pertaining to the particulars of employee resignations. Moreover, the ideas espoused above are drawn, in the main, from specialist industry bodies and lobbying groups that may wish to present a certain narrative. Consequently, it is impossible to test the validity of such conclusions (Noonan, 2015).

Likewise, as discussed in the empirical chapters of the book, banks have responded to changing regulatory stipulations concerning variable remuneration by employing a series of policy tools that have effectively allowed institutions to mitigate the effects of new rules. In particular, role-based pay allowances have allowed banks to circumvent restraints on pay. Indeed, many of the banks have explicitly cited the introduction of role-based pay as being a direct response to tougher regulations introduced by CRD IV. However, were rules concerning role-based allowances to change in the future, then this may very well see an exodus of employees for higher rewarding markets not subject to the same regulatory standards and which could potentially leave UK banks ill-equipped to deal with the increasingly complex nature of markets.

Peer-to-Peer Learning

Though the empirical section of the book found some evidence of peer-to-peer learning, which may indeed be indicative of a positive learning experience, peer-to-peer learning can also be an impediment to future learning unless lessons are quickly assimilated and transposed into an institution's underlying theories-in-use. For instance, the most prominent examples of peer-to-peer learning can be found in cases where banks have recruited key agents from rival organisations, thus resulting in the acquisition of knowledge gained through past experiences. Likewise, banks that have appointed experts from particular fields in which there has been found to be institutional weaknesses or shortcomings, such as HSBC's recruitment of a number of experts with backgrounds in the prevention of financial crime, may similarly benefit from peer-to-peer learning. However, in both instances, this 'adjacent information' remains with the individual in question unless special attention is paid to the task of assimilating this knowledge into the institution. However, the transfer of knowledge is largely dependent upon the individual expert that holds the relevant information and their ability to exercise their agency and affect learning and change within an organisation. Consequently, without the necessary policy tools to implement change gained through the transfer of knowledge, an institution's ability to learn from peer-to-peer learning may be impeded.

Concluding Thoughts and Future Directions

The focus of my research and the conclusions reached in the book, aided by the analytical framework laid out in the Introduction, is significant as it offers the reader an empirically rich, bank-centric contribution to the current literature on financial reform post GFC. Moreover, by utilising the expanded version of historical institutionalism first developed by Bell (2011), Bell and Feng (2014) and Bell and Hindmoor (2015), and upon which my own work expands, I have been able to place the banks at the centre of the analysis. In this respect, this research offers political economists, and beyond, a unique vantage point from which to study bank learning and post-crisis reform.

While Bell and Hindmoor's (2015) theoretical work is grounded within the broader tradition of historical institutionalism, I have sought to explore the margins of this framework and which has allowed my research to move between structural, institutional and agential explanations of learning. This has been particularly useful when faced with tricky and difficult concepts. In this respect, by exploring the boundaries of Bell and Hindmoor's (2015) work I have been endowed with the intellectual tools that have allowed me the freedom to differentiate and address the non-exclusive and mutually shaping relationship between contextual factors.

However, the theoretical approach adopted by my research is also problematic. The expanded version of historical institutionalism presented by Bell and Hindmoor (2015) upon which my work builds is generally loose or even capacious. My own theoretical framework has done little to address this problem and may even be guilty of adopting a more expansive framework than the original presented by the authors. Such an approach may present problems for future researchers who may need to invest time and energy exploring the limits of the framework especially when faced with certain situational specifics which are not easily identifiable. Therefore, such theoretical considerations should be taken into account by future researchers.

Despite this, the theoretical framework developed here has meant that I have been free to study and explore the preference shaping interactions between structures, institutions and agents in detail. Indeed, such an approach to the research has stressed the need to consider the mediating forces between structural and institutional reform and those key preference-shaping agents placed at key junctures of the political economy. By studying how banks and bankers have responded to weaknesses stressed by the GFC, we are able to gain greater insight into how these systemically important institutions and actors may shape the future stability of financial markets.

The aim of this book was to investigate if and to what extent banks in the UK have learned lessons from the GFC and explain why these shifts have, or have not, taken place. The account of post-crisis bank learning presented here has found that different banks have learned very different lessons and that these institutional variations are best explained by competing structural, institutional and agential factors. Indeed, the research does not proffer a sole explanation as to the extent to which banks have learned. Likewise, I do not believe that any one of these various structural, institutional or agential factors should be ascribed greater gravitas in explaining the learning trajectory of banks in this study. There is no one-size-fits-all answer that can be applied to the research question, to the banks in general or to individual institutions. Instead, the analysis suggests that there is present a great deal of inter- and intra-bank variation in the post-crisis learning experience of institutions. Indeed, we should consider the myriad of issues that have shaped the dynamics of institutional responses to the crisis on a bank-by-bank basis. The conclusions offered by the book are important as they stress the need to examine the non-exclusive and mutually shaping relationship between contending contextual factors and the extent to which these have shaped the learning trajectory of banks and the impact thereof on financial stability.

References

Baker, A. (2015). *The bankers paradox: The political economy of macroprudential regulation* (SRC Discussion Paper No. 37). The London School of Economics and Political Science.

Bell, S. (2011). Do we really need a new 'constructivist institutionalism' to explain institutional change? *British Journal of Political Science, 41,* 883–906.

Bell, S., & Feng, H. (2014). How proximate and 'meta-institutional' contexts shape institutional change: Explaining the rise of the People's Bank of China. *Political Studies, 62,* 197–215.

Bell, S., & Hindmoor, A. (2015). *Masters of the universe, slaves of the market.* Cambridge, MA: Harvard University Press.

Bessis, J. (2015). *Risk management in banking* (4th ed.). Chichester: Wiley.

Brummer, A. (2015). *Bad banks: Greed, incompetence and the next global crisis.* London: Random House Business

Capitalism: A love story. (2009). Hollywood, CA. Overture Films, Paramount Vantage.

Margin Call. (2011). New York, NY: Before the Door Pictures, Benaroya Pictures, and Washington Square Films

Noonan, L. (2015, May 28). Banks face pushback over surging compliance and regulatory costs. *Financial Times.* Available at: https://www.ft.com/content/e1323e18-0478-11e5-95ad-00144feabdc0.

Parker, E., & Gupta. M. (2015, October 18). Too much regulation creates bank brain drain. *Financial Times.* Available at: https://www.ft.com/content/4dfc4190-719f-11e5-9b9e-690fdae72044.

The Big Short. (2015). Hollywood, CA. Paramount Pictures.

Thomson Reuters. (2016). *Thomson Reuters regulatory intelligence: The cost of compliance 2016.* Available online at: https://risk.thomsonreuters.com/en/resources/special-report/cost-compliance-2016.html.

Turner, A. (2016). *Between debt and the devil, money, credit, and fixing global finance.* Princeton, NJ: Princeton University Press.

Bibliography

Acharya, V., & Richardson, M. (2009a). *Restoring financial stability: How to repair a failed system*. New Jersey: John Wiley & Sons.

Acharya, V., & Richardson, M. (2009b). Causes of the financial crisis. *Critical Review, 21*(2), 195–210.

Acharya, V., & Schnabl, I. (2009). How Banks Played the Leverage Game. In V. Acharya & M. Richardson (Eds.), *Restoring financial stability: How to repair a failed system* (pp. 83–100). New Jersey: John Wiley & Sons.

Acharya, V., Philippon, T., Richardson, M., & Roubini, N. (2009). Prologue: A bird's eye view—The financial crisis of 2007–2009. In V. Acharya & M. Richardson (Eds.), *Restoring financial stability: How to repair a failed system* (pp. 1–56). New Jersey: John Wiley & Sons.

Action Aid. (2013a, November 20). Barclays must stop promoting the use of tax havens in Africa—ActionAid REPORT. *Action Aid*. Available at: https://www.actionaid.org.uk/latest-news/barclays-must-stop-promoting-the-use-of-tax-havens-in-africa-actionaid-report.

Action Aid. (2013b, December 11). Barclays respond but deny promoting investment in Africa through tax havens. *Action Aid*. Available at: http://www.actionaid.org/2013/12/barclays-respond-deny-promoting-investment-africa-through-tax-havens.

Admati, A., & Hellwig, M. (2013). *The bankers new clothes*. Princeton NJ: Princeton University Press.

Agius, M. (2010) Barclays corporate governance report: Group chairman's introduction. In *Barclays [Barclays banking group PLC] Annual report and accounts 2009*. Available at: https://home.barclays/content/dam/home-bar

A. Barber, *UK Banks and the Lessons of the Great Financial Crisis*, Building a Sustainable Political Economy: SPERI Research & Policy, https://doi.org/10.1007/978-3-030-70254-0

clays/documents/investor-relations/annualreports/ar2009/barclays-plc-annual-report-2009.pdf, pp. 151–152.

Agur, I. (2013, January). *Wholesale bank funding, capital requirements and credit rationing* (IMF Working Paper No. 13/30). Available at: https://www.imf.org/en/Publications/WP/Issues/2016/12/31/Wholesale-Bank-Funding-Capital-Requirements-and-Credit-Rationing-40285.

Aldrick, P. (2009, October 19). RBS pays £5m for 11 bankers. *The Telegraph*. At: http://www.telegraph.co.uk/finance/newsbysector/banksandfinance/6379051/RBS-pays-5m-for-11-bankers.html.

Aldrick, P. (2013, August 3). HSBC vows to limit impact of EU bonus cap. *The Telegraph*. Available at: http://www.telegraph.co.uk/finance/newsbysector/banksandfinance/10222839/HSBC-vows-to-limit-impact-of-EU-bonus-cap.html.

Allison, I. (2014, October 15). European banking authority tightens rules on 'fixed pay' bonus cap dodge. *International Business Times*. At: http://www.ibtimes.co.uk/european-banking-authority-tightens-rules-fixed-pay-bonus-cap-dodge-1470171.

Anderson, S. (2013). A history of the past 40 years in financial crises. In International financing review, 2000 issue 40 years in review. Thomas Reuters (pp. 48–52). Available at: http://edition.pagesuite-professional.co.uk/Launch.aspx?EID=b2eb69c3-7774-4d35-a0ff-c70b03f7288f.

Archer, M. (1988). *Culture and agency: The place of culture in social theory*. Cambridge: Cambridge University Press.

Archer, M. (1995). *Realist social theory: The morphogenetic approach*. Cambridge: Cambridge University Press.

Archer, M. (2000). *Being human: The problem of agency*. Cambridge: Cambridge University Press.

Archer, M. (2003). *Structure, agency and the internal conversation*. Cambridge: Cambridge University Press.

Archer, M. (2007). *Making our way through the world*. Cambridge: Cambridge University Press.

Archer, M. (2012). *The reflexive imperative in late modernity*. Cambridge: Cambridge University Press.

Argyris, C., & Schon, D. A. (1978). *Organizational learning: A theory of action perspective*. Reading, MA: Addison-Wesley Publishing.

Arygris, C., & Schon, D. A. (1996). *Organizational learning II: Theory, method, and practice*. Reading, MA: Addison-Wesley Publishing.

Argyris, C., Putnam, R., & Smith, D. (1985). *Action science*. San Francisco: Jossey-Bass.

Armitage, J. (2014, March 6). Banks could be wiped out by the 'role-based allowances'. *The Independent*. http://www.independent.co.uk/news/bus

iness/comment/banks-could-be-wiped-out-by-the-rolebased-allowances-9172081.html.

Armstrong, R. (2019, December 10). HSBC to pay $192m penalty in US tax evasion case. *Financial Times*. Available at: https://www.ft.com/content/e7d51ec4-1b99-11ea-97df-cc63de1d73f4.

Arnason, G. (2012, August 6). HSBC sells ship brokerage and consultancy arm to management. *Financialnews.co.uk*. Available at: http://www.financial-news.co.uk/6752/2012/08/hsbc-sells-ship-brokerage-and-consultancy-arm-to-management/.

Arnold, A. (2014a, May 14). HSBC cuts chairman's bonus with £1m Cap. *The Financial Times*. At: http://www.ft.com/cms/s/0/53f928e0-db7f-11e3-a460-00144feabdc0.html?siteedition=uk#axzz3alh4vVZ7.

Arnold, M. (2014b, June 24). HSBC continues banking retreat with sale of swiss assets to LGT. *Financial Times*. Available at: http://www.ft.com/cms/s/0/cd4ab6de-fbb7-11e3-ad9b-00144feab7de.html#axzz4Bjy08QER.

Arnold, M. (2015a, March 26). RBS agrees to sell coutts international to swiss bank UBP. *Financial Times*. Available at: http://www.ft.com/cms/s/0/a2f7e3ea-d3c3-11e4-99bd-00144feab7de.html#axzz41C1UVFL5.

Arnold, M. (2015b, October 16). Barclays to speed up investment bank cuts. *Financial Times*. Available at: https://next.ft.com/content/0b971e08-7418-11e5-bdb1-e6e4767162cc#myft:saved-articles:page.

Arnold, M. (2015c, July 8). Barclays fires jenkins after clash over investment banking unit. *Financial Times*. Available at: https://next.ft.com/content/74fed7c6-2537-11e5-9c4e-a775d2b173ca#myft:saved-articles:page.

Arnold, M. (2015d, February 25). HSBC chiefs grilled by MPs over tax scandal. *Financial Times*. Available at: https://www.ft.com/content/0ee7112c-bd1a-11e4-b523-00144feab7de.

Arnold, M. (2017a, October 26). RBS settles DoJ fraud claims over mortgage-backed securities. *Financial Times*. Available at: https://www.ft.com/content/2231f092-f991-3eef-9ebe-4a46ed6ddf9f.

Arnold, M. (2017b, May 10). Barclays chief apologises to shareholders for trying to identify whistleblower. *Financial Times*. Available at: https://www.ft.com/content/a5f8caed-9677-326f-bd69-a1fe72155e40.

Arnold, M. (2017c, May 10). Barclays chief Jes staley apologises for pursuit of whistleblower. *Financial Times*. Available at: https://www.ft.com/content/aa0fa830-3572-11e7-bce4-9023f8c0fd2e.

Arnold, M. (2017d, May 11). Barclays rejigs top management at investment banking arm. *Financial Time*. Available at: https://www.ft.com/content/47d37ce2-366b-11e7-bce4-9023f8c0fd2e.

Arnold, M. (2017e, December 11). US lifts threat of prosecution against HSBC. *Financial Times*. Available at: https://www.ft.com/content/58775414-de5a-11e7-a8a4-0a1e63a52f9c.

Arnold, M. (2018a, January 18). HSBC agrees to $101.5m US forex settlement. *Financial Times*. Available at: https://www.ft.com/content/5c7223ca-fca8-11e7-9b32-d7d59aace167.

Arnold, M. (2018b, April 16). HSBC announces private banking shake-up. *Financial Times*. Available at: https://www.ft.com/content/c5556682-418f-11e8-803a-295c97e6fd0b.

Arnold, M., & Croft, J. (2017, May 3). RBS investors advised to vote against pay policy. *Financial Times*. Available at: https://www.ft.com/content/fa35e1ca-3023-11e7-9555-23ef563ecf9a.

Arnold, M., & England, A. (2016, May 5). Barclays makes £600m from stake sale in African subsidiary. *Financial Times*. Available at: http://www.ft.com/cms/s/0/109031b8-1212-11e6-91da-096d89bd2173.html#axzz4GA9DEhts.

Arnold, M., & Jenkins, P. (2015, October 13). Barclays set to pick Jes Staley as chief executive. *Financial Times*. Available at: https://next.ft.com/content/31fbe252-7122-11e5-9b9e-690fdae72044.

Arnold, M., & Jenkins, P. (2016, May 2). Barclays' risk officer in France alleges laundering and mis-selling failures. *Financial Times*. Available at: http://www.ft.com/cms/s/0/981b083e-1054-11e6-839f-2922947098f0.html#axzz4GpAcMw00.

Arnold, M., & Shubber, K. (2018, March 29). Barclays agrees to pay $2bn to settle US mis-selling claims. *Financial Times*. Available at: https://www.ft.com/content/358a35da-3359-11e8-ac48-10c6fdc22f03.

Arnold, M., Barker, A., & Toplensky, R. (2016, December 7). Trio of big banks hit back at EU's Euribor-rigging fine. *Financial Times*. Available at: https://www.ft.com/content/372aacae bc71 11e6 8b15 b8b81dd5d080.

Arnold, M., Croft, J., & Binham, C. (2018, May 21). UK court dismisses charges against barclays over qatar deal. *Financial Times*. Available at: https://www.ft.com/content/b1a78a9a-5ce0-11e8-ad91-e01af256df68.

Ashby, S. (2010, January). *The 2007–09 financial crisis: Learning the risk management lessons*. Available at: https://www.nottingham.ac.uk/business/businesscentres/crbfs/documents/researchreports/paper65.pdf.

Ashwin, P. (2008). Accounting for structure and agency in 'close-up' research on teaching, learning and assessment in higher education. *International Journal of Educational Research, 47,* 151–158.

Augar, P. (2018). *The bank that lived a little: Barclays in the age of the very free market*. London: Allen Lane.

Baert, P. (1998). *Social theory in the twentieth century*. Cambridge: Polity Press.

Baker, A. (2013). The new political economy of the macroprudential ideational shift. *New Political Economy, 18*(1), 112–139.

Baker, A. (2015). *The bankers paradox: The political economy of macroprudential regulation* (SRC Discussion Paper No. 37). The London School of Economics and Political Science.

Baily, M., Holmes, S., & Bekker, W. (2015, May 26). *The big four banks: The evolution of the financial sector, part I*. Brooking Institute. Available at: https://www.brookings.edu/wp-content/uploads/2016/06/big_four_banks_evolution_financial_sector_pt1_final.pdf.

Bandura, A. (1977). Self-efficacy: Towards a unifying theory of behavioural change. *Psychological Review, 84*(2), 191–215.

Bank of England [bankofengland.co.uk]. *Remuneration code—About*. Available at: http://www.bankofengland.co.uk/pra/Pages/supervision/activities/aboutremuneration.aspx.

Bank of England [bankofengland.co.uk]. *The financial policy committee's approach to setting the countercyclical capital buffer a policy statement*. April 2016. Available at: http://www.bankofengland.co.uk/financialstability/Documents/fpc/policystatement050416.pdf.

Bank of England. (2015, November). *The failure of HBOS plc (HBOS) a report by the Financial Conduct Authority (FCA) and the Prudential Regulation Authority (PRA)*. Bank of England. Available at: http://www.bankofengland.co.uk/pra/Documents/publications/reports/hbos.pdf.

Barclays [Barclays Banking Group PLC]. (2007). *Annual report and accounts 2007*. Available at: https://www.home.barclays/content/dam/barclayspublic/docs/InvestorRelations/AnnualReports/AR2007/2007-barclays-plc-annual-report.pdf.

Barclays [Barclays Banking Group PLC]. (2011). *Annual report and accounts 2011*. Available at: https://www.home.barclays/content/dam/barclayspublic/docs/InvestorRelations/AnnualReports/AR2011/barclays-plc-annual-report-2011.pdf.

Barclays [Barclays Banking Group PLC]. (2012). *Annual report and accounts 2012: Building the 'go-to' bank*. Available at: https://www.home.barclays/content/dam/barclayspublic/docs/InvestorRelations/AnnualReports/AR2012/2012-barclays-plc-annual-report.pdf.

Barclays [Barclays Banking Group PLC]. (2013a). *Integrity Barclays' response to the salz review*. Available at: https://www.home.barclays/content/dam/barclayspublic/documents/news/471-392-250413-salz-response.pdf.

Barclays [Barclays Banking Group PLC]. (2013b, February 12). *Becoming the 'go-to' bank Barclays strategic review executive summary*. Available at: https://www.home.barclays/content/dam/barclayspublic/docs/Microsites/Transform/barclays-strategic-review-executive-summary.pdf.

Barclays [Barclays Banking Group PLC]. (2013c). *Annual report and accounts 2013*. Available at: https://www.home.barclays/content/dam/barclayspublic/docs/InvestorRelations/AnnualReports/AR2013/2013-barclays-annual-report-final.pdf.

Barclays [Barclays Banking Group PLC]. (2013d, February 12). *Press release: Barclays announces the outcome of its strategic review and sets out commitments for 2015*. Available at: https://www.home.barclays/content/dam/barclaysp ublic/docs/Microsites/Transform/barclays-strategic-review-announcement. pdf.

Barclays [Barclays Banking Group PLC]. (2014a, December 31). *Barclays PLC results announcement*. Available at: https://www.home.barclays/content/ dam/barclayspublic/docs/InvestorRelations/ResultAnnouncements/2015% 20FY%20Results/Barclays_FY_2014_Results.pdf.

Barclays [Barclays Banking Group PLC]. (2014b, May 8). *Barclays PLC Barclays announces group strategy update*. Available at: https://www.home.barclays/ content/dam/barclayspublic/docs/InvestorRelations/IRNewsPresentations/ 2014News/Barclays-group-strategy-update.pdf.

Barclays [Barclays Banking Group PLC]. (2014c). *Barclays PLC annual report and accounts: Helping people their ambitions—In the right way*. Available at: https://www.home.barclays/content/dam/barclayspublic/docs/InvestorR elations/AnnualReports/AR2014/Barclays_PLC_Annual_Report_%202014. pdf.

Barclays [Barclays Banking Group PLC]. (2015a). *Annual report and accounts 2015*. Available at: https://www.home.barclays/content/dam/barclaysp ublic/docs/InvestorRelations/AnnualReports/AR2015/Barclays_PLC_Ann ual_Report_%202015.pdf.

Barclays [Barclays Banking Group PLC]. (2015b). *Barclays PLC strategic report 2015*. Available at: https://www.home.barclays/content/dam/barclaysp ublic/docs/InvestorRelations/AnnualReports/AR2015/Barclays_PLC_Str ategic_Report_2015.pdf.

Barclays [Barclays Banking Group PLC]. (2015c, November 26). *Press release: Barclays announces settlement with the FCA*. Available at: http://www.new sroom.barclays.co.uk/r/3272/barclays_announces_settlement_with_the_fca.

Barclays [Barclays Banking Group PLC]. (2016). *Annual report and accounts 2016: Building the bank of the future*. Available at: https://home.barclays/ content/dam/home-barclays/documents/investor-relations/reports-and-eve nts/annual-reports/Barclays-PLC-Annual-Report-2016.pdf.

Barclays [Barclays Banking Group PLC]. (2017). *Annual Report and accounts 2017, positioned for growth, sharing and success*. Available at: https://www. home.barclays/content/dam/home-barclays/documents/investor-relations/ annualreports/ar2017/Barclays%20PLC%20Annual%20Report%202017.pdf.

Barclays [Barclays Banking Group PLC]. (2018). *Annual report and accounts 2018: Creating opportunities to rise*. Available at: https://home.barclays/con tent/dam/home-barclays/documents/investor-relations/reports-and-events/ annual-reports/2018/2018-barclays-plc-annual-report.pdf.

Barnett, M., & Duvall, R. (2005). Power in international politics. *International Organization, 59*(1), 39–75.

BBC [BBC News Online]. (2003, Tuesday 4 March). Buffett warns on investment 'time bomb'. *BBC News*. Available at: http://news.bbc.co.uk/1/hi/2817995.stm.

BBC News Online. (2013, December 11). RBS fined $100m by US for Iran sanctions violations. *BBC News*. Available at: http://www.bbc.co.uk/news/business-25341882.

BBC News Online. (2015, December 16). RBS outlines williams & glyn sale plans. *BBC News*. Available at: http://www.bbc.co.uk/news/uk-scotland-scotland-business-35111705.

BBC [BBC Radio 4]. (2013, February 12). *The today programme: Barclays 'will be judged by actions'*. Available at: http://www.bbc.co.uk/news/uk-21424240.

BBC News. (2012a, September 14). RBS confirms it will sell off direct line insurance. *BBC News*. At: http://www.bbc.co.uk/news/business-19596192.

BBC News. (2012b, May 11). HSBC sells South American units to banco GNB sudameris. *BBC News*. Available at: http://www.bbc.co.uk/news/business-18043315.

BBC News. (2013, February 6). RBS: The embarrassing transcripts. *BBC News*. http://www.bbc.co.uk/news/business-21358362.

BBC News. (2014a, November 20). RBS fined £56m over 'unacceptable' computer failure. *BBC News*. http://www.bbc.co.uk/news/business-30125728.

BBC News. (2014b, August 27). RBS fined £14.5m over mortgage advice by FCA. *BBC News*. http://www.bbc.co.uk/news/business-28948518.

BBC News. (2014c, April 6). Barclays sells its united Arab Emirates retail business. *BBC News*. Available at: http://www.bbc.co.uk/news/business-26915911.

BBC News. (2015a, May 27). Libor: What is it and why does it matter? *BBC News*. http://www.bbc.co.uk/news/business-19199683.

BBC News. (2015b, February 10). HSBC bank 'helped clients dodge millions in tax'. *BBC News*. http://www.bbc.co.uk/news/business-31248913.

BBC News. (2017, June 20). Barclays charged with fraud in Qatar case. *BBC New*. Available at: http://www.bbc.co.uk/news/business-40338220.

BBC Panorama. (2015, February 9). *The bank of tax cheats*. BBC 1. http://www.bbc.co.uk/iplayer/episode/b052sk1h/panorama-the-bank-of-tax-cheats-panorama.

BCBS (Basel Committee on Banking Supervision). (2010). *An assessment of the long-term economic impact of stronger capital and liquidity requirements*. Basel: Bank of International Settlements.

Bell, S. (2011). Do we really need a new 'constructivist institutionalism' to explain institutional change? *British Journal of Political Science*, *41*, 883–906.

Bell, S., & Feng, H. (2014). How proximate and 'meta-institutional' contexts shape institutional change: Explaining the rise of the people's bank of China. *Political Studies* 62, 197–215.

Bell, S., & Hindmoor, A. (2014). The ideational shaping of state power and capacity: Winning battles but losing the war over bank reform in the US and UK. *Government and Opposition, 49*(3), 342–368.

Bell, S., & Hindmoor, A. (2015a). *Masters of the universe, slaves of the market*. Cambridge, MA: Harvard University Press.

Bell, S., & Hindmoor, A. (2015b). Masters of the universe but slaves of the market: Bankers and the great financial meltdown. *British Journal of Politics and International Relations, 17*(1), 1–22.

Bell. S., & Hindmoor, A. (2015c). Taming the city? Ideas, structural power and the evolution of British banking policy amidst the great financial meltdown. *New Political Economy, 20*(3), 454–474.

Bell, S., & Hindmoor, A. (2018). Are the major global banks now safer? structural continuities and change in banking and finance since the 2008 crisis. *Review of International Political Economy, 25*(1), 1–27.

Bernanke, B. (2009, November 17). *Testimony before the national commission on the causes of the financial and economic crisis in the United States*. Available at: http://som.yale.edu/sites/default/files/files/Bernanke_Ben_Financial_Crisis_Inquiry_Commission_11-17-09.pdf.

Bernanke, B. (2010, September 2). *Statement by Ben S. Bernanke before the financial crisis inquiry commission [transcript]*. Available at http://fcic-static.law.stanford.edu/cdn_media/fcic-testimony/2010-0902-Bernanke.pdf.

Bernanke, B. (2012, April 13). *Some reflections on the crisis and the policy response*. Speech at the Russell Sage Foundation and the Century Foundation Conference on Rethinking Finance, New York. Available at http://www.federalreserve.gov/newsevents/speech/bernanke20120413a.htm.

Bernanke, B., Geithner, T., & Paulson, H. (2019). *Firefighting: The financial crisis and its lessons*. London: Profile Books.

Bernstein, J. (2019). *The laundromat: Inside the panama papers investigation of illicit money networks and the global elite*. New York: MacMillan.

Bessis, J. (2015). *Risk management in banking* (4th ed.). Chichester: John Wiley & Sons.

Bhaskar, R. (1979). *The possibility of naturalism*. Harvester: Brighton.

Bhaskar, R. (1993). *Dialectic: The pulse of freedom*. London: Verso.

Binham. C. (2016, February 19). Barclays Qatari deal turns into tale of two battles. *Financial Times*. Available at: http://www.ft.com/cms/s/0/18cc5926-d728-11e5-829b-8564e7528e54.html#axzz4GM2flvfG.

Binham, C. (2017a, March 23). City watchdog relaunches probe into Barclays' cash call. *Financial Times*. Available at: https://www.ft.com/content/073efae2-0e2c-11e7-b030-768954394623.

Binham, C. (2017b, March 23). Qatari connection casts long shadow over Barclays. *Financial Times*. Available at: https://www.ft.com/content/daddа8fa-0d58-11e7-a88c-50ba212dce4d.

Binham, C. (2018a, January 17). Rogue RBS unit told to 'let customers hang themselves'. *Financial Times*. Available at: https://www.ft.com/content/ecbca106-fbab-11e7-a492-2c9be7f3120a.

Binham, C. (2018b, January 30). RBS drops challenge to scathing report about restructuring unit. *Financial Times*. Available at: https://www.ft.com/content/c1b36dbc-05d0-11e8-9650-9c0ad2d7c5b5.

Binham, C. (2018c, February 8). RBS chair hits back against allegations of misleading UK parliament. *Financial Times*. Available at: https://www.ft.com/content/0116c31e-0cc5-11e8-8eb7-42f857ea9f09.

Binham, C. (2018d, May 11). Barclays CEO Jes Staley fined £640,000 over whistleblowing scandal. *Financial Times*. Available at: https://www.ft.com/content/86089810-5502-11e8-b24e-cad6aa67e23e.

Binham, C., & Dunkley, E. (2015, November 26). Attempted 'elephant deal' costs Barclays £72m. *The Financial Times*. Available at: http://www.ft.com/cms/s/0/9d77d27c-9461-11e5-bd82-c1fb87bef7af.html#axzz4GSlHG8s3.

Binham, C., & Dunkley, E. (2017, October 16). RBS excludes thousands of small businesses from compensation. *Financial Times*. Available at: https://www.ft.com/content/351172aa-b035-11e7-aab9-abaa44b1e130.

Binham, C., & Jenkins, A. (2014, May 11). UK fraud office steps up probe into Barclays' dealings with Qatar. *Financial Times*. Available at: http://www.ft.com/cms/s/0/cda8004e-d7a1-11e3-80e0-00144feabdc0.html#axzz31UZn5j85.

Binham, C., & Tetlow, G. (2017, June 27). Bank of England tells lenders to increase capital buffers by £11.4bn. *Financial Times*. Available at: https://www.ft.com/content/9bc99294-5b1b-11e7-9bc8-8055f264aa8b.

Binham, C., & Thompson, B. (2017, August 17). *FDIC sues Barclays, RBS and other banks over libor*. Available at: https://www.ft.com/content/46d51cbe-8360-11e7-a4ce-15b2513cb3ff.

Binham, C., Arnold, M., Noonan, L., & Chon, G. (2015, May 15). Forex rigging settlement: 10 things you need to know. *Financial Times*. Available at: http://www.ft.com/cms/s/0/a9c85836-fb09-11e4-9aed-00144feab7de.html#axzz41YViGO3G.

Birkland, T. (2009). Disasters, lessons learned, and fantasy documents. *Journal of Contingencies and Crisis Management, 17*(3), 146–156.

BIS [Bank for International Settlements]. (2006). *Part 2: The first pillar—Minimum capital requirements*. Available at: https://www.bis.org/publ/bcbs128b.pdf.

BIS [Bank for International Settlements]. (2010, December). *Basel III: A global regulatory framework for more resilient banks and banking systems* (rev June 2011). Available at: http://www.bis.org/publ/bcbs189.htm.

BIS [Bank for International Settlements]. (2018). *Basel III monitoring report march 2018*. Available at: https://www.bis.org/bcbs/publ/d433.pdf.

Blackden, R. (2012, July 12). HSBC's 'money-laundering' apology. *The Telegraph*. At: http://www.telegraph.co.uk/finance/newsbysector/banksandfinance/9393874/HSBCs-money-laundering-apology.html.

Blair, T. (2005, May 26). Full text: Tony blair's speech on compensation culture. *The Guardian*. Available at: http://www.theguardian.com/politics/2005/may/26/speeches.media.

Blinder, A. (2014). *After the music stopped: The financial crisis, the response, and the work ahead*. New York: Penguin Books.

BloombergBusiness.com. (2015, February 27). *Lloyds banking group PLC: 'People'*. At: http://www.bloomberg.com/research/stocks/people/person.asp?personId=2461671&ticker=LLOY:LN.

Blyth, M. (1997). Any more bright ideas? The ideational turn of comparative political economy. *Comparative Politics* 29, 229–250.

Blyth, M., & Matthijs, M. (2017). Black Swans, Lame Ducks, and the mystery of IPE's missing macroeconomy. *Review of International Political Economy, 24*(2), 203–223.

Boin, A., & Fishbacher-Smith, D. (2011). The importance of failure theories in assessing crisis management: The *Columbia* space shuttle disaster revisited. *Policy and Society, 30*(2011), 77–87.

Booth, S., & Anderberg, E. (2005). Academic development for knowledge capabilities: Learning, reflecting and developing. *Higher Education Research & Development, 24*(4), 373–386.

Bootle, R. (2011). *The trouble with markets*. London: Nicholas Brealey.

Bourke, J. (2015, November 19). Barclays fined another $150m over forex-rigging scandal. *The Independent*. Available at: http://www.independent.co.uk/news/business/news/barclays-fined-150m-more-over-forex-rigging-scandal-a6740011.html.

Bracken, P., Bremmer, I., & Gordon, D. (2005). *Managing strategic surprise: Lessons from risk management and risk assessment*. Cambridge: Cambridge University Press.

Bradford, H. (2012, July 27). Barclays Makes employees watch video to ensure libor rigging 'never happens again'. *The Huffington post*. Available at: http://www.huffingtonpost.com/2012/07/27/barclays-libor-video_n_1710895.html.

Bray, C. (2016, April 28). Barclays to sell credit card business in Portugal and Spain. *The New York Times*. Available at: http://www.nytimes.com/2016/

04/29/business/dealbook/barclays-sell-credit-card-business-spain-portugal.html?_r=0.

Brazier, A. (2017, Monday 24 July). *'Debt strikes back' or 'the return of the regulator'?*. Alex Brazier executive director, financial director for financial stability strategy and risk member of the financial policy committee bank of England University of Liverpool, Institute for Risk and Uncertainty. Available at: http://www.bankofengland.co.uk/publications/Documents/speeches/2017/speech992.pdf.

Brinded, L. (2012, July 30). Libor fixing scandal: HSBC faces six rate probes as CEO admits bank's failure. *International Business Times*. At: http://www.ibtimes.co.uk/hsbc-libor-fixing-scandal-euribor-money-laundering-368151.

Brinded, L. (2013, November 1). Mis-selling PPI scandal: RBS compensation pot hits £2.6bn. *International Business Times*. At: http://www.ibtimes.co.uk/rbs-mis-selling-ppi-results-ross-mcewan-518833.

Brinded, L. (2014a, August 8). RBS scraps controversial GRG unit criticised in tomlinson report. *International Business Times*. Available at: http://www.ibtimes.co.uk/rbs-scraps-controversial-grg-unit-criticised-tomlinson-report-1460346.

Brinded, L. (2014b, June 12). Mis-selling derivatives scandal: HSBC compensates victims £139,000 on average. *International Business Times*. At: http://www.ibtimes.co.uk/mis-selling-derivatives-scandal-hsbc-compensates-victims-139000-average-1452403.

Brinded, L. (2015, July 8). The fired Barclays CEO had two nicknames inside the bank that tell you why he was forced out. *Business Insider UK*. Available at: http://uk.businessinsider.com/barclays-ceo-antony-jenkins-left-because-of-his-lack-of-investment-banking-understanding-2015-7.

Brindley, B., Butler, D., Clutterbuck, B., Johnson, B., Lewis, P., Owen, G., Sidwell, G., Walters, R. M., Wood, A., & Wright, M.(2008). *Oxford dictionary of finance and banking*. Oxford: Oxford University Press.

British Bankers Association [BBA]. (2014, May). *The cyber threat to banking: A global industry challenge*. Available at: https://www.bba.org.uk/wp-content/uploads/2014/06/BBAJ2110_Cyber_report_May_2014_WEB.pdf.

British Bankers Association [BBA]. (2015, November). *Winning the global race, the competitiveness of the UK as a centre for international banking*. Available at: https://www.bba.org.uk/news/reports/winning-the-global-race/#.VqtrObfcuM8.

British Bankers Association [BBA]. (2016, January). *BBA briefing: Reforms since the financial crisis*. Available at: https://www.bba.org.uk/news/reports/bba-briefing-reforms-since-the-financial-crisis/#.VqtvzbfcuM8.

Brown, G. (2005, November 28). Full text: Gordon brown's speech to the CBI. *Financial Times*. Available at: http://www.ft.com/cms/s/2/9073a120-600d-11da-a3a6-0000779e2340.html#axzz3ttxP5SYf.

Brown, G. (2010). *Beyond the crash: Overcoming the first crisis of globalisation.* London: Simon & Schuster.

Brown, G. (2017). *Gordon brown my life, our times.* London: Bodley Head.

Brummer, A. (2015). *Bad banks: Greed, incompetence and the next global crisis.* Random House Business: London.

Buck, T., & Sharman, A. (2014, September 1). Barclays loses £500m on sale of Spanish business. *Financial Times.* Available at: http://www.ft.com/cms/s/0/fae5d374-3147-11e4-8313-00144feabdc0.html#axzz4GA9DEhts.

Buiter, W. (2009, January 13). *Treasury select committee, minutes of evidence.* Available at: http://www.publications.parliament.uk/pa/cm200809/cmselect/cmtreasy/uc144-i/uc14402.htm.

Bustamante, M. C., & Donangelo, A. (2014, February). *'Product market competition and industry returns' financial markets group* (Discussion Paper No. 728). At: http://www.lse.ac.uk/fmg/workingPapers/discussionPapers/fmgdps/DP728-final.pdf.

Butcher, S. (2016, March). *Jes Staley's rose-tinted vision for Barclays' investment bank.* Efinancialcareer.com. Available at: http://news.efinancialcareers.com/uk-en/237824/jes-staleys-strategy-for-barclays-investment-bank/.

Caetano, A. (2014, September 10). Defining personal reflexivity: A critical reading of archer's approach. *European Journal of Social Theory, 15*(1), 93–115.

Cameron, G. (2014, January 27). RBS sets aside £3.1bn for new mortgage and PPI claims. *The Herald Scotland.* Online Edition. At: http://www.heraldscotland.com/news/13142627.RBS_sets_aside___3_1bn_for_new_mortgage_and_PPI_claims/.

Cangelosi, V., & Dill, W.R. (1965). Organizational learning. Observations toward a theory. *Administrative Science Quarterly, 10*(2), 175–203.

Capitalism: A Love Story. (2009). Hollywood, CA: Overture Films, Paramount Vantage.

Carney, M. (2016, February). *Bank of England inflation report press conference* [online]. Available at: http://www.bankofengland.co.uk/publications/Pages/webcasts/latest.aspx.

Carney, M. (2017a, September 28). *Opening remarks to the bank of England 'independence—20 years on'.* Conference Remarks given by Mark Carney, Governor of the Bank of England. Available at: https://www.bankofengland.co.uk/-/media/boe/files/speech/2017/opening-remarks-at-the-boe-independence-20-years-on-conference.pdf?la=en&hash=4D7358410C6E5852A401EC6EF0DEEE7A00D4F0F9.

Carney, M. (2017b, Tuesday). *Financial stability report press conference* [online]. Available at: https://www.bankofengland.co.uk/-/media/boe/files/financial-stability-report/2017/transcript-june-2017.pdf?la=en&hash=AF4E73FFEE23818E5CC4B3D8B479968E2AF9ADFD.

Carney, M. (2017c, April 20). *What a difference a decade makes*. Remarks at the institute of International Finance's Washington Policy Summit, the Reagan Centre, Washington DC [online]. Available at: https://www.bankofengland.co.uk/-/media/boe/files/speech/2017/what-a-difference-a-decade-makes.

Chon, G., & Martin, K. (2015, November 18). Barclays fined $150m over electronic forex trading. *Financial Times*. Available at: http://www.ft.com/cms/s/0/4afc8ea6-8e09-11e5-a549-b89a1dfede9b.html#axzz4GSlHG8s3.

Christensen, J., Shaxson, N., & Wigan, D. (2016). The finance curse: Britain and the world economy. *The British Journal of Politics and International Relations, 18*(1), 255–269.

CityAm. (2012, October 2). *HSBC sells property advice unit*. CityAm. Available at: http://www.cityam.com/article/hsbc-sells-property-advice-unit.

Clark. A. (2009, January 10). Lloyds forfeits $350m for disguising origin of funds from Iran and Sudan. *The Guardian*. Available at: https://www.theguardian.com/business/2009/jan/10/lloyds-forfeits-350m-to-us.

Clark, A. (2010, August 16). Barclays fined $298m for sanction breaking. *The Guardian*. Available at: https://www.theguardian.com/business/2010/aug/16/barclays-fined-for-sanction-breaking.

Clark, D. (2016). *The global financial crisis and austerity: A basic introduction*. Bristol: Polity Press.

CMA [Competition & Markets Authority]. (2016). *Retail banking Market investigation: Final report august 2016*. Available at: https://assets.publishing.service.gov.uk/media/57ac9667e5274a0f6c00007a/retail-banking-market-investigation-full-final-report.pdf.

CMC Market. (2019, December 3). Lloyds share price: Is the bank a safe bet with Brexit on the horizon?. *CMC Markets*. Available at: https://www.cmcmarkets.com/en-gb/opto/lloyds-share-price-is-the-bank-a-safe-bet-with-brexit-on-the-horizon.

Coates, S. (2013, March 12). Lloyds plays it simple with St James's place sale. *The Times*. Available at: http://www.thetimes.co.uk/tto/business/industries/banking/article3711088.ece.

Cohan, W. (2009). *House of cards: A tale of Hubris and wretched excess on wall street*. New York: Doubleday.

Cohan, W. (2011). *Money and power: How goldman sachs came to Rule the world*. New York: Doubleday.

Columbia Accident Investigation Board [CAIB]. (2003). *Columbia accident investigation report*. Available at: http://www.nasa.gov/columbia/home/CAIB_Vol1.html.

Cortell, A., & Peterson, S. (1999). Altered states: Explaining domestic institutional change. *British Journal of Political Science, 29*(1) (January), 177–203.

Cotterill, J. (2017, May 31). Barclays to sell £1.6bn stake in African unit. *Financial Times*. Available at: https://www.ft.com/content/5b67ec64-7fa8-389d-ac49-7c7c08aedee9.

Crouch, C. (2011). *The strange non-death of neoliberalism*. Cambridge: Polity Press.

Croft, J., & Binham, C. (2020, February 28). London jury clears 3 former Barclays bankers of fraud charges. *Financial Times*. Available at: https://www.ft.com/content/d0bc7fd4-5a19-11ea-a528-dd0f971febbc.

Darling, A. (2011). *Back from the brink*. London: Atlantic Books.

Darling, A. (2017, September). Between a rock and a hard place: 10 years on from Northern rock. *Resolution Foundation* [online]. Available at: https://www.youtube.com/watch?v=hBTI4GQT_OI&feature=youtu.be.

Davies, H. (2010). *The financial crisis: Who is to blame?*. Cambridge: Polity Press.

Davies, P., Rabinovitch, S., & Robinson, G. (2012, December 5). HSBC sells ping an stake to Thai group. *Financial Times*. Available at: http://www.ft.com/cms/s/0/e193282a-3e7a-11e2-829d-00144feabdc0.html#axzz4APxrj9ee.

Day, P., & Klein, R. (1989). Interpreting the unexpected: The case of AIDS policy making in Britain. *Journal of Public Policy, 9*(3), 337–353.

Decisionmarketing.co.uk. (2015, September 28). *RBS accused of falsifying data*. Available at: http://www.decisionmarketing.co.uk/news/rbs-accused-of-falsifying-data.

Department of Financial Services [New York State Department of Financial Services]. (2018, December 18). *DFS fines Barclays bank plc and New York branch $15 million following whistleblower investigation*. DFS Press Release. Available online at: https://www.dfs.ny.gov/reports_and_publications/press_releases/pr1812181.

DoJ [United States Department of Justice]. (2018, March 29). *Barclays agrees to Pay $2 billion in civil penalties to resolve claims for fraud in the sale of residential mortgage-backed securities*. Press Release Available at: https://www.justice.gov/opa/pr/barclays-agrees-pay-2-billion-civil-penalties-resolve-claims-fraud-sale-residential-mortgage.

Desoete, A., Roeyers, H., & De Clercq, A. (2003). Can offline metacognition enhance mathematical problem solving? *Journal of Educational Psychology, 95*, 188–200.

Deutsch, K. W. (1963). *The nerves of government*. New York: Free Press.

Diamond, B. (2012, June 12). *Barclays press release 28 June 2012: Letter from bob diamond, Barclays chief executive*. Barclays Media Relations, Press Release. Available at: http://www.newsroom.barclays.co.uk/r/2306/letter_from_bob_diamond__barclays_chief_executive.

DiMaggio, P., & Powell, W. (1983). The iron cage revisited: Institutional isomorphism and collective rationality in organizational fields. *American Sociological Review, 48*(2), 147–160.

Dodgson, M. (1993, May). Organizational learning: A review of some literatures. *Organization Studies, 14*, 375–394.

Duncan, R., & Weiss, A. (1979). Organisational learning: Implications for organisational design. In B. M. Staw & L. L. Cummings (Eds.), *Research in organisational behaviour* (pp. 75–123). Greenwish, CT: JAI Press.

Dunkley, E. (2016a, February 26). RBS piles up £50bn in losses since crisis. *Financial Times*. Available at: http://www.ft.com/cms/s/0/2b9428ec-dc58-11e5-a72f-1e7744c66818.html#axzz41YViGO3G.

Dunkley, E. (2016b, December 28). Williams & Glyn sale faces bank of England review. *Financial Times*. Available at: https://www.ft.com/content/739cfc9e-cd17-11e6-864f-20dcb35cede2.

Dunkley, E. (2016c, April 30). RBS sale of Williams & Glyn among most prolonged in HISTORY. *Financial Times*. Available at: https://www.ft.com/content/c842fc72-0e08-11e6-ad80-67655613c2d6.

Dunkley, E. (2016d, August 2). UK banks face more than £1bn in extra PPI costs. *The Financial Times*. Available at: http://www.ft.com/cms/s/0/2e997baa-5886-11e6-9f70-badea1b336d4.html#axzz4GpAcMw00.

Dunkley, E. (2017a, July 12). RBS to pay £4.2bn for mis-sold US mortgage-backed securities. *Financial Times*. Available at: https://www.ft.com/content/49872ce2-6702-11e7-8526-7b38dcaef614.

Dunkley, E. (2017b, October 23). UK watchdog publishes review of alleged abuses by RBS unit. *Financial Times*. Available at: https://www.ft.com/content/68b3d138-b7fc-11e7-8c12-5661783e5589.

Dunkley, E. (2017c, July 26). RBS deal with EU pushes UK closer to selling stake. *Financial Times*. Available at: https://www.ft.com/content/ac6fe344-721f-11e7-aca6-c6bd07df1a3c.

Dunkley, E. (2017d, September 18). Brussels approves RBS plan for boosting competition. *Financial Times*. Available at: https://www.ft.com/content/95eb931d-680f-3141-90c1-9ee8b1019911.

Dunkley, E. (2017e). UK Government No Longer Largest Shareholder in Lloyds. *Financial Times Online*. Available at: https://www.ft.com/content/9cc4c9e6-d64d-11e6-944b-e7eb37a6aa8e.

Dunkley, E., & Arnold, M. (2015a). RBS plans to sell Williams & Glyn next year. *The Financial Times*. http://www.ft.com/cms/s/0/87cc4f28-a3c7-11e5-873f-68411a84f346.html#axzz41C1UVFL5.

Dunkley, E., & Arnold, M. (2015b, August 4). Sale of RBS stake marks start of the UK's biggest privatisation. *Financial Times*. Available at: https://www.ft.com/content/8a09333a-39e3-11e5-8613-07d16aad2152.

Dunkley, E., & Jenkins, P. (2017, May 18). How Lloyds came back from the brink. *Financial Times*. Available at: https://www.ft.com/content/34e57e76-3a87-11e7-821a-6027b8a20f23?myftTopics=TnN0ZWluX09OX0ZvcnR1bmVDb21wYW55X0xMT1k%3D-T04%3D#myft:my-news:grid.

Dunkley, E., Barrett, C., & Aglionby, J. (2014, November 20). Royal bank of Scotland fined £56m for IT meltdown. *The Financial Times*. At: http://www.ft.com/cms/s/0/3e8d7d5e-7084-11e4-9129-00144feabdc0.html#axzz3j5Int9H2.

Dunkley, J. (2015, February 18). HSBC tax avoidance scandal: Timeline of Britain's biggest banking leak. *The Independent*. At: http://www.independent.co.uk/news/business/comment/hsbc-tax-avoidance-scandal-timeline-of-britains-biggest-banking-leak-10054442.html.

Driga, I., & Dura, C. (2014). *The financial sector and the role of banks in economic development*. Annals of the University of Petrosani, pp. 598–603. Available at: http://www.upet.ro/simpro/2014/proceedings/09%20-%20ECONOMICS%20AND%20PUBLIC%20ADMINISTRATION/9.2.pdf.

Eatwell, J. (2009). Practical proposals for regulatory reform. In P. Subacchi & A. Monsarrat (Eds.), *New ideas for the London summit: Recommendations to the G20 leaders* (pp. 11–15). London: Royal Institute for International Affairs Chatham, The Atlantic Council.

Easterby-Smith, M., & Araujo, L. (1999). Organizational learning: Current debates and opportunities. In M. Easterby-Smith, B. Burgoyne & L. Araujo (Eds.), *Organizational learning and the learning organization* (pp. 1–21). London: Sage.

Edmondson, A., & Moingcon, B. (1999). Learning, trust and organizational change. In M. Easterby-Smith, J. Burgoyne & L. Araujo (Eds.), *Organizational learning and the learning organization: Developments in theory and practice* (Chapter 9, pp. 157–176). London: Sage Publications.

El Radi, A. (2014, August). *Enhancing quality of capital under basel III. Ahmad El Radi METAC banking supervision advisor*. Beirut: Lebanon. Available at: http://www.imfmetac.org/Upload/Link3_753_105.pdf.

Elkjaer, B. (1999). In search of a social learning theory. In M. Easterby-Smith, B. Burgoyne & L. Araujo (Eds.), Organizational learning and the learning organization: Developments in theory and practice (Chapter 5, pp. 75–91). London: Sage Publications.

Ellul, A., & Yerramilli, V. (2010, January). *Stronger risk controls, lower risk: Evidence from U.S. bank holding companies* (Axa Working Paper Series No. 1 Discussion Paper No. 646). Available at: http://www.lse.ac.uk/fmg/workingPapers/discussionPapers/Stronger%20Risk%20Controls,%20Lower%20Risk%20Evidence%20from%20US%20Bank%20Holding%20Companies.pdf.

Engelen, E., Erturk, I., Froud, J., Johal, S., L, A., Moran, M., et al. (2011). *After the great complacence: Financial crisis and the politics of reform*. Oxford: Oxford University Press.

Erturk, I. (2017). Shadow banking: A story of the doppelganger (the Double) in science of finance. *Journal of Cultural Economy* (16 November 2016), 1–16.

Etheredge, L. S. (1981). Government learning: An overview. In S. Long (Ed.), *The hand-book of political behaviour* (Vol. 2, pp. 73–161). New York: Plenum Press.

European Banking Authority [EBA]. (2014, October 15). Opinion of the European Banking Authority on the application of Directive 2013/36/EU (Capital Requirements Directive) regarding the principles on remuneration policies of credit institutions and investment firms and the use of allowances. EBA/Op/2014/10. European Banking Authority. Available at: https://www.eba.europa.eu/documents/10180/657547/EBA-Op-2014-10+Opinion+on+remuneration+and+allowances.pdf.

Evans, M. (2015, February 9). HSBC 'helped wealthy clients evade millions in tax'. *The Express*. At: http://www.express.co.uk/news/uk/557025/HSBC-accused-evade-tax-millions-wealthy-clients.

Evans, R. (2011, January 11). NatWest and RBS fined £2.8m for poor complaint handling. *The Telegraph*. At: http://www.telegraph.co.uk/finance/personalfinance/bank-accounts/8252180/NatWest-and-RBS-fined-2.8m-for-poor-complaint-handling.html.

Eversheds Sutherland. (2016, January 28). Remuneration and the EBA final guidelines on sound remuneration policies. *Eversheds Sutherland International. Online Report*. Available at: http://www.eversheds-sutherland.com/global/en/what/articles/index.page?ArticleID=en/Employment_and_labour_law/BA_Final_Guidelines_on_sound_remuneration_policies.

Fallon, I. (2015). *Black horse ride: The inside story of Lloyds and the banking crisis*. London: The Robson Press.

Fama, E. (1970). Efficient capital markets: A review of theory and empirical work. *Journal of Finance, 25*(2), 383–417.

Farrell, S. (2015, September 25). Government reduces stake in Lloyds banking group. *The Guardian*. Available at: http://www.theguardian.com/business/2015/sep/25/government-sells-further-stake-lloyds-banking-group-share.

Farrell, S. (2016, February 3). The price of PPI: What the banks have set aside to pay for mis-selling. *The Guardian*. Available at: https://www.theguardian.com/money/2014/feb/03/ppi-banks-misselling.

FCA [Financial Conduct Authority]. (2012). 'Barclays fined £59.5 million for significant failings in relation to LIBOR and EURIBOR' FCA Press Release First published: 27/06/2012 Last updated: 22/03/2013. Available at: https://www.fca.org.uk/news/press-releases/barclays-fined-%C2%A3595-million-significant-failings-relation-libor-and-euribor.

FCA [Financial Conduct Authority]. (2013a, July 24). *Royal bank of Scotland fined £5.6m for failing to properly report over a third of transactions*. Press Release. Online At: https://www.fca.org.uk/news/rbs-fined.

FCA [Financial Conduct Authority]. (2013b, December 11). *FCA fines Lloyds banking group firms a total of £28,038,800 for serious sales incentive failings*. FCA News/Press Release. Available at: http://www.fca.org.uk/news/press-releases/fca-fines-lloyds-banking-group-firms-for-serious-sales-incentive-fai lings.

FCA [Financial Conduct Authority]. (2014a, November 20). *FCA fines RBS, natwest and ulster bank ltd £42 million for IT failures*. Press Release. Online At: http://www.fca.org.uk/news/fca-fines-rbs-natwest-and-ulster-bank-ltd-42m-for-it-failures.

FCA [Financial Conduct Authority]. (2014b, August 27). *FCA fines RBS and natwest for failures in mortgage advice process*. Press Release. Online At: https://fca.org.uk/news/fca-fines-rbs-and-natwest-for-failures-in-mortgage-advice-process.

FCA [Financial Conduct Authority]. (2014c, July 28). *Lloyds banking group fined £105m for serious LIBOR and other benchmark failings*. Available at: https://www.fca.org.uk/news/lloyds-banking-group-fined-105m-libor-benchmark-failings.

FCA [Financial Conduct Authority]. (2014d, November 11). *Final notice from FCA to HSBC bank plc, reference number: 114216*. FCA Online. Available at: https://www.fca.org.uk/publication/final-notices/final-notice-hsbc.pdf.

FCA [Financial Conduct Authority]. (2015, June 15). *Recovery and resolution directive*. Available at: https://www.fca.org.uk/firms/markets/international markets/eu/rrd.

FCA [Financial Conduct Authority]. (2016). *Financial conduct authority: Ring-fencing*. First published: 14 September 2016; Last updated: 1 June 2020. Available at: https://www.fca.org.uk/consumers/ring-fencing.

FCA [Financial Conduct Authority]. (2017). *FCA handbook: SYSC 19C.3 remuneration principles*. Online. Available at: https://www.handbook.fca.org.uk/handbook/SYSC/19C/3.html?date=2017-09-01.

Ferrarini, G., & Ungureanu, M. C. (2011, December 15). Bankers' pay after the 2008 crisis: Regulatory reforms in the US and the EU. *Journal of Banking Law and Banking, 6*(11), 1–13. Available at: http://www.academia.edu/1630936/Bankers_Pay_after_the_2008_Crisis_Regulatory_Reforms_in_the_US_and_the_EU.

Financial Policy Committee. (2014). *The financial policy committee's powers to supplement capital requirements: A policy statement*. London: Bank of England. Available at: http://www.bankofengland.co.uk/financialstability/Documents/fpc/policystatement140113.pdf.

Fleetwood, S. (2008). Institutions and social structures. *Journal for the Theory of Social Behaviour, 38*(3).

FPC [Financial Policy Committee]. (2017). *Bank of England financial stability report executive summary June 2017*. Available at: http://www.bankofengland.co.uk/publications/Documents/fsr/2017/fsrjun17sum.pdf.

FINMA [Financial Market Supervisory Authority]. (2017, February 2). FINMA sanctions coutts for 1MDB breaches. *FINMA*. Available at: https://www.finma.ch/en/news/2017/02/20170202-mm-coutts/.

Fiol, C. M., & Lyles, M. A. (1985). Organizational learning. *Academy of Management Review, 10*(2), 803–813.

Fiske, S. T., & Taylor, S. E. (1991). *Social cognition*. New York: McGraw-Hill.

Forbes.com. (2015, March 19). *RBS Close to a deal with UBP for Sale of coutts international*. Forbes. Available at: http://www.forbes.com/sites/greatspeculations/2015/03/19/rbs-close-to-a-deal-with-ubp-for-sale-of-coutts-international/#4eb822d7104c.

Ford, J. (2018, September 26). Lloyds accused of ignoring police whistleblower request in HBOS probe. *Financial Times*. Available at: https://www.ft.com/content/28ae208a-c0d8-11e8-8d55-54197280d3f7.

Ford, J. (2019a, December 10). Business victims of HBOS fraud in line for bigger payout. *Financial Times*. Available at: https://www.ft.com/content/918d9c1a-1b64-11ea-97df-cc63de1d73f4.

Ford, J. (2019b, December 20). HBOS fraud victims to receive £35,000 special payout. *Financial Times*. Available at: https://www.ft.com/content/c1061c40-2273-11ea-92da-f0c92e957a96.

Ford, J., & Binham, C. (2019, May 3). Lloyds bows to pressure from watchdog by reviewing HBOS redress. *Financial Times*. Available at: https://www.ft.com/content/6768de62-6dbe-11e9-80c7-60ee53e6681d.

Forstater, M. (2007). *Little book of big ideas economic*. London: A&C Black Publishers.

Fraser, I. (2014). *Shredded: Inside RBS the bank that broke Britain*. Birlinn: Edinburgh.

Friedman, Jeffrey. (2009). A crisis of politics, not economics: Complexity, ignorance and policy failure. *Critical Review, 21*(2–3), 127–183.

Frogman, J. (1997). Socially irresponsible and illegal behavior and shareholder wealth: A metaanalysis of event studies. *Sage, 36*(3), 221–249.

FSA [Financial Services Authority]. (2011). *FSA fines RBS and natwest £2.8m for poor complaint handling*. Press Release. Online At: http://www.fsa.gov.uk/pages/Library/Communication/PR/2011/003.shtml.

FSA [Financial Services Authority]. (2012). *Coutts fined £8.75 million for anti-money laundering control failings*. Press Release. http://www.fsa.gov.uk/library/communication/pr/2012/032.shtml.

FSB [Financial Stability Board]. (2016, November 21). *2016 List of Global Systemically Important Banks (G-SIBs)* [online]. Available at: https://www.fsb.org/wp-content/uploads/2016-list-of-global-systemically-important-banks-G-SIBs.pdf.

FSB [Financial Stability Board]. (2017, November 21). *2017 List of Global Systemically Important Banks (G-SIBs)* [online]. Available at: https://www.fsb.org/wp-content/uploads/P211117-1.pdf.

Gale, A. (2016, March 1). What is Jes Staley's strategy for Barclays? *Management Today*. Available at: http://www.managementtoday.co.uk/jes-staleys-strategy-barclays/article/1380329.

Gamble, A. (2014). *Crisis without end? The unravelling of western prosperity*. London: Palgrave Macmillan.

Garside, J., Leigh, D., Ball, J., & Pegg, D. (2015, February 9). Ex-HSBC boss Stephen green: The ethical banker with questions to answer. *The Guardian*. http://www.theguardian.com/business/2015/feb/09/ex-hsbc-boss-stephen-green-the-ethical-banker-with-questions-to-answer.

Geithner, T. (2017). Are we safe yet: How to manage financial crises? *Foreign Affairs, 96*(1), 54–72.

Giddens, A. (1988). *Central problems in social theory*. London: Macmillan.

Giddens, A. (1995). *The constitution of society*. Cambridge, UK: Polity.

Global Witness. (2009, March). *Undue diligence how banks do business with corrupt regimes*. A report by global witness. Available at: https://www.globalwitness.org/documents/14621/undue_diligence_lowres.pdf.

Global Witness. (2011, June 22). Barclays account used by dictator's son to buy €18m of artwork with suspect funds. *Global Witness*. Available at: https://www.globalwitness.org/en-gb/archive/barclays-account-used-dictators-son-buy-18m-artwork-suspect-funds/.

Goff, S. (2014, May 23). HSBC shareholders revolt on pay. *The Financial Times*. http://www.ft.com/cms/s/0/a05f4f0a-e27a-11e3-89fd-00144feabdc0.html#axzz3aJKWzcCW.

Goff, S., & Scannell, K. (2014, July 28). 'Reprehensible' Lloyds under fire from carney. *The Financial Times*. Available at: https://www.ft.com/content/f0d55584-1640-11e4-93ec-00144feabdc0.

Goodway, N. (2015, March 21). Lloyds sells 50% of TSB to sabadell for £1.7bn. *Independent*. Available at: http://www.independent.co.uk/news/business/news/lloyds-sells-50-of-tsb-to-sabadell-for-17bn-10124603.html.

Gov.uk. (2012). Government action halts banking tax avoidance schemes. *Press release from: HM treasury and the Rt Hon David Gauke MP*. Available at: https://www.gov.uk/government/news/government-action-halts-banking-tax-avoidance-schemes.

Gowan, P. (2009). Crisis in the heartland. *New Left Review, 55*, 5–30.

Gracie, A. (2014, June 10). *Managing cyber risk—The Global banking perspective*. Speech given at British Bankers' Association Cyber Conference, London. Available at: http://www.bankofengland.co.uk/publications/Documents/speeches/2014/speech735.pdf.

Grandhi, K. (2016, May 3). Barclays France alleged to be involved in money laundering and mis-selling. *International Business Times*. Available at:http://www.ibtimes.co.uk/barclays-france-alleged-be-involved-money-laundering-mis-selling-1557899.

Gray, A. (2013, December 9). Lloyds sells St. James's place stake for £670m. *The Financial Times*. Available at: http://www.ft.com/cms/s/0/835c1dee-60f1-11e3-916e-00144feabdc0.html#axzz47ItLdg1G.

Green, S. (2010). *Group chairman's statement: 2009: A year of transition*. In HSBC [HSBC Holdings PLC] Annual report and accounts 2009: Strong, steadfast, sustainable. Available at: www.hsbc.com/-/media/hsbc-com/.../financialresults/2009/hsbc2009ara0.pdf, pp. 8–11.

Greenspan, Alan. (2013). *The map and the territory: Risk, human nature, and the future of forecasting*. London: Allen Lane.

Gup, B. (2004). What does too big to fail mean? In B. Gup (Ed.), *Too big to fail: Policies and practices in government bailouts* (pp. 29–49). London: Praeger.

Haldane, A. (2011, October 24). *Control rights (and wrongs)*. Speech to the Wincott Annual Memorial Lecture, Westminster. Available at http://www.bankofengland.co.uk/publications/Documents/speeches/2011/speech525.pdf.

Haldane, A. (2012a, April 14). *Financial arms races, based on a speech to institute for new economic thinking*, Berlin. Available at http://www.bankofengland.co.uk/publications/Documents/speeches/2012/speech565.pdf.

Haldane, A. (2012b, October 25). *On being the right size*. The 2012 Beesley Lectures, Institute of Economic Affairs. Available at http://www.bankofengland.co.uk/publications/Documents/speeches/2012/speech615.pdf.

Haldane, A. (2012c, October 29). *A leaf being turned*. Occupy Economics, Socially Useful Banking, London. Available at http://www.bankofengland.co.uk/publications/Documents/speeches/2012/speech616.pdf.

Haldane, A., & Alessandri, P. (2009, September 25). *Banking on the state*. Paper presented to the Federal Reserve Bank of Chicago Twelfth Annual International Banking Conference on 'The International Financial Crisis: Have the Rules of Finance Changed'. Chicago. Available at http://www.bis.org/review/r091111e.pdf.

Haldane, A., & Madouros, V. (2012, August 31). *The dog and the frisbee*. Speech to the Federal Reserve Bank of Kansas City's 366th Economic Policy Symposium on 'The Changing Policy Landscape'. Jackson Hole, Wyoming. Available at http://www.bis.org/review/r120905a.pdf.

Haldane, A., & May, R. (2011). Systemic risk in banking ecosystems. *Nature, 469*(20), 351–355.

Haldane, A., Brennan, S., & Madouros, V. (2010). What is the contribution of the financial sector: Miracle or mirage? In A. Turner et al. (eds.), *The future of finance: The LSE report* (Chapter 2, pp. 64–105). London: The London School of Economics and Political Science.

Hale, G., & Santos, J. (2013). *Do banks propagate debt market shocks?* Federal reserve bank of San Francisco (Working Paper 2010–08). Available at: http://www.frbsf.org/economic-research/files/wp10-08bk.pdf.

Hall, P. (1993). Policy paradigms, social learning, and the state: The case of economic policymaking in Britain. *Comparative Politics, 25*(3) (April), 275–296.

Hall, P., & Soskice, D. (2001). *Varieties of capitalism: The institutional foundations of comparative advantage*. Oxford: Oxford University Press.

Halversson, E. (2010). *The "silo effect"—Symptoms, causes, cure and prevention*. Offshore Investment February 2010 issue 203. Available at: http://www.offshoreinvestment.com/pages/index.asp?title=issue_203#sthash.lGcyRLgo.dpuf.

Hampton, M. P., & Christensen, J. E. (2002). Offshore pariahs? small island economies, tax havens and the reconfiguration of global finance. *World Development, 30*(9), 1657–1673.

Härle, P., Lüders, E., Pepanides, T., Pfetsch, S., Poppensieker, T., & Stegemann, U. (2010). *Basel III and European banking: Its impact, how banks might respond, and the challenges of implementation*. McKinsey and Co and EMEA Banking.

Hartwig, M. (2007). *Dictionary of critical realism*. London: Routledge (online)

Hastie, R., & Kumar, P. A. (1979). Person memory: Personality traits as orga nizing principles in memory for behaviors. *Journal of Personality and Social Psychology, 37*(1), 25–38.

Hawkes, S., & Armstrong, A. (2013, December 11). Lloyds fined £28m for 'sell or be demoted' incentive plan. *The Telegraph*. Available at: http://www.telegraph.co.uk/finance/newsbysector/banksandfinance/10510228/Lloyds-fined-28m-for-sell-or-be-demoted-incentive-plan.html.

Hay, C. (2006). Globalization in public policy. In M. Rein, M. Moran & R. Goodin (Eds.), *Oxford handbook of public policy*. Oxford: Oxford University Press.

Hay, C. (2013). *The failure of anglo-liberal capitalism*. London: Palgrave Macmillan.

Helleiner, E. (2014). *The status quo crisis: Global financial governance after the 2008 meltdown*. Oxford: Oxford University Press.

Hindmoor, A. (2006). *Rational choice*. London: Palgrave Macmillan.

Hindmoor, A., & McConeell, A. (2013a). Why didn't they see it coming warning signs, acceptable risks and the global financial crisis. Political Studies, *61*(3), 543–560.

Hindmoor, A., & McConeell, A. (2013b). Luck, systematic luck and business power: Lucky all the way down or trying hard to get what it wants without trying?. *Political Studies, 61*(4), 834–849.
HM Treasury. (2015a). *Banking for the 21st century: Driving competition and choice*. https://www.gov.uk/government/uploads/system/uploads/attachment_data/file/416097/Banking_for_the_21st_Century_17.03_19_40_FINAL.pdf.
HM Treasury. (2015b, October). *Senior managers and certification regime: Extension to all FSMA authorised persons*. Available at: https://www.gov.uk/government/uploads/system/uploads/attachment_data/file/468328/SMCR_policy_paper_final_15102015.pdf.
Hodgson, G. (2006). What are institutions. *Journal of Economic Issues, 40*(1), 1–25.
Hosking, P. (2014, September 29). Lloyds sacks staff and claws back bonuses over rate-rigging. *The Times*. Available at: http://www.thetimes.co.uk/tto/business/industries/banking/article4221170.ece.
HSBC [HSBC Holdings PLC]. (2007). *Annual report and accounts 2007*. At: http://www.hsbc.com/investor-relations/financial-and-regulatory-reports#page-3.
HSBC [HSBC Holdings PLC]. (2008). *Annual report and accounts 2008*. At: http://www.hsbc.com/investor-relations/financial-and-regulatory-reports#page-3.
HSBC [HSBC Holdings PLC]. (2009). *Annual report and accounts 2009*. At: www.hsbc.com/-/media/hsbc-com/.../financialresults/2009/hsbc2009ara0.pdf.
HSBC [HSBC Holdings PLC]. (2010). *Annual report and accounts 2010*. At: https://www.hsbc.co.uk/1/PA_esf-ca-app-content/.../annual_results2010_full.pdf.
HSBC [HSBC Holdings PLC]. (2011a). *Annual report and accounts 2011*. At: http://www.hsbc.com/investor-relations/financial-and-regulatory-reports#page-2.
HSBC [HSBC Holdings PLC]. (2011b, May 10). *HSBC 2011 investor day: Group strategy presentation*. Available at: http://www.hsbc.com/investor-relations/events-and-presentations/investor-day-2011.
HSBC [HSBC Holdings PLC]. (2012a, July 16). *HSBC statement on testimony before the United States senate permanent subcommittee on investigations*. HSBC Media Release. Available at: http://www.hsbc.com/news-and-insight/media-resources/media-releases/2012/statement-psi-hearing.
HSBC [HSBC Holdings PLC]. (2012b). *Annual report and accounts 2012*. http://www.hsbc.com/investor-relations/financial-and-regulatory-reports#page-2.

HSBC [HSBC Holdings PLC]. (2013a). *Annual report and accounts 2013*. http://www.hsbc.com/investor-relations/financial-and-regulatory-reports#page-1.

HSBC [HSBC Holdings PLC]. (2013b, December 10). *HSBC news release: HSBC to sell minority stake in bank of shanghai*. Available at: http://www.hsbc.com/~/media/HSBC-com/InvestorRelationsAssets/StockExchangeAnnouncements/2013/december/sea-131210-hsbc-to-sell-minority-stake-in-bank-of-shanghai.

HSBC [HSBC Holdings PLC]. (2014). *Annual report and accounts 2014*. At: http://www.hsbc.com/investor-relations/financial-and-regulatory-reports#page-1.

HSBC [HSBC Holdings PLC]. (2015a). *Annual report and accounts 2015: Value of the network connecting customers to opportunities*. Available at: https://www.hsbc.com/-/files/hsbc/investors/investing-in-hsbc/all-reporting/subsidiaries/2015/annual-results/hsbc-bank-plc/hsbc-bank-plc-annual-report-and-accounts-2015.pdf.

HSBC [HSBC Holdings PLC]. (2015b). *HSBC's swiss private bank progress update—January 2015*. Press Release. Available at: http://www.hsbcprivatebank.com/~/media/pdf/update-on-the-swiss-private-bank.

HSBC [HSBC Holdings PLC]. (2016). *Annual report and accounts 2016: connecting customers to opportunities*. Available at: https://www.hsbc.com/-/files/hsbc/investors/investing-in-hsbc/all-reporting/group/2016/annual-results/hsbc-holdings-plc/170221-annual-report-and-accounts-2016.pdf.

HSBC [HSBC Holdings PLC]. (2017a, December 11). *HSBC holdings plc expiration of 2012 deferred prosecution agreement*. Available online at: https://www.hsbc.com/media/media-releases/2017/hsbc-holdings-plc-expiration-of-2012-deferred-prosecution-agreement.

HSBC [HSBC Holdings PLC]. (2017b). *Annual reports and accounts 2017: Connecting customers to opportunities*. Available at: https://www.hsbc.com/-/files/hsbc/investors/hsbc-results/2017/annual/hsbc-holdings-plc/180220-annual-report-and-accounts-2017.pdf.

HSBC [HSBC Holdings PLC]. (2018). *Annual report and accounts 2018: Connecting customers to opportunities*. Available at: https://www.hsbc.com/-/files/hsbc/investors/hsbc-results/2018/annual/hsbc-holdings-plc/190219-annual-report-and-accounts-2018.pdf.

HSBC [Online]. *About HSBC: Leadership: Kathleen casey profile*. Available at: http://www.hsbc.com/about-hsbc/leadership/kathleen-casey.

HSBC.com. [HSBC Holdings PLC—Online]. *HSBC home—Our approach—Corporate governance—Board committees*. Available at: http://www.hsbc.com/investor-relations/governance/board-committees.

Huber, G. P. (1991). Organisational learning: The contributing process and the literature. *Organization Science, 2*(2), 88–115.

Ianfraser.org. (2016, April 29). *RBS boss ross mcewan answers critics live on LBC.* Available at: http://www.ianfraser.org/rbs-boss-ross-mcewan-answers-critics-live-on-lbc/.

IIF Working Group on Cumulative Impact. (2010). *Interim report on the cumulative impact on the global economy of proposed changes in the banking regulatory framework*, (IIF).

Immelmann, K. (1975). Ecological significance of Imprinting and early learning. *Annual Review of Ecology & Systematics* (6), 15–37.

Inman. P. (2009, December 2). RBS warns cap on bonuses will lead to exodus of top staff. *The Guardian.* http://www.theguardian.com/business/2009/dec/02/rbs-warns-over-bonus-cap.

Insley. J. (2011, January 11). NatWest and RBS fined £2.8m over complaint handling failures. *The Guardian.* At: http://www.theguardian.com/money/2011/jan/11/natwest-rbs-fined-complaint-handling-failures.

International Monetary Fund [IMF]. (2015, October). *Vulnerabilities, legacies, and policy challenges risks rotating to emerging markets.* International Monetary Fund Global Financial Stability Report. Available at: http://www.imf.org/external/pubs/ft/gfsr/2015/02/index.htm.

International Monetary Fund [IMF]. (2017, April). *Global financial stability report: Getting the policy mix right.* Available at: https://www.imf.org/en/Publications/GFSR/Issues/2017/03/30/global-financial-stability-report-april-2017.

Jaeger. J. (2013, February 4). *HSBC creates financial system vulnerabilities committee, appoints new director.* At: https://www.complianceweek.com/blogs/scuttlebutt/hsbc-creates-financial-system-vulnerabilities-committee-appoints-new-director#.VZ_M67fbKM8.

Jakab, Z., & Kumhof, M. (2015, May). Bank of England (Working Paper No. 529). *Banks are not intermediaries of loanable funds—And why this matters.* Available at: http://www.bankofengland.co.uk/research/Documents/workingpapers/2015/wp529.pdf.

James, S., & Quaglia, L. (2020). *The UK & multi-level financial regulation: From post-crisis reform to Brexit.* Oxford: Oxford University Press.

Jenkins, A. (2013, December 2). *Antony jenkins group chief Executive Barclays letter to Richard Miller executive director ActionAid UK.* Available at: http://www.actionaid.org/sites/files/actionaid/barclays_response.pdf.

Jenkins, A. (2015). Barclays Press Release 20 May 2015: *Barclays announces foreign exchange and ISDAfix settlements.* Statement by Barclays Group Chief Executive. Barclays Media Relations Press Release. Available at: http://www.newsroom.barclays.co.uk/r/3171/barclays_announces_foreign_exchange_and_isdafix_settlements_.

Jenkins, P. (2010, September 24). Geoghegan set to quit HSBC by year-end. *Financial Times*. http://www.ft.com/cms/s/0/ed47fc0c-c73c-11df-aeb1-00144feab49a.html#axzz3fUZNGgJ5.

Jenkins, P. (2015, February 13). Lord green always wrestled with god and mammon. *The Financial Times*. http://www.ft.com/cms/s/0/1866aace-b3a0-11e4-a6c1-00144feab7de.html#axzz3dzIIoEGW.

Jenkins, P. (2018, June 1). UKFI goes out without any RBS bang. *Financial Times*. Available at: https://www.ft.com/content/f1f03cb6-64ef-11e8-a39d-4df188287fff.

Jitendra, A. K., Griffin, C. C., Haria, P., Leh, J., Adams, A., & Kaduvettoor, A. (2007). A comparison of single and multiple strategy instruction on third-grade students' mathematical problem solving. *Journal of Educational Psychology, 99*(1), 115–127.

Johal, S., Moran, M., & Williams, K. (2014). Power, politics and the city of london after the great financial crisis. *Government and Opposition, 49*(3), 400–425.

Jones, B. D. (1999). Bounded rationality. *Annual Review of Political Science, 2*, 297–321.

Jones, B. D., & Baumgartner, F. R. (1993). *Agendas and instability in American politics*. Chicago: University of Chicago Press.

Jones, B. D., & Baumgartner, F. R. (2005). *The Politics of attention: How government prioritizes problems*. Chicago: University of Chicago Press.

Jones, B. D., & Baumgartner, F. R. (2009). *Agendas and instability in American politics* (2nd ed.). Chicago: Chicago University Press.

Justice.gov. (2012). 'Statement of facts' case 1:12-cr-00763-ILG Document 3-3 Filed 12/11/12. http://www.justice.gov/sites/default/files/opa/legacy/2012/12/11/dpa-attachment-a.pdf.

Kahn, P., Qualter, A., & Young, R. (2012). Structure and agency in learning: A critical realist theory of the development of capacity to reflect on academic practice. *Higher Education Research & Development, 31*(6) (December), 859–871.

Kar-Gupta, S. (2012, March 26). *Coutts fined 8.75 million pounds for money laundering failures*. Reuters U.K. Online At: http://uk.reuters.com/article/2012/03/26/uk-coutts-fine-idUKBRE82P0BL20120326.

Karpoff, J. M. (2012). Does reputation work to discipline corporate misconduct? In Timothy Pollock & Michael Barnett (Eds.), *The oxford handbook of corporate reputation*. Oxford: Oxford University Press.

Kashyap, A. (2010, February 27). *Lessons from the financial crisis for risk management*. Paper Prepared for the Financial Crisis Inquiry Commission. Available at: http://faculty.chicagobooth.edu/anil.kashyap/research/papers/lesson_for_fcic.pdf.

Kay, J. (2016). *Other people's money*. London: Profile Books.

Kerr, P. (2010). Espoused theories and theories-in-use of information literacy: A model for reflection and evaluation. *Proceedings of the American Society for Information Science and Technology, 46*(1), 1–7.

Keohane, D., & Arnold, M. (2017, November 14). HSBC agrees to pay €300m to settle probe into tax evasion. *Financial Times*. Available at: https://www.ft.com/content/7d228060-c959-11e7-ab18-7a9fb7d6163e.

Kindleberger, C. P., & Aliber, R. Z. (2011). *Manias, panics, and crashes, a history of financial crises*. Basingstoke: Palgrave Macmillan.

King, A. (2000). The accidental derogation of the lay actor a critique of giddens's concept of structure. *Philosophy of the Social Sciences, 30*(3), 362–383.

King, A. (2004). *The structure of social theory*. London: Routledge.

King, A. (2005). Structure and agency. In A. Harrington (Ed.), *Modern social theory* (pp. 215–232). Oxford. Oxford University Press.

King, M. (2009, March 17). *Finance—A return from risk*. Speech to the Worshipful Company of International Bankers. London. Available at http://www.bis.org/review/r090319a.pdf.

King, M. (2016). *The end of alchemy: Money banking and the future of the global economy*. London: Little Brown.

Knight, J., & Dunkley, J. (2014, February 27). RBS sells direct line stake on eve of revealing losses. *The Independent*. http://www.independent.co.uk/news/business/news/rbs-sells-direct-line-stake-on-eve-of-revealing-losses-9155966.html.

Kollewe, J. (2010, Wednesday 3 November). Profile: New Lloyds chief antónio horta-osório. *The Guardian*. http://www.theguardian.com/business/2010/nov/03/profile-lloyds-chief-antonio-horta-osorio.

Kollewe, J. (2014, February 26). Royal bank of scotland plans to sell remaining 28% stake in direct line. *The Guardian*. Available at: https://www.theguardian.com/business/2014/feb/26/royal-bank-scotland-sell-stake-direct-line.

Kollewe, J., Treanor, J., & Hickey, S. (2014, November 12). Banks pay out £166bn over six years: A history of banking misdeeds and fines. *The Guardian*.http://www.theguardian.com/business/2014/nov/12/banks-fined-200bn-six-years-history-banking-penalties-libor-forex.

Krippner, G. (2011). *Capitalizing on crisis: The political origins of the rise of finance*. Cambridge, MA: Harvard University Press.

Krugman, P. (2009). *The return of depression economics and the depression of 2008*. New York. W.W: Norton.

Lall, R. (2012). From failure to failure: The politics of international banking regulation. *Review of International Political Economy, 19*(4), 609–638.

Lambert, R. (2011, December 12). Unchecked excess: The lessons of RBS failure. *Financial Times*. Available at: http://www.ft.com/cms/s/0/c91ca412-24b6-11e1-ac4b-00144feabdc0.html#axzz40R7UIlfX.

Lawrence, F. (2009, March 20). Macho poker bets, summary sackings and an 'electric chair'. *The Guardian*. Available at: https://www.theguardian.com/business/2009/mar/20/barclays-guardian-tax-claim.

LBC [Leading Britain's Conversation]. (2015, November 24). RBS is a 'changed' business say ross mcewan LBC interview. Available at: https://www.youtube.com/watch?v=w5AgQQF76HA.

Levitt, B., & March, J. G. (1988). Organisational learning. *Annual Review of Sociology, 14*, 319–340.

Lewin, J. (2016, March 15). RBS slashing 448 investment banking jobs. *Financial Times*. Available at: https://www.ft.com/content/86aaa6da-d176-3b8e-95d6-322067f0a66d.

Lewis, M. (2011). *The big short*. London: Penguin.

Lloyds [Lloyds Banking Group]. (2008). *Annual report and accounts 'creating the UK's best financial services provider'*. Available at: http://www.lloydsbankinggroup.com/globalassets/documents/investors/2009/2009_lbg_ra.pdf.

Lloyds [Lloyds Banking Group]. (2009). *Annual report and accounts 2009 'creating the UK's best financial services provider'*. Available at: http://www.lloydsbankinggroup.com/globalassets/documents/investors/2009/2009_lbg_ra.pdf.

Lloyds [Lloyds Banking Group]. (2010a). *Annual report and accounts 2010 'creating the UK's best financial services provider'*. Available at: http://www.lloydsbankinggroup.com/globalassets/documents/investors/2010/2010_lbg_ra.pdf.

Lloyds [Lloyds Banking Group]. (2010b). *Lloyds banking group press release, 3 November 2010: Appointment of new chief executive officer*. Available at: http://www.lloydsbankinggroup.com/globalassets/documents/investors/2010/2010nov3_lbg_new_ceo.pdf.

Lloyds [Lloyds Banking Group]. (2011a, June 30). *Lloyds banking group plc outcome of strategic review*. Available at: http://www.lloydsbankinggroup.com/globalassets/documents/investors/2011/2011jun30_lbg_strategic_review_transcript.pdf.

Lloyds [Lloyds Banking Group]. (2011b, October 4). *Presentation given by António Horta-Osório group chief executive at bank of America Merrill Lynch conference*, 'The Financial Crisis: Key Questions, Reality and Responses'. London. Available at: http://www.lloydsbankinggroup.com/globalassets/documents/investors/2011/2011oct4_lbg_boamlconf_london.pdf.

Lloyds [Lloyds Banking Group]. (2011c). *Annual report and accounts 2011 'becoming the best bank for customers'*. Available at: http://www.lloydsbankinggroup.com/globalassets/documents/investors/2011/2011_lbg_randa.pdf.

Lloyds [Lloyds Banking Group]. (2012). *Annual report and accounts 'becoming the best bank for customers'*. Available at: http://www.lloydsbankinggroup.

com/globalassets/documents/investors/2012/2012_lbg_randa_interactive.pdf.

Lloyds [Lloyds Banking Group]. (2013). *Annual report and accounts 'becoming the best bank for customers'*. Available at: http://www.lloydsbankinggroup.com/globalassets/documents/investors/2014/2013_lbg_interactive_annual_report.pdf.

Lloyds [Lloyds Banking Group]. (2014a). *Annual report and accounts 2014: Becoming the best bank for customers*. Available at: http://www.lloydsbankinggroup.com/globalassets/documents/investors/2014/2014_lbg_annual_report.pdf.

Lloyds [Lloyds Banking Group]. (2014b, July 28). *Settlements reached on legacy LIBOR and BBA Repo rate issues*. Press Release. Available at: http://www.lloydsbankinggroup.com/Media/Press-Releases/2014/lloyds-banking-group/settlements-reached-on-legacy-libor-and-bba-repo-rate-issues/.

Lloyds [Lloyds Banking Group]. (2015a). *Annual report and accounts 2015 'becoming the best bank for customers'*. Available at: http://www.lloydsbankinggroup.com/globalassets/documents/investors/2015/2015_lbg_annual_report_v3.pdf.

Lloyds [Lloyds Banking Group]. (2015b, June 30). *Sale of TSB banking group PLC*. Available at: http://www.lloydsbankinggroup.com/globalassets/documents/investors/2015/2015jun30_tsb_sale.pdf.

Lloyds [Lloyds Banking Group]. (2016). *Annual report and accounts 2016, helping Britain prosper*. Available at: https://www.lloydsbankinggroup.com/globalassets/documents/investors/2016/2016_lbg_annual_report_v2.pdf.

Lloyds [Lloyds Banking Group]. (2017a). *Annual report and accounts 2017, helping Britain prosper*. Available at: http://www.annualreports.co.uk/HostedData/AnnualReportArchive/L/LSE_LLOY_2017.pdf.

Lloyds [Lloyds Banking Group]. (2017b, May 17). *2017 Press releases: Lloyds banking group returns to full private ownership*. Lloyds Press Release. Available at: https://www.lloydsbankinggroup.com/Media/Press-Releases/press-releases-2017/lloyds-banking-group/lloyds-banking-group-returns-to-full-private-ownership/.

Lloyds [Lloyds Banking Group]. (2018). *Annual report and accounts 2018, helping Britain prosper*. Available at: https://www.lloydsbankinggroup.com/globalassets/documents/investors/2018/2018_lbg_annual_report_v2.pdf.

Lloyds [Lloyds Banking Group]. (2019a, October 31). *2019 press releases: Juan colombas to retire during Q3 2020*. Lloyds Press Release. Available at: https://www.lloydsbankinggroup.com/globalassets/documents/investors/2019/2019oct31_lbg_board_change.pdf.

Lloyds [Lloyds Banking Group]. (2019b, December 10). *2019 Press releases: Lloyds banking group responds to the outcome of assurance review*. Lloyds Press Release. Available at: https://www.lloydsbankinggroup.com/Media/Press-

Releases/2019-press-releases/lloyds-banking-group/lloyds-banking-group-responds-to-the-outcome-of-assurance-review/.

Lloydsbank.com. (2014). *Lloyds bank Switzerland—Post-closure contact details April 2014 update*. LloydsBankingGroup.com. Available at: https://international.lloydsbank.com/LloydsBankSwitzerland/.

Lloydsbankinggroup.com [Lloyds Banking Group]. (2013, May 29). *LLOYDS banking group announces the sale of its international private banking operations*. Press Release Full Transcript. Available at: http://www.lloydsbankinggroup.com/globalassets/documents/media/press-releases/lloyds-banking-group/2013/2905_pb_sale.pdf.

LloydsBankingGroup.com. (2016). *Our history LloydsBankingGroup.com*. Available at: http://www.lloydsbankinggroup.com/our-group/our-heritage/our-history/.

Lopez, J., & Scott, J. (2000). *Social structure*. Buckingham: Open University Press.

Lumsden, G. (2011, May 25). *Watchdog slams bank of Scotland with £3.5m fine*. CityWire. Available online: http://citywire.co.uk/money/watchdog-slams-bank-of-scotland-with-3-5m-fine/a494775.

Lucas, R. (1980). Equilibrium in a pure currency economy. *Economic Inquiry, 18*(2), 203–220.

Lysandroua, P., & Nesvetailova. A. (2014). The role of shadow banking entities in the financial crisis: A disaggregated view. *Review of International Political Economy, 22*(2), 1–23.

Macartney, H., & Calcagno, P. (2019). All bark and no bite: The political economy of bank fines in Anglo-America. *Review of International Political Economy, 26*(4), 630–665.

Macaskill, A., & Choudhury, A. (2010, September 24). *Gulliver's promotion at HSBC marks ascent of investment bankers*. Bloomberg.com. http://www.bloomberg.com/news/articles/2010-09-24/gulliver-s-promotion-at-hsbc-signals-ascent-of-investment-bankers-in-u-k-.

Macaskill, A., & White, L. (2017, May 11). RBS defends directors' bonuses in response to criticism. *Reuters*. Available at: https://www.reuters.com/article/us-rbs-agm/rbs-defends-directors-bonuses-in-response-to-criticism-idUSKBN1871RP.

MAG (FSB/Basel Committee Macroeconomic Assessment Group). (2010). *Assessing the macroeconomic impact of the transition to stronger capital and liquidity requirements*. Basel: Bank of International Settlements.

Makortoff, K. (2020, July 15). Claim amanda staveley in charge of Abu Dhabi Barclays deal 'a fantasy', court told. *The Guardian*. Available at: https://www.theguardian.com/business/2020/jul/15/claim-amanda-staveley-in-charge-of-abu-dhabi-barclays-deal-a-fantasy-court-told.

Makortoff, K., & Julia Kollewe, J. (2019, September 9). PPI claims: Lloyds and Barclays face billions of pounds in extra charges. *The Guardian*. Available at: https://www.theguardian.com/business/2019/sep/09/lloyds-ppi-claims.

Margin Call. (2011). *Before the door pictures, benaroya pictures, and washington square films*. New York, NY.

Marquis, C., & Tilcsik, A. (2013, January 9). *Imprinting: Toward a multilevel theory*. Harvard Business School (Working Paper. No. 13-061).

Martin, I. (2014). *Making it happened: Fred goodwin and the men who blew up the British economy*. London: Simon & Schuster.

Marton, F. (1975). On non-verbatim learning. I. Level of processing and level of outcome. *Scandinavian Journal of Psychology, 16*(1) (September), 273–279.

Marton, F., & Saljo, R. (1976). On qualitative differences in learning. I. outcome and process. *British Journal of Educational Psychology, 46*, 4–11.

Matthew, J. (2015, March 27). RBS confirms sale of coutts international to Swiss Bank UBP. *International Business Times*. Available at: http://www.ibtimes.co.uk/rbs-confirms-sale-coutts-international-swiss-bank-ubp-1493780.

May, P. J. (1992). Policy learning and failure. *Journal of Public Policy, 12*(4), 331–354.

Mayer, M. (1999, Thursday 20, May). *The dangers of derivatives*. The Brookings Institute. Available at: https://www.brookings.edu/opinions/the-dangers-of-derivatives/.

Mayer, R. E. (1999). *The promise of educational psychology: Vol. 1. learning in the content areas*. Upper Saddle River, NJ: Merrill Prentice Hall.

Mazur, R. (2013, January 2). *How to halt the terrorist money train*. NYTimes.com. http://www.nytimes.com/2013/01/03/opinion/how-bankers-help-drug-traffickers-and-terrorists.html?_r=4.

McBride, J. Alessi, C., & Sergie, M. (2015, May 21). *Understanding the libor scandal*. CFR.org. Available at: http://www.cfr.org/united-kingdom/understanding-libor-scandal/p28729.

McDonald, O. (2019). *Holding bankers to account: A decade of market manipulation, regulatory failure and regulatory reforms*. Manchester: Manchester University Press.

McEwan, R. (2014, April 17). RBS responds to clifford chance report into allegation of systematic fraud. *RBS*. Available at: http://www.rbs.com/news/2014/04/clifford-chance-report-into-allegations-of-systematic-fraud.html.

McEwan, R. (2015a, October 30). RBS news 2015: RBS completes sale of citizens financial group inc. Stake. *RBS*. Available at: http://www.rbs.com/news/2015/october/rbs-completes-sale-of-Citizens-Financial-Group.html.

McEwan, R. (2015b, May 20). Royal bank of Scotland plc reaches foreign exchange settlements. *RBS*. Available at: http://www.rbs.com/news/2015/may/rbs-plc-reaches-foreign-exchange-settlements.html.

McEwan, R. (2018, August 14). The royal bank of Scotland group plc—Declaration of interim dividend. *RBS News and Opinion*. Available at: https://www.rbs.com/rbs/news/2018/08/the-royal-bank-of-scotland-group-plc-declaration-of-interim-div.html.

McLannahan, B. (2015, October 30). Citizens financial breaks free of royal bank of Scotland shackles. *The Financial Times*. Available at: http://www.ft.com/cms/s/0/7be28b06-7f18-11e5-93c6-bba4b4b36134.html#axzz41C1UVFL5.

McLannahan, B. (2016, July 12). Osborne intervened in US HSBC money-laundering probe, report says. *Financial Times*. Available at: https://www.ft.com/content/2be49f84-47c9-11e6-b387-64ab0a67014c.

Méaulle, M. (2011). *The basel III agreement: A critical survey*. Brussels: Foundation for European Progressive Studies.

Medland, D. (2013, June 5). Whistleblowing almost killed me. *Financial Times*. Available at: http://www.ft.com/cms/s/0/2dd0f0de-ab70-11e2-8c63-00144feabdc0.html?siteedition=uk#axzz35SZlyUbZ.

Megaw, N. (2017, November 21). HSBC fined record $51m by Hong Kong authorities over lehman-linked products. *Financial Times*. Available at: https://www.ft.com/content/48dd91ce-0efd-37e7-8747-893f3c028d43.

Megaw, N. (2018a, August 15). US investigation highlights extent of wrong-doing at RBS. *Financial Times*. Available at: https://www.ft.com/content/614f9b4c-a07d-11e8-85da-eeb7a9ce36e4.

Megaw, N. (2018b, June 5). UK government takes £2.1bn loss with RBS stake sale. *Financial Times*. Available at: https://www.ft.com/content/5d8eab1e-6889-11e8-b6eb-4acfcfb08c11.

Megaw, N. (2019a, September 4). RBS to take hit of up to £900m from late PPI claims. *Financial Times*. Available at: https://www.ft.com/content/0c8d4e84-cede-11e9-99a4-b5ded7a7fe3f.

Megaw, N. (2019b, September 20). UK lender RBS appoints alison rose as chief executive. *Financial Times*. Available at: https://www.ft.com/content/26229e04-db6c-11e9-8f9b-77216ebe1f17.

Menon, J. (2010, September 25). *HSBC replaces three most senior executives as green steps down*. Bloomberg.com. http://www.bloomberg.com/news/articles/2010-09-23/hsbc-chief-geoghegan-said-to-step-down-from-bank-be-replaced-by-gulliver.

Meyer, J., & Rowan, B. (1977). Institutionalized organizations: Formal structure as myth and ceremony. *American Journal of Sociology, 83*(2), 340–363.

Minsky, M. (1975). A framework for representing knowledge. In P. Winston (Ed.), *The psychology of computer vision*. New York: McGraw-Hill.

Mishkin, F. S. (2004). *The economics of money, banking, and finance* (7th ed.). Pearson: Addison-Wesley.

Moore, J., & Goodway, N. (2015, July 9). Antony jenkins fired: Investors cheer Barclays' shock move to get rid of chief executive. *Independent*. Available at: http://www.independent.co.uk/news/business/news/antony-jenkins-fired-investors-cheer-barclays-shock-move-to-get-rid-of-chief-executive-10376705.html.

Moore, P. (2015). *Crash bank wallop: The memoirs of the HBOS whistle-blower*. London: New Wilberforce.

Moshinsky, B. (2016a, April 27). Barclays is selling Off 74 French branches. *Business Insider UK*. Available at: http://uk.businessinsider.com/barclays-is-selling-off-74-french-branches-2016-4.

Moshinsky, B. (2016b, March 1). Barclays internal memo: Here's CEO Jes Staley's message to staff. *Business Insider UK*. Available at: http://uk.businessinsider.com/barclays-internal-memo-heres-ceo-jes-staleys-message-to-staff-2016-3.

Mugge, D. (2011). From pragmatism to dogmatism: European Union governance, policy paradigms and financial meltdown. *New Political Economy, 16*(2), 185–206.

National Audit Office. (2010). *Maintaining the financial stability of UK banks: Update on the support schemes*. Available online at: https://www.nao.org.uk/wp-content/uploads/2010/12/1011676es.pdf.

National Audit Office. (2018). *The return of Lloyds banking group to private ownership*. Report by the Comptroller and Auditor General Ordered by the House of Commons to be printed on 21 June 2018. Available online at: https://www.nao.org.uk/wp-content/uploads/2018/06/The-return-of-Lloyds-Banking-Group-to-private-ownership.pdf.

Neate, R. (2013, May 24). HSBC suffers investor revolt over pay. *The Guardian*. Available at: https://www.theguardian.com/business/2013/may/24/hsbc-chairman-apologises-scandals.

Neate, R. (2014, August 13). HSBC awards 15 top bankers £7.1m in move to sidestep bonus rules. *The Guardian*. http://www.theguardian.com/business/2014/aug/13/hsbc-executive-pay-allowance-bonuses-banks.

Neate, R. (2016a, January 31). Barclays and credit suisse pay biggest ever fines for dark pool trading. *The Guardian*. Available at: https://www.theguardian.com/business/2016/jan/31/barclays-and-credit-suisse-to-pay-biggest-ever-fines-for-dark-pool-trading.

Neate, R. (2016b, July 11). HSBC escaped US money-laundering charges after osborne's intervention. *The Guardian*. Available at: https://www.theguardian.com/business/2016/jul/11/hsbc-us-money-laundering-george-osborne-report.

Noona, L. (2015, May 28). Banks face pushback over surging compliance and regulatory costs. *Financial Times*. Available at: https://www.ft.com/content/e1323e18-0478-11e5-95ad-00144feabdc0.

Noonan, L., Binham, C., & Giles, C. (2017a, April 10). Barclays blamed BoE over lowering of libor rate, claims BBC. *Financial Times*. Available at: https://www.ft.com/content/f7b6b39a-1dcf-11e7-a454-ab04428977f9.

Noonan, L., Megaw, N., Binham, C., Thompson, J., Dunkley, E., & Jenkins, P. (2017b, April 10). Barclays chief censured for attempt to identify whistle-blower. *Financial Times*. Available at: https://www.ft.com/content/155df86c-1db8-11e7-b7d3-163f5a7f229c.

North, D. (1990). *Institutions, institutional change and economic performance*. New York: Cambridge University Press.

Obermaier, F., & Obermayer, B. (2017). *The Panama papers: Breaking the story of how the rich and powerful hide their money*. London: Oneworld Publications.

Pachico, E. (2012, Friday 14, December). *Sinaloa cartel bought Narco Plane Via HSBC bank*. InsightCrime.org. http://www.insightcrime.org/news-briefs/sinaloa-cartel-bought-narco-plane-via-hsbc-bank.

Palan, R., Murphy, R., & Chavagneux, C. (2009). *Tax havens: How globalization really works*. Cornell: Cornell University Press.

Parker, E., & Gupta, M. (2015, October 18). Too much regulation creates bank brain drain. *Financial Times*. Available at: https://www.ft.com/content/4dfc4190-719f-11e5-9b9e-690fdae72044.

Parker, G., & Jenkins, P. (2013, February 2). RBS to cut bonuses to pay US libor fine. *Financial Times*. Available at https://www.ft.com/content/a0dc728a-6d2f-11e2-889d-00144feab49a.

Parliamentary Commission on Banking Standards (PCBS). (2013). *Changing banking for good. (HC 175-I, First Report of Session 2013–14)—Volume 1: summary, and conclusions and RECOMMENDATIONS*. London: TSO. Available at http://www.parliament.uk/documents/banking-commission/Banking-final-report-volume-i.pdf.

Partington, R. (2015, March 6). Lloyds's Horta-Osorio tops HSBC boss as best-paid bank CEO. *Bloomberg*. Available at: http://www.bloomberg.com/news/articles/2015-03-06/lloyds-s-horta-osorio-tops-hsbc-boss-as-best-paid-u-k-bank-ceo.

Patrick, M. (2015, July 8). Barclays fires chief executive antony jenkins. *The Wall Street Journal*. Available at: http://www.wsj.com/articles/barclays-chief-executive-antony-jenkins-to-leave-bank-1436335989.

Pendry, L. (2008). Social cognition. In M. Hewstone, W. Stroebe & K. Jonas (Eds.), *Introduction to social psychology: A European perspective*. Fourth Edition. Oxford: Blackwell.

Perman, R. (2013). *HUBRIS, How HBOS wrecked the best bank in Britain*. Birlinn Limited: Edinburgh.

Perrin, S. (2014, December 2). Rebuilding lloyds banking group: Interview with Antonio Horta-Osorio. *ICAS*. Available at: http://icas.org.uk/News/Lat

est-News/Rebuilding-Lloyds-Banking-Group-Interview-with-Antonio-Horta-Osorio/.

Pickford, J. (2014, August 29). RBS fine over mortgage advice failures 'might not be last'. *The Financial Times*. http://www.ft.com/cms/s/0/55a1f8b2-2ecb-11e4-a054-00144feabdc0.html#axzz3in2bVkIS.

Pierson, P. (1994). *Dismantling the welfare state? Reagan, thatcher, and the politics of retrenchment*. Cambridge and New York: Cambridge University Press.

Press Association. (2014, August 27). RBS fined £14.5m over mortgage advice. *Press Association Guardian*.http://www.theguardian.com/business/2014/aug/27/rbs-fined-mortgage-advice.

ProactiveInvestors.com. (2011, February 25). *Lloyds returns to profit 2010, income up 3%*. Available at: http://www.proactiveinvestors.co.uk/companies/news/21712/lloyds-returns-to-profit-2010-income-up-3-25897.html.

Prudential Regulation Authority [Bank of England]. *Remuneration code—About*. Available at: http://www.bankofengland.co.uk/pra/Pages/supervision/activities/aboutremuneration.aspx.

Prudential Regulation Authority [Bank of England]. (2017, April). *Supervisory statement|SS2/17 remuneration*. Available at: https://www.bankofengland.co.uk/-/media/boe/files/prudential-regulation/supervisory-statement/2017/ss217.

PwC [Pricewaterhouse Coopers]. (2013, July). *Regulatory brief: EU bonus cap to take effect January 1st 2014*. Available at: http://www.pwc.com/us/en/financial-services/regulatory-services/publications/assets/fs-reg-brief-eu-bonus-cap.pdf.

PwC [Pricewaterhouse Coopers]. (2015, June 26). *First take: A publication of PwC's financial services regulatory practice*. Available at: https://www.pwc.com/us/en/financial-services/regulatory-services/publications/assets/eu-final-bonus-compensation-rule.pdf.

Quinn, J. (2013, September 27). RBS to create new challenger bank under revived 'Williams & Glyn's' brand. *The Telegraph*. http://www.telegraph.co.uk/finance/newsbysector/banksandfinance/10322675/RBS-to-create-new-challenger-bank-under-revived-Williams-and-Glyns-brand.html.

Quinn, J., & Wilson, H. (2011, January 8). RBS chief Stephen Hester awarded a £2.5m bonus. *The Telegraph*.http://www.telegraph.co.uk/finance/newsbysector/banksandfinance/8248374/RBS-chief-Stephen-Hester-awarded-a-2.5m-bonus.html.

Ramskogler, P. (2015). Tracing the origins of the financial crisis. *OECD Journal: Financial Market Trends, 2014/2*. Available at: http://www.oecd-ilibrary.org/finance-and-investment/tracing-the-origins-of-the-financial-crisis_fmt-2014-5js3dqmsl4br?crawler=true.

Rankin, J. (2013, July 24). RBS fined £5.6m by FCA for 'pervasive' reporting failures. *The Guardian*. http://www.theguardian.com/business/2013/jul/24/rbs-fined-fca-share-dealing-reporting-failure.

Rayner, G. (2009, January 20). Banking bailout: The rise and fall of RBS. *The Telegraph*. Available at: http://www.telegraph.co.uk/finance/newsbysector/banksandfinance/4291807/Banking-bailout-The-rise-and-fall-of-RBS.html.

Resnick, P., Zeckhauser, R., Swanson, J., & Lockwood, K. (2006). The value of reputation on eBay: A controlled experiment. *Experimental Economics, 9*(2), 79–101. https://doi.org/10.1007/s10683-006-4309-2.

Royal Bank of Scotland. (1998). *Royal bank of Scotland annual report and accounts 1998*. Available at: https://investors.natwestgroup.com/reports-archive/archived.

RBS.com [Royal Bank of Scotland]. (2015, May 20). Royal bank of Scotland plc reaches foreign exchange settlements. *RBS*. Available at: http://www.rbs.com/news/2015/may/rbs-plc-reaches-foreign-exchange-settlements.html.

RBS [Royal Bank of Scotland]. (2007). *Annual report and accounts 2007*. Available at: http://www.investors.rbs.com/~/media/Files/R/RBS-IR/annual-reports/rbs-group-accounts-2007.pdf.

RBS [Royal Bank of Scotland]. (2008). *Annual report and accounts 2008*. Available at: http://www.investors.rbs.com/~/media/Files/R/RBS-IR/annual-reports/rbs-group-accounts-2008.pdf.

RBS [Royal Bank of Scotland]. (2009a). *Annual report and accounts 2009*. Available at: http://investors.rbs.com/~/media/Files/R/RBS-IR/annual-reports/rbs-group-accounts-2009.pdf.

RBS [Royal Bank of Scotland]. (2009b, November 27). Proposed accession to the asset protection scheme and B Share and dividend access share issues. *RBS Investor Relation*. Available at: https://investors.natwestgroup.com/~/media/Files/R/RBS-IR-V2/corporate-actions/asset-protection-scheme-and-b-share-issuance/asset-protection-scheme-and-b-share-issuance-1.pdf.

RBS [Royal Bank of Scotland]. (2010). *Annual report and accounts 2010*. Available at: http://www.investors.rbs.com/~/media/Files/R/RBS-IR/annual-reports/rbs-group-annual-report-and-accounts-10.pdf.

RBS [Royal Bank of Scotland]. (2011). *Annual report and accounts 2011*. Available at: http://www.investors.rbs.com/~/media/Files/R/RBS-IR/annual-reports/annual-report-2011.pdf.

RBS [Royal Bank of Scotland]. (2012). *Annual report and accounts 2012*. Available at: http://www.investors.rbs.com/~/media/Files/R/RBS-IR/annual-reports/annual-report-2012.pdf.

RBS [Royal Bank of Scotland]. (2013). *Annual report and accounts 2013, serve customers well*. This is our purpose. Available at: http://www.investors.rbs.com/~/media/Files/R/RBS-IR/2013-reports/annual-report-and-accounts-2013.pdf.

RBS [Royal Bank of Scotland]. (2014a). *Annual report and accounts 2014, earning our customers' trust*. Available at: http://investors.rbs.com/~/media/Files/R/RBS-IR/2014-reports/annual-report-2014.pdf.

RBS [Royal Bank of Scotland]. (2014b, April 25). *The royal bank of Scotland group plc, 25th April, 2014 annual report and accounts 2013, strategic report 2013, pillar 3 disclosure 2013*. Available at: http://hsprod.investis.com/ir/rbs1/ir.jsp?page=news-item&item=1745474709094400.

RBS [Royal Bank of Scotland]. (2015). *Annual report and accounts 2015, building a strong, simple, fair bank*. Available at: http://www.investors.rbs.com/~/media/Files/R/RBS-IR/results-center/annual-report-2015.pdf.

RBS [Royal Bank of Scotland]. (2016). *Annual report and accounts 2016, creating a simple, safe, customer-focused bank*. Available at: https://investors.natwestgroup.com/~/media/Files/R/RBS-IR-V2/results-center/annual-report-2016.pdf.

RBS [Royal Bank of Scotland]. (2017). *Annual report and accounts 2017, becoming simple, safe and customer focused*. Available at: https://investors.natwestgroup.com/~/media/Files/R/RBS-IR-V2/results-center/annual-report-2017.pdf.

RBS [Royal Bank of Scotland]. (2018). *Annual report and accounts 2018, building a simple, safe and more customer focused bank*. Available at: https://investors.natwestgroup.com/~/media/Files/R/RBS-IR-V2/results-center/annual-report-2018.pdf.

RBS [Royal Bank of Scotland]. (2019). *Annual report and accounts 2019, we champion potential, helping people, families and businesses to thrive*. Available at: https://investors.rbs.com/~/media/Files/R/RBS-IR/results-center/annual-report-2019.pdf.

RBS Online. (2013, December 4). *RBS reaches settlement with the European commission*. Available at: http://www.rbs.com/news/2013/12/rbs-reaches-settlement-with-the-european-commission.html.

Reinhart, C., & Rogoff, K. (2009). *This time is different: Eight centuries of financial folly*. Princeton New Jersey: Princeton University Press.

Relbanks.com. *Banks around the world: The 50 largest banks in the world*. Available at: https://assets.publishing.service.gov.uk/media/57ac9667e5274a0f6c00007a/retail-banking-market-investigation-full-final-.

Rennison, J. (2016, 31). Barclays and credit suisse to pay $154m over dark pools. *The Financial Times*. Available at: http://www.ft.com/cms/s/0/d160fc2a-c84c-11e5-be0b-b7ece4e953a0.html#axzz4GSlHG8s3.

Reuters UK. (2011, May 25). Lloyds' bank of Scotland arm fined 3.5 million pounds. *Reuter UK*. Available at: http://uk.reuters.com/article/uk-lloyds-fsa-fine-idUKTRE74O25X20110525.

Reuters. (2016a, July 7). Libor-rigging trial: Ex-Barclays traders jailed for two to six years. *The Guardian*. Available at: https://www.theguardian.com/

business/2016/jul/07/libor-rigging-trial-ex-barclays-traders-jailed-merchant-pabon-mathew-johnson.

Reuters. (2016b, January 12). Six bankers charged: UK begins euribor rigging case. *CNBC*. Available at: http://www.cnbc.com/2016/01/12/.

Ridley, K. (2016, January 13). Euribor 6 face 2017 trial in UK, charged with rate-rigging plot. *Reuters*. Available at: http://uk.reuters.com/article/uk-court-euribor-britain-idUKKCN0UR1GQ20160113.

Ring, S. (2016, July 8). *Baseball bats, lies and libor: The fall of a career Barclays man*. Bloomberg. Available at: http://www.bloomberg.com/news/articles/2016-07-07/baseball-bats-lies-and-libor-the-fall-of-a-career-barclays-man.

Rixen, T. (2013). Why reregulation after the crisis is feeble: Shadow baking, offshore financial centres, and jurisdictional competition. *Regulation and Governance, 7*(4), 435–459.

Roberts, R., & Kynaston, D. (2014). *The lion wakes: A modern history of HSBC*. London: Profile Books.

Rose, R. (1991). What is lesson-drawing? *Journal of Public Policy, 11*(1), 3–30.

Rose, R. (1993). *Lesson-drawing in public policy: A guide to learning across time and space*. Chatham, New Jersey: Chatham House Publishers.

Rose, R. (2005). *Learning from comparative public policy: A practical guide*. London: Routledge.

Ross, A. (2017, February 2). Coutts sanctioned by swiss regulator over 1MDB. Financial Times. Available at: https://www.ft.com/content/27e0771d-b086-37a4-bb09-a5c54b8a880d.

Ross, S., Westerfield, R., & Jaffe, J. (1996). *Corporate finance*. Boston: Irwin.

Ruddick, G. (2012, February 26). HSBC set to claw back 'mis-selling' bonuses. *The Telegraph*.http://www.telegraph.co.uk/finance/newsbysector/banksandfinance/9107147/HSBC-set-to-claw-back-mis-selling-bonuses.html.

Rushe, D. (2011, August 10). HSBC sells US credit cards to capital one. *The Guardian*. Available at: https://www.theguardian.com/business/2011/aug/10/hsbc-sells-us-credit-card-business-to-capitalone.

Rushton, K. (2014, October 11). Cyber-criminals could spark next financial crisis. *The Telegraph*. Available at: http://www.telegraph.co.uk/finance/newsbysector/banksandfinance/11156260/Cyber-criminals-could-spark-next-financial-crisis.html.

Sabatier, P. A. (1988). An advocacy coalition framework of policy change and the role of policy-orientated learning therein. *Policy Sciences, 21*, 129–168.

Sabato, G. (2009, August). *Financial crisis: Where did risk management fail? article in SSRN electronic journal*. Available at: https://www.researchgate.net/publication/228126967_Financial_Crisis_Where_did_Risk_Management_Fail.

Salmon, J. (2015a, May 1). *Lloyds sells TSB to Spanish bank sabadell—And loses a staggering £2.5bn*. Thisismoney.co.uk. Available at: http://www.thisismoney.

co.uk/money/markets/article-3064784/Lloyds-sells-TSB-Spanish-bank-Sabadell-loses-staggering-2-5billion.html.

Salmon, J. (2015b, January 14). *'Lloyds braced for rage over boss' windfall: Horta-Osorio's £7m pay 'sticks in the throat'*. Available at: http://www.thisismoney.co.uk/money/markets/article-2909002/Lloyds-braced-rage-boss-windfall-Horta-Osorio-s-7m-pay-sticks-throat.html.

Salmon, J. (2016, November 27). Barclays is fined £72m for secret deals with mega-rich: Bank shamed over no-questions-asked policy that left Britain vulnerable to financial crime. *The Daily Mail*. Available at: http://www.dailymail.co.uk/news/article-3335743/Barclays-fined-72m-secret-deals-mega-rich-Bank-shamed-no-questions-asked-policy-left-Britain-vulnerable-financial-crime.html.

Salz, A. (2013, April). *Salz review: An independent review of Barclays' business practice*. Available at: http://online.wsj.com/public/resources/documents/SalzReview04032013.pdf.

Samuels, B. (2019). *FCA remuneration code guide*. Kervin & Barnes Solicitors Online Resources. Available at: https://www.kervinandbarnes.co.uk/resources/fca-remuneration-code-guide/.

Savage, R. (2015, October 28). Jes Staley won't return Barclays to big, brash investment banking. *Management Today*. Available at: http://www.managementtoday.co.uk/jes-staley-wont-return-barclays-big-brash-investment-banking/article/1370451.

Scannell, K. (2013, December 11). RBS settles US sanctions case with $100m pact. *Financial Times*. Available at: http://www.ft.com/cms/s/0/a28f9064-6291-11e3-bba5-00144feabdc0.html#axzz41YViGO3G.

Schafer, D., & Arnold, M. (2014, April 13). City bankers to evade EU bonus cap with 'role-based' allowances. *Financial Times*.http://www.ft.com/cms/s/0/02213446-c19d-11e3-b95f-00144feabdc0.html#axzz3hlYESIG9.

Schäfer, D., & McCrum, D. (2012, May 21). Barclays to sell £3.8bn blackrock stake. *The Financial Times*. Available at: http://www.ft.com/cms/s/0/0422a6c0-a332-11e1-8f34-00144feabdc0.html#axzz4GA9DEhts.

Schäfer, D., Jenkins, A., & Binham, C. (2013, September 16). *Barclays contests £50m fine for breach of listing rules*. Available at: http://www.ft.com/cms/s/0/2e565e1e-1ebf-11e3-b80b-00144feab7de.html#axzz4GM2flvfG.

Schmidt, V. (2008). Discursive institutionalism: The explanatory power of ideas and discourse. *Annual Review of Political Science* (11), 303–326.

Scuffham, M. (2014, February 21). *RBS to shrink investment bank and cut 30,000 jobs—Sources*. Reuters Online UK edition. http://uk.reuters.com/article/2014/02/21/uk-rbs-restructuring-idUKBREA1K0FR20140221.

Scuffham, M. (2015, February 27). *RBS shrinks investment bank, posts 3.5 billion-pound loss*. Reuters Online UK edition. http://uk.reuters.com/article/2015/02/27/uk-rbs-results-idUKKBN0LU0HO20150227.

Selznick, P. (1957). *Leadership in administration: A sociological interpretation.* New York: Harper & Row.

SFO [Serious Fraud Office]. (2020, February 20). *Former Barclays executives acquitted of conspiracy to commit fraud.* SFO Press Release. Available online at: https://www.sfo.gov.uk/2020/02/28/former-barclays-executives-acquitted-of-conspiracy-to-commit-fraud/.

Shankleman, M. (2009, March 11). Barclays 'corrupt regime' claim. *BBC News.* Available at: http://news.bbc.co.uk/1/hi/business/7936335.stm.

Shapiro, I. (2004). Problems, methods, and theories in the study of politics, or: What's wrong with political science and what to do about it. In I. Shapiro, R. Smith, & T. Masoud (Eds.), *Problems and methods in the study of politics* (pp. 19–41). Cambridge: Cambridge University Press.

Shaxson, N. (2012). *Treasure islands: Tax havens and the men who stole the world.* London: Vintage.

Shaxson, N. (2018). *The finance curse: How global finance is making us all poorer.* London: Bodley Head.

Shubber, K. (2018a, March 6). RBS in $500m mis-selling settlement with New York state. *Financial Times.* Available at: https://www.ft.com/content/fb30c9c8-2181-11e8-a895-1ba1f72c2c11.

Shubber, K. (2018b, October 9). HSBC finalises $765m settlement over securities sales. *Financial Times.* Available at: https://www.ft.com/content/0d73cd4c-cbe6-11e8-b276-b9069bde0956.

Simon, H. A. (1957). *Models of man.* New York: John Wiley and Sons.

Simon, H. A. (1958). *Administrative behaviour* (2nd ed.). New York: Macmillan.

Simon, H. A. (1959). Theories of decision-making in economics and behavioural science. *The American Economic Review, XLIX*(3), 253–283.

Simon, H. A. (1983). *Reason in human affairs.* California: Stanford University Press.

Simon, H. A. (1985). Human nature in politics: The dialogue of psychology with political science. *The American Political Science Review, 7*(2) (June), 293–304.

Simon, H. A. (1995). Rationality in political behaviour. *Political Psychology, 16*(1) Special Issue: Political economy and political psychology (March), 45–61.

Simon, H. A. (1998). *The sciences of the artificial* (3rd ed.). Cambridge, MA: MIT Press.

Simonian, H. (2011, December 21). Credit suisse buys HSBC's Japan private bank. *Financial Times.* Available at: http://www.ft.com/cms/s/0/bd7670b8-2bad-11e1-b194-00144feabdc0.html#axzz4BSfOfq71.

Slater, S. (2015, July 31). Barclays cuts 150 investment bank jobs under cost-cutting plan. *Reuters.* Available at: http://www.reuters.com/article/us-barclays-employment-investmentbank-idUSKCN0Q51ES20150731.

Slater, S., & Scuffham, M. (2015, March 3). Barclays will cut investment bank again if performance doesn't improve. *Reuters*. Available at: http://uk.reuters.com/article/uk-barclays-results-idUKKBN0LZ0H820150303.

Smith, M. K. (2011, 2013). Chris argyris: Theories of action, double-loop learning and organizational learning. *The encyclopaedia of informal education*. Available at: http://infed.org/mobi/chris-argyris-theories-of-action-double-loop-learning-and-organizational-learning/. Accessed 11 April 2014.

Smythe, C. (2013, July 3). *HSBC judge approves $1.9B drug-money laundering accord*. Bloomberg.com. http://www.bloomberg.com/news/articles/2013-07-02/hsbc-judge-approves-1-9b-drug-money-laundering-accord.

Sorkin, A. (2009). *Too big to fail: Inside the battle to save wall street*. London: Allen Lane.

Staley, J. (2016). Investor relations media centre: 'Accelerating the delivery of our strategy' group chief executive Jes Staley. *Barclays*. Available at: http://www.media.barclays.co.uk/player-standalone/?id=167779-5153926&width=604&height=340.

Steger, A. (2011, January 26). *Barclays financial planning arm to close*. Citywire.co.uk. Available at: http://citywire.co.uk/new-model-adviser/news/barclays-financial-planning-arm-to-close/a466159.

Steinmo, S. (2012). Historical institutionalism. In D. Della Porta & M. Keating (Eds.), *Approaches and methodologies in the social sciences*. Cambridge: Cambridge University Press.

Stiglitz, J. (2010). *Freefall: America, free markets and the sinking of the world economy*. New York: W.W. Norton.

Stinchcombe, A. L. (1965). Social structure and organizations. In J. G. March (Ed.), *Handbook of organizations* (pp. 142–193). Chicago: Rand McNally & Co.

Streeck, W. (2009). *Re-forming capitalism: Institutional Change in the German political economy*. Oxford: Oxford University Press.

Sweller, J., Chandler, P. Tierney, P., & Cooper, M. (1990). Cognitive load as a factor in the structuring of technical material. *Journal of Experimental Psychology, 119*, 176–192.

S&P Global. (2018, April 6). *S&P global market intelligence: Data dispatch: The world's 100 largest banks* [online]. Available at: https://platform.mi.spglobal.com/web/client?auth=inherit#news/article?id=44027195&cdid=A-44027195-11060.

Tax Justice Network. (2011, June 22). FSA reveals British banks are failing to turn down corrupt funds. *Tax Justice Network*. Available at: http://taxjustice.blogspot.co.uk/2011/06/fsa-reveals-british-banks-are-failing.html.

Telegraph [The]. (2009, August 13). RBS spends more than £10m hiring two bankers. *The Telegraph*. http://www.telegraph.co.uk/finance/newsbysector/

banksandfinance/6020004/RBS-spends-more-than-10m-hiring-two-bankers.html.

Telegraph.co.uk. (2014, March 14). *Libor: FDIC sues Barclays, RBS, HSBC, Lloyds and BBA*. http://www.telegraph.co.uk/finance/libor-scandal/10699359/Libor-FDIC-sues-Barclays-RBS-HSBC-Lloyds-and-BBA.html.

Tett, G. (2015). *The silo effect: The peril of expertise and the promise of breaking down barriers*. New York: Simon & Schuster.

The Big Short. (2015). *Hollywood*. CA: Paramount Pictures.

The Economist. (2009a, December 3). *Silo but deadly*. Available at: http://www.economist.com/node/15016132.

The Economist. (2009b, June 12). BlackRock and a hard PLACE, Barclays sell BGI. *The Economist Online Extra*. Available at: http://www.economist.com/node/13848711.

Thomas, H., & Braithwaite, T. (2011, July 31). HSBC will sell 195 US branches. *Financial Times*. Available at: http://www.ft.com/cms/s/0/199e0fc8-bbb9-11e0-a7c8-00144feabdc0.html#axzz4APxrj9ee.

Thompson, J. (2013, January 30). HSBC sets up crime-fighting unit. *Financial Times*.http://www.ft.com/cms/s/0/270cc020-6ade-11e2-9871-00144feab49a.html#axzz3fUZNGgJ5.

Thompson, J., & Kortekaas, V. (2013, May 31). HSBC recruits ex-head of MI5 to shore up financial crime defence. *Financial Times*.http://www.ft.com/cms/s/0/e337b62a-c9dd-11e2-8f55-00144feab7de.html#axzz3fUZNGgJ5.

Thomson Reuters. (2016). *Thomson reuters regulatory intelligence: The cost of compliance 2016*. Available online at: https://risk.thomsonreuters.com/en/resources/special-report/cost-compliance-2016.html.

Tims, A., & Collinson, P. (2015, October 3). HSBC has wrecked our lives, say customers frozen out and unable to switch. *The Guardian*. Available at: https://www.theguardian.com/money/2015/oct/03/hsbc-derisking-account-frozen-marie-shaun-langley.

Titcomb, J. (2015, May 20). Barclays handed biggest bank fine in UK history over 'Brazen' currency rigging. *The Telegraph*. Available at: http://www.telegraph.co.uk/finance/newsbysector/banksandfinance/11619188/Barclays-handed-biggest-bank-fine-in-UK-history-over-brazen-currency-rigging.html.

Tooze, A. (2018). *Crashed: How a decade of financial crises changed the world*. London: Allen Lane.

Tomlinson, L. (2013). *Banks' lending practices: Treatment of businesses in distress*. Available Online at: http://www.tomlinsonreport.com/docs/tomlinsonReport.pdf.

Treanor, J. (2009, December 15). RBS chief blasts 'politicisation' of bank. *The Guardian*.http://www.theguardian.com/business/2009/dec/15/rbs-bank-bonuses.

Treanor, J. (2010a, February 26). Bonuses: RBS admits that more than 100 bankers awarded over £1m each. *The Guardian*.http://www.theguardian.com/business/2010/feb/25/bonus-rbs-bankers.

Treanor, J. (2010b, February 25). Analysis: Royal bank of Scotland and bankers' bonuses. *The Guardian*.http://www.theguardian.com/business/2010/feb/25/royal-bank-of-scotland-bonuses-analysis.

Treanor, J. (2010c, April 27). Lloyds banking group returns to profit. *The Guardian*. Available at: http://www.theguardian.com/business/2010/apr/27/lloyds-banking-group-returns-to-profit.

Treanor, J. (2011a, May 5). Lloyds U-turn on £3bn payment protection bill drags it into the red. *The Guardian*. Available at: https://www.theguardian.com/business/2011/may/05/lloyds-loss-payment-protection-costs.

Treanor, J. (2011b, July 18). Barclays faces large loss in Russian exit. *The Guardian*. Available at: https://www.theguardian.com/business/2011/jul/18/barclays-faces-large-loss-russian-exit.

Treanor, J. (2012a, March 26). Queen's banker fined for poor money laundering checks. *The Guardian*.http://www.theguardian.com/business/2012/mar/26/coutts-fined-money-laundering-checks.

Treanor, J. (2012b). RBS unveils direct line insurance IPO. *The Guardian*.http://www.theguardian.com/business/2012/sep/14/rbs-direct-line-insurance-ipo.

Treanor, J. (2012c, June 28). Barclays fined £290m as bid to manipulate interest rates is exposed. *The Guardian*. Available at: https://www.theguardian.com/business/2012/jun/27/barclays-chief-bob-diamond-bonus-fine.

Treanor, J. (2012d, December 11). Bleak day for British banking as libor arrests follow record fine for HSBC. *The Guardian*. Available at: https://www.theguardian.com/business/2012/dec/11/banking-libor-fine-hsbc.

Treanor, J. (2013a, September 27). RBS sells 314 branches to church-backed corsair consortium. *The Guardian*.http://www.theguardian.com/business/2013/sep/27/rbs-branches-church-corsair-consortium.

Treanor, J. (2013b, March 11). Lloyds to raise £400m selling part of St. James's place stake. *The Guardian*. Available at: http://www.theguardian.com/business/2013/mar/11/lloyds-bank-sell-stake-st-james-place.

Treanor, J. (2013c, April 3). Barclays tax avoidance division generated £1bn a year—Salz review. *The Guardian*. Available at: https://www.theguardian.com/business/2013/apr/03/barclays-tax-avoidance-salz-review-scm.

Treanor, J. (2014a, November 20). RBS fined £56m for IT breakdown. *The Guardian*. Available at: https://www.theguardian.com/business/2014/nov/20/royal-bank-of-scotland-it-breakdown-56m-pounds-fine.

Treanor, J. (2014b, May 8). Barclays to cut 19,000 jobs as it scales back investment arm. *The Guardian*. Available at: https://www.theguardian.com/

business/2014/may/08/barclays-to-cut-19000-jobs-scale-back-investment-bank-antony-jenkins.

Treanor, J. (2014c, February 24). HSBC hands allowances to hundreds of bankers to avoid EU bonus cap. *The Guardian*.http://www.theguardian.com/business/2014/feb/24/hsbc-bankers-multimillion-pound-eu-bonus-cap.

Treanor, J. (2015a, October 15). UK government waters down financial regulation regime. *The Guardian*. Available at: http://www.theguardian.com/business/2015/oct/15/financial-accountability-regime-will-not-be-fully-operational-until-2018.

Treanor, J. (2015b, March 3). RBS could cut 14,000 staff in retreat from US and Asia. *The Guardian*.http://www.theguardian.com/business/2015/mar/03/rbs-could-cut-14000-staff-us-asia-ross-mcewan.

Treanor, J. (2015c, July 8). Barclays fires chief executive antony jenkins. *The Guardian*. Available at: https://www.theguardian.com/business/2015/jul/08/barclays-fires-chief-executive-antony-jenkins.

Treanor, J. (2015d, November 26). Barclays fined £72m over 'elephant deal'. *The Guardian*. Available at: https://www.theguardian.com/business/2015/nov/26/barclays-fined-72m-elephant-deal-fca.

Treanor, J. (2016, November 7). RBS to set up compensation fund for small businesses. *The Guardian*. Available at: https://www.theguardian.com/business/2016/nov/07/rbs-to-set-up-compensation-fund-for-small-businesses.

Treanor, J., & Rushe, D. (2014, June 26). Barclays investigated in US over 'dark pool' activities. *The Guardian*. Available at: https://www.theguardian.com/business/2014/jun/26/barclays-investigated-dark-pool-new-york-trading.

Treasury Committee [House of Commons Treasury Committee]. (2009). *Banking crisis. Volume II: written evidence*. London: The Stationery Office. Available at: https://publications.parliament.uk/pa/cm200809/cmselect/cmtreasy/144/144ii.pdf.

Treasury Select Committee [House of Commons Treasury Committee]. (2014). *Project verde: Sixth report of session 2014–2015 volume I*. London: The Stationery Office.

Treasury Select Committee [House of Commons Treasury Committee]. (2018, January 9). *Ross mcewan RBS GRG—Correspondence between ross McEwan and Rt Hon Nicky Morgan MP*. Available Online at: https://www.parliament.uk/documents/commons-committees/treasury/Ross-McEwan-RBS-GRG-090118.pdf

Trotman, A. (2015, October 29). RBS to sell off final stake in US bank citizens. *The Telegraph*. Available at: http://www.telegraph.co.uk/finance/newsbysector/banksandfinance/11964598/RBS-to-sell-off-final-stake-in-US-bank-Citizens.html.

True, J. L., Jones, B. D., & Baumgartner, F. R. (2007). Punctuated equilibrium theory. In P. Sabatier (Ed.), *Theories of the policy process*. Cambridge, MA: Westview Press.

Tucker, P., Hall, S., & Pattani, A. (2013). Macroprudential policy at the bank of England. *Bank of England Quarterly Bulletin, Bank of England, 53*(3), 192–200.

Tuckman, B. (2016). Derivatives: Understanding their usefulness and their role in the financial crisis. *Journal of Applied Corporate Finance, 28*(1), 62–71.

Turner, A. [Turner Review]. (2009). *The turner review: A regulatory response to the global banking crisis*. London: FSA. Available at http://www.fsa.gov.uk/pubs/other/turner_review.pdf.

Turner, A. (2012, March 14). *Shadow banking and financial instability*. CASS Lecture 2012. CASS Business School. Available at: https://corpgov.law.harvard.edu/2012/04/16/shadow-banking-and-financial-instability/.

Turner, A. (2016). *Between debt and the devil, money, credit, and fixing global finance*. Princeton, NJ: Princeton University Press.

Tversky, A., & Kahneman, D. (1974). Judgement under uncertainty: Heuristics and biases. *Science, 185*(4157) (September 27), 1124–1131

UEAPME. (2010, October 27). *New capital requirements for banks (Basel III)*. UEAPME Press Release.

UK Finance. (2018, September). *United Kingdom's banking sector: Facts & figures* [online]. Available at: https://www.ebf.eu/united-kingdom/.

UKFI [UK Financial Investments Ltd]. [Online]. Press Release Archives 2011–2015. Available at: http://www.ukfi.co.uk/index.php?URL_link=press-releases&Year=2015.

Urry, J. (2014). *Offshoring*. London: Polity Press.

Usher, R., & Bryant, I. (1989). *Adult education as theory, practice and research: The captive triangle*. London: Routledge.

US Department of the Treasury. (2013, December 11). *Treasury department reaches $33 million settlement with the royal bank of Scotland Plc*. Available online at: https://www.treasury.gov/press-center/press-releases/Pages/jl2239.aspx.

van der Zwan, N. (2014). Making sense of financialisation. *Socio-Economic Review, 12*, 99–129.

Verity, A. (2016, February 1). Barclays and credit suisse are fined over US 'dark pools'. *BBC News*. Available at: http://www.bbc.co.uk/news/business-35456219.

Verity, A. (2017, January 30). HBOS: A highly unusual fraud case. *BBC News*. Available at: https://www.bbc.co.uk/news/business-38796087.

Vygotsky, L. S. (1962). *Thought and language*. Cambridge, MA: MIT Press.

Vygotsky, L. S. (1978). *Mind and society: The development of higher mental processes*. Cambridge, MA: Harvard University Press.

Wallace, T. (2016a, January 28). George osborne delays final sell-off of Lloyds shares due to market turmoil. *Telegraph*. Available at: http://www.telegraph.co.uk/finance/newsbysector/banksandfinance/12127179/George-Osborne-delays-final-sell-off-of-Lloyds-shares-due-to-market-turmoil.html.

Wallace, T. (2016b, February 27). Barclays' new boss to support US investment bank with more hiring. *The Telegraph*. Available at: http://www.telegraph.co.uk/business/2016/02/26/barclays-new-boss-to-support-us-investment-bank-with-more-hiring/.

Wallace, T. (2016c, March 7). Barclays hires nine M&A executives to bolster investment bank. *The Telegraph*. Available at: http://www.telegraph.co.uk/business/2016/03/07/barclays-hires-nine-ma-executives-to-bolster-investment-bank/.

Watkins, D. (1983). Depth of processing and the quality of learning outcomes. *Instructional Science, 12*, 49–58.

Weardon, G. (2011, May 5). How the PPI scandal unfolded. *The Guardian*. Available at: https://www.theguardian.com/business/2011/may/05/how-ppi-scandal-unfolded.

Weick, K. E., & Roberts, K. H. (1993). Collective mind in organizations: Heedful interrelating on flight decks. *Administrative Science Quarterly, 38*(3), 357–381.

Weinland, D. (2016, April 7). Barclays to sell Asia wealth division to OCBC for $320m. *Financial Times*. Available at: http://www.ft.com/cms/s/0/1e8923dc-fc74-11e5-b3f6-11d5706b613b.html?siteedition=uk#axzz4GA9DEhts.

Werdigier, J. (2009, February 26). Record loss at royal bank of scotland. *The New York Times*.http://www.nytimes.com/2009/02/27/business/worldbusiness/27rbos.html?_r=0.

Weyland, K. (2008). Toward a new theory of institutional change. *World Politics, 60*(2), 281–314.

Wilson, H. (2011, December 5). HSBC hit with record fine over investment mis-selling. *The Telegraph*.http://www.telegraph.co.uk/finance/newsbysector/banksandfinance/8936729/HSBC-hit-with-record-fine-over-investment-mis-selling.html.

Wilson, H. (2012, March 7). HSBC sells insurance businesses for $914m. *The Telegraph*. Available at: http://www.telegraph.co.uk/finance/newsbysector/banksandfinance/9128234/HSBC-sells-insurance-businesses-for-914m.html.

Wilson, H. (2013a, July 24). RBS fined £5.6m over reporting failures. *The Telegraph*.http://www.telegraph.co.uk/finance/newsbysector/banksandfinance/10199474/RBS-fined-5.6m-over-reporting-failures.html.

Wilson, H. (2013b, May 29). Lloyds continues sale of private banks. *Telegraph*. Available at: http://www.telegraph.co.uk/finance/newsbysector/banksandfinance/10087830/Lloyds-continues-sale-of-private-banks.html.

Wilson, H., Aldrick, P., & Ahmed, K. (2011, May 6). Royal bank of Scotland investigation: The full story of how the 'world's biggest bank' went bust. *The Telegraph*. Available at: http://www.telegraph.co.uk/finance/newsbysector/banksandfinance/8496654/Royal-Bank-of-Scotland-investigation-the-full-story-of-how-the-worlds-biggest-bank-went-bust.html.

Wintour, P. (2015, February 26). HSBC scandal caused horrible damage to reputation, says chairman. *The Guardian*.http://www.theguardian.com/business/2015/feb/25/hsbc-scandal-horrible-damage-reputation-chairman.

Wolf, M. (2015). *The shifts and the shocks*. London: Penguin.

Woods, S. (2017, May). *Looking both ways*. Speech given by Sam Woods Sam Woods, Deputy Governor, Prudential Regulation and Chief Executive Officer, Prudential Regulation. Available at: http://www.bankofengland.co.uk/publications/Documents/speeches/2017/speech988.pdf.

Woodward, R. (2006). Offshore strategies in global political economy: Small islands and the case of the EU and OECD harmful tax competition initiatives. *Cambridge Review of International Affairs, 19*(4) (December).

Wooley, P. (2010). Whay are financial markets so inefficient and exploitative—And a suggested remedy. In A. Turner et al. (eds.), *The future of finance: The LSE Report* (Chapter 3, pp. 105–130). London: The London School of Economics and Political Science.

World Bank. (2017). *Global financial development database*. Washington, DC: The World Bank Group. Retrieved from http://data.worldbank.org/data-catalog/global-financial-development.

Wursthorn, M., & Stynes, T. (2015, June 8). Stifel to buy Barclays's U.S. wealth management Ops. *The Wall Street Journal*. Available at: http://www.wsj.com/articles/stifel-to-buy-barclays-u-s-wealth-management-ops-1433766107.

Z/Yen and CDI. (2018). *The global financial centres index 23*. Z/Yen Group/China Development Institute: London/Shenzhen.

Index

A. Barber, *UK Banks and the Lessons of the Great Financial Crisis*, Building a Sustainable Political Economy: SPERI Research & Policy, https://doi.org/10.1007/978-3-030-70254-0

T

U

V

W

The manufacturer's authorised representative in the EU is Springer Nature Customer Service Centre GmbH, Europaplatz 3, 69115 Heidelberg, Germany. If you have any concerns regarding our products, please contact ProductSafety@springernature.com

Printed and bound by CPI Group (UK) Ltd, Croydon, CR0 4YY
30/09/2026
02225701-0014